A HISTORY OF
MEDIEVAL
EUROPE

A HISTORY OF
MEDIEVAL
EUROPE

From Constantine to Saint Louis

by

R. H. C. DAVIS

Professor of Mediaeval History,
University of Birmingham,
and formerly Fellow of Merton College, Oxford.

LONGMAN

LONGMAN GROUP LIMITED
London

Associated companies, branches and representatives
throughout the world

First published 1957
Revised Edition 1970
First published in paperback 1972
Fifth impression in paperback 1978

ISBN 0 582 48208 9

Printed in Great Britain by
Richard Clay (The Chaucer Press) Ltd, Bungay, Suffolk

FOR
E. M. D.

PREFACE

I N the History Department at University College, London, it
was, and still is, the custom to make all ' modernists ' attend
a course of lectures on Medieval European History. No
examination was involved and the purpose of the course was
officially described as ' mere broadening '. The lecturer was
allotted twenty-five lectures and invited to talk about the things
he thought important. It was a challenge which could not fail
to be stimulating, and so far as I myself am concerned it has
led to the writing of this book.

My thanks are due to all my former colleagues whose advice
was sought, and freely given, on points too numerous to be set
out in detail. They will, I hope, excuse me if I tender them my
thanks *en bloc*. I owe a particular debt of gratitude to the
Honourable David Roberts of Christ's Hospital who, before his
untimely death, did far more to shape the pattern of this book
than he would ever admit. I have also to thank Mr. Philip D.
Whitting, G.M., of St. Paul's School for reading a large part of
the typescript and making many valuable suggestions, Mr. J.
Campbell of Merton College for reading the proofs and detect-
ing many errors, and Mrs. A. Munro for the exemplary skill
and patience which she showed in typing the whole manuscript.

R. H. C. D.

28 December 1956

In this revised edition some errors have been corrected, the
lists of books for further reading have been revised, and three
short appendices have been added.

R. H. C. D.

16 March 1970

CONTENTS

ix

PART II

THE HIGH MIDDLE AGES (900–1250)

Contents xi

MAPS

PLATES

xiii

ACKNOWLEDGMENTS

We are indebted to the following for permission to reproduce copyright material :

Messrs. Jonathan Cape Ltd. for extracts from *The Travels of Ibn Jubayr*, translated by R. J. C. Broadhurst ; The Clarendon Press, Oxford, for extracts from *History of the Franks by Gregory of Tours*, translated by O. M. Dalton ; and Columbia University Press for extracts from *Correspondence of Pope Gregory VII*, translated by E. Emerton (1932).

ABBREVIATIONS

C.M.H.	*Cambridge Medieval History.*
Migne, *P.L.*	*Patrologia Cursus Completus, series latina*, ed. J. P. Migne.
M.G.H.	*Monumenta Germaniae Historica.*
M.G.H.S.S.	*Scriptores Rerum Germanicarum in usum scholarum ex Monumentis Germaniae Historicis recusi.*
R.S.	Rolls Series.

Part I
THE DARK AGES

INTRODUCTION

THE civilization that we call European is not spread evenly over the continent of Europe, nor is it confined to Europe. Sometimes it has expanded and sometimes it has contracted. Kinglake came to the end of ' wheel-going Europe' and started his exploration of ' the Splendour and the Havoc of the East' in the Moslem quarter of Belgrade; that was in 1844. Farther east there are lands that have once been European. The natives of Syria call modern Europeans, their houses, transport, clothes, and sanitation ' franji', because until the modern age they had known no European colonists since the crusaders or Franks. Even in Greece, Europeans are called Franks, since Greece was conquered by crusaders in the thirteenth century. On the southern shores of the Mediterranean, in Algeria, Tunisia, and Tripolitania, Europeans are called ' Roumi', because the previous exponents of European civilization were Romans. European civilization moves. Under the Greeks and the Romans it was based on the Mediterranean. By the sixteenth century it had shifted to the Atlantic seaboard, to the Netherlands, England, France, and Spain. In one sense, the history of medieval Europe is the history of this movement of civilization, northwards from the Mediterranean.

The Roman Empire was Mediterranean and embraced all its shores. It was not localized. Just as the second city of Greece was Alexandria, in Egypt, so the Emperor Constantine founded a ' new Rome' at Constantinople and called its people ' Romans'. The Emperor Diocletian had built his palace at Split on the Dalmatian coast; one of the most famous schools of Roman law was at Beyrouth, in Syria, and the third largest Roman amphitheatre in the world is still to be seen in the Tunisian village of El Djem. Few of the great Romans of imperial times were of Roman stock. The Emperor Trajan was a Spaniard; Septimius

3

Severus was a native of Leptis Magna in Tripolitania. Most significant of all was St. Paul; his parents were Jews, but he was a Roman citizen because he had been born in the Greek city of Tarsus, which was on the coast of Asia Minor and was capital of the Roman province of Cilicia. He died at Rome, after he had undertaken missionary journeys over the greater part of the eastern Mediterranean.

The Mediterranean was not only the centre of the Roman Empire; it was what made the Empire possible. The magnificence of Roman roads is apt to make us think that Rome was primarily a land-power and to make us forget that Rome could not defeat Carthage until she was a sea-power. Rome depended on the sea. The corn for her bread came from Sicily and Egypt, and an outbreak of piracy in the middle sea could endanger her very existence.

Before the age of railways, motor-cars, and aeroplanes, all great civilizations depended on water-transport. The earliest civilizations grew up on rivers, where the hazards of navigation seemed less terrifying than on sea. For civilization depends on cities where men are spared the trouble of growing their own food and can devote their lives to specialized trades or arts; cities can only obtain their material needs by trading; trading requires transport; and transport is far more difficult over land than over water. To transport goods overland one needs roads and bridges, relays of horses and carts, and stopping-places where both man and beast can find food and rest in peace; it requires stupendous organization. To travel over water one needs nothing more than a boat.

In a boat, one can sail down the Nile and into the Mediterranean, the paradise of early sailors. It was neither too big nor too little. It was big enough to contain the marvels of the world, the golden apples of the Hesperides, the cave of Cumae and the pillars of Hercules; and yet it was small enough for the fearful mariner never to be far from sight of land. It invited exploration. The Greeks nosed their way along its shores in search of new lands and new markets, founding cities as they went, as at Cyrene on the African shore, or as at Naples ($N\varepsilon\acute{a}\pi o\lambda\iota\varsigma$ = the new city) in southern Italy where their cities became known as *Magna Graecia*. In Spain they founded the great market of

Emporion and the city of Hemeroskopeion (' the watch-tower of the day '). Nor were the Greeks alone. Phoenicians from Tyre had founded Carthage, and Carthaginians founded Cadiz. Exploration and trading went hand in hand. Trading led to cities and cities to civilization.

The Romans conquered the cities and the civilization, with the Mediterranean. They made an Empire out of the economic unit that existed already, and called the Mediterranean ' our sea ', *mare nostrum*. They then set about defending it, for the sea was vulnerable from the land. Any invader who marched overland and conquered a portion of its shore, could build a fleet and disrupt the economic unity on which the Empire depended. Fortunately, the Mediterranean had natural defences on three sides. On the west and on the south were the Atlantic and the Sahara, both equally impassable. On the east, the Syrian desert formed a barrier against the Persians except at its northern extremity which was defended by the fortress of Nisibis. The weak frontier was on the north. If the Romans had only had to defend Italy, they could have made the Alps their frontier ; but they had to defend the whole of the north Mediterranean shore. To protect the shores of Greece and Dalmatia they advanced to the Danube which they made a frontier against the Goths. To protect their province on the Mediterranean coast of Gaul, they advanced into northern Gaul ; to secure northern Gaul they occupied Britain and advanced eastwards to the Rhine. Augustus decided that the advance should go no farther, and in consequence the northern frontier of the Empire followed the lines of the Rhine and Danube with only a small extension to the east in the region of the Neckar. A longer frontier could not have been devised. To garrison it, the Romans recruited Syrians, Armenians, Dalmatians, Spaniards, and even German auxiliaries. The frontier was the military centre of the Empire, for its purpose was not just the defence of Gaul or Illyricum, but of the whole Mediterranean. The Romans knew that once a rival power reached the shores of ' their ' sea, it could shatter their economy and so bring an end to their Empire and their civilization.

The fact that Mediterranean civilization depended on the unity of that sea made it vulnerable from within as well as from without. It was essential to keep the Mediterranean peoples at peace with one another. It was the triumph of the Romans that they discovered how to do this with the least possible military effort. They knew that all the Mediterranean peoples had a common interest in the commerce of their sea, and they believed in men. They believed that all men had by nature an instinctive knowledge of what was right and what was wrong, and they believed that it was possible to frame laws in accordance with the standard of nature. They distinguished between custom which was of no more than local significance, and law which appertained to justice and was consequently of universal significance. They would have found the greatest difficulty in understanding the way in which we now think it natural for different civilized states to have different laws. Of course they did not expect all men to share their law at once, but they did expect all *civilized* men to share it. Roman law was aiming at absolute justice as ordained by nature, and men whose reason was educated would recognize it naturally. For centuries their confidence was justified ; but Roman civilization was to be shaken when barbarian invaders claimed that their own laws were particular to themselves, since they were not founded on nature and reason, but on the dictates of their own divine ancestors.

It always has been that different races find self-expression in their religion as well as in their laws. But the Romans were convinced of the common humanity of all men, and just as they postulated a *jus gentium*, or law that was common to all peoples, so they postulated that there must be a common religion. They thought that, just as there were different languages with different words for the same object, so the differences between the gods of different peoples were differences only of names. They identified Zeus with Jupiter, Baal with Saturn, and the Celtic Mapon with Apollo. Julius Caesar reported that the Gauls paid most deference to Mercury, and after him to Apollo, Jupiter, and Minerva, ' and about them their ideas correspond fairly closely with those current among the rest of mankind '. The statement shows a magnificent belief in the universal humanity of man, since it implied that even barbarians knew by instinct something of the truth discovered by civilized man. But the belief depended on pantheism. There had to be many recognized gods it all the gods of the barbarians were to be found equivalents in the Roman pantheon ; and any new gods had to be content to take their place alongside deities that were already numerous. What could not be tolerated was a religion that claimed to have a monopoly of truth—that claimed not only that it was right, but that all other religions were wrong. Just as the Roman Empire embraced all Mediterranean peoples and gave them Latin names, so Roman religion embraced all gods and required that they also should observe the *pax Romana*.

The structure of the Roman Empire was based on the unity of the Mediterranean, its peoples and its gods. In the following chapters we will see how that unity was broken. It was first cracked by the claim of the Christian Church to be the guardian of absolute truth, because that claim made religious compromise impossible. It was further cracked by the determination of barbarian invaders to prefer the law of their ancestors to the law of reason, since that preference implied the superiority of loyalty to one's race over loyalty to the civilized world. It was shattered when traders lost the freedom of the sea. When that happened, the greater part of Europe reverted to an agricultural economy in which there was no place for the cities that made men civilized.

I

CONSTANTINE THE GREAT:
THE NEW ROME AND CHRISTIANITY

CONSTANTINE the Great was proclaimed Caesar by the imperial troops at York on the death of his father in 306. At that date the Roman Empire was ruled by two emperors (*augusti*) and two junior colleagues (*caesars*), and the Christian religion was proscribed. Constantine's sphere was Gaul and Britain, but he set out to conquer the whole Empire for himself, to have the Christians as his allies, and even to become a Christian himself. By 312 he had defeated one of his rivals, Maxentius, at the battle of the Milvian Bridge and had made himself master of Rome and the whole West; he attributed his victory to the fact that in obedience to a vision, his army had fought under the sign of the cross. By 324 he had defeated all his rivals and was sole emperor of the East as well as of the West until his death in 337. He was a superstitious man, and cruel—in Gaul he had shocked public opinion by giving barbarian kings to the beasts, along with their followers by the thousand, and in 326 he had his wife and son put to death—with nothing of the philosopher about him, but his reign stands out as decisive in the history of the Roman Empire. For it was he who founded Constantinople, the New Rome of the East; and it was he who was the first emperor to become a Christian, and who first posed the problem, which was to be fundamental for all medieval history, of the relationship between Church and State.

The foundation of Constantinople marked an important stage in the development of the Roman Empire. Rome had ceased to be convenient as the capital of the Roman Empire, and a new Rome was needed, more suitable for the pressing necessity of defending the Empire from the barbarians. The northern

8

frontier along the Rhine and the Danube, and the eastern frontier against Persia, were in perpetual danger of attack, and it was necessary for the emperor to have a headquarters from which he could send effective help quickly to any threatened sector. For such a purpose Rome was useless ; its position was central, but that only meant that it was equally remote from every frontier province. Nor was it possible to find any single headquarters that was convenient for directing campaigns on both the Rhine and the Euphrates. Consequently, it had become necessary by the end of the third century A.D. to have two emperors and two imperial headquarters, one in the East and one in the West, so that the whole of the Roman Empire might be defended effectively. In the West the imperial headquarters were usually in North Italy, at Milan or Ravenna, but it was no serious inconvenience to keep Rome as an extra capital. In the East it was different. A new Rome was needed, and Constantine founded it.

The site chosen by Constantine was a Greek city called Byzantium which, after several vicissitudes, had been largely destroyed by the emperor Septimius Severus. In 325 it was little more than a fishing village. Constantine had hit on the site after an attempt to build his New Rome on the site of Troy. He planned it on a huge scale from the very start (325). The Christian tradition is that he marked out its boundaries in person, spear in hand and guided by a celestial vision. Forty thousand Gothic *foederati* were employed on the buildings, and Greece was ransacked for works of art, such as the serpent-column from Delphi (already eight hundred years old), so as to adorn the city and give it the appearance of being, like Rome, a centre of the ancient world. Within five years the new Rome was sufficiently advanced to be dedicated. In most ways it was the image of its older counterpart. It had its hippodrome with its green and blue factions, its seven hills, its forum, its senate, its quaestors, and its praetorian prefect. To mark the fact that the two Romes were still part of one empire, each of them had one of the two consuls which had to be elected each year.

The similarity between the old Rome and the new has been stressed because Constantine did not in any way intend this city to be the capital of a new empire. It was a new capital for the old empire. Historians have found it convenient to call the eastern part of the Empire, which did not collapse with the barbarian invasions but survived till 1453, ' Byzantine '. The convention is useful, but it must not blind us to the fact that the Greek-speaking citizens of Constantine's capital called themselves 'Ρωμαῖοι, Romans. Similarly their empire was 'Ρωμαῖος, and their Church, which we now call the Greek or Orthodox Church, is called 'Ρωμαῖος still.

There were, of course, differences between the old Rome and the new. The new Rome had no strong pagan traditions, and it was supposed to have no pagan temples, being Christian from the start. Nor did it possess the republican traditions of the old Rome ; the imperial palace was a central feature of the new Rome and it was designed so as to inspire awe. In the first and second centuries the emperors had prided themselves on seeming no more than the first citizens of Rome, but since the third century they had begun to cultivate a more oriental *mystique* of empire. They had worn a diadem in public, dressed ever more lavishly in bejewelled cloth of gold. They gave solemn audiences, and those who received the favour prostrated themselves at their feet. At Rome, where Brutus had killed Julius Caesar, such *adoratio* might have seemed out of place, and consequently emperors like Diocletian had tended to live away from the capital at such places as Nicomedia. With the foundation of New Rome, the court could return to the capital.

The greatest difference of all, however, was that the new Rome had a purpose, which the old Rome no longer had. The new Rome, Byzantium, was a fortress situated at the strategic centre of the Eastern Empire, on the western shore of the Bosphorus at its entry to the Sea of Marmora. It controlled the passage from Europe to Asia and from the Black Sea to the Mediterranean, and could serve as a base for the armies that manned both the Persian and the Danube frontiers. It was also a naval base, and from it the whole of the eastern Mediterranean could be controlled. It was built to stand sieges and it stood them. Except for the half-century after its capture by the Venetians in the Fourth Crusade of 1204, Byzantium remained impregnable till 1453 when the last of the Roman emperors fell fighting in the breach that the Turks had made in the walls. Till then it had been the eastern bulwark of Christian Europe and the pre-condition of its survival. The reason why the Moslems did not overrun the Balkans and march on Vienna till the fifteenth and sixteenth centuries was that for eight hundred years Byzantium, the city of Constantine the Great, was standing in their way.

Even more important than the foundation of the city, however, was the fact that Constantine the Great was the first emperor to be converted to Christianity. This was a decisive change in imperial policy and was bound to provoke opposition, especially from the governing classes. For Christianity was an oriental religion, and new. It was not the religion of any particular people, for though it had started amongst Jews it had been denounced by the Jewish authorities. It was extreme in its claims, and intolerant; Christians believed that they had a monopoly of truth and that it was consequently their duty to convert non-Christians. Most of the converts were Greeks, and they were strongest in the towns, especially amongst artisans and slaves— a feature which was considered particularly unfortunate by the senatorial families of Rome. More alarming was the fact that the religion spread rapidly, and up the social scale too, slaves infecting their mistresses with the mysterious new faith. Such converts tended to be particularly embarrassing. They did not mind what company they kept, so long as it was Christian, and nobody could hope to reason with them. How could one, when they insisted on believing that a man who had been executed by a Roman governor in Palestine was God? To those who did not understand it, the new religion seemed superstitious, emotional, and revolutionary.

Tacitus, for example, had charged the Christians with ' hatred of the human race ' (*odium generis humani*). This was because they seemed to take a delight in denouncing as false the established beliefs and conventions of civilized society, and put the interests of their religion even above that of the State. Most educated people were sceptical about the reality of the pagan gods, but they complied with the normal religious usages because it was in the interests of society that they should do so. The Christians, on the other hand, would never have considered the argument of *raison d'état*. There were indeed Christians who served the Empire, either in the army or in the magistrature, but they were always liable to come out with a conscientious objection. They would not burn a pinch of incense at the altar of an emperor ; one Christian soldier even refused to wear a laurel wreath on the occasion of a *donativum*, even though the penalty was death.

What was still more infuriating to the pagan authorities was that the Christians took everything so seriously. They assumed that everyone who burnt incense on the altar of an emperor was committing himself to belief in the emperor's divinity, when in fact he was only observing the conventions of society. Educated pagans were prepared to conceal their own scepticism so that the masses might not be disturbed in their beliefs, but the Christians thought it wicked to leave the masses undisturbed in false beliefs. They preached to ' the weavers, the fullers, and the shoemakers '.

> I do not address myself to those who have been trained in the schools or the libraries [wrote Tertullian] ; it is to you others that I speak, simple and ignorant souls, who have learnt only what can be picked up in the streets and in taverns.

The Christians loved their fellow-men so much that they wished to ' save ' the masses. That was what made Tacitus so angry ; the safety of the state required that the masses should not be disturbed. The Christians were putting loyalty to their religion above loyalty to the State.

In such circumstances it was not surprising that some emperors persecuted Christianity. There were long periods when the Church was left in peace and there were shorter periods, as in the reign of Alexander Severus (222–35), when Christians were even prominent at court ; but whenever the safety of the Empire was threatened, the qualifications made by Christians in the support that they gave to the cause of the ' human race ' brought odium and persecution on them. Persecution merely encouraged fanaticism. The book of the *Revelation of St. John*, in which the Roman Empire is represented as ' the beast ', is only one example of the apocalyptic fervour which was created by persecution. The *magisterium* of the Church condemned voluntary or provoked martyrdom, but only with indifferent success. Eusebius in his

Ecclesiastical History [1] records one case of three Christians who were living in the country and who

> reproached themselves for their carelessness and sloth, because, instead of hastening to secure the crown of martyrdom, they were proving contemptuous of the prize, though the present opportunity was bestowing it upon such as yearned with a heavenly desire. But when they had taken counsel thereon, they started for Caesarea, appeared before the judge, and met the above-mentioned end [of martyrdom].

Further evidence of the fervour with which some Christians greeted the last persecution (302–5) is to be found in the case of Andronicus. The magistrate had had the bread and meat of sacrifice thrust into Andronicus's mouth, so that he should not have to pay the penalty of martyrdom.

'May you be punished, bloody tyrant, both you and those who have given you power to defile me with your impious sacrifices!' shouted Andronicus. 'One day you will know what you have done to the servants of God.' 'Accursed scoundrel,' replied the magistrate, 'do you dare to curse the emperors who have given the world such long and profound peace?' 'I have cursed them and I will curse them,' was the reply, 'these public scourges, these drinkers of blood that have turned the world upside-down.'[2]

Yet the Emperor Constantine became a Christian. Those historians who have stressed the fanaticism of Christianity and who would have it that Andronicus was typical of the majority have, not unnaturally, doubted the sincerity of Constantine in linking himself to such a cause. But all the evidence goes to show that Constantine was sincere in his religion, and that the reason why he was not frightened of Christianity was because his sphere of office had been in the West, where there had been much less persecution, and where, in consequence, Christianity had less of the martyrs' fanaticism.

Constantine was convinced that God had given him the Empire—Professor Norman Baynes has shown that the fact is patent in his letters—and late in his life he even became convinced

---

[1] Bk. vii. xii. The translation is J. E. L. Oulton's (Loeb Classics, ii. 167).
[2] Quoted from J. B. Firth, *Constantine the Great* (Heroes of the Nations series), London, 1905, p. 31.

that the only reason why he had won the battle of the Milvian Bridge, and thus overthrown one of his four imperial rivals, was the effect of divine intervention. He thought that he had been commanded by Christ to make a banner modelled on the Christian monogram which he had seen in the sky; and he was convinced that this banner, the *labarum*, had given him the victory. Though the story is suspect, it has its symbolic significance; for when, in the following year, he persuaded one of his remaining colleagues to tolerate Christianity, his reason was ' that thus the supreme Divinity, to whose worship we freely devote ourselves, might continue to vouchsafe His favour and beneficence to us '.

It would, of course, have been impossible for him to gain popular support if he had been explicit in his Christianity. The Christians were only a minority, and the senatorial aristocracy, the civil service, and the army were predominantly pagan. Constantine therefore kept his Christianity as a sort of open secret. He would avow it to those of his officials who were themselves Christians, but otherwise spoke and acted with a degree of ambiguity. He referred not to Christ but to the ' supreme divinity '. He was not formally baptized until he was on his deathbed. He retained the imperial title of *pontifex maximus* although he never exercised that pagan office, which was confined to Rome and was not reproduced in Constantinople. One of the advantages of his new capital, indeed, was that it enabled him to make a break with the religious traditions of pagan Rome, but even there he was careful not to be too compromisingly Christian. Typical of his public conduct was the column which he erected in his own honour in his new capital. On the column was an antique Greek statue that had once represented Apollo, but which now had a new head representing Constantine. On the head was a radiated crown; in the right hand was a lance and in the left a globe surmounted with a cross. The inscription read ' To Constantine shining like the sun '. Christians believed that his glory shone because of the cross; pagans could think, if they liked, that their emperor was likening himself to Apollo. There was a similar ambiguity about the coins struck to celebrate his funeral. They showed the image of a four-horsed chariot being drawn up to heaven, from which a hand was extended in greeting. It could have been taken to represent either Elijah or the deification of the emperor.

On one point, however, Constantine was emphatic. Whether as a servant of Christ or as *pontifex maximus*, he considered that he had the right and the responsibility to see that the Christian Church behaved in an orderly and peaceful way. In the Roman Empire the government of religion had always been an imperial prerogative, and Constantine thought that as God had entrusted him with the government of all earthly things, He would punish him if he did not enforce the divine laws by helping to preserve the harmonious unity of the Church.

The difficulty was how to do it, for the Church seemed full of disputes. One, the Donatist controversy, was brought to his notice within six months of the victory of the Milvian Bridge (312). It arose out of a double-election to the see of Carthage which was recognized as the ecclesiastical capital of the imperial 'diocese' of Africa. The two candidates represented different elements of the population. One, Caecilian, represented the Romanized population of the Carthaginian sea-board. The other, Majorinus, soon to be succeeded by Donatus who gave his name to the whole party, represented, in effect, the Numidians of the interior who were traditionally anti-Roman. A further complication was that Caecilian, as befitted a member of the Romanized community, had condemned the passion, which was particularly noticeable in Africa, for voluntary or provoked martyrdom. The Donatists took the opposite point of view, and strained every nerve to identify Caecilian with the *lapsi*, or those who had relapsed from Christianity under threat of persecution. They claimed that Caecilian had submitted to consecration by a *traditor*, that is to say, by a bishop who had surrendered the gospel books to the imperial authorities in order to save his skin. Such a traitor to Christ, they said, had forfeited all right to be a bishop, and any consecration performed by him was null and void.

Caecilian disputed the truth of the allegations made against him, but the important point was that there was no acknowledged authority to which he could appeal. Normally such an affair would have been judged by a council of the bishops of Africa, but such a council could only be summoned by the metropolitan, and the whole dispute was as to who that metropolitan was, Caecilian or Donatus. The Church of Rome had some sort of primacy in the Roman world, but its powers were undefined, and the Donatists, suspecting that it would be against them, did not wish to acknowledge it. They appealed instead to the emperor, on three successive occasions. The first time, they asked him to appoint Gaulish bishops to hear the dispute, for Gaul, they said, being the only province that had escaped Diocletian's persecution, was the only place where impartial judges could be found in a matter concerning *traditores*. Constantine agreed to their request and appointed the bishops of Autun, Cologne, and Arles to join the Bishop of Rome and one other to settle the dispute. The Bishop of Rome demonstrated his independence by summoning a further fifteen Italian bishops to hear the case, and the council thus formed decided in favour of Caecilian. There the matter should have rested, but the Donatists refused to accept the decision and kept on appealing to the emperor. He, for his part, kept on trying to produce an authority which the Donatists would accept. He summoned a general council of the bishops of the Western Empire to Arles (314), and when the Donatists would not accept its adverse decision, even judged the case himself (316). It was then, and only then, that the Donatists asked what business the emperor had to meddle with the Church. Constantine's reply was to banish the Donatist leaders and to confiscate their churches :

> I am going to make plain to them what kind of worship is to be offered to the Divinity. . . . What higher duty have I, in virtue of my imperial office and policy than to dissipate errors and repress rash indiscretions, and so to cause all to offer to Almighty God true religion, honest concord, and due worship ?

The disadvantages inherent in such an attitude towards the Church became more generally apparent during the Arian controversy, which flared up in 323, and was of the utmost importance for the whole of Christendom, since it involved the central point of Christian doctrine, the divinity of Christ. Arius was a priest of Alexandria, where the spirit of philosophical inquiry was especially strong, and the theory which he made famous was a model of dialectic. If, he said, Christ was the son of God, He must be younger than God, and therefore lesser than God. One of the attributes of God was eternity—the quality of having no beginning and no end—but Christ was not eternal for he had a beginning. Therefore He was not wholly God. Such views were naturally denounced by the Bishop of Alexandria, and Arius was excommunicated. He fled first to Palestine and then to Nicomedia, stirring up trouble amongst all those who were jealous of the Bishop of Alexandria's authority, and having his decisions reversed by rival councils of bishops. At the same time he popularized his views by putting them into ballad form so that they could be sung by sailors and shopkeepers. The controversy spread far and wide, and in all classes of society. Gregory of Nazianzus has described the *furore* that it made in Constantinople :

> Ask a tradesman how many obols he wants for some article in his shop and he replies with a disquisition on generated and ungenerated being. Ask the price of bread today, and the baker tells you ' the Son is subordinate to the Father '. Ask your servant if the bath is ready and he makes answer ' the Son arose out of nothing '. ' Great is the only begotten ' declare the Catholics, and the Arians reply ' But greater is He that begot.' [1]

This was the situation as Constantine found it when he became emperor of the East as well as the West. By heroic efforts he had succeeded in reuniting the whole Roman Empire, only to find that the Church was rent in twain. The situation was clearly intolerable. He did not understand the importance of the point at issue in the controversy—he said that the theological question at issue was frivolous and should never have been asked, much less answered—but was only too painfully aware of the fact that religious strife could easily lead to civil disorder or even war. He was afraid, as he put it, that if he did not restore unity to the Church, God would be moved to wrath against him personally.

The difficulty was that most of the churches of the East had already taken sides in the dispute. Ecclesiastical councils held at Alexandria and Antioch had condemned Arius, rival councils at Nicomedia and Caesarea had upheld him. To impose any final decision on the Church it would be necessary to have a general council of the whole Church, summoned by a neutral

---

[1] As quoted in J. B. Firth, *Constantine the Great*, p. 206.

authority to a place which was not too obviously committed to either side. In 325, therefore, Constantine himself summoned a general council of the Church to meet at Nicaea. It was the first general council of the Church that had ever been held. It is claimed, and with some probability, that as many as 318 bishops attended. They came from all parts of the Empire, the imperial authorities having provided them with travelling facilities. There were delegates from the Bishop of Rome, and a Spaniard—Hosius, Bishop of Cordova—acted as Constantine's religious adviser.

The part that Constantine played in the council was large, for he not only summoned it, but also presided over it, even though he had not yet been baptized. He showed suitable humility by refusing to be seated without the consent of the assembled bishops, but he addressed them in Latin, which was the official language of the Empire, instead of in Greek, which was the language of the Church. It was, moreover, the authority of his support that led to the acceptance by the council of the *homoousion* clause, wherein Christ was declared to be one in essence with the Father—' God from God, Light from Light, True God from True God, Begotten not created '—and it was the emperor who declared that those who would not accept this creed should be exiled.

Only two of the assembled bishops refused to subscribe, and it seemed as if the Council of Nicaea had been a triumphant success. In point of fact, however, it had not succeeded in bringing peace to the Church. The Arians were not really content to accept its decision, and intrigued against it in every possible way. They had friends at court and were able to persuade Constantine that he would never obtain peace in the Church until Arius had been re-admitted to its communion. Consequently Constantine, in his capacity as emperor, welcomed a vague submission by Arius that he adhered to the faith and thought of the Church ' all investigations and subtle arguments set aside ', and himself decided that Arius should be re-admitted to the Church.[1] Then, finding

---

[1] The exact details of how the Arians gained Constantine's ear are not known. Nor is it certain whether or not he re-assembled the Council of Nicaea in 327, in order to re-admit him to the Church. The problem is discussed by G. Bardy, in Fliche and Martin, *L'Histoire de l'Eglise*, iii. 100.

that the Athanasians were offended, he began to veer from side to side. On the advice of Athanasius he over-ruled a council of bishops. Then he changed his mind, sent Athanasius into exile at Trèves, and ordered the Bishop of Constantinople to give Arius communion in his cathedral. In fact the order never took effect, because Arius died on his way to the cathedral ; Athanasius, who believed the worst of his enemies, said that his death occurred in a public lavatory.

At that point we may leave the history of the Arians, since what concerns us is not their subsequent fortunes but the attitude of the emperor to the Church. He had taken a leading part in the most important general council of the early Church, although he was still unbaptized. He had adopted a theological formula, which he had subsequently striven to undermine, and had finally summoned further councils to endorse his subsequent vacillations. He styled himself ' equal of the apostles ', but his main concern was the imperial concern for religious unity rather than for religious truth.

The difference between Church and Empire was a difference of emphasis, not of aim. Both Church and Empire wanted Christian unity and the establishment of the Kingdom of God, but while the Church thought that unity could best be attained by purely religious means, emperors thought that God could best be worshipped by means of a united Empire. The reasonable compromise was to allow both Church and Empire to work towards the same goal by different means, but this involved the demarcation of the respective spheres of Church and State. Hosius of Cordova (who had apparently held different views at the Council of Nicaea) expressed the view that was to become general in a letter which he wrote to Constantine's son, Constantius, in 355 :

Do not interfere in matters ecclesiastical, nor give us orders on such questions, but learn about them from us ! For into your hands God has put the kingdom ; the affairs of the Church He has committed to us. If any man stole the Empire from you he would be resisting the ordinance of God : in the same way, you on your part should be afraid lest, in taking upon yourself the government of the Church, you incur the guilt of a grave offence. ' Render unto Caesar the things that are Caesar's, and unto God the things

that are God's.' We are not permitted to exercise an earthly rule ;
and you, Sire, are not authorized to burn incense.[1]

This dichotomy was the consequence of the conversion of
the Empire to Christianity. In the pagan Empire the problem had
not arisen because the Empire was in some sense a religion in
itself and every emperor was a potential god. But Christians
did not venerate the State for its own sake ; they wanted to trans-
form it into something far greater and far holier, in order to
bring about the Kingdom of God on earth. The history of
the Middle Ages is in large measure the attempt of the Church
to consecrate the State and make it acceptable unto God. It is
also the record of its failure, because Church and State could not
agree as to what were the things that were Caesar's and what
were the things that were God's.

Further Reading

EDWARD GIBBON. *The Decline and Fall of the Roman Empire* (especially
    chapters 15 and 16, first published in 1776).
N. H. BAYNES. *Constantine the Great and the Christian Church* (Pro-
    ceedings of the British Academy, xv. London. 1929).
EUSEBIUS OF CAESAREA. *Church History* (trans. J. E. L. Oulton). Loeb
    Classics, 1932.
B. J. KIDD. *Documents Illustrative of the History of the Church.* 2 vols.
    London. 1923.
J. LEBRETON and JACQUES ZEILLER. *The History of the Primitive Church*
    (tr. E. C. Messenger). 4 vols. London. 1948. (The French
    edition is vol. ii of *L'Histoire de l'Eglise*, edited by A. Fliche
    and V. Martin.)
A. H. M. JONES. *Constantine the Great and the Conversion of Europe.*
    (Teach Yourself History series). London. 1948.
A. ALFÖLDI. *The Conversion of Constantine and Pagan Rome.* Oxford.
    1948.
W. H. C. FREND. *Martyrdom and Persecution in the Early Church.*
    Oxford. 1965.

---

[1] *Documents of the Christian Church*, ed. Henry Bettenson. The World's Classics,
O.U.P., 1943, p. 27.

II

THE BARBARIAN INVASIONS

THE barbarian invaders who crossed the northern frontiers of the Roman Empire were Germanic peoples who were being driven westwards by a Mongol people called the Huns. The Huns did not settle permanently within the Empire; the Germans did. The Germanic peoples must therefore be our first concern, and they can be divided into two main groups, the West Germans and the East Germans. To the West Germans belonged the Franks, the Angles, and the Saxons; to the East Germans the Goths, the Vandals, the Gepids, the Burgundians, and the Lombards. The West Germans had acquired a settled form of agricultural life before they invaded the Empire, but the East Germans were still nomadic. Consequently, while the invasions of the West Germans took the form of steady advances which were systematically consolidated, those of the East Germans took the form of spectacular but spasmodic ' wanderings '.

The East Germans came from Scandinavia; the Goths may have come from what are now the Swedish provinces of East and West Gautland, and the Burgundians from the Danish island of Bornholm (Borgundarholmr). It was probably during the last five centuries before Christ that they crossed over the Baltic into Germany, apparently because the climate of Scandinavia, which had previously been temperate, was growing extremely severe. The Goths were the last of the East Germans to leave Scandinavia and their arrival on the mainland of Europe accentuated the lack of East German *lebensraum*. Had they been prepared to settle down, to clear wasteland and forest and to cultivate the land intensively, there might have been land enough for everyone, for the total population of the East German peoples does not seem to have been unduly numerous. (The Vandals

are said to have numbered about 80,000 in 429 A.D., and the
Heruls, who were a lesser people, could not muster more than
about 4,500 warriors in the sixth century.) But the East Germans
were not agriculturalists; they were primarily herdsmen, and
since they were unable or unwilling to improve the land, they
had always to be on the move in search of fresh pastures. It
was this nomadic condition that was the basic reason for those
restless migrations which the Germans have so aptly called the
Völkerwanderung or 'wanderings of peoples'. The Goths
travelled as far as the Black Sea where, about the middle of the
second century A.D., they settled in two groups, the Ostrogoths
in the Don basin and the Visigoths in Dacia, north of the lower
Danube. It was while there that they were converted to Arian
Christianity by Ulfilas (311–81), the descendant of one of the
Cappadocian captives whom they had made slaves.

The Gothic settlement in the Black Sea region might have
become permanent had it not been for the Huns. The Huns
were Mongols and came from Asia. Quite possibly there had
been some climatic change in central Asia similar to the climatic
change in Scandinavia, for we know that China suffered from
barbarian invasions from the west just as much as the Roman
Empire suffered from barbarian invasions from the east. It has
even been claimed that the Huns themselves had invaded China
before they turned westwards, for it is thought that they were
the same people as the *Hiong-nu*, who invaded China early in the
fourth century, only to be driven southwards and westwards by
yet more ferocious barbarians from the north. If so, they had
migrated across the whole breadth of Asia before they reached
the Don basin *c.* 375 A.D. There they defeated the Ostrogoths,
and began to drive all the Germanic peoples southwards and
westwards on to, and into, the Roman Empire.

The most dramatic entry into the Roman Empire was that of
the Visigoths (376), who implored the Emperor Valens to grant
them asylum from the Huns by allowing them to cross the Danube
and cultivate the waste lands of Thrace. Since resistance to such
a request would have been difficult, the emperor granted it, and
the Visigoths crossed the Danube. Unfortunately the imperial
authorities found that the task of regulating and feeding these
refugees was beyond their resources, and the Visigoths took to

arms. The emperor collected an army from the east and marched on them without waiting for the arrival of the reinforcements which he had summoned from the west, and at Hadrianople his army was completely defeated, and he himself was killed (378).

The battle of Hadrianople can be taken as marking the end of an epoch. For although the Visigoths were subsequently ' pacified ' for a short while, the emperor had no option but to give them land on which to settle. He promised to provide them with food and markets so long as they remained peaceful, and concentrated all his efforts not on resisting the barbarians but on controlling them by economic means.

Such ' economic warfare ' could only be practised as long as the barbarians were prevented from gaining control of the Mediterranean. The imperial authorities recognized this fact; they did everything in their power to lure or repel barbarians away from the Mediterranean ports, and it was made a capital offence to teach barbarians the art of ship-building. None the less one barbarian people, the Vandals, did succeed in crossing to Africa. They had crossed the Rhine frontier into Gaul in 406–7, and had subsequently made their way to Spain where, for a short while, they had been settled as *foederati* or allies of the Empire. In 425, however, they captured Cartagena and became masters of the imperial fleet in Spanish waters. Four years later they crossed over to Africa, allegedly at the invitation of a rebellious Roman general, Count Boniface, and by 439 they had conquered the coastline as far east as Carthage, thus winning control of the greater part of the North African corn supply, together with a splendid base for themselves as a sea power. By 455 their fleet was strong enough to sail to the Tiber and sack Rome. The emperor could only make a treaty with them, and buy their corn, though this must have been a heavy financial burden since he had previously received the corn of North Africa free as imperial tribute ; but he had obviously lost his stranglehold on the food supplies of the Empire, since henceforth neither the food nor the sea over which it had to be transported was indisputably his.

There remained to the Empire the possibility of creating a balance of power among the barbarians themselves. It was, for

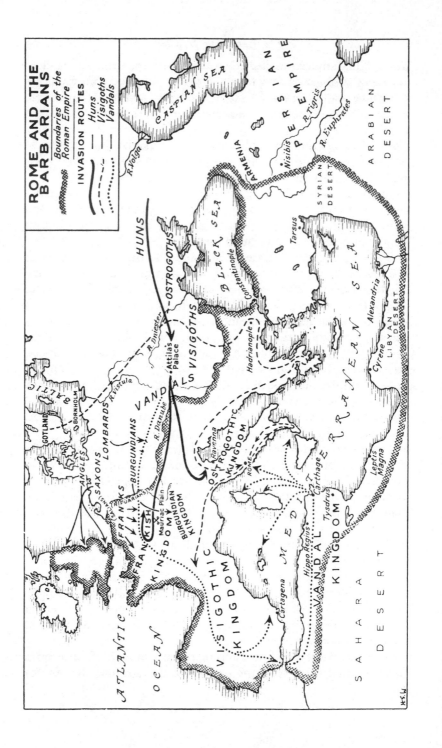

ROME AND THE
BARBARIANS

Boundaries of the
Roman Empire

INVASION ROUTES
——— Huns
— — — Visigoths
··········· Vandals

CASPIAN SEA

PERSIAN EMPIRE

ARABIAN DESERT

R.Volga

ARMENIA

R.Tigris

Nisibis

R.Euphrates

SYRIAN DESERT

HUNS

OSTROGOTHS

BLACK SEA

Constantinople

Tarsus

Alexandria

LIBYAN DESERT

Cyrene

Hadrianople

VISIGOTHS

VANDALS

Attila's Palace

R.Dniester

BALTIC

GOTLAND

BORNHOLM

R.Vistula

SAXONS LOMBARDS

R.Danube

BURGUNDIANS

ANGLES

FRANKS

(SALIAN) (RIPUARIANS)

FRANKISH KINGDOM

Mauriac Plain

BURGUNDIAN KINGDOM

Ravenna

OSTROGOTHIC KINGDOM

ROME

MEDITERRANEAN SEA

Leptis Magna

ATLANTIC OCEAN

VISIGOTHIC KINGDOM

Cartagena

Hippo Regius

Carthage

Tysdrus

VANDAL KINGDOM

SAHARA DESERT

H.S.W.

example, an obvious part of imperial policy to embroil the Vandals with the Visigoths. But it was not enough simply to keep the Germanic peoples who were already within the Empire at logger-heads with each other; it was necessary to make the Germanic peoples as a whole feel the necessity for imperial support, and such a feeling could be kept alive only by fear of the Huns. It was from the Huns that the Germans had fled to the west, and the Huns had not ceased to pursue them. Under their king, Attila, ' the scourge of God ', the Huns had created a formidable empire for themselves and had forced the more easterly Germans, such as the Ostrogoths, to become their vassals. It paid the Romans to do everything in their power to make the Germans fear the Huns still more ; thus the Roman general Aëtius went out of his way to keep on friendly terms with the Huns so as to be able to use their power against the Goths. But such a policy had its dangerous moments. When Attila the Hun invaded Gaul and besieged Orleans, Aëtius was forced to ally with the Visigoths in order to oppose him. But although he then defeated Attila in a battle at the ' Mauriac plain ' near Troyes (often wrongly called the ' battle of Chalons ') (451), he refused to follow up his victory and crush the power of the Huns, since an overwhelming victory would have upset the balance of power and left him at the mercy of the Goths. As a result, Attila was strong enough to invade Italy in the following year.

Aëtius had risked everything to preserve the balance of power, and yet the balance of power was eventually destroyed—not because Italy had been devastated, but because of Attila's unexpected death in 453. The empire of the Huns had been built solely on his personal pre-eminence, and on his death it collapsed. His Germanic vassals promptly revolted against their Hunnish masters, defeated them utterly, and forced them to flee to the region north of the lower Danube. Thenceforward the Germans had no one to fear but themselves.

It was not surprising, therefore, that in 476 Odovacar, the barbarian general of an imperial army that consisted almost entirely of East Germans, felt strong enough to depose Romulus, the last Roman emperor in the West. He arranged for the Roman senate to send an embassy to the Emperor Zeno at Constantinople, declaring that there was no need for a separate emperor in the

West; one emperor was enough, and it was preferable to have him at a distance. Zeno was asked to confer upon Odovacar the rank of Patrician and to entrust him with the administration of Italy. He granted the request; Italy remained part of the Empire, but was to be governed by a barbarian.

It is for this reason that the year 476 has often been taken to mark the end of the Roman Empire in the West. By then the barbarians were obviously supreme. Odovacar ruled in Italy, the Vandals in Africa; the Visigoths controlled not only south-west Gaul but also most of Spain; and the Burgundians were established in the western Alps and the Rhone valley. The West Germans also had by then made their most important advances; the Anglo-Saxons were in process of settling Britain, and the Franks had advanced from the lower Rhine far into northern Gaul. Yet in spite of these facts it would be an exaggeration to say that in the year 476 the Roman Empire in the West ' came to an end '. We have already seen that Odovacar had been entrusted with the administration of Italy by the surviving emperor and at the request of the Roman senate. Similarly all the barbarian kings, with the exception only of the Vandals and the Anglo-Saxons, professed obedience to the Roman emperor and were delighted to receive imperial honours. The series of Roman consuls remained unbroken; the senate still met from time to time, and the noble families and rich landowners of the Empire did not lose their influence entirely. Even in the sixth century there were still patrician families in Rome, who played a great part in the government of both the city and the Church, as did Pope Gregory the Great (590–604).

It would, in short, be a great mistake to consider the barbarian invasions as a cataclysmic event. ' Barbarization ' was a very gradual and a very complex development, and it is impossible to say when the Roman Empire came to an end, for from a strictly legal point of view it continued to exist at Constantinople until 1453. The battle of Hadrianople (378) and the sack of Rome by Alaric the Goth (410) were, like the deposition of Romulus Augustus, single events that were important not so much for their own sakes as for their symbolic value. They were like milestones marking the distance that had already been covered on the road to the new Europe.

Those who used to think of the barbarian invasions as a sudden calamity causing the immediate destruction of Roman towns, Roman life, and the Roman Empire, underestimated or ignored four salient features of the period. The first was that by the beginning of the fifth century the Roman Empire had been suffering from economic decline for at least two centuries ; the second was that the Romans were already being ' barbarized '; the third was that the barbarians were already being Romanized; and the fourth was the precise manner in which the barbarian settlements were made. Each of these factors must be discussed in turn, however briefly.

The economic decline of the Roman Empire has attracted a great deal of attention among historians. Its primary cause seems to have been that the Roman economy was unproductive. Rome had grown rich simply on the spoils of war. Its population consumed the corn-tribute of Africa and Sicily, and did not produce any manufactured goods in return ; it simply enjoyed the bread and circuses, and its chief trade was money-lending. Such an economy could have been maintained only by a policy of perpetual conquest and enlargement of the Empire. Once the frontier of the Empire was stabilized, the profits of war declined sharply, and the emperors had a struggle to raise enough money even to pay the army its wages. In such circumstances the easiest, and most disastrous, expedient was to debase the coinage, and this the emperors did. The *denarius*, which in the second century had been of silver, was by the end of the third century a silver-washed bronze coin, and, in relation to gold, its value had fallen to a fortieth. Indeed, the most permanent feature of the later Roman Empire was that the purchasing-power of money was declining steadily, and that the decline continued not just for ten years or twenty but for centuries. As a result the only prudent course for a rich man was to invest his money in land. For unlike money, land retained its value. The owner of a great estate could live in luxury in his villa, secure from the worst evils of monetary inflation. He had workshops in which his slaves could make the necessary agricultural implements, and he could, if necessary, pay his taxes and buy his luxuries with goods in kind.

This drift of the wealthy from the towns to the country had

serious consequences for the civilization of the Empire. For Roman policy had always been to persuade the barbarian peoples whom they conquered to live in towns, since to them town-life *was* civilization. But now, in the third century, they were unable to make town-life attractive. When the wealthy retired to their villas, the tradesmen in the towns lost their custom and were anxious to depart in their turn. Thus it happened that, in the third century, many Roman towns actually shrunk in area (Bordeaux from 175 to 56 acres and Autun from 500 to 25). The parts that were no longer inhabited fell into ruins.

The situation was made worse by the fact that the total population of the Empire was declining. The causes for this decline are unknown,—it might simply have been caused by the higher state of civilization—but as a fact it is unquestionable.[1] One modern estimate is that the population fell by about one-third, from 70 millions to 50 millions. This might not have had such serious consequences if the Empire had contracted its frontiers or reduced its responsibilities to a level suited to the smaller population, but no such reduction was made. In Rome itself, for example, the State continued to distribute bread, wine, oil, and pork, either free or at nominal prices. But with the reduced population, the difficulty was to find sufficient ship-owners to transport the goods to Rome, and corn-traders, oil-merchants, bakers, and pork-butchers to arrange for its distribution on terms which the State could afford. The imperial authorities, therefore, tried to maintain a sufficient staffing of these essential services by organizing the relevant traders into hereditary guilds called *collegia*. The bakers, for example, were enrolled in a *collegium* of their own and had to bake for the rest of their lives; even a baker's son had no option but to be a baker too, and was not allowed to marry anyone but a baker's daughter. This incredible system was, by the beginning of the fifth century, applied to almost all trades in almost all towns of the Empire; and men working at the most unpleasant jobs—in the mines, quarries, or arms-factories—were branded, so as to be recognized

---

[1] See A. H. M. Jones, *The Later Roman Empire* (Oxford, 1964), p. 1041. Working from the evidence of tombstones, he shows that ' in Africa, of 100 boys of 10, 85 survived to 22, 74 to 32, 58 to 42, 47 to 52, and 36 to 62 ', but these figures are necessarily silent about the number of still births or the number of boys who never reached the age of ten. He adds that ' A population with so high a death-rate would have required a very high birth-rate even to maintain its numbers ', and draws a comparison with conditions in India in 1914.

the more easily if they should escape. The worst fate of all was to be enrolled among the *curiales* ; for the *curiales* had to serve as town-councillors and were held responsible for the provisioning of the town and for the payment of the full quota of taxes from its dependent territory, no matter whether any lands had fallen out of cultivation or not. The pagan Emperor Maxentius (306–12) had punished Christians by enrolling them as *curiales*, and the Christian Emperor Honorius (395–423) punished apostate Christians in exactly the same way.

By the third century A.D. it was clear that if the Roman Empire was to survive it needed more wealth and more people. Wealth was always elusive, but people, at any rate, could be imported. All prisoners taken in frontier-warfare were normally sold as slaves, and it was consequently as slaves that people of barbarian stock first became a common sight in the Roman Empire.

It was probably the vast barbarian slave-population that was responsible for the barbarization of the Romans, for barbarian slaves were employed in almost every department of life. In the third century, we are told, they were to be seen in crowds, sitting in the market-places of Gaul, waiting to be distributed among the provincials ' in order to build again the places which perhaps they themselves had laid waste '. In the fourth century, Synesius, Bishop of Cyrene (in North Africa), declared that there was ' hardly a household of means without a Goth or a Scythian as cook or house-servant, butler or steward ' [1] and it is clear that these slaves were influencing their masters considerably. In the last days of the Republic and in the early days of the Empire, the slaves of Rome had tended to be Greek, and the Romans had fallen under the spell of Greek culture. Now that the slaves were barbarian, the Romans took to barbarian fashions. The most enduring proof of this fact is to be seen in art. Even in Rome itself, the beginnings of medieval art are to be found a century and more before the advent of Alaric and his Goths. As an example of this fact we give an illustration of some of the carvings from the arch of Constantine at Rome, erected in, or soon after, 312. Either from lack of money, or

---

[1] The whole passage, a manifesto against barbarian control of the Empire, is printed in translation by A. A. Vasiliev, *History of the Byzantine Empire, 324–1453,* 2nd English edition, Oxford, 1952, pp. 92–3.

from lack of skilled carvers, or both, Constantine was not able to afford many new carvings for the adornment of his arch, and had to make do with many secondhand pieces removed from earlier monuments of the first and second centuries. The carvings on the circular plaque in the illustration, for example, are such secondhand carvings, and are still in an imperial Graeco-Roman tradition. The relief showing Constantine addressing his troops, on the other hand, was carved for the occasion, and is hardly classical at all; it gives the impression that the carver was not interested in the form of the human figure, and it resembles not so much the works of the Greeks as the carvings that are to be found over the doorways of eleventh- and twelfth-century churches in Italy (Plate I).

Just as the barbarians influenced art, so also they influenced men's fashions. The Emperor Honorius (395–423) found it necessary to forbid the wearing in Rome ' of gaily-coloured sleeveless coats, wide trousers, and long hair in the barbarian manner ', and this was hardly surprising, for the great military leaders of the Empire in his time were themselves barbarians. Stilicho, the general who virtually ruled the Empire and who opposed Alaric the Goth, was himself a Vandal.

Stilicho's position as ' master of both services ' shows that ' barbarization ' had affected even the army. In point of fact the ' Roman ' armies that confronted the barbarians were, for the most part, themselves composed of barbarians, either Germanic or Hun. To a certain extent this was no innovation in an empire whose armies had always been cosmopolitan. Just as the British were, until recently, able to make use of their Indian army, and just as the French still have a large number of colonial troops, so the Romans had made a practice of garrisoning the provinces of their Empire with troops from other provinces. The garrison of Britain consisted of troops from Gaul, Spain, the Danube, Dalmatia, and even Palmyra in the Syrian Desert, while Britons in their turn were (in the second century) deported to Germany to settle and defend the region of the Main, the Neckar, and the Odenwald. What was new, towards the end of the fourth century, was that barbarians who entered the imperial service were often settled and employed on the frontiers nearest to their own people. The strain on the Roman military machine was so great that there was no opportunity for complicated exchanges of garrison. Every commander recruited whomsoever he could on the spot ; and, as we shall presently see, if he could recruit a whole tribe he would recruit it *en bloc*.

Although this ' barbarization ' of the army was carried out on a very large scale, we should not imagine that in consequence the imperial armies were traitorous. Barbarians in the imperial forces served the Empire loyally—it is one of the surprising facts of history. They introduced certain Germanic customs, as when they elevated the emperor of their choice on a shield as Germans did with their elected kings, but they became none the less imperial soldiers. Just as they helped to ' barbarize ' the Empire, so service in the Roman army helped to Romanize them, and this process of Romanization should not be overlooked.

It is dangerously easy to imagine the barbarian peoples as ' barbarians ' not just in the original sense of ' foreigners ' but in the modern sense of people who hate civilization and wish to destroy it. The barbarian peoples did not understand the imperial civilization very well, but they certainly did not hate it. All of them except the Franks and the Anglo-Saxons had adopted Christianity before they crossed the imperial frontiers. It is true that their Christianity was of the heretical Arian brand, for they had been converted while in eastern Europe at a time when the eastern part of the Empire was predominantly Arian, but the fact that they had been converted at all shows that they did not hate all things civilized. Indeed, Theodoric the Ostrogoth, as we shall presently see, was outstanding in his desire to restore the city of Rome and its monuments, and was a great patron of art and literature.

The historian who has recently done most (some would say too much) to stress the extent of Roman civilization acquired by the Germanic peoples, is Alfons Dopsch. In *The Economic and Social Foundations of European Civilization* he has demonstrated that even on the very frontiers of the Empire the German settlements often made no great break in the previous way of life. The great landowners lost their possessions, but the Germans who took over from them were often sufficiently romanized to continue something of the previous Roman organization. The household and agricultural implements, even the masonry, the vinedressers' tools and the coopers' tools of the early German period are identical with those of the late Roman period, because, for a hundred years and more, the Germans had been learning the useful arts from the Romans. Even more striking are the instances in which the great imperial domains (*saltus*) were taken over by German tribal dukes and passed to the Frankish kings, who sometimes held them still, as royal domain, as late as the ninth century. The Latin word *villa* became corrupted and was used by the Germans as a place-name, as in *Weiler* or *Gebweiler*. Most places with such names commemorate Roman civilian settlements, and a striking instance of continuity is provided in some of them where in the later Middle Ages the German-speaking inhabitants still used field-names derived from the Latin. Even in the towns, though there the break with the Roman past was certainly greater than in the countryside, Dopsch has been able to make a case for some sort of survival throughout the Dark Ages, as in the cases of Cologne, Strassburg, Augsburg, and Regensburg. The barbarians came not to destroy the Empire but to enjoy it, even though the way in which they enjoyed it necessarily brought about its downfall.

This brings us to our fourth point, the actual way in which the barbarians settled in the Empire. Most of them were settled by imperial authority as allied troops or *feoderati*. *Feoderati* were peoples whose chiefs had signed a treaty with the emperor whereby they agreed to fight for him in return for being settled on imperial territory. In civil matters they kept a certain amount of independence, often living under their own laws and being governed by their own kings, but in military affairs they were subject to the imperial commands. The emperor made himself responsible for their upkeep by quartering them on some specific territory in the same way as he might arrange for the quartering of other imperial troops. It was this quartering on the land that was in fact the beginning of the barbarian settlements, but the technical term for it was *hospitalitas*, or 'hospitality'.

Hospitalitas included not only board and lodging, but also the provision of horses, fodder, and clothes. As a way of paying, keeping, and equipping soldiers it was simpler for the emperor than for the districts concerned. Its burden was especially heavy since Roman and barbarian soldiers alike were not confined to

(*a*) Hadrianic Plaque, *c.* 117–38: Sacrifice to Apollo

(*b*) Constantinian relief: Constantine addresses the people

I. TWO RELIEFS FROM THE ARCH OF CONSTANTINE
IN ROME

II. POPE LEO III's MOSAIC IN THE LATERAN PALACE

St. Peter is shown investing Leo III with the pallium (spiritual authority) and Charlemagne with the banner (temporal authority)

barracks but normally lived ' out ' with their wives, families, and slaves. In order to provide for them, landed proprietors might have to surrender one-third of their house and of the produce of their land. Sidonius Apollinaris, for example, complained to a friend of the heavy burden of the ' hospitality ' which he had to provide for Burgundians. He disliked their language, their songs and their smell (they spread butter on their hair and breathed garlic and onions in his face), and his house was invaded ' as if he were an old grandfather or foster-father, by a crowd of giants, so many and so big that not even the kitchen of Alcinous could support them '.

From receiving as *hospitalitas* a proportion of the produce of the land, it was but a short step to receiving a portion of the land itself. Since the barbarians were mainly quartered on the greater landlords, it followed that they soon acquired a portion of many of the greater estates, receiving rents in money or in kind from the tenants of the previous Roman landlords. Their settlement did not usually upset the existing tenurial arrangements. On the contrary, they were anxious to determine the precise rights of the property to which they had fallen heirs. Their desire was to receive the necessities of life from their tenants, not to create a social revolution.

Consequently it was possible for Roman citizens to shut their eyes to the immensity of the changes that were going on about them. They could not fail to realize that they were living in a time of crisis, but they could, if they chose, ignore the extent and the permanence of the ' barbarization ' that had already taken place. They themselves continued to be subject to Roman law, and to pay the old Roman taxes ; and if those taxes went to the treasure of a Frankish or Visigothic king, instead of to the emperor, they were none the less the habitual taxes that had previously been paid to Rome. The barbarians themselves were careful to keep up appearances. Because it was a rule of Roman law that certain public documents should be written on papyrus, the chancery of the Merovingian kings of the Franks used papyrus in Gaul until the end of the seventh century. They wanted to ' do things properly '

Orosius has a story that Ataulfus, the brother-in-law of Alaric the Goth, was intimate with a certain citizen of Narbonne, a grave, wise and religious person who had served with distinction under Theodosius, and often remarked to him that in the first ardour of his youth he had longed to obliterate the Roman name and turn all Roman lands into an empire which should be, and should be called, the Empire of the Goths, so that what used to be commonly known as ' Romania ' should now be ' Gothia ', and that Ataulfus should be what Caesar Augustus had once been. But now that he had proved by long experience that the Goths, on account of their unbridled barbarism, could not be induced to obey the laws, and yet that, on the other hand, there must be laws, since without them the Commonwealth would cease to be a Commonwealth, he had chosen, for his part at any rate, that he would seek the glory of renewing and increasing the Roman name by the arms of his Gothic followers, and would be remembered by posterity as the restorer of Rome, since he would be its changer.[1]

Such ambitions were by no means rare among the 'barbarians', but even though a Gothic or a Frankish king might honestly desire to continue the Roman Empire in some form or other, there were two factors which tended to cut him off from Roman citizens, and to keep the barbarians as peoples apart, at once outsiders and intruders. These two factors were religion and law.

We have already mentioned that all the Germanic peoples except the Franks and the Anglo-Saxons were Arian Christians. We cited their Christianity as evidence of their romanization. We must now point out that their Arianism, accidentally though they had acquired it, served as an impenetrable barrier between them and the Roman citizens of the West. For the Western Church had never been Arian. It considered, and rightly so, that Arianism was founded on a sort of logical pun and that it cut at the roots of the Christian faith, since it denied that the divine nature in Christ was purely divine, and reduced Him to the status of a demi-god. It considered that, while the heathen were ignorant, the Arians were blasphemous ; compared with the simpleminded beliefs of the heathen, the subtle and enticing doctrines of the Arians were as the wiles of the devil. It therefore treated the Arians as outcasts. It is often hard for an irreligious age to recognize that religion has in fact been capable of dividing men

[1] Orosius vii. 43 ; translation based on that of T. Hodgkin in *Theodoric the Goth* (Heroes of the Nations series), Putnam, 1897, pp. 4-5.

as effectually as political doctrine or economic status, but unless the fact is recognized the history of the Middle Ages will remain a meaningless labyrinth. For the present it must be sufficient to point out that the two barbarian peoples who were responsible for the rise of the papacy were the only two Germanic peoples who had never been Arian and who were in fact heathen when they entered the Empire—the Franks and the Anglo-Saxons ; and that of all the peoples of Europe it was the Anglo-Saxons who preserved classical learning in the eighth century and the Franks who revived the Roman Empire in the ninth. They were able to do this because they had been received into the community of the Roman world, since they were not tainted with Arianism.

The second factor was law. In the Roman Empire the civil and military powers had been kept severely apart, except in the person of the emperor himself. The Germans had, of necessity, been accepted as his soldiers, and had been, in theory at least, under his military control ; but they had never been absorbed into the civilian government of the Empire. They had lived under their own kings and had been governed by their own laws, which were of a very peculiar type. Their principal feature was the *wergeld* system. *Wergeld* meant ' worth-money ', and a man's *wergeld* varied according to his rank ; it represented the sum of money that would have to be paid as compensation to his kindred by the family of anyone who should happen to murder him. The reason for the system was this. In the primitive Germanic society, everyone was secure in the knowledge that he could call on his whole kindred to avenge any wrong done to him. The ruling principle was an eye for an eye and a tooth for a tooth. If a man was murdered it was the sacred duty of his kindred to avenge him by hunting down the murderer and killing him, often together with a suitable number of his kindred. In this way blood-feuds had become the scourge of Germanic society, and there was a crying need for some method by which the murderer's kinsmen could buy off the wrath of the murdered man's kinsmen without loss of honour. It was in order to provide such a method that the Germanic laws contained elaborate tariffs of *wergelds*. A king was worth more than a noble, a noble more than a freeman, a freeman more than a slave, and a slave more than an ox. There was also a regular tariff for lesser injuries. Thus, in the laws of King Ethelbert of Kent (dating from the end of the sixth century) it was laid down that the compensation due for each of the four front teeth was 6*s.*, for the tooth next to them 4*s.*, for the tooth next to that 3*s.*, and for the rest 1*s.* each.

The system had its disadvantages, for the tariff was usually different for different peoples, that of the Visigoths varying from that of the Burgundians, and both being different from those of the Salian and Ripuarian Franks. But the Romans had to tolerate the system even though they regarded it as barbarous, because it was the only sort of law that the Germanic peoples understood. The real difficulty was that, as the Germans were allowed to retain their own laws even within the Empire, law ceased to be territorial and became personal. Franks lived by Frankish law wherever they might be (the Salian Franks had one code and the Ripuarian Franks another), Visigoths lived by Visigothic law, Burgundians by Burgundian law, and Roman citizens by Roman law. In every part of the Empire, therefore, the legal situation was intensely complicated, especially if, as might easily have happened in Gaul, a Frank went to law with a Visigoth over land that he had acquired from a Roman citizen. The fact that a Frankish king might have had the dignity of a consul granted to him by the emperor did not alter the situation in the least. The grant might, or might not, imply recognition of the Frankish king's authority over Roman citizens, but it neither removed Frankish law from the one nor Roman law from the other.

Although it does credit to the barbarians' respect for Roman civilization that they left Roman citizens in the enjoyment of Roman law, the fact that they themselves retained their own laws and instituted the doctrine of ' personal law ' was disastrous for the Empire. As a political institution, the Empire could not be maintained solely by polite theories as to the sub-ordination of barbarian kings to a distant emperor, or by the continued existence of people who wished to enjoy the luxuries of civilization. In the last resort the Roman State was founded on obedience to Roman law. Law was the bond of civil society and the State was but a fellowship of law—the sentiments are those of Cicero, but they are valid for all time. The barbarians

might never cease to dream, like Ataulf the Goth, ' of renewing
and increasing the Roman name ', but so far as the West was
concerned the Roman *respublica* ceased to have any real meaning
when rival systems of law jostled with each other within the frontiers of the Empire.   For then the concept of nationality had
triumphed over the Roman conception of the *gens humana*.

Further Reading

N. D. FUSTEL DE COULANGES. *Histoire des Institutions Politiques de
l'Ancienne France ; l'Invasion Germanique et la fin de l'empire*
(ed. C. Jullian, Paris, 1891).   Still fresh and valuable in spite
of exaggerations.

J. B. BURY. *History of the Later Roman Empire from the death of Theodosius I to the death of Justinian.* 2 vols. The indispensable
narrative history. London. 1923.

S. DILL. *Roman Society in the last century of the Western Empire.* London.
1898.

F. LOT. *La Fin de Monde Antique.* Paris. 1927 (new ed. 1951).

ALFONS DOPSCH. *The Economic and Social Foundations of European
Civilization* (abridged and translated from the German by
M. G. Beard and Nadine Marshall). London. 1937.

F. W. WALBANK. *The Decline of the Roman Empire in the West.* London.
1946. Useful for economic history.

P. COURCELLE. *Histoire Littéraire des grandes invasions germaniques.*
Paris. 1948.

J. M. WALLACE-HADRILL. *The Barbarian West, 400 1000.* (Hutchinson's University Library). London. 1952.

A. H. M. JONES. *The Later Roman Empire, 284-602.* 3 vols.
Oxford. 1964.

SIDONIUS APOLLINARIS. *Letters and Poems.* The first of two volumes,
edited and translated by W. B. Anderson, appeared in the Loeb
Classics. London. 1936.

III

THREE REACTIONS TO THE BARBARIAN
INVASIONS

BECAUSE the barbarian invasions were not sudden, but gradual, it was possible for many Roman citizens to ignore their significance. Though they bewailed the fact that the times were not as good as they once had been, they tried to go on living as if nothing had changed. But every now and again a sudden shock would wake them up to reality and force them to acknowledge the extent of what had already decayed or been destroyed. It was only the more woeful preachers, like Salvian, who insisted on reminding everyone in season and out of season that the barbarians were no longer at the gates but within them. Most people tried to imagine that things were not so bad as they seemed. Nevertheless it was necessary for everyone to adjust himself to the new circumstances. It might be done in a moment of clear-sightedness, or in a moment of panic, or blindly and unconsciously, but it had to be done somehow; and at our distance of time it is possible to pick out three general types of reaction. One could retreat into oneself and, like St. Augustine, concentrate simply on the kingdom of God; or one could collaborate with the barbarians in the belief that the better of them would appreciate Roman civilization and be content to live in amity with the Romans; or one could fight back, as did the Emperor Justinian. Many people, of course, reacted first in one way and then in another; but the three main types are most conveniently treated in isolation and in turn.

1. St. AUGUSTINE (354–430)

From 396 to 430 St. Augustine was Bishop of Hippo Regius (Bône) in North Africa, and the shock that awakened him to the fact that the Roman Empire was falling was the sack of Rome by Alaric the Goth (410). The damage done to the buildings of Rome by Alaric was not nearly so severe as that which later barbarians were to do, but the fact that a hostile army had entered Rome was in itself overwhelming. Refugees fled to North Africa and created panic there. It was believed that Alaric would cross the sea from Italy and invade Africa for the sake of its corn-supplies, and consequently some people (including a whole convent of nuns) evacuated themselves to Egypt. When the danger from Alaric disappeared, a new threat came, this time from the Vandals. In 409 they invaded Spain, and more refugees arrived in Africa. Augustine was asked whether it was legitimate for the Christian clergy to flee or whether they should stay at their posts and be persecuted by the Arian Vandals. He replied that they might flee only if they could take their entire congregations with them ; if any of the Christian community was left behind the clergy should remain with them. Twenty years later Augustine had to make the same decision for himself. The Vandals had crossed into Africa and were besieging Hippo Regius. Augustine remained at his post. He died before the city fell.

It was in this atmosphere that ' The City of God ' (*De Civitate Dei*) was written. Its twenty-two books were written over a period of thirteen years (413–26) and show the changing moods of its author. As we might expect, it is not consistent in all its various parts, and consequently it has often been misunderstood, particularly in the later Middle Ages. But it is an intensely moving book, for it shows Augustine wrestling with the central problem of his time, why God had allowed the Roman Empire to fall.

To the pagans the answer was clear. They were convinced that the Empire had been destroyed because it had deserted the pagan gods and become Christian. Some, apparently, insisted that the Christians were bad citizens who would not play their part in defending the Empire. Others, and these seem to have been the most numerous, simply insisted that Rome had fallen because it had deserted its tutelary gods—Jupiter and the rest. The pagan gods had defended Rome while Rome had remained faithful to them ; when it had deserted them they had turned upon it and destroyed it.

These accusations had to be answered, and St. Augustine was the man to answer them. He had a firm grasp of pagan learning, for he had only been converted to Christianity at the age of thirty-two, and he was a rhetorician. He met the pagans on their own ground and searched history for examples of calamities that had befallen mankind in the pre-Christian era. Had pagan empires never fallen? Had the pagan gods saved Troy from destruction? Had they been powerless to prevent the disasters to Roman arms at Cannae and the Caudine forks?

A mere rhetorician might have been content with the cheap *tu quoque*. But Augustine was anxious to go further and discover the truth. For him it was not enough to declare that the Goths would still have sacked Rome even if Rome had still been pagan. He felt it was his duty to explain why the Christian God had allowed it to be sacked. That was his difficulty. He could not pretend that the rule of the barbarians was preferable to that of Rome, for he was convinced that it was not. Nor could he argue that God was not responsible for the fall of Rome, for he was convinced that God was omnipotent, controlling and ordaining not only what happened in Heaven but also what happened on earth. God was both almighty and righteous. Therefore He had willed the sack of Rome, and it had been righteous. Mortal men might be incapable of seeing why, but that was simply because they could not see eternity at a glance.

What makes St. Augustine's work so moving is that he was not prepared to stop at this point, declaring the will of God to be inscrutable and unknowable. He was dismayed to find that it was God's will that the Roman Empire should fall. But instead of questioning God's righteousness, he questioned his own faith; for the very fact that he was dismayed showed him how little he understood the will of God. Consequently he tried to see the fall of the Roman Empire as God would have seen it, in the perspective of eternity; and when he had done that, he saw that he had been mistaken in thinking that the fall of Rome really mattered, since in the eyes of God no earthly city, kingdom, or empire was a supreme good in itself. In a famous passage he illustrated this point by means of a demonstration that even Rome, for all its virtues, had not been a true state (*respublica*) because it had not been founded on justice. (See Book XIX, chapters

21–4.) For justice was ' that virtue which distributes to everyone that which is its own ', and the Roman Empire had not given to God the things that were God's.

The point that Augustine was trying to make was that for the Christian, or even for the virtuous pagan, justice was more important than the State.

> Set aside justice, then, and what are kingdoms but great bands of brigands ? For what are brigands' bands but little kingdoms? For in brigandage the hands of the underlings are directed by the commander, the confederacy of them is sworn together, and the pillage is shared by law among them. And if those ragamuffins grow up to be able enough to keep forts, build habitations, possess cities, and conquer adjoining nations, then their government is no longer called brigandage, but graced with the eminent name of a kingdom, given and gotten not because they have left their practices but because they use them without danger of law. Elegant and excellent was that pirate's answer to the great Macedonian Alexander, who had taken him ; the king asking him how he durst molest the seas so, he replied with a free spirit : ' How darest thou molest the whole earth ? But because I do it only with a little ship, I am called brigand : thou doing it with a great navy art called emperor.' (Book IV, chapter 4.) [1]

There was, thought Augustine, nothing sanctified about the state ; it was only a convention. That was why he did not consider that, in the eyes of God, the fall of the Roman Empire mattered. What did matter was that justice should not be destroyed.

To Augustine the embodiment of justice was the ' City of God '. This was not, as later ages were to think, the papacy or the Church Militant on earth. It was the whole body of the faithful, whether in Heaven or on earth. He referred to life on earth as a ' pilgrimage ' or ' pilgrimage amongst the wicked ', and his conception was that for the true citizen of God's city this pilgrimage was but a moment in eternity, a period of trial and temptation in which his loyalty was tested. The Fall of Man, his Original Sin, had made justice unattainable on earth. What should be of concern to the Christian, therefore, was not the palliation of the necessary

<hr>

[1] The translation is that of John Healey (1620), as reprinted in Everyman's Library (1945).

evils of this world, but steadfast loyalty to Christ who alone could offer salvation :

> What does it matter in respect of this short and transitory life under whose dominion a man lives as long as he be not impelled to acts of impiety or injustice ?

Consequently he counselled Christians to obey whatever powers might be, and to suffer even the barbarians if it was God's will that they should overrun the Empire. *Da quod jubes, et jube quod vis*, was his prayer. In this respect his attitude was faithfully reflected, centuries later, by Martin Luther.

> For though they take our life,
> Goods, honour, children, wife,
> Yet is their profit small.
> These things shall vanish all.
> The city of God remaineth.

It is easy to claim that Augustine was making a tame surrender of all the solid benefits that Rome had won for mankind. But to do so would be unjust. It was largely due to his inspiration that the Christian Church, and much of classical culture too, survived the Dark Ages. His ideals were in line with the monastic ideal that expected a man to retreat from the world in order to save his soul, to become a citizen of the City of God, fighting the battles not of the world but of the spirit. In later chapters we will have to notice the debt that medieval and modern civilization owes to monasticism, and then it may be appreciated that Augustine's attitude was not defeatist at all. Rome had fallen, but Christ had risen.

2. THEODORIC THE OSTROGOTH

An alternative to withdrawal from the world in face of the barbarian invasions was a policy of collaboration. This policy was implicit in the whole imperial system of recruiting barbarians as *foederati*, but it found its most spectacular expression in Italy at the end of the fifth, and beginning of the sixth, century. In Italy the conditions were specially favourable for successful collaboration. The Italians had been forced to admit that military power had passed to the barbarians, for Rome ' the unconquer-

able ' had been sacked first by Alaric the Goth and then by the
Vandals. It was useless for the Italians to try to repel the
barbarians. If they were to save anything of their civilization
they would have to absorb them into their society and educate
them. This could only be a practical policy, however, if the
barbarians wanted to educate themselves and to discipline themselves to the rule of law. Hence the importance of the fact
that Italy was ruled by an outstandingly ' good ' barbarian,
Theodoric the Ostrogoth.

Theodoric was the son of Theudemir, one of three brothers
who were kings of the Ostrogoths. He was probably born in
453 or 454. At that time the Ostrogoths were settled as *foederati*
in Pannonia (*i.e.* on the middle Danube), and Theodoric might
have been educated as an ordinary barbarian had it not been
for the fact that in 461 he was sent to Constantinople as a hostage
for the good behaviour of his people. There he remained for
ten years. He was treated well, for he attracted the attention
of the Emperor Leo I, and it is probable that special efforts
were made to educate him in ' the Roman way of life '. What
the exact form of that education might have been, we do not
know ; it is quite possible that he never learnt to read or write.
But it can hardly be doubted that the very fact of living in Constantinople must have made an enormous impression on the boy.
The account which Jordanes, a Goth and a younger contemporary of Theodoric, gives of the visit of Athanaric to Constantinople in 380, may be quoted as giving some indication of
the wonder with which the Goths regarded that city :

> Entering the royal city and marvelling thereat, ' Lo, now I behold ',
> he said, ' what I have often heard of without believing, the wonder
> of so great a city.' Then turning his eyes this way and that, behold-
> ing the situation of the city and the concourse of ships, now he
> marvels at the long perspective of the walls, then he sees the multi-
> tudes of various nations like the wave gushing forth from one
> fountain which has been fed by divers springs, then he beholds the
> marshalled ranks of soldiery. ' A God ', said he, ' without doubt
> a God upon Earth is the Emperor of this realm, and whoso lifts
> his hand against him, that man's blood be on his own head.' [1]

[1] Quoted from T. Hodgkin, *Theodoric the Goth* (Heroes of the Nations series),
1897, p. 38.

None the less, when Theodoric returned to his own people (471) he immediately proved his worth as a warrior, and when, on his father's death (474), he became King of the Ostrogoths, he continued the traditional policy of his people as *foederati*, ever mistrustful of the emperor and ever ready to revolt against him.   On one occasion he threatened Thessalonika, on others he captured Dyrrachium, devastated Thessaly, and even (in 487) marched on Constantinople.   He was clearly a dangerous man to have so close to the capital of the Empire, and in order to get rid of him the Emperor Zeno gave him a commission to invade Italy and to subdue, in his name, the barbarian Odovacar.

Odovacar had been possessed of Italy since 476, when he had persuaded the senate to declare that there was no further need for a Roman emperor in the West.   He had ruled the country in the name of the (eastern) Roman emperor and with the collaboration of well-born Romans such as Liberius and the elder Cassiodorus who acted as his ministers.   Subsequently he had, so far as the Emperor Zeno was concerned, grown too powerful and independent ; he had apparently annexed Dalmatia and was thought to be plotting against the emperor himself. Zeno therefore resorted to what was by now the time-honoured device of Roman policy.   Faced with two dangerous barbarian enemies, he incited them to fight each other.   All that he had to do was to promise Theodoric that if he overthrew Odovacar he could govern Italy himself until ' the emperor should come to claim the supremacy '.

It probably came as a great surprise to Zeno that the victory of Theodoric and his Ostrogoths was both decisive and rapid. Theodoric marched on Italy in 488.   By 490 he had won control over most of the country.   In 493, having made peace with Odovacar, he murdered him at a banquet, and his position was secure.   He gave to his followers that portion of the land (one-third) that had previously been enjoyed by Odovacar's army, and took over Odovacar's position as governor of Italy.   The senate and the Italian people transferred their allegiance to him, and he was able to employ many of the ministers who had previously served under Odovacar.   His invasion does not seem to have caused any serious break in the civil administration of Italy.

Theodoric had conquered Italy in the name of the emperor,

and he was careful to conform, in outward appearance at least, to the constitutional theory that he was ruling not in his own name but in that of the Roman emperor. He gave himself the title of King (*rex*) but did not state what he was king of, the Goths or Italy. He did not date official edicts by the year of his own reign but by that of the emperor. On the coins that he struck, the effigy and name on the obverse were almost invariably those of the emperor, though Theodoric's monogram might be figured on the reverse. He was correct in his dealings with the Roman senate, and (as Odovacar had done before him) nominated a consul annually and forwarded the nomination to the emperor. He did not make any laws (which only emperors could do) but issued edicts. On the other hand, he wore the purple and enforced the *adoratio*, so that those to whom he gave audience prostrated themselves before him as they did before the emperor ; and in his letters he allowed his officials to declare that he ruled ' with the help of God ', in spite of the fact that, in this respect, divine assistance was an imperial prerogative.

The constitutional position, therefore, was such that Romans did not necessarily feel any conflict between loyalty to the emperor and acceptance of Theodoric's rule. Theodoric was able to lay great stress on the fact that he was a military commander and that it was his prime duty to defend Italy from other barbarian invaders. He therefore made his capital not at Rome but at Ravenna, where he built his own palace and his own churches without fear of breaking age-old traditions. The visitor to the church of S. Apollinare Nuovo can still see mosaics which illustrate the splendour and brilliance of Theodoric's court, and this experience will help him to understand why Theodoric's government was at first popular in Italy. There were two main reasons.

The first was that Theodoric cared for civilization in a way that Odovacar had not. This does not mean that Odovacar had wished to destroy civilization in Italy, but only that he had done nothing to save it. The natural tendency in fifth-century Italy was for city-life to decay. The population had decreased and was decreasing, so that it was both difficult and unnecessary to keep all the houses, or all the quarters, of a town in good repair. This would have been the case even if no damage at all had been done to the towns by the barbarian invasions ; it was simply that the ordinary maintenance works were not carried out. Bushes and trees had grown up in the aqueducts, so the water-supply of Rome was both scanty and foul. Public buildings such as the Colosseum and the theatre of Pompey were in ruins, great blocks of stone which had fallen from the decrepit buildings littered and obstructed the streets, and bands of thieves stole the bronze statues that adorned the city, to melt them down for the sake of the metal. From this state of ruin, Theodoric was determined to rescue Italy. Several of the letters in which he ordered the repair of various cities or monuments have survived, and show the wide range of his activities in this direction. ' For what ', he asked, ' is more worth-while our doing than to construe the repair [of Rome] which constantly stands as an ornament of our state ? ' It was an attitude that brought fresh hope to Italy.

The second reason for his popularity, and it was even more important than the first, was his insistence that Romans and Goths should live and work in partnership. The Romans had the skill, the education, and the civilization that the Goths lacked ; the Goths had the vigour and public spirit that the Romans had lost. If only the two peoples could work in partnership there might yet be hope of a revived commonwealth. But such a partnership, if it were to endure, would need to be founded on justice. It was important not only that Theodoric himself should have the reputation of being a most specially just king, but also that he should insist on having only one law in his kingdom. There was to be ' one law and equal discipline ' for ' all that was in alliance in Italy '.

> With us, the rules of law are the same for all, Goths and Romans. The only difference between the one people and the other is that the Goths assume military responsibility in the common interest so that you, O Romans, can enjoy in peace the benefits of the Roman state (*civitatis*).[1]

To declare that the Goths should be subject to Roman law was not as simple a matter as to declare that in the twentieth

---

[1] *Variae*, viii. 3. The words are those of Cassiodorus, put into the mouth of Athalaric, Theodoric's grandson and successor.

century an Englishman living in Italy should be subject to Italian law. For Germanic law stood for a way of life which was different from that implied by Roman law, and was regarded by the Germanic peoples as their birthright. It rested on notions of kinship, compurgation and *wergelds* and represented a whole complex of loyalties and values that were totally foreign to the Romans. To forswear one's law was to forswear the tradition of one's ancestors. Theodoric saw this clearly and considered that the acceptance of Roman law was the rejection of ' barbarism ' or the ' Gentile ' way of life.

> Understand, he declared, that men progress not so much by bodily violence as by reason, and that those who deserve the greatest praise are those who excel others in justice.[1]

He might in some ways be compared to a missionary endeavouring to convert his followers to a new way of life.

His success, however, was only partial. In law, for example, though he succeeded in submitting his people to Roman law (with the result that the Ostrogoths, alone of Germanic peoples, lost their own law), he did not succeed in making them justiciable to the same courts as the Romans. The Roman rule was that soldiers and their families were justiciable to military courts, and only civilians to the civil courts, and in Theodoric's Italy the Goths were all soldiers and the Romans all civilians. The presidents of the military courts were Gothic counts, and so it followed that Goths were justiciable only to Goths, even though the law involved was Roman. For the Romans, the situation was more complex, for while cases amongst themselves were heard in the civil courts, cases involving both Romans and Goths went to the military courts. In such cases it was necessary for the Gothic count to be assisted by a Roman assessor, but the system may well have seemed somewhat inequitable.

Just as the Romans and Goths had one law but different law courts, so also they were both Christian but had different creeds and different churches, for the Goths were Arians. In the earlier part of his reign Theodoric does not seem to have considered that this religious division was important. He believed in religious toleration since it was impossible to make people

---

[1] Cassiodorus, *Variae*, iii. 17.

accept a new belief simply through fear of force. He did not confiscate any churches for the use of Arians, but built new ones ; and as his capital was not at Rome but at Ravenna it was possible to reduce to a minimum the amount of friction that rival churches would necessarily engender.

This religious policy was doomed to failure, since, although it was apparently a policy of toleration, it was also a policy of racial segregation. It was founded on the assumption that all Goths would be Arians and that all Romans would be Catholics, in much the same way as other Germanic leaders would have considered that every people should have its own law. Had Theodoric been convinced that Arianism was truer than Catholicism, he might at least have allowed the Arian clergy to proselytize among the Roman Catholics, but the evidence suggests that he was opposed to any such attempt. He apparently thought that, just as the Goths were by nature warriors and the Romans skilled in the arts, so Arianism was the badge of the Goths and Catholicism of the Romans. Religion was one of the signs that showed that the Goths had not accepted the Roman way of life in its entirety, and that they were not so willing as might at first have appeared to forswear the beliefs of their ancestors.

In the early part of Theodoric's reign, the religious difference was less important than in the later part. This was partly because when Theodoric first took possession of Italy there was no alternative power that was Catholic. The emperor was a Monophysite, the Franks were heathen, and the Visigoths, Burgundians, and Vandals were Arian. Later in his reign, however, the situation changed. Between 496 and 506 the Franks were converted to Catholic Christianity, and in 518 there was once again an orthodox emperor in Constantinople. The way was open for the emperor to ally himself with the Franks in an attempt to overthrow the Ostrogothic kingdom in the name of Catholic Christianity. An ominous precedent occurred in 507 when the Franks, with the enthusiastic support of the Gallo-Roman Catholics, had defeated the Visigoths at Vouillé and annexed Aquitaine. One bishop wrote to Clovis, King of the Franks, urging him to ' spread the light ' of his new faith to the nations about him. ' Where *you* fight ', he wrote, ' *we* conquer.'

Knowledge that the Catholics of Italy might be enticed into such an anti-Arian alliance cast a gloom over the last years of Theodoric's reign. In 523 he forbade Italians to carry arms and began to show nervousness at the relationship between the senate and the Emperor Justin. In theory the senate had both a right and duty to keep in touch with the emperor, who was still recognized as the supreme ruler of Italy. In practice, however, the emperor was a potential enemy, and any but the most formal correspondence between him and the senate was bound to be mistrusted by Theodoric. In 523 he thought that one such correspondence had in fact been treasonable, and the main accusation was eventually levelled against the philosopher Boëthius who had previously been 'master of the offices'. With the evidence at our disposal it is impossible to say whether Boëthius was innocent or guilty of the charges levelled against him. The fact that while in prison awaiting execution he wrote the *Consolation of Philosophy* has perhaps prejudiced subsequent generations in his favour, and led them to assume that in condemning him the senate was simply being subservient to the whim of a tyrant,[1] but the fact that Boëthius's successor as master of the offices was Cassiodorus, is proof that there were at least some Romans left who still, even after 523, wanted to collaborate with the Goth.

In 525-6 the close relationship between the Roman Catholic Church and the Emperor Justin I caused further difficulties. Theodoric was anxious to use his position as an Arian ruling over Catholic subjects in order to protect the position of the Arians whom the emperor was persecuting in the East. Consequently he sent the Pope, John I, on an embassy to Constantinople to demand toleration for the Arians. Distasteful as the mission must have been to the Pope, he accomplished it with some success, but in doing so he enjoyed a personal triumph which was not to Theodoric's liking. He was received in Constantinople with the very greatest honour, and amid scenes of great enthusiasm officiated in person at the coronation of the emperor. Legally, there was nothing wrong in this, for his king, Theodoric, was theoretically subject to the emperor, but

---

[1] The *Consolation of Philosophy* also shows that his Christianity was only skin-deep, and that his real belief was in the pagan philosophers of Greece.

in practice such a coronation could only be interpreted as express-
ing the Pope's desire for a revival of imperial power at the
expense of Theodoric's. On his return to Italy, therefore,
John I was imprisoned by Theodoric, and, since he was in a
weak state of health, he died in prison. To make matters worse,
Theodoric decreed that on 30 August 526, all the Catholic churches
of Italy should be handed over to the Arians. The decree was
never executed, however, for on that very day Theodoric died.
The Catholics regarded his death as a divine dispensation.

The kingdom of the Ostrogoths did not come to an end with
Theodoric's death. He was succeeded by his grandson Athalaric
(526–34), though, since he was only a boy, the real power belonged to his mother, Amalasuntha. She was Theodoric's
daughter and carried even further his policy of civilizing the Goths,
with Cassiodorus as her main adviser. In doing so, however,
she lost the support of the more conservative elements among
her own people. Her difficulties are well illustrated by the
complaints that some of her nobles are said to have made to her
on the subject of the education of her son :

> O lady, you are not dealing justly by us, nor doing that which
> is expedient for the nation, in your way of educating your son.
> Letters and book-learning are very different from manly courage
> and fortitude, and to hand a lad over to the teaching of greybeards
> is generally the way to make him a coward and a caitiff. He who
> is to do daring deeds and win glory in the world must be emancipated
> from fear of the pedagogue and be practising martial exercises.
> Your father Theodoric would never suffer his Goths to send their
> sons to the grammarian-school, for he used to say : ' If they fear
> their teacher's strap now they will never look on sword or javelin
> without a shudder.' And he himself, who won the lordship of
> such wide lands, and died King of so fair a Kingdom which he
> had not inherited from his fathers, knew nothing even by hearsay
> of this book-learning. Therefore, lady, you must say ' good-bye '
> to these pedagogues, and give Athalaric companions of his own
> age, who may grow up with him to manhood and make of him a
> valiant king after the pattern of the barbarians.[1]

The issue as here set forth by a Greek historian of the sixth century
brings to life some of the real difficulties involved in a policy of

---

[1] Procopius trans. Hodgkin, *op. cit.*, 307–8.

collaboration. Whether these difficulties were fundamental and would have involved the policy in inevitable failure we cannot tell, for the collapse of the Ostrogothic kingdom was eventually brought about not by any internal force but by the reconquest of Italy by the emperor Justinian.

From the Roman side, the advantages and disadvantages of collaboration are best seen in the career of Marcus Aurelius Cassiodorus Senator, commonly known as Cassiodorus. He belonged to a noble Roman family, but was an enthusiastic supporter of the policy of collaboration. He had learnt the policy from his father, who had served both Odovacar and Theodoric. He himself had shown his enthusiasm for the ' middle way ' in his support of Theodoric even after the execution of Boëthius (whom he succeeded as master of the offices), and in his support for Amalasuntha in her Romanizing policy ; and when the Emperor Justinian invaded Italy to reconquer it from the Goths, Cassiodorus remained faithful to his chosen course. He continued to serve his Gothic master until the initial Byzantine victories seemed decisive. Then, making his way to Constantinople, he did his utmost to effect a reconciliation between the Goths and the ' Romans '. Even as late as 551, he was still there, urging moderation on the imperial government, not because he loved the Goths more than the Romans, but because he loved them both.[1] It was only after the General Narses had been sent to Italy with orders to crush the Goths completely, that Cassiodorus realized the failure of his hopes. He left Constantinople, returned to his ancestral home at Squillace and, retreating from the tribulations of political life, founded a monastery which he called *Vivarium*. He ordered his monks to lay great stress on learning, for he was convinced that the barbarians had come to stay, and that the most important task that he could perform would be to transmit the culture of the ancient world to the new. For that reason, manuscripts of the classics were sedulously copied at *Vivarium*. In his earlier days he had, perhaps with an eye to promotion, written a *History of the Goths* (now lost), but his two most important and typical works were the *Variae* and the *Institutions*. The *Variae* (or *Epistolae variae*) was a collection of official

---

[1] See A. Momigliano, ' Cassiodorus and Italian Culture of his Time ', *Proceedings of the British Academy*, xli (1955), 207–45.

letters written by Cassiodorus for Theodoric and his successors ;
it was intended as a sort of handbook for the future civil servant,
to help him perform his functions in correct form and with a
proper sense of style.   It was a conscious effort to pass on a
tradition, as also was the *Institutions*.   This latter book, composed
after the fall of the Ostrogothic Kingdom, was written for his
monastery of *Vivarium*, and was an epitome of pagan and Christian learning with practical advice for their study.

But though he had a real enthusiasm for learning, it must not
be imagined that he was a classical writer himself.   On the con-
tary, he was a most admirable example of the fact that the pattern
of men's thought had changed.   It was not simply that Cassiodorus found an interest in new subjects, such as Gothic history,
but even more that he deliberately cultivated a style that was
difficult, pompous, and verbose.   This style was used even in
official letters.   A good example comes from one that he wrote
for Theodoric complaining of the riotous behaviour of the spec-
tators at the circus, and ordering them to behave themselves in
future :

> You are accustomed to fill the air with mellifluous cries, and to
> shout with one voice so that even the beasts delight to hear it.   The
> voices that you raise are sweeter than an organ, and thus you make
> the concave theatre resound as if with the harmony of the lute, so
> that anyone would think it was music rather than shouting.   Is
> it fitting that in such a setting there should be brawls and violent
> fights ?   Be happy and cast off your madness !   Rejoice and shut
> out your anger ! [1]

The point of such language, as Cassiodorus himself said, was that
while the gift of speech was given to all men, the only quality that
distinguished the educated from the uneducated was the orna-
mentation of style.   Had Cassiodorus written with brevity and
lucidity, the uneducated might have thought that they were as
learned as he, and have lost their respect for letters.   But incomprehensible language increased the esteem in which he was
held.

In his attitude to knowledge, which again was profoundly
medieval, Cassiodorus caught something of this same infection.

[1] *Variae*, i. 31.

If the distinguishing mark of the learned was that they read books, it would seem to follow that the learning to be had in books was sounder than any knowledge that might be acquired by personal observation. He stated in all seriousness that the elephant had no knees, that once prostrate upon the ground it could not rise unaided, that it paid homage to good rulers but not to bad, and that ' when requested to do so, it exhales its breath, which is said to be a remedy for the headache '. If challenged as to the truth of these statements he would probably have replied that they were certainly true because he had read them in a book ; and if by any chance he had subsequently seen an elephant he would probably have said that it was not a ' real ' elephant, since ' real ' elephants had no knees.

This uncritical adoration of book-learning was one of the most significant features of the so-called ' Dark Ages '. There is a popular fallacy that the cause of the Dark Ages was the fact that the barbarians destroyed the civilization which they found, burning cities, breaking statues, and casting works of classical authors to the flames. In point of fact, the men who ushered in the Dark Ages were men like Theodoric and Cassiodorus, who were intent on restoring the cities, preserving the statues, and transcribing the classics. Their adoration of the ancient world was matched only by their inability to understand it, for by the time that they were born, classical culture was already dead. They were the first of the great medievals and began to build a new civilization in an attempt to restore the old.

3. RECONQUEST : THE EMPEROR JUSTINIAN (527-565)

A third possible reaction to the barbarian invasions was to fight back, and to go on fighting in an attempt to reconquer what had been lost. Within the boundaries of the Western Empire, such a reaction was rare, but in the Eastern or Byzantine Empire it was predominant. Constantinople (or Byzantium) had been built not only as a capital but also as a fortress. Its people believed that it had been founded by the will of God and that it was protected by Him, and they fought in its defence with the confidence born of religious conviction. In its political ideals, as in its art and literature, Byzantium was intensely conservative, and showed no desire to compromise with the new forces at work in the world, since it considered that the Empire provided the only conceivable satisfactory way of life.

Justinian himself was slightly more conservative still, for he was not a Greek or easterner by birth, but a Latin-speaking Illyrian. He came of peasant-stock and had risen to power because his uncle Justin had, after a successful army career, usurped the Empire (518). Not only was he the last Latin-speaking emperor, he was also the last who framed his policies with a view to Latin rather than Greek interests. Whereas the typical Greek based the defence of the Empire on the conviction that the greatest menace to its existence came from Persia, Justinian was convinced that the more real menace came from the Germanic peoples in the West. Consequently it was his ambition (to quote his own words) to reconquer ' the countries possessed by the ancient Romans, to the limits of the two oceans '. He aimed at reviving the Roman Empire in the fullness of its splendour.

In this task he was assisted by one of the most remarkable women of all history, the Empress Theodora, ' whose strange elevation ', wrote Gibbon, ' cannot be applauded as the triumph of female virtue '. According to the *Secret History* of Procopius, on which Gibbon based his famous account of her, she was the daughter of a Cypriot, Acacius, the master of the bears in the hippodrome. After his death, his three daughters were ' successively devoted to the public and private pleasures of the Byzantine people '. It was as a slapstick comedian in the theatre that Theodora first made her name, but her beauty was ' the subject of more flattering praise and the source of more exquisite delight '.

> Her features were delicate and regular ; her complexion, though somewhat pale, was tinged with a natural colour ; every sensation was instantly expressed by the vivacity of her eyes ; her easy motions displayed the graces of a small but elegant figure ; and either love or adulation might proclaim, that painting and poetry were incapable of delineating the matchless elegance of her form. But this form was degraded by the facility with which it was exposed to the public eye, and prostituted to licentious desire. Her venal charms were abandoned to a promiscuous crowd of citizens and strangers of every rank, and of every profession ; the fortunate

lover who had been promised a night of enjoyment, was often driven from her bed by a stronger or more wealthy favourite ; and when she passed through the streets, her presence was avoided by all who wished to escape either the scandal or the temptation.[1]

The story of how she advanced herself from this profession to that of empress must be read in Gibbon or Procopius. But there can be no doubt that when she had attained that exalted station, she proved herself to be not only virtuous but also a woman of mettle. In the year 532 the riots between the blue and the green factions in the hippodrome developed to such an extent that a large part of Constantinople was wrecked by fire and a usurper was proclaimed emperor. Justinian prepared for flight, and was only checked by Theodora who, according to Procopius, spoke in terms such as these :

> May I never exist without this purple robe and may I never live to see the day on which those who meet me shall not address me as ' Queen '. If you wish, O Emperor, to save yourself, there is no difficulty ; we have ample funds. Yonder is the sea, and there are the ships. Yet reflect whether, when you have once escaped to a place of security, you will not prefer death to safety. *I* agree with an old saying that ' Empire is a fair winding-sheet '.[2]

The saying might, as the event turned out, be applied to the whole of Justinian's reign, for he recovered the throne which he had nearly lost and then proceeded to reconquer the West. To embark on any such policy required courage. It was fifty years since Odovacar had taken control of Italy, and a hundred since the Vandals had conquered Africa, yet Justinian considered that what had once belonged to the Empire should belong to it still. At the beginning of his reign he had to face a war with Persia, but he was so anxious to realize his plans in the West that in 532 he made an ' endless peace ' with Chosroes. In point of fact it was neither glorious—for it included the payment of eleven thousand pounds of gold—nor enduring, since it lasted only eight years ; but it served Justinian's purpose by giving him a respite in which to plan his great enterprise in the West.

Justinian's advisers were not unanimous in favour of his plan

---

[1] E. Gibbon, *Decline and Fall of the Roman Empire*, ch. xl.
[2] Procopius, xxiv, 33–7, as quoted by J. B. Bury, *op. cit.*, ii. 45.

for a reconquest of the West. He himself, however, regarded
his project somewhat as a crusade to rescue the Catholics from
Arian rule. According to Procopius, one of the deciding factors
that determined Justinian to send an expedition to Africa, was
the intervention of a bishop who declared that God had revealed
to him in a dream that the emperor should ' rescue the Christians
in Libya from tyrants ' and that He himself would aid him. In
point of fact the Catholics did give him assistance, although in
Italy it was not nearly so whole-hearted as might have been expected. What was far more important was the help that Justinian
received from the divisions among the barbarians themselves.

There were four main barbarian powers in the West. The
Vandals ruled Africa, the Visigoths Spain and part of southern
France, the Franks northern and western France, and the Ostrogoths Italy. While Theodoric had ruled in Italy, he had attempted
by means of marriage alliances to form an Arian *bloc* in the West,
but he had failed, and by 532 the Ostrogoths were on bad terms
with both the Franks and the Vandals. This was a great matter
for Justinian, for it meant that when he despatched his armada
against Vandal Africa, it was able not only to pass Sicily unmolested, but also to collect supplies and intelligence there (533).

The armada consisted of 500 transports and 92 escort-vessels.
The army, under the command of Belisarius, consisted of 10,000
foot-soldiers and 5,000 cavalry. It was an army of mercenaries
consisting of Huns, Herules, Lombards, Isaurians, Persians,
and other barbarian elements, and it must have seemed pitifully
small for its task. But Belisarius was considerably helped by the
fact that the Vandals were divided amongst themselves. Their
lawful king, Hilderic, had pursued a policy that was complaisant
towards his Catholic subjects and the Empire (for his mother
was the daughter of the Emperor Valentinian III). He had thus
incurred the opposition of many of his fellow-countrymen, and
in 530 he had been deposed and imprisoned by his cousin Gelimer.
In consequence, Belisarius was able to claim that he was not
going to war with the Vandals, but ' only attempting to overthrow your tyrant who . . . keeps your king a prisoner '. After
the imperial victory of *Ad Decimum*, outside Tunis, however, it
transpired that Gelimer had had Hilderic executed as soon as he
had heard the news of Belisarius's landing, and consequently

the imperialists were relieved of the embarrassment of restoring a Vandal king. By the further victory of Tricamaron (December 533) the Vandal power was virtually broken, and in March of the following year Gelimer surrendered. Africa was restored as a province of the Empire.

Before proceeding to the conquest of Italy, Belisarius returned to Constantinople, for he was anxious to show his loyalty to the emperor. It would not have been difficult for him to set himself up as an independent king in the same way as Theodoric had done, for his army was composed of barbarians, and about 1,500 of his 5,000 cavalry were his personal retainers (*bucellarii*) who would, no doubt, have supported him even against the emperor. But Belisarius was a genuine imperialist and repeatedly made it clear that, no matter what his subordinates or his enemies might suggest, he was fighting not for himself but for the Empire.

In 535–40 he was entrusted with the reconquest of Italy from the Ostrogoths. Here, as in Africa, he was assisted by the divisions of the barbarians. The Franks were indifferent to the collapse of Ostrogothic power in Italy (if anything, they rather welcomed it), and the Ostrogoths were, like the Vandals, divided among themselves. The Romanizing policy of Theodoric had been continued, and perhaps extended by his daughter Amalasuntha. She had therefore met with much opposition from the more reactionary element among the Goths and had at one point contemplated flight to Constantinople. In 534 she was imprisoned by her husband, Theodahad, on an island in Lake Bolsena, where soon afterwards she was strangled in her bath. As soon as he had heard of her imprisonment, Justinian had written to Amalasuntha assuring her of his protection, and in 535 his armies landed in Italy as her avengers. The support that his armies received, however, was not as great as might have been expected—the greatest enthusiasm for the imperial cause being in Sicily where no Goths had settled. The Pope, of course, was imperialist, but in Naples the Gothic and imperialist parties were about equal. Cassiodorus, Roman though he was, served the Gothic kings Theodahad (535–6) and Witigis (536–40), in the same way as he had served Theodoric and Amalasuntha. Belisarius had to fight his way up the peninsula—and he was besieged in Rome for a year (537-8)—before he had secured the capture of Ravenna and the surrender of King Witigis (540). When the surrender was accomplished, two of its features were especially remarkable. Witigis was not treated as a traitor or usurper, but was pensioned off to an estate on the Persian frontier with the title of patrician, almost as if he were a Roman. The Goths, on the other hand, endeavoured to treat with Belisarius as if he were the general of just another barbarian army. They offered him the throne of Italy, so that he might rule in semi-independence, like Odovacar or Theodoric, and in point of fact they surrendered only on the understanding that Belisarius had accepted their offer. He had in fact deceived them, for he was a devoted imperialist, but it came as a surprise to most people that he had resisted the temptation.

In 540 Justinian's power was at its acme. Africa seemed to be at peace, and Italy was apparently reconquered (though there was still trouble to come). It is true that the Empire had not yet regained its greatest extent in the West, for, in 550, divisions amongst the Visigoths were to make it possible for the imperialists to occupy south-east Spain. It is true also that in this very year (540) the second Persian war broke out and Antioch was sacked. None the less, it was at this point of Justinian's reign that the fortunes of his empire seemed brightest.

And bright they may well have seemed, for Justinian had not confined his revival of the Empire to the mere reconquest of lost territories. He considered it his duty to revive its whole spirit. This made it necessary for him to see that the Empire did not fail in its proper task, the provision of a just and uniform rule of law. The difficulty was that Roman law had become so vast in bulk that lawyers and magistrates, especially in the provinces, found it almost impossible to establish what in fact was ' good law ' on any given point, and consequently their judgements varied greatly. Justinian therefore resolved to recodify the law in such a way that reference to it should be practical and convenient.

The result was the production of the *Corpus Juris Civilis*. This work, which in the standard printed edition runs to 2,200 pages, was produced in five years (528-33) by a commission of lawyers, at the head of which was the quaestor Tribonian. It reduced the size of the necessary library for a lawyer from 106 to 5½ volumes, and it consisted of three separate parts, the *Code*, the *Digest* or *Pandects*, and the *Institutions*. The *Code* was a collection of imperial constitutions (or ' statute law ') from which all contradictions or obsolete laws had been removed. Similar codes had been made previously, notably under Theodosius II in 438, but Justinian's code was, of course, more up-to-date. A greater work by far was the *Digest* or *Pandects* which dealt with the *responsa prudentium* or ' answers ' of learned lawyers, which carried the weight of imperial authority and were in many ways comparable to our ' case law '. The ' opinions ' of the learned lawyers were not always in harmony with each other, and it was the rule that in such cases the majority was to prevail. But how was the lawyer or magistrate to find his way about these learned ' answers ', even to count them ? The *Digest* provided the solution. It was divided into fifty books and dealt with specific legal points one by one, grouping together the relevant ' answers ' of the wise lawyers. Most of these lawyers had lived in the second or third century A.D., but nobody before had attempted a comprehensive *digest* of their ' answers ', because the task had seemed too immense. ' Like sailors crossing the mid-ocean,' wrote Justinian in the preface, ' we have now, by the favour of Heaven, completed a work of which we once despaired.' All that remained to be done was to write a short handbook for students, the *Institutions*, ' whereby you may be enabled to learn your first lesson in law no longer from ancient fables, but grasp them by the light of imperial learning '.

The *Corpus Juris Civilis* was an achievement to make any emperor famous. It showed a tremendous belief in the virtue of society as it existed. Roman law was no sudden invention but had grown up gradually, shaping itself to conformity with every new development in Roman society. It embodied the beliefs and conventions of a thousand years. When codified by Justinian it gave a picture not only of imperial government as it should be, and of a state of society as it was, but also of a common-sense philosophy of life. From the ' answers ' of the wise lawyers it is still possible to trace the development of political ideas in the second, third, and fourth centuries A.D. ; and when medieval lawyers studied with admiration the logical arrangement of Roman law, they imbibed with their legal admiration the political ideas of the ancient world. That was the way in which Justinian's work influenced later centuries.

There can be little doubt that the *Corpus Juris Civilis* influenced Justinian's own age in much the same way, giving a new force to the old beliefs that upheld the Empire and the society for which it stood. The mere fact that the emperor had thought it worth while to go to so much trouble to make the *Corpus*, gave his subjects confidence that he still regarded the Empire as a permanent institution. The completion of the work betokened a new energy and determination to succeed in the highest places. Similar encouragement was given by Justinian's buildings, to which he attached importance. When Procopius wished to bestow the most fulsome praise on his emperor, it was *The Buildings* that he wrote, and he had to divide his work into six books in which were described respectively (1) the churches and other buildings erected in Constantinople, (2) the cities built or restored on the Persian frontier, (3) those built in Armenia and the Caucasus, (4) those in the Balkans, including Greece, (5) those in Asia Minor, and (6) those in Egypt and North Africa. The very number of the buildings provokes admiration. The frontier fortresses of North Africa, stretching in a chain from Tripolitania to Algeria, the fortified cities of the eastern frontier, the Danube defences, and the walls which once traversed the pass of Thermopylae and the isthmus of Corinth, bear witness to the determination of the emperor to defend his empire, and to the gargantuan effort that it entailed.

Besides building fortresses, Justinian was intent on beautifying the existing cities, thus adding to the lustre of his empire. The buildings erected were of a very high artistic quality and inaugurated the golden age of Byzantine art. Most famous of them was the Cathedral of the Holy Wisdom (Hagia Sophia) at Constantinople, the work of two architects, Anthemius of Tralles and Isidore of Miletus. It was built to replace the cathedral that had been burnt in the Nika revolt (532) and it was dedicated in 537, though the dome, which is its central feature, had to be rebuilt in 558. The effect of this dome, when seen from within, is awe-inspiring; one feels lost in its vastness. As Procopius put it :

Whenever one goes there to pray, one's heart is lifted up to God and finds itself in heaven. . . . And this happens not only when one visits it for the first time ; everyone gets this same impression every time he goes there, as if each visit were his first.[1]

In Italy, Justinian's most famous buildings are the basilica of S. Apollinare in Classe, and the church of S. Vitale in Ravenna itself, and they outshine even the monuments of Theodoric. Their mosaics were made of thousands of glass cubes which reflect the light in different directions and bathe the whole church in coloured light. In San Vitale the dominant colours are green and gold, and ' you would imagine ', as Procopius wrote of Hagia Sophia, ' that it was illuminated not merely from without by the sun, but that radiance springs also from within it '. And there, on either side of the chancel, are portrayed, with staring eyes and rigid form, the Emperor Justinian, the Empress Theodora, and their courts. The emperor is surrounded by ministers, clergy, and soldiers. The Empress Theodora, with seven ladies of her court, stands in the most gorgeous apparel by a fountain at the entrance of a church. Surely one should exclaim that Justinian was a truly glorious emperor and his reconquest magnificent !

The church of San Vitale was consecrated in 547. In that year the Goths were once again in possession of a large part of Italy. They had a new and able king, Totila (541–52), who in 546 had retaken Rome and had only desisted from razing it to the ground on the plea of Belisarius. By 550 the only important Italian towns that remained to the imperialists were Ravenna, Ancona, Otranto, and Crotona. To make matters worse, the Franks had taken Marseilles, and Justinian, in order to buy their doubtful support, had confirmed their right to it, for (as Procopius put it) ' the Franks never felt that they held Gaul securely unless the emperor had ratified their title '. The Herules had occupied Belgrade, the Lombards had crossed the Danube into Noricum and Pannonia, and the Persians had sacked Antioch (540). Even Africa, which had seemed subdued in 534, had remained, thanks to the Berbers and a mutiny in the imperialist armies, a theatre of war till 548. To add to all these woes, the whole Empire suffered from a great pestilence in 542–3. This pestilence

[1] *Buildings*, 1. i. 61–2 (tr. Ure, *op. cit.*, 223).

was apparently the bubonic plague, and the mortality which it caused seems to have been as great as the Black Death of the fourteenth century.

The gloom of the later part of Justinian's reign was not, however, entirely unrelieved. Antioch was recovered and Africa was pacified. Even a new conquest was made when, in 550, Justinian was able to profit from dissensions among the Visigoths in order to conquer the south-eastern province of Spain, which included Cartagena, Malaga, and Cordova. In 552 a new army was sent to Italy under the command of the eunuch Narses, and by 554 he had been able to defeat Totila and reduce the country to subjection. Italy was then, after nineteen years of war, able to enjoy fourteen years of peace. Even on the Persian frontier there was peace from 557. But the peace that hung over the last years of Justinian's Empire had been brought about by exhaustion rather than by any settlement of differences. Italy had been devastated by the rival armies, Rome had been besieged three times and had been won and lost three times by each side. Milan was razed to the ground and all its adult males massacred by the Goths and Burgundians (539). The civilization and the cities of Italy, which Theodoric had done so much to restore, were ruined. So far as Italy was concerned, it was Justinian's wars that marked the beginning of the ' Dark Ages '. In reconquering the West, Justinian had in fact destroyed it ; of him it could be said more truly than of any other emperor, that ' he made a desert and called it peace '.

The cost of the reconquest was enormous. Even if it is viewed from no other point of view than that of finance, it was excessive. Justinian's armies were mercenary, and had to be paid, though the pay was almost always in arrears. Armies were needed in Persia, Africa, Italy, Spain, and Thrace, and though generals like Belisarius would themselves recruit a large number of personal retainers (*bucellarii*), the cry was always for more men and more supplies. When Belisarius returned to Italy in order to attempt the defence of his conquests against Totila, he wrote to Justinian as follows (545) :

I arrived in Italy without men, horses, arms or money. The provinces cannot supply me with revenue for they are occupied by the enemy ; and the numbers of our troops have been diminished by large desertions to the Goths. No general could succeed in these circumstances. Send me my own armed retainers and a large host of Huns and other barbarians ; and send me money.[1]

Justinian did not invent any new taxes, though he increased the imperial estates by fair means and foul, but he applied the existing system of taxation over-rigorously. Most serious of the taxes was the land-tax and the way in which neighbouring landlords were made responsible for the taxes of land that had been deserted and allowed to fall out of cultivation. This became especially burdensome as the wars progressed, especially after the great plague of 542. An idea of the ubiquity of the tax-gatherer is given by the fact that it was considered a virtue on the part of the emperor that he remitted one year's tribute to cities which were actually taken by the enemy. It was not surprising that the name of John of Cappadocia, the praetorian prefect who was in charge of finance in the early part of Justinian's reign, should have been almost universally hated. But the real blame for the financial exactions of the reign lay, not on John, but on Justinian, for it was he who insisted on reconquering the lost provinces at the same time as the Slavs were attempting to advance into the Balkans and the Persians were on the offensive. Faced with wars on two fronts, he elected to fight a third war on a third front also, because he was a dreamer of dreams.

His dream was that the whole Empire should be liberated from barbarians. He found it a disgrace that Italy should be ruled, even in his name, by Ostrogothic kings, and he determined to reconquer the lost provinces by force of Roman arms. But there were no armies which were truly Roman. If the West had fallen to the barbarians, the East had allowed the barbarians to infiltrate into the imperial government itself. The armies that reconquered the lost provinces of the West, that set out to liberate their fellow-citizens and fellow-Catholics from a barbarian and heretical 'tyranny', were themselves composed of Huns, Isaurians, Lombards, Persians, Gepids, and Herules. Imperialist troops might change sides (as after Totila's second siege of Rome) and Gothic troops might be employed, as they regularly were, to fight for the emperor against the Persians. So far as the Italians were concerned, the war was fought between two

[1] Quoted from J. B. Bury, *History of the Later Roman Empire*, 1923, ii. 235.

armies that were equally foreign and equally barbarian, and it was hardly surprising that they referred to the imperialist government not as ' Roman ' but as ' Greek '. In a general sense there were no Romans left.

Justinian's dream was therefore unrealistic. It was also dangerous. For the Goths had, as *foederati*, performed a service for the Italians in defending their frontiers against other barbarians, and this defence was no nominal matter. The Franks, the Alemanni, and the Lombards were all advancing southwards on Italy, the Franks actually invading it twice in Justinian's reign (539 and 553). If Justinian was to defend Italy, he had to garrison it permanently, and that was just what he could not afford to do. In order to get sufficient troops to defeat the Goths, the eunuch Narses had had to recruit a force from amongst the Lombards, thus increasing the temptation of that people to invade Italy themselves, which they did two years after Justinian's death. It would thus be true to say that Justinian had not in any way improved the position of Italy. He had made it worse.

He had, however, regarded his mission as religious as well as political and military. He viewed himself as the deliverer of Catholics from Arian rule, the emperor who was to re-unite all true Christians under his rule, and who would ' close all the roads which lead to error and place religion on the firm foundations of a single faith '. But even the idea of a united Christian Church with a harmonious agreement on theology was a chimera. Justinian thought that it could be achieved by means of force and imperial legislation. He soon discovered his mistake. The East, and particularly Egypt, was enthusiastic in support of Monophysitism [1] which the West abhorred, and neither East nor West was prepared to compromise its religious beliefs for the sake of political unity. Hence Justinian's difficulties. If he was to win the support of the Catholics in the West, he had

---

[1] Monophysitism (the doctrine of Eutyches) was the belief that Christ had only one nature. It was argued that though Christ was both the son of God and the son of the Virgin Mary, yet the Divine absorbed the human nature and made it one. This doctrine was opposed to (i) Nestorianism which held that Christ had two distinct natures, one human and one divine, the Virgin being the mother only of the human Christ, and God being the father of the divine nature in Christ ; (ii) Catholic Christendom which held that Christ was of both natures, but that the two natures were indivisible.

to be anti-Monophysite, and in 536 he went so far as to allow Pope Agapetus to depose Anthimus the patriarch of Constantinople, who was a secret Monophysite. But if he was to keep the East at peace, and if he was to serve the wishes of the Empress Theodora, it was necessary for him to please the Monophysites also, and when Pope Agapetus died soon after his deposition of Anthimus he thought that his opportunity had come.

He thought that to solve his theological difficulties he had only to nominate a more complaisant Pope, his candidate (or rather the Empress Theodora's) being the deacon Vigilius. The Romans, however, did not wait for an imperial nomination. They were still under Ostrogothic rule and elected, with the approval of King Theodahad, a certain Silverius. Such independence did not suit the imperialists, and after they had captured Rome and were being besieged in it by the Goths, they charged Silverius with treachery, alleging that he had plotted to hand over the Lateran gate to the Goths. They deposed him and appointed Vigilius in his place. In the East such high-handed interference was normal, but in the West it was not, and Vigilius soon found that he had to choose between the support of the Western churches or the support of the emperor. He was summoned to Constantinople and asked to subscribe to the Edict of Three Chapters which contained a compromise-formula for the Monophysites. Three times he resisted the demand, and three times he gave way—resistance giving way to acquiescence as the imperialist armies were more victorious in Italy. On his way back to Rome he died and his successor was an imperial nominee, Pelagius, who could not assemble for his consecration as many as three bishops from the West. The bishops of Tuscany would not admit his name into the sacramental liturgy, and Childebert, King of the Franks, required him to make a complete confession of the orthodox faith. Imperial diplomacy could find no remedy for the fact that while the East was predominantly Monophysite, the West was not; for East and West were determined not to agree.

Justinian's heroic attempt to re-unite the Roman world in one Empire and one Church, simply served to show that the Roman world had disappeared. It had not been destroyed by any particular invasion; it had not ceased to exist at any particular moment; it had simply faded away. Of that there was no dispute. For who, in the sixth century, were the Romans? Were they the people of Rome, battered and besieged, now under Gothic, now under imperialist rule? Or were they the members of the imperial court—Justinian who was an Illyrian, Belisarius who was a Thracian, the eunuch Solomon who came from Mesopotamia, and the eunuch Narses whose origin was unknown? By birth it was Cassiodorus who was the noblest Roman of them all, but he had served the Ostrogoths and then, when the imperialists were victorious, had retired from the world to his monastery of *Vivarium*.

Justinian is one of the most enigmatic figures in history. The reader of the *Corpus Juris Civilis* and the visitor to Constantinople or Ravenna cannot but stand amazed at the breadth of his vision and the magnificence of his achievement. The reader of the official histories of Procopius, let alone of his *Secret History*, must be astonished that, in the midst of so much intrigue and so many dangers, Justinian accomplished anything at all. But the historian of Europe is forced to admit that by undertaking a reconquest of the West when all his forces were needed to defend his Empire on the Persian and Slavonic frontiers, Justinian exhausted the resources of his Empire in pursuit of a policy which could not possibly succeed.

Further Reading

PETER BROWN. *Augustine of Hippo*. London. 1967.

ST. AUGUSTINE. *The City of God*, translated by John Healey (1620), with an Introduction by Sir Ernest Barker (Everyman's Library, 1945). 2 vols.

NORMAN H. BAYNES. *The Political Ideas of St. Augustine's ' De. Civitate Dei '* (Historical Association. London. 1936).

T. HODGKIN. *Theodoric the Goth* (Heroes of the Nations series). London. 1891.

T. HODGKIN. *The Letters of Cassiodorus*. London. 1896. Free translations from the *Variae*.

A. MOMIGLIANO. ' Cassiodorus and Italian Culture of his Time '. *Proceedings of the British Academy*, xli (1955), 207–45.

CHRISTIAN COURTOIS. *Les Vandales et l'Afrique*. Paris. 1955.

A. A. VASILIEV. *History of the Byzantine Empire*, 324–1453 (2nd English edition). Oxford. 1952.

P. N. URE. *Justinian and his Age.* London. 1951.

J. B. BURY. *A History of the Later Roman Empire from the death of Theodosius I to the death of Justinian.* 2 vols. London. 1923.

PROCOPIUS. *The Persian, Vandal and Gothic Wars, The Buildings* and *The Secret History,* with a translation by H. B. Dewing (Loeb Classics). 7 vols.

IV

THE CHURCH AND THE PAPACY

And if a man consider the originall of this great
Ecclesiasticall Dominion, he will easily perceive
that the *Papacy*, is no other, than the *Ghost* of the
deceased *Romane Empire*, sitting crowned upon the
grave thereof.

THOMAS HOBBES, 1651.

THE origins of ecclesiastical organization and Papal power
are questions of intense controversy. None the less the
medieval historian cannot afford to ignore them, for in
many ways it was the Church that made the Middle Ages. In
the present chapter an attempt will be made to explain some of
the main factors that contributed to the organization of Church
and Papacy in the first six centuries of the Christian era.

1. DEVELOPMENT OF ECCLESIASTICAL ORGANIZATION
UP TO THE END OF THE FIFTH CENTURY

The missionary work of the Christian Church was undertaken
by the apostles, who formed a sort of travelling ministry. They
founded churches, or Christian communities, in various cities
of the Empire, such as Corinth, Ephesus, Thessalonika, and Rome,
and the epistles of St. Paul show clearly the intimate relationship
between such churches and their founders. St. Paul felt he had
a clear responsibility for the churches he had founded, even when
he had moved on to different parts of the Empire.

By the second century the travelling ministry of the apostles
had ended. Christendom was organized into local churches,
each one under a bishop. Normally the units of the Christian

68

Church corresponded to the units of imperial administration, the sphere of one church and its bishop being a ' city ' (*civitas*). Such ' cities ' were more or less the size of our counties, since they consisted of a town and dependent countryside, but most of the Christians would live in the town, the countryfolk (*pagani*) being normally identified with non-Christians. The bishop's duties, however, were very different from those of the modern diocesan, because he had no parishes and no parish-clergy to supervise. In the second century he could be compared to the rector of a large modern parish. He might have a body of assistant clergy and might hold services at many different places within his territory, but the Church of his ' city ' was one and undivided, and he alone represented it before God. The more important sees had large bodies of assistant clergy—in Rome, for example, we know that by the year 251 the bishop was assisted by forty-six presbyters and seven deacons. The presbyters formed his council and assisted him in his spiritual work of teaching the faith. The deacons acted more or less as his clerks or secretaries, distributed the church's alms for him, and reported to him any offences that might require disciplinary action. The bishop was the head of the community. He was supposed to know his flock individually and by name. He alone could admit new members to the Church by conferring baptism. He alone could utter sentence of excommunication. He alone could preside at the Eucharist. It was he who was the apostles' representative and the embodiment of the Faith.

The significance of the bishop's position was due to the fact that many churches were founded by the apostles before the four Gospels were written. (According to Sir Frederic Kenyon, the earliest of them, St. Mark's, would have been written *c.* 65 A.D., and the latest, St. John's, *c.* 95 A.D.) The early Church's teaching, therefore, could not be founded exclusively on Holy Writ. Even after the Gospels had been written they were not considered superior to the living tradition of the Church, since they were simply attempts to put that tradition into writing, and there was no official Canon of Scripture in the West till 382. It was therefore a matter of real importance that a bishop should have received oral instruction in the Faith from a recognized authority, such as one of the apostles or their pupils. The

' apostolic succession ' was not a formula but a living reality and a necessity. At Rome, for example, Clement, the third bishop in succession from the Apostles, had, according to Irenaeus, ' himself seen the blessed apostles, and had conferred with them, and had still their preaching sounding in his ears and their tradition before his eyes ; not alone, for there were still many left who had been taught by the apostles '. Irenaeus himself (*c.* 170) was Bishop of Lyons, and he had been taught in Smyrna by St. Polycarp (*c.* 69–155) who had conversed with St. John and others of the apostles who had known Christ.

In theory, there was no doubt that all bishops were equal. They were all successors of the apostles, said St. Jerome, whether bishop of Rome or of Gubbio ; consequently the translation of a bishop from one see to another was inconceivable. But in spite of this recognition of equality, and side by side with it, certain churches had come to occupy positions of privilege, their bishops having taken the lead in assembling local councils of bishops to discuss matters on which a common policy was desirable. The most common of these councils were those in which the bishops of one imperial province assembled.[1] The most convenient meeting-place was the province's *metropolis* or capital city, and the most natural president was that city's bishop, the *metropolitan.* Metropolitan sees therefore acquired a certain importance in every imperial province, and the Council of Nicaea (325) recognized the fact. In the East it became a definite rule that every time the emperor created a new province in his Empire, a new metropolitan see was created for the Church automatically. In the West, however, though the provinces of archbishops (as metropolitans were subsequently called) were normally a faithful reflection of the administrative geography of the Roman Empire, this rule was not so strictly observed.

There were two different schools of thought in the fourth century as to why certain churches were, and should be, more important than others. On the one hand there was the view that the importance of a see derived from its importance in the imperial administration. On the other hand there was the view that the importance of a see depended on the strength of its apostolic

[1] Some idea of the size of these provinces is given by the fact that in Roman Gaul there were 17 provinces containing 112 ' cities '.

tradition and the significance of its founder. Both arguments were applicable to the three great sees of Antioch, Alexandria, and Rome. All three claimed to have been founded by St. Peter, the prince of the apostles, either in person (as in the case of Antioch and Rome) or through the agency of St. Mark (as in the case of Alexandria). All three were important centres of the Empire; Antioch was capital of the vast ' diocese ' of the Orient,[1] Alexandria was the capital of Egypt and the intellectual centre of the Hellenistic world, and Rome, of course, was the imperial city.

There were, however, certain practical difficulties which prevented the whole-hearted acceptance of either argument by the entire Church. If the organization of the Church did in fact reflect that of the State, it would follow that the Divine Society of the Church had been made to conform to the pattern of a worldly empire that was necessarily transient. Moreover, it would follow that changes in the organization of the Empire should be reflected by changes in the organization of the Church. It was in consequence of this view that in 381 the Council of Constantinople declared that ' the bishop of Constantinople shall have primacy of honour after the bishop of Rome, because this town is the new Rome '. Just as Constantine had transferred the senate, the consulate, and the seat of empire, so that they co-existed in both the old Rome and the new, so (according to the Council) the Church of Rome had had some of its power transferred to the new capital.[2]

But was it really right that the emperor's unilateral action in founding a new capital city should affect the established order of the Church ?

The alternative explanation, by means of Petrine authority, is best known in connection with the Church of Rome, and is most impressively displayed in St. Peter's basilica. Round the base

---

[1] A ' diocese ', in the terminology of the fourth-century Empire, was an administrative district comprising several provinces. The Empire was divided into six prefectures ; the prefectures into ' dioceses ' ; the ' dioceses ' into provinces ; the provinces into ' cities ' (*civitates*) ; and the ' cities ' into *urbes, oppida, castra, pagi*, and *vici*. It is important not to confuse imperial dioceses with the later ecclesiastical use of the word to denote a bishop's ' city '.

[2] Thus John, Patriarch of Constantinople at the end of the sixth century, wrote : ' I hold the most holy Church of the old and the new Rome to be one. I define the see of the Apostle Peter and this of the imperial city to be one see.'

of the dome are written the words from St. Matthew's gospel (xvi. 18–19)

TU ES PETRUS ET SUPER HANC PETRAM AEDIFICABO
ECCLESIAM MEAM ET TIBI DABO CLAVES REGNI CAELORUM

and on the walls are inscribed the names of the popes stretching in unbroken succession from St. Peter to Paul VI. The claim of the Roman Catholic Church is that Christ instituted St. Peter as head of the Church, that St. Peter was the founder and first Bishop of Rome, and that the popes are his successors.[1] This doctrine, which was first adumbrated by St. Cyprian (Bishop of Carthage 248–58), was officially adopted by the Papacy at a Roman council held under Pope Damasus I in 382. In reply to the Council of Constantinople it declared that the Roman primacy rested not on any 'synodal decisions' but on Christ's promise to St. Peter. It set up a sort of hierarchy of Petrine sees of which the first was Rome, the second Alexandria, and the third Antioch. Constantinople was not mentioned.

It is significant that both theories, imperialist and Petrine, were formulated after the initial development of the Church hierarchy had taken place; they were advanced as explanations of what had already happened. The four sees of Rome, Alexandria, Antioch, and Constantinople were, in the middle of the fourth century, undeniably pre-eminent in the Church, even though they were subsequently to have rivals in Jerusalem and Milan. The only question that remained was how these four sees were to organize their relations with each other. Would

---

[1] The historical basis of this claim has, of course, been hotly disputed. There is fairly general agreement amongst modern scholars as to the probability that St. Peter went to Rome, and was martyred and buried there *c.* 64 A.D. It does not necessarily follow, however, that St. Peter was either the founder or the first Bishop of Rome : St. Paul's epistles, which contain much information about the early Church in Rome, do not suggest that it had been founded by St. Peter, or even that it had, at that date, any significant connection with him. St. Cyprian (*c.* 248–58) was the first writer to refer to St. Peter alone as the founder of the Roman Church. Before that date, reference had always been made to the *two* apostles, Peter and Paul, as if the Church of Rome had, in the first two centuries, considered that it owed an equal debt to both. Would it have done so, if it had already held the doctrine of Petrine authority ? The controversy can be studied in T. G. Jalland, *The Church and the Papacy* (1944) (Anglican), E. Caspar, *Geschichte des Papsttums*, 2 vols. (1930) (Protestant), and P. Batiffol, *Le Siège Apostolique* (1924) (Roman Catholic).

they be equals, or would one of them become supreme amongst the others? And if so, which? It is easy, in the twentieth century, to declare that the leadership would obviously pass to Rome since it was the only one of the four sees that was *both* of Petrine origin *and* in the imperial city, but in the fifth century any such logical conclusion could hardly have been foreseen. For the Church was closely linked with the Empire, and Rome was at the mercy of the barbarians.

To the citizen of the Christian empire, it might well have seemed that Alexandria was the see which was most likely to win the leadership of the whole Church. It claimed to have been founded by St. Peter through the agency of St. Mark, who was buried there. It was the centre of early monasticism, the see of St. Athanasius, and the intellectual and cultural capital of the Hellenistic world. It was suspected by the other churches of the East of having what might be described as 'Papalist' ambitions. Its bishop had absolute control over the churches of the six provinces of Egypt, confirming all elections to vacant sees, and consecrating all bishops himself; and it was thought that he would like to have similar powers over an even wider area. At the great councils of the Church the Egyptian 'party' was always formidable, and nearly always in opposition to the 'party' of Constantinople, which also made no secret of its desire to have the ruling voice in the government of the imperial Church. Both parties were prepared to seek support from Rome which, to them, seemed venerable but harmless and remote, surrounded by heretical Germans in the distant West.

In the fifth century it would have seemed inconceivable that two centuries later it would be, not Rome, but Alexandria and Antioch that were ruled by a non-Christian people. But even before the Moslems had delivered the *coup de grâce* to the most formidable of Rome's rivals, the Papacy was gaining a position of supremacy. For its real strength lay in what was thought at the time to be its weakness—in the fact that Rome was remote from the imperial government and likely to fall into the hands of the barbarians. While Alexandria and Constantinople were subject to imperial interference in the ordinary routine of ecclesiastical affairs, Rome was free. In the East the emperor attempted to control the Church and would himself propound theological compromises in an attempt to preserve the unity of the Empire and its Church. But in Rome theology was formulated quite independently. The Papacy was neither imperial nor anti-imperial. Situated in the remote fastnesses of the West, it was unmoved by the political and theological rivalries of Alexandria and Constantinople, and it claimed for itself a non-imperial and other-worldly authority.

But though Rome had all the advantages of being free from effective imperial control, it also enjoyed all the advantages of being the Imperial City. So far as the barbarians were concerned, no lack of effective power could alter the fact that it was the name of Rome that they had been taught to revere and obey, and that the city, even in its ruins, represented to them the very essence of empire and civilization. That city had now been deserted by the Emperor, and its most important citizen was the Pope.[1] It was the Pope, Leo I, who (together with the praetorian prefect of Italy) persuaded Attila to retreat from Italy in 452, and three years later, when the Vandals sacked Rome, it was the same Pope who intervened to save the three oldest basilicas from being plundered and the whole city from being burnt down. To the barbarians, the Papacy represented the magic and the power of the Roman name. And this was important, for the Roman Catholic Church grew to its greatness as the Church not only of Rome, but of the barbarians.

2. BENEDICTINE MONASTICISM

A more strictly religious reason for the development of the Papacy was its connection with Benedictine monasticism, which, both directly and indirectly, gave it much of its proper character. St. Benedict of Nursia lived from *c.* 480 to *c.* 543 in Italy, his life coinciding with the period of the Ostrogothic kingdom and the earlier phases of Justinian's reconquest. From 535 Italy was being devastated by the rival armies of Justinian and the Ostrogoths, and in 542–3 there was the great plague, in which

---

[1] The word 'pope' is a translation of *papa*, father. From the fourth century to the ninth bishops were commonly known as *papa*, and in Greece the word is used to this day in addressing an ordinary priest. The word began to be used as the special designation of the Bishops of Rome and Alexandria in the fifth century.

St. Benedict himself may have died. Roman order had, so it seemed, gone for ever, and with it all chance of being able to live a Christian life in the towns. St. Benedict determined, therefore, to retreat to the waste places, where invasions, murders, and the vices bred by a decrepit urban economy would all be unknown. Many hermits had made such a retreat before, but St. Benedict did not approve of their excesses. To be a hermit one needed special qualifications, and St. Benedict was proposing what he called ' a school for beginners ', an institution in which quite ordinary people could lead a Christian life.

> We are about to institute a school for the service of God in which we hope nothing harsh nor burdensome will be ordained . . . so that [we] never leaving His school, but preserving in the monastery until death in His teaching, may share, by our patience, in the sufferings of Christ, and so merit to be partakers in His kingdom.
> (*Prologue of the Rule, tr.* Gasquet, pp. 6–7.)

' Nothing harsh nor burdensome ' may strike some readers as a deliberate understatement, but St. Benedict did not intend it to be taken as such. What he understood by a harsh or burdensome monastic life was that of the monks of Egypt who, from the beginning of the fourth century, whether living as a group of hermits after the example of St. Anthony, or in a communal life after the example of St. Pachomius, made feats of endurance one of the objects of their life. St. Macarius of Alexandria, for example, could not bear to be outdone, and ' if he ever heard of anyone having performed a work of asceticism he was all on fire to do the same '. This ambition to set up new ' records ' of asceticism had spread, by the fifth century, to most of the provinces of the East, and had reached absurd proportions. St. Symeon the Stylite stood on a platform on top of a pillar for thirty-three years ; he had no protection from the summer sun nor from winter frosts, and never sat or lay down. St. Daniel the Stylite (409–93) was his disciple and beat his ' record ' by remaining on his platform (which was on two columns) for thirty-three years and three months. It was not for men such as this that St. Benedict drew up his Rule, but for ordinary men, ' beginners ', who desired to enter a ' school for the service of God '.

There were, of course, others who had stressed the value of

the cenobitic, or communal, life before. Even in Egypt, and as early as 315, St. Pachomius had founded a *cenobium* with detailed rules of a common life. Fifty years later St. Basil, with whose Rule St. Benedict was familiar, had developed the idea and had even declared the cenobitic life to be superior to the eremitic. But while St. Pachomius and St. Basil had both been insistent that their *cenobia* should be self-sufficient communities, they had not developed the idea of the monastery as a corporate body to the same extent as St. Benedict. He, in the very first sentences of his Rule, spoke of the monk's 'work of obedience' and of giving up his own will, both to God and the community which served Him. He did not approve of monks who moved from one monastery to another as they pleased. On entering the monastery, the monk became a member of that particular community, and he took the vow of 'stability' to remain in that particular monastery until death. He was forthwith divested in the church of his own garments and clothed in those of the monastery. He no longer had anything that was his own. 'He must know that he has henceforth no power even over his own body.'

Within the monastery, the ruling idea was humility. In the seventh chapter of the Rule, St. Benedict discoursed at length on this virtue and the twelve steps by means of which it was to be attained, but it is also the theme of the whole Rule. Humility was learnt, in the first place, by praising God—'Not unto us, O Lord, not unto us, but unto thy name give glory.' For this reason much of the Rule was devoted to precise liturgical instructions. The ninth chapter, for example, set out how many psalms were to be said in the night hours :

In the winter season, having first said the verse, *O God incline unto mine aid*; *O Lord make haste to help me*, the words *O Lord, Thou shalt open my lips and my mouth shall declare Thy praise* are then to be said thrice. After this the third Psalm is to be said with a *Gloria*; after which the ninety-fourth Psalm, with an antiphon, is to be recited or sung, followed by a hymn, and then six psalms with their antiphons. When these are ended and a versicle said, let the abbot give a blessing ; and then, all being seated, let three lessons from the book placed on the lectern be read by the brethren in turns. Between these lessons three responsories are to be sung, two without a *Gloria*. After the third lesson, however, let the cantor add the *Gloria* to the responsory, and as soon as he begins it, let all rise from their seats out of honour and reverence to the Holy Trinity.[1]

This, it should be observed, is only part of the instructions given for one of the seven services or ' offices ' of the day. On ordinary days in winter, one of St. Benedict's monks would have spent about four hours in the ' oratory ' performing the *Opus Dei*, quite apart from any additional time that he might devote to private prayer or spiritual exercises.

A second way of learning humility was by implicit obedience. The monk was not allowed to disobey his superior, whether abbot or prior, even if he thought that what he was being ordered to do was wrong. It was the good monk's desire not to live as he himself willed, but to be ruled by an abbot, and he strove to obey him as promptly ' as if the command had come from God '. One chapter of the Rule is devoted to what a monk should do when ordered to do something impossible. He might, at the proper time, ' without show of pride, resistance or contradiction ' state the reason why he found his task impossible, but if the abbot or prior persisted in his command, the monk had no option but, trusting in God's help, to obey.

Closely allied to obedience was St. Benedict's insistence that all property was to be shared in common.

No one, without leave of the abbot, shall presume to give, or receive, or keep as his own, anything whatever : neither book nor tablets, nor pen : nothing at all. For monks are men who can claim no dominion even over their own bodies or wills. All that is necessary, however, they may hope for from the Father of the monastery ; but they shall keep nothing which the abbot has not given or allowed. All things are to be common to all, as it is written, *Neither did any one say or think that aught was his own* (*c*. xxxiii).[2]

A monk might not even receive letters or presents from his parents without the abbot's permission ; and even then the abbot was expressly empowered to allot such presents to whichever monk he wished, regardless of the monk to whom they were sent. For absolute submission to the abbot was one of the works of humility.

[1] Tr. Gasquet, pp. 36–7. [2] *Ibid.*, p. 65.

Humility was also learnt by working in the fields. Both Romans and Goths abhorred the manual work of agriculture as fit only for slaves, but monks were the slaves of God. It is true that St. Benedict apparently did not intend that they should do all their agricultural work themselves. Additional hired labour would have been necessary, especially in summer, when the monastic timetable made it difficult for the monks to begin their field work sufficiently early to avoid the heat of the day. But it is clear that St. Benedict envisaged agricultural work as the normal work for a monk, and that the abbot described in a letter of St. Gregory's as mowing the hay with his monks, was typical.

St. Benedict's Rule was a sensible rule for people who wished to live the Christian life as a community. It had regard for the practical details as well as the general principle of monastic life. It laid down that the monks should sleep in separate beds in a common dormitory, with the amount of bedclothes varied to suit the individual monk's condition of life. The kitchen work was to be done by the monks in turn, and ' on Saturday he who ends his weekly service must clean up everything '. The daily meal was to consist of two cooked dishes ' so that he who cannot make his meal of one may make his meal of the other '. Instructions were given for the care of the sick and regulations for clothing, though in this matter much was left to the discretion of the abbot, ' since in cold regions, more is needed and in warm regions less '. There was in fact a spirit of humanity in St. Benedict's Rule ; it did not attempt to make the monastic life more difficult than was necessary. Gregory the Great relates that when a neighbouring hermit chained himself to a rock, St. Benedict rebuked him, saying : ' If thou be God's servant, let the chain of Christ, not any iron chain hold thee.'

It was here, perhaps, that the main achievement of Benedictine monasticism lay, because it succeeded in diverting religious en- thusiasm from ' record-breaking ' feats of asceticism into the life of an ordered community. In the East, notwithstanding St. Basil's attempt to establish the communal life as the best life for monks, it continued to be thought that monks who were particularly holy would naturally want to withdraw from the monastery to a hermitage. In the West, monasticism followed more practical lines. With very little adaptation it could become a powerful instrument for the strengthening of the Church, and in the pontificate of Pope Gregory I ('the Great') it made its first great contribution to the development of the Papacy.[1]

3. POPE GREGORY THE GREAT (590–604)

In the pontificate of Gregory I (590–604) the Papacy begins to emerge in its medieval form. In it the first steps taken towards the organization of an ordered hierarchy of the Western Church under the direct control of the Pope, and the first developments that led to the creation of a Papal State, were to be seen. Paradoxically, however, Gregory the Great was essentially a conservative man, embodying in himself all the diverse traditions of *Romania*. *Romania* was a word which came into use in the fourth century to express the Roman as opposed to the barbarian way of life. Exponents of its traditions included Augustine who was an African, Cassiodorus who was a Roman, Justinian who was an Illyrian, and the Christian Church which had its roots in Judaism. Each represented, no matter how much he might differ from the others, a way of life that was foreign to the barbarian world. Pope Gregory the Great represented them all.

He was by birth a Roman of good senatorial family, and his great-great-grandfather had been Pope Felix III (483–92). His father had a large house on the *Clivus Scauri* in Rome, and he himself was *praefectus urbis* in 573. But the city in which he had

---

[1] St. Benedict had drawn up his Rule for the monasteries that he had founded himself. Of these there may not have been more than three—Subiaco, Monte Cassino, and Terracina. There was no thought of a monastic *Order*. The fame of his Rule was largely due to the publicity given to it in the dialogues of Pope Gregory the Great. But in the seventh and eighth centuries it seems to have been more widely known in Gaul and England than in Italy. See Appendix I.

It should also be noted that though the interpretation of the Rule given here is the traditional interpretation, an alternative interpretation is that the Rule set out only what St. Benedict thought was 'the minimum standard of evangelical life, which could be demanded of all, but which proficients could transcend while yet fulfilling'. For this latter view, see M. D. Knowles, *The Monastic Order in England*, p. 10. The traditional view is well, and in my opinion conclusively, put by Cuthbert Butler, *Benedictine Monachism*, 2nd ed., 1924, pp. 389–93. Both writers were themselves Benedictine monks at Downside.

held this once-glorious office had lost its splendour and was falling into ruins. Quite apart from the disasters of the fifth century, it had been besieged and captured three times in Justinian's Gothic War, during which Gregory himself had been born (*c.* 540).

> She that once appeared the mistress of the world [wrote Gregory], we have seen what has become of her, shattered by everything that she has suffered from immense and manifold misfortunes—the desolation of her inhabitants and the menace of her enemies. Ruins on ruins. . . . Where is the senate? Where the people? All the pomp of secular dignities has been destroyed. . . . And we, the few that we are who remain, every day we are menaced by scourges and innumerable trials. . . . No more senate, no more people, but for that which still survives, sorrows and groanings, multiplied every day. Rome is deserted and in flames, and as for her buildings we see them fall down of their own accord.[1]

One of the main reasons for his pessimism was that the imperial power in Italy was declining rapidly. In 568, only fourteen years after the end of the Gothic War, the Lombards invaded Italy under their king Alboin. They crossed the Alps with their families, goods, and chattels and within ten years had occupied large parts of Italy and had completely disrupted the imperial administration. But neither they nor the imperial forces were strong enough to win a decisive victory. Though some Lombard forces made their settlements as far south as Spoleto and Benevento, the emperor's representative, the Exarch, was able to maintain a tenuous control over a strip of territory that stretched across Italy from Venice and Ravenna on the east coast to Rome and Naples on the west. It was exposed to attack from both north and south, its lines of communication were often cut, and its permanent defence was impossible. It was a pitiable remnant of imperial power. Gregory compared it to an eagle that had gone bald.

> Man has only his head that is bald; but the eagle becomes bald all over its body, and when it grows old it loses all its feathers, including those of its wings.[2]

[1] Quoted from P. Batiffol, *St. Grégoire le Grand* (1928), p. 4.
[2] Quoted from Batiffol, English ed., pp. 91–2.

In Gregory's opinion, the decay of imperial power, of *Romania*, and of civilization all betokened that the world was rapidly drawing to its end. The Kingdom of Heaven was at hand.

> That, my dear brethren, even if the Gospel should be silent about it, the world itself would proclaim. These very ruins serve as its voice. Beaten down by so many blows, the ancient kingdom has fallen from its glory and shows us now another kingdom, which is coming, which is already near. The present world is bitter for those who love it, and its decay teaches us that we ought not to love it. If your house were shaken by a tempest and threatened to fall down, you who lived in it would take flight. You loved it when it was standing firm, but you would hasten to leave it when it began to fall down. If then, when the world is still sinking beneath us, we still love it and cling to it, it is because we wish to perish with it.[1]

Gregory became a monk. He founded six monasteries on the estates he had inherited in Sicily, and himself entered a seventh, dedicated to St. Andrew, which he had founded in his father's house on the *Clivus Scauri* in Rome. What was important, however, was that he became a monk of the Benedictine type. He was, as Professor Knowles puts it, ' saturated with the traditions of St. Benedict's life ', and accepted his ruling-principles wholeheartedly ; the monk was to be humble, obedient, and a member of a community—' he must know that he has henceforth no power even over his own body '.

There was more than one community to which St. Gregory belonged, however, for his monastery of St. Andrew was within the greater community of the Roman Church, and when in 579 Pope Pelagius II made him a deacon and ordered him to go as papal envoy (*apocrisiarius*) to Constantinople, he obeyed. The main reason for his mission was to beg the Emperor Maurice to send reinforcements for the defence of Italy.

> The territory around Rome (*partes romanae*), wrote the pope, is without any garrison. The Exarch writes that he can do nothing for us, being unable to defend the region of Ravenna himself. May God bid the emperor to come to our aid at the earliest possible moment in the perils which are closing in upon us, before the army

---

[1] Quoted from Batiffol, English ed., p. 83.

of that impious nation, the Lombards, shall have seized the lands which still form part of the empire.[1]

Gregory stayed in Constantinople for the best part of six years (579–85), but he got no help from the emperor, who was too preoccupied with troubles on the Eastern frontier to think of sending re–inforcements to the West. Rome had to defend itself as best it could, under the leadership of the Pope. That it did not fall to the Lombards, Gregory considered to be something of a miracle, attributable to ' the protection of the blessed Peter, prince of the Apostles '.

In 590 Pope Pelagius II died and the Roman people elected Gregory to succeed him, though he was not consecrated till the imperial consent had been received from Constantinople. He was at first unwilling to accept the office, and attempted to escape from the city, but in the *Regula Pastoralis* he later made it clear that he would have considered that he had failed in his duty to God if he had refused consecration, even for the sake of the contemplative life. He scorned the ambition that sought high office for its own sake, but declared that humility was not genuine when it resisted the command of God. He accepted the Papacy and endeavoured to serve God's Church with the same obedience that he would have given to his abbot as a monk. His official title was *servus servorum Dei*, servant of the servants of God.

His attitude to his office is best seen in his attitude to the Church's property, St. Peter's patrimony. He supervised its administration with care and efficiency, but considered that he held the wealth derived from it in trust for the whole community. When a beggar died of hunger in the streets of Rome, Gregory held himself responsible and suspended himself from his priestly functions. He is even said to have had a register drawn up to show the names of persons of every age, sex, and profession who were in receipt of regular allowances from his treasury. Previously such distributions of bread or money had been the responsibility of the emperor. But the imperial administration had broken down, and the need was great. Just as an abbot ruled his monastery in all things both spiritual and temporal, so Gregory cared for all the needs of the people of Rome, who were his

---

[1] Quoted from Batiffol, English ed., p. 41.

flock. He was able to do so, because the patrimony of St. Peter was large and included many estates in Sicily, which was still at peace, not having been invaded by the Lombards.

The wealth of the Church was, indeed, increasing. In many cities, landowners who found it impossible to pay their taxes surrendered their land to the bishop. In this way the bishops, whose bishoprics were in any case coincident with the administrative districts of the ' cities ', found themselves shouldering the responsibilities of the city's *curia*; they might be responsible for the maintenance of the town walls, the aqueducts, or other public buildings. Gregory himself found that he was even acting as the emperor's banker, advancing the wages for the imperial troops, or the money to be paid as tribute to the Lombards. As the administration of the Empire broke down, so the Church stepped in to save as much as could be saved of *Romania*, and the logical development of this process was reached in the eighth century when it was found that the Pope was a temporal as well as a spiritual ruler, being in possession of the Papal States.

Amongst the most immediate of the secular responsibilities that fell on Gregory was the defence of Rome. The emperor was in Constantinople and could spare no reinforcements, and the exarch was preoccupied with the defence of Ravenna. In moments of emergency Gregory found it necessary not only to protest when the exarch moved troops away from Rome, but to appoint military commanders. When all else failed, he would write to the local bishop asking him to see that the citizens were compelled to do their turns of guard-duty on the walls of the town. Nobody thought that he was thereby usurping the imperial prerogative. His actions were not questioned until he began to formulate a policy that was contrary to that of the emperor. This was that peace would have to be made with the Lombards. There was no doubt that he would have preferred to continue the fight if there had been any chance of success. But if the emperor was unable to send reinforcements, success was impossible. The only way he had been able to save Rome from being sacked had been by entering into negotiations with the Lombard Duke of Spoleto whom he described as ' the unspeakable Ariulf '. When the emperor blamed him for his

' simplicity ' in pursuing such a policy, Gregory replied in a letter that was full of indignation :

> My pious lord may think all the evil he wants of me, provided that, for the sake of the usefulness of the Republic and for the cause of Italy's deliverance, he will not listen to every one who comes along, but will deign to believe *facts* rather than *words*.[1]

Roman, imperialist, and conservative though he was, Gregory saw that he was living in a new world. It was no use lamenting the past. It was no use, even, to retreat to a monastery if it was only to shut one's eyes to what was happening in the world. The barbarians had come to stay. The Roman Empire in the West, at any rate in the form in which Gregory knew it, was in the last stages of decrepitude. If the Pope, as St. Peter's successor, was to guard the interests of the Church, and to see that the Faith survived in its purity, it was obviously his duty to convert the barbarians. They might be ' unspeakable ' and unclean ; they might represent everything that was repugnant to the conception of *Romania* ; but Gregory accepted with due humility the fact that God must have willed that these barbarians should overcome the Empire, and that it was his duty as Pope to watch over their Faith.

This was no easy matter. Previously the Church had relied to a very large extent on the assistance of the imperial government for the summoning of Church councils and the enforcing of their decisions, for we have already seen how the Emperor Constantine summoned the councils of Arles and Nicaea and mobilized the civil government against the Donatists in Africa. But at the end of the sixth century there were few parts of the West in which the imperial authorities were capable of helping the Church ; it was only in Africa that Gregory received any effective help. He had, therefore, as in the defence of Rome from the Lombards, to improvise his own organization. What he did was to make use of the officials who were charged with the administration of the lands of St. Peter's patrimony. They were primarily bailiffs or estate agents, but as they were scattered all over Italy and Sicily it was only natural for the Pope to use them as his agents in all matters. They were all directly under

---

[1] Quoted from Batiffol, English ed., pp. 244-5.

his control, and he frequently wrote to them as often as once a month. They kept him informed on all matters that concerned the Church, and consequently Gregory's supervision of the Church in Italy was effective.

Outside Italy, however, where the Pope had no territorial interests, the problem of supervision was more difficult. In Gaul the problem was particularly acute. The Bishop of Arles remained in close touch with the Papacy, but otherwise the Gallic Church was administered almost as a department of state by the Frankish kings. They regarded the churches of Gaul as ' theirs ', and while they listened respectfully to the Pope, they did not consider it either necessary or desirable that he should exercise any regular oversight of ' their ' bishops. To Gregory, however, it seemed that papal supervision was an urgent necessity. The spiritual life of the Frankish Church had been eaten away by gross simony ; the bishops appointed by the kings included youths and laymen whose conduct was sometimes notorious, and the reason for their appointment was not the interest of the Church so much as royal favour. Gregory thought that some remedy for this state of affairs might be found if the marriage of clergy were forbidden and if the Frankish Church held annual councils in which to review its faith and morals. He wrote to the bishops and sent a special envoy to bring to the notice of all—ecclesiastics, kings, and the notorious Queen Brunhild herself—the absolute necessity of enforcing Church discipline. He was heard politely and with respect, but nothing in the way of reform was accomplished.

It was clear, therefore, that unless the Church were to become an object of scandal, it would have to elaborate its own machinery of government. It was no longer sufficient for the Papacy to claim the ' primacy ' of the Church ; it had to govern it, and to control even the remotest parts of the Church by its own central authority. The first steps towards such a central control were taken by Gregory in the organization of his mission to England. His original plan had been to buy young English slaves, educate them in the monasteries of Gaul, and then send them back to England to convert their heathen countrymen. But in the event he abandoned this plan in favour of another which ensured direct papal control of the mission. The man he sent out, Augustine, was not English, knew nothing of the country, and could not speak a word of the language. He had very few, if any, of the conventional qualities of a missionary, but he was a monk, and what was more, he was Gregory's monk from his own monastery. He had the virtue of obedience. He obeyed the instructions that the Pope had given him and, when confronted with unforeseen difficulties, wrote back to Rome for further advice, his questions, and Gregory's answers, being preserved in Bede's *Ecclesiastical History*. The conversion of the English was therefore Gregory's own achievement, even though he worked through the agency of Augustine.

Gregory also planned the administration of the new Church himself. It was to consist of two provinces, corresponding to the former imperial provinces of Upper and Lower Britain, and in each there was to be a metropolitan and twelve bishops. The metropolitan sees were to have been at London and York, the two most important cities in Roman Britain, but Canterbury had to be substituted for London because the East Saxons who controlled London reverted to paganism. Gregory's intention, therefore, was to set up a provincial organization similar to that found in all parts of the Empire, but with the difference that the metropolitan was to derive his power from the Pope. He laid it down that the badge of office of the metropolitan was the *pallium*—a band of white wool—and that it could be bestowed by the Pope alone. He sent Augustine's *pallium* out to him, but the subsequent custom was for the newly-elected metropolitan (*i.e.* archbishop) to go to Rome to receive the *pallium* in person, after having made a written profession of faith. In this way Gregory established what was to be the pattern of the government of the Church, bishops being supervised by their archbishop, and archbishops by the Pope.

The whole scheme was a most original adaptation and combination of institutions that already existed. The *pallium*, for example, had previously been bestowed—originally by the emperor and subsequently by the Pope in his name—simply as a mark of special honour or favour, and similarly the title of archbishop had been purely honorary. Metropolitan bishops had, as we have already seen, been prominent in their provinces since the fourth century, but hitherto it had not been necessary for them to be confirmed in their office by the Pope or to be subject to his control. Gregory's scheme for England, however, meant that the English Church was controlled by the Papacy more closely than any other Church outside Italy ; and for their part, the English delighted in being regarded as the special servants of the Apostolic See. When, in the eighth century, the English sent missions to the Germans north and east of the Franks, the first step of the leading missionaries was to go to Rome to acquire the Pope's sanction for the enterprise. Both Willibrord and Wynfrith were consecrated bishops in Rome, and the Pope gave them new names, Clement and Boniface, to mark their reception into the Roman community. After the success of their mission, the one founded an archbishopric at Utrecht and the other at Mainz, and both received their *pallia* from the Pope. They had introduced Gregory's centralized pattern of Church organization to continental Europe, and they were eventually responsible for establishing an effective papal supremacy over the Frankish Church. In this way the organization of the medieval Church as a centralized body controlled and supervised from Rome was built up.

' I know of no bishop ', wrote Gregory, ' who is not subject to the Apostolic See when a fault has been committed.' He felt himself to be the head of the Church and responsible for its good order. None the less, he was sufficiently conservative to respect the rights of other bishops, and even of the other patriarchs. He firmly rejected the title of ' universal bishop ', not only because it had been usurped by the Bishop of Constantinople, but also because he thought that any bishop who desired such a title must be ' the forerunner of Antichrist '.

I do not wish [he wrote] for an honour that would be conferred upon me at the expense of the honour of my brothers [*i.e.* other bishops]. My honour is that of the universal Church. It is also the solid authority of my brothers. I am honoured when the honour due to my brothers is refused to none of them. If Your Holiness treats me as *papa universalis*, you disqualify your own rank as bishop, by assuming that I am universal.[1]

It is difficult to say which is the more impressive, the evident modesty of the words or the grandeur of the central assumption.

[1] Quoted from Batiffol, English ed., p. 257.

There is, of course, much more that could be said of Gregory's pontificate, and of his relations with the great sees of the East and the other churches of the West. But it is hoped that enough has been said to show why he was regarded as the very type of what a Pope should be. It was not simply that he was a particularly virtuous and religious man, nor simply that he was renowned throughout the Middle Ages as the author of the *Regula Pastoralis* which was the standard handbook on the duties of a bishop to his flock. What made him so specially great was that, at a time when the imperial power was crumbling and when the world seemed to be coming to an end, Gregory undertook the task of saving the Church. But for him it might easily have decayed like the Empire : in Italy it might have become nothing more than a landed interest, and in the kingdom of the Franks a royal possession. Gregory reformed it, organized it, and gave it an independent existence. He translated the theory of papal *principatus* into the practical terms of papal supremacy. Even if the Moslems had not obliterated the rival churches of Alexandria and Antioch, the Papacy would almost certainly have enjoyed the position which it subsequently held in Christendom, for it alone had given to the Church an organization that was independent of the Empire or any other lay power. That was the achievement of Gregory the Great.

Further Reading

A. FLICHE and V. MARTIN (eds.). *Histoire de l'Eglise depuis les origines jusqu'à nos jours.* 24 vols. Paris. 1934 and after. This is now the standard history of the Church. The relevant volumes for this chapter are 1-5.

CUTHBERT BUTLER. *Benedictine Monachism.* London, 2nd ed. 1924.

PIERRE BATIFFOL. *Saint Grégoire le Grand.* Paris. 1928. (English translation by John L. Stoddard, London. 1929.)

WILLHELM LEVISON. *England and the Continent in the Eighth Century.* Oxford. 1946. This has much information about Gregory's influence on the English Church.

ABBOT JUSTIN MCCANN (ed.). *The Rule of St. Benedict.* London, 1952, with a translation. Another translation, with an Introduction by Cardinal Gasquet, is in vol. xxv of ' The Medieval Library '. London. 1936.

V

ISLAM

THE Prophet Mohammed, founder of Islam, was a younger contemporary of Pope Gregory the Great. When he died in 632 A.D. his religion and his empire were confined to the Arabian desert and its two cities of Mecca and Medina. In the next twelve years his followers overwhelmed the Persian Empire, and conquered Syria and Egypt which had hitherto belonged to the Byzantine Empire; their dominion extended from Ispahan in the East to Tripolitania in the West. Within a hundred years of Mohammed's death, their conquests were wider still. In the East they had advanced to India. In the Mediterranean they had extended their rule to the whole north African coastline and Spain as well. Only two powers had been able to resist them. In the eastern Mediterranean the Byzantine Empire continued to defend most of what is now Turkey, and its capital city, Constantinople, which had to withstand the full weight of the attack, survived several sieges, notably in 717. In the West Charles Martel, leader of the Franks, defeated them in 732 at the battle of Poitiers and drove them back to the foothills of the Pyrenees. The problem of security in the Mediterranean world had changed dramatically, and the danger-spot had shifted from the West to the East; the perils that confronted Rome now seemed trivial when compared with those that confronted Constantinople. Three patriarchates of the Christian Church, those of Alexandria, Antioch, and Jerusalem, had fallen to the Moslems, who were now the rulers of what had once been the most Christian part of the Roman Empire. The great strongholds of Christianity were to become almost wholly Moslem and the language spoken in what had once been some of the foremost centres of the Hellenistic world was to be not Greek but Arabic. Such a revolution requires an explanation.

1. THE PROPHET MOHAMMED (*c.* 570-632)

Mohammed was born in Mecca, which was then a heathen city, about the year 570 A.D. He came of a good but impoverished family of the tribe of the Quraysh, and earned his living, like a great many other Meccans, by trading with Syria. It was thus that he came into contact with Judaism and Christianity. At the age of twenty-five he married the wealthy widow of whose camels he had charge, and at the age of forty he received the call to be Prophet.

It is most important for non-Moslems to realize that Mohammed never claimed to be a god and that his followers have never worshipped him as such. His claim was that he was the Prophet, inspired to utter messages which were of divine origin. In this respect he was in the tradition of the Hebrew prophets, whom he freely admitted to have been true prophets also. The correct name for his religion is not Mohammedanism but Islam ; *Islam* is an Arabic word meaning ' submission to the will of God '. Those who follow his religion are called Moslems ; *Moslem* is an Arabic word meaning ' one who submits to the will of God '. The fact that the Arabic word for God is *Allah* should not be allowed to obscure the fact that the God worshipped by the Moslems is the same as the God worshipped by Jews and Christians. These two peoples were specially protected by the Moslems as ' the people of the book '. The difference between Mohammed's teaching and that of Christianity was that he denied that Jesus Christ was the Son of God ; he thought Him a prophet and an apostle sent by God, but he insisted that He was only a man. His attitude to the Jews was that though God had revealed His will to them, they had not obeyed it.

For about twelve years Mohammed preached in Mecca, with little success. The Meccans were polytheists and had a vested interest in their pagan sanctuary (which included the *Kaaba*) because it was an object of pilgrimage for the surrounding bedouin tribes. Eventually in 622, Mohammed considered it was no longer safe for him to stay in Mecca, and he fled to the city of

Medina, 280 miles to the north-east, where he had already converted a number of Jews to the Faith. The flight was the decisive
moment in his career, and it is the event from which Moslems
reckon the date of the year, in the same way as Christians reckon
from the birth of Christ.[1] It is called the *Hejira*, which does not
mean ' flight ' or ' migration ' so much as ' the breaking of old
ties ' ; for once at Medina, Mohammed decided to break the ties
of kindred, and fight to impose his religion on his own people
by force. After eight years of desultory combat he entered Mecca
in triumph. The Meccans accepted his religion, and the *Kaaba*
was purified of its pagan associations and made the central shrine
of Islam. Two years later (632), Mohammed died, just as he
was planning one of the first Moslem expeditions against the
Syrian frontier.

The aspects of Mohammed's teaching which are most widely
known in the West are those that reflect the conceptions of the
barbarian Arabic society of his day—the subjugation of women,
the licence for a man to have four wives at once, and his conception of the fleshly delights of Paradise. These aspects are real, but
they are not so significant as those other aspects of his teaching
that are comparable to the teaching of the extreme forms of
Protestantism. There were to be no priests, because man needed
no mediator between himself and God. There were to be no
graven images of any sort ; representational art was forbidden.
There was to be no ritual. The duties laid on the faithful were
prayer (five times a day), almsgiving, fasting for one month
in the year, and the pilgrimage to Mecca once in a lifetime.

It is also, of course, obligatory for the Moslem to know the
Koran, which is regarded as the Word of God—an accurate copy
of what was written in heaven. It is an article of faith that it
was revealed to Mohammed, and he apparently recited it in a
trance, each chapter or *sura* being a single revelation. Several
of the *suras* can be dated accurately because they contain clear
references to events in the Prophet's life or to decisions that he
had made or was about to make, and it is generally noticed that

[1] Dates calculated from the Hejira (A.H.) are not easily converted into dates A.D.,
because the Moslem year is made up of 12 *lunar* months and consequently consists
of only 354 days. It follows also that in the Moslem calendar, there is no fixed
relation between the months and the seasons ; the month of Ramadan, in which
Moslems fast from dawn to dusk, may occur in winter or summer.

there is a difference in tone between those *suras* that were ' revealed ' before and after the *hejira*. In the latter there is a new insistence on the need for a holy war (*iihad*) to convert the peoples of Arabia to the true faith, and a marked hardening in the attitude towards Christians and Jews. It is freely stated in the Koran that the authority of one *sura* is sometimes contradicted by a contrary passage in another, but where the chronology is confused (which is very often) it is impossible to say which of two contradictory statements should abrogate the other.

In consequence of these inconsistencies, the genuineness of Mohammed's prophetic inspiration has sometimes been denied. Most scholars, however, would probably agree that Mohammed showed all the genuine marks of inspiration. The account of his Call, for example, that is given by Ibn Ishak (*d.* 768) has the genuine ring of apocalyptic prophecy.[1]

> In the year that Mohammed was called to be a prophet, he went to Mount Hira with his family in the month of Ramadhan in order to devote himself to solitary religious exercises. ' One night ', the Prophet states, ' Gabriel came to me with a cloth and said : Recite ! I answered, I cannot recite ! So he choked me with the cloth until I believed that I should die. Then he released me and said Recite ! (*Iqra !*) The prophet hesitated, and twice again the angel repeated the harsh treatment. Then finally Mohammed asked : What shall I recite ? The angel said : Recite thou in the name of the Lord who created—who created man from clots of blood. Recite thou ! For the Lord is the most beneficent, who has taught the use of the pen,—has taught man what he knoweth not.'
>
> *   *   *
>
> ' I awoke ', said Mohammed, ' from my sleep, and it was as if they had written a message in my heart. I went out of the cave, and while I was on the mountain, I heard a voice saying : O Mohammed, thou art Allah's apostle and I am Gabriel ! I looked up and saw Gabriel in the form of a man with crossed legs at the horizon of heaven. I remained standing and observed him, and moved neither backwards nor forwards. And when I turned my gaze from him, I continued to see him on the horizon, no matter where I turned.'

It is one thing to be inspired, and another to have a message. But no student of the Koran or of early Islamic history could

[1] I quote it as given by Tor Andrae, *Mohammed, the Man and his Faith* (London 1936), p. 57.

possibly doubt the force of Mohammed's message. It was that there was only one God and that He must be obeyed. Mohammed believed that God had predestined the course of human affairs, so that no amount of human rebelliousness could possibly make any difference. Those who obeyed God's will and who fought for His cause would have victory. Those who attempted to disobey it would fail in the attempt and would perish. But *Islam* was not simply obedience to God in a narrowly religious sense. It embraced the whole of life in all its aspects. Moslems have always found it hard to appreciate the Western distinction between Church and State, or religion and politics. To them as to the Jews of the Old Testament, there was no such distinction. There was but one society, which was governed in all things by God through the mouth of his prophet ; obedience to him was a religious duty and disobedience would be punished by force. After the Prophet's death the ruler of Islam was the caliph ; the word meant ' deputy ' or ' representative ' and denoted the man to whom the Prophet's leadership had been deputed. Consequently it is sometimes said that a caliph was a sort of Moslem pope and emperor combined, but the description is only partly accurate, for it must be remembered that Islam had no priesthood, and though the caliph might require absolute obedience over all other Moslems, his office gave him no power of binding and loosing. He acted as *Imām* or leader of the daily prayers in the mosque, but anyone could take his place ; it is expressly stated that a slave, a nomad of the desert, a callow youth, or the son of a prostitute might act as *Imām*. There was no Moslem Church, because there was no clergy and no distinction between the spiritual and the secular.

> The Apostle of God said : Whoso obeys me, obeys God, and whoso rebels against me, rebels against God ; whoso obeys the ruler, obeys me ; and whoso rebels against the ruler, rebels against me.

2. THE CONQUESTS

The speed of the Moslem conquests was remarkable. By 634 the conquest of Arabia was more or less complete, and in the same year Palestine and Syria were invaded. Damascus and

Emessa (Homs) surrendered in 635, and a huge Byzantine army which attempted to recover them was defeated decisively at the battle of the Yarmouk (636). After that, only a few of the more important Hellenized towns offered any serious resistance ; Acre, Tyre, Sidon, Beyrouth, and Laodicea fell in 637, Jerusalem and Antioch in 638, and Caesarea in 640. The conquest of the Persian Empire was being undertaken at the same time. Ctesiphon, the capital, fell in 637, Rakka in 639, Mosul in 641, Kazvin and Rai (near Teheran) in 643, Hamadan and Ispahan in 644. Farther west, Egypt and the north African coastline as far west as Cyrenaica were taken from the Byzantines in 639–42, and after a temporary halt the Berber countries of Maghrib were attacked. Here resistance was stronger and it was twenty-five years before the Moslems were able to effect the subjugation of Tunisia and the surrender of Carthage (670–95), but, once defeated, the Berbers became ardent Moslems and joined their new masters in the conquest of Spain from the Visigoths (711–20). An attempt to advance into northern France was frustrated by Charles Martel, King of the Franks, at the battle of Poitiers (732), and a final limit was put to Islamic expansion in the west.[1] But the most extraordinary fact about the conquests was that, with the exception of Spain, they were all permanent, the countries concerned being Islamic to this day. This is all the more remarkable, since the Moslem conquests had not been of uncivilized outposts of the ancient world, but of the main centres of Persian and Hellenistic civilization. Their conquests had taken them straight from the mud huts of Medina or the tents of the desert, to the wonders of Ctesiphon, the Museum of Alexandria, and the summer-resorts of the Byzantine court. Even though many of the Moslems had probably fought as Byzantine auxiliaries, and understood the organization and tactics of the imperial army, their achievement was remarkable. In a few decisive battles they had won, with insignificant armies, an empire that was comparable to that of Alexander the Great ; and this, even though they had started out on their conquests with no premeditated plan of campaign. What is the explanation of these startling successes?

A first step would be to explain where so many Arabs came

---

[1] But they conquered Sicily in the ninth century and from there began a movement northwards into southern Italy.

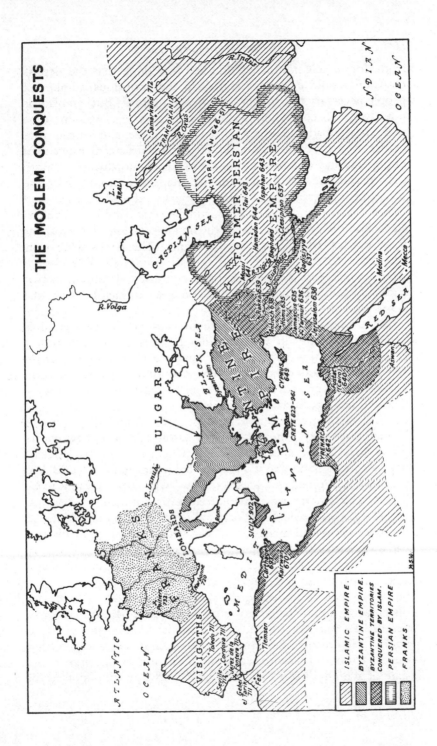

THE MOSLEM CONQUESTS

INDIAN OCEAN

R. Indus

Samarkand 712

TRANSOXANIA

R. Oxus

L. ARAL

KHORASAN 646-51

FORMER PERSIAN EMPIRE

Rai 643

Ispahan 643

Hamadan 644

Baghdad

Ctesiphon 637

CASPIAN SEA

Mosul 641

CARTPO

R. Euphrates

Qadisiyya 637

R. Volga

Takrit 639

Medina

Mecca

Antioch 638

Damascus 635

R. Tigris

Homs 635

Yarmuk 636

Jerusalem 638

BLACK SEA

Byzantium

BYZANTINE EMPIRE

RED SEA

BULGARS

R. Tanais

CYPRUS 649

Cairo 640

Aswan

MEDITERRANEAN SEA

CRETE 823-961

CYRENAICA 642

LOMBARDS

Rome

SICILY 902

Carth 643

Kairwan 670

FRANKS

Narbonne 720

VISIGOTHS

Toledo 711

Cordova 711

Seville

Xeres de la Frontera 711

Gebel el Tarik 711

Fez

Tilemsen

ATLANTIC OCEAN

ISLAMIC EMPIRE.

BYZANTINE EMPIRE.

BYZANTINE TERRITORIES
CONQUERED BY ISLAM.

PERSIAN EMPIRE

FRANKS

M.S.W.

from, for at first sight it would seem incredible that the deserts
of Arabia could ever have contained the enormous number of
people necessary to conquer two great empires. But Arabia was
not always so completely a desert as it now is. At some time
in the past it had undoubtedly been more fertile, and for centuries
before the birth of Mohammed there had been a steady movement
of population from the south of the peninsula northwards. Both
the Persian and the Roman empires had been troubled by the
consequent pressure on their frontiers and had endeavoured
to stabilize the situation by organizing Arabic tribes into ' buffer-
states ' on their borders. With the first successes of the Moslems
these border tribes joined the invaders. The Arabs who overwhelmed the two empires had not all emigrated from central
Arabia together. They represented centuries of migration that
had only temporarily been halted on the frontier between the
desert and the sown.

Till the beginning of the seventh century the two empires
had little difficulty in withstanding the pressure of the Arabs.
But when the Moslem attack was launched they were both in an
exceptionally weak condition. They had only just emerged from
a disastrous war in which the Persian Empire had been totally
defeated and the Byzantine Empire completely exhausted. The
two rulers involved were King Chosroes II and the Emperor
Heraclius (610–41), and the war had lasted for twenty-two years
(606–28). During the course of it, Chosroes and his Persians
had occupied Syria and Egypt for ten years, and at Jerusalem
the Jews had joined in a massacre of all who were thought to be
loyal to the Empire (614), the current estimate being that 57,000
people had been killed. Worse still, the Persians had captured
the True Cross and carried it off as a spoil of war. The disaster
had awakened a true crusading fervour in the Emperor Heraclius.
Even though the Persians had advanced as far as Chalcedon and
were preparing to join the Avars in a siege of Constantinople,
he determined to leave the defence of his capital to God and
his citizens, and marched his army across Asia Minor eastwards,
invaded Persia itself, and advanced almost to the gates of Ctesiphon. He crushed the power of Persia and was resposible for
the overthrow of Chosroes and the reduction of his empire to a
state of anarchy (628). He regained the lost provinces of Egypt

and Syria. He reluctantly consented to a massacre of the Jews in Jerusalem—in penance for which the Coptic Church of Egypt still keeps the first week of Lent as 'the fast of Heraclius'—and recovered the True Cross intact. The religious fervour of the emperor had been rewarded. The heathen Persians had been defeated for ever, and Heraclius might well have likened himself to a second Constantine, defeating the heathen in the name of the Lord.

The Persian war revealed both the strength and the weakness of the Byzantine Empire on the eve of the Moslem invasion ; it identified itself with Christianity and it was Greek ('*Ρωμαῖος*). The question that concerned the inhabitants of Syria and Egypt was whether their love of Christianity was more powerful than their hatred of the Greeks. For the Hellenization of these countries in the ancient world was as superficial as their European-ization is today. There were Hellenized towns like Alexandria, Antioch, Caesarea, and Jerusalem, but they were few, and out-side them the Greeks were hated by the natives as interlopers—as alien rulers with an alien civilization. The great mass of the population was Semitic—Phoenician, Jew, or Arab. When unrestrained by the common tie of Christianity, their detestation of the Greeks knew no bounds, as is illustrated by the part played by the Jews in the massacre of Jerusalem. But Christianity made, or could make, a difference ; the Christians had not actually joined forces with the Persians, but, swayed by conflicting emo-tions, had remained passively neutral, while the Persians had endeavoured to win popularity by tolerating, or even indulging, their heresies.

The main difficulty, from the imperial point of view, was that while Christianity was the only force that could unite the diverse elements of the Empire, the Christian Church was itself divided. Worse still, the divisions in the Church seemed to follow the same lines as the divisions in the Empire, for the Greeks and the Semites would hardly ever agree on matters of theology. The Greeks tended to elaborate the doctrine of the Trinity and the Semites to insist on the oneness of God. The resulting difficulties were particularly well illustrated by the case of the Monophysites in Egypt. The central tenet of Monophysitism was, as its name suggests, that Christ had only one nature ; His divine nature was thought to have absorbed His human nature entirely, so that He had only the appearance and not the reality of a human body.

As this theory cut at the roots of the doctrine of the Incarnation, it was not surprising that it was declared heretical. But the trouble was that in Egypt it was supported by the greater part of the Church, so that the only way of deposing heretical bishops was by invoking the imperial authority; and even then the deposed bishops continued to rule over 'underground' Churches. In most cities there were two Churches, two bishops, and two bodies of clergy. On the one hand, there was the official or orthodox Church which was protected by the State, enjoyed all the ecclesiastical revenues, and was popularly called ' Melkite ' (or the King's) Church. On the other hand, there was the proscribed Church of the Monophysites; it was called Coptic— a word derived from Αἴγυπτος, the Greek word for ' Egyptian '. The names describe them both admirably, for they were divided not only doctrinally but also socially and racially. The one was the Church of the Greek ruling class, ' the King's friends ', and the other was the Church of the Egyptians.

The Emperor Heraclius was well aware of the dangers of this situation, especially as the Persians had exploited it. Relations between the Melkites and the Copts had to be improved somehow, and he endeavoured to do it by means of a theological compromise. He and his religious advisers declared that the question whether Our Lord's nature was single or twofold should be dismissed as irrelevant and its discussion forbidden; the doctrine on which the Church was now to insist was that Christ had only one will. The compromise was ingenious, even if somewhat cynical, but neither the Melkites nor the Copts would accept it, because they did not want a compromise.[1] Heraclius therefore determined to impose it by force. He appointed a bishop called Cyrus to be both Patriarch of Alexandria and Viceroy of Egypt, and empowered him to persecute all those who would not accept the official Church. His cruelty became legendary. It is said, for example, that when the brother of the Coptic patriarch was captured, he was put to death by drowning, after a period

---

[1] In Syria, however, the ' Monothelite ' (*i.e.* one-will) doctrine had a certain measure of success, and it has survived there in the Maronite Church.

of torture in which lighted torches were held against him ' till the fat dropped down from both his sides to the ground '.

In these circumstances, it was hardly to be expected that either the Coptic or the Syrian Monophysites would feel any particular loyalty to the Empire, or any violent hatred of the Moslems. Indeed the Moslems, being Arabs, were racially akin to them, and might even have been regarded as brethren in heresy. Moreover, they tolerated both Christians and Jews. Contrary to the legend that is current in the West, the terms which they offered to Christian peoples such as the Egyptians were lenient. They demanded that they should pay tribute and accept an inferior status, but guaranteed them their lives, their property, and their freedom of worship. Every religious community, whether orthodox or heretical, Melkite or Coptic, was protected in the possession of the property which it had held on the eve of the conquest. The only restrictions were that crosses were not to be displayed in public, that Islam was not to be reviled, and that no attempts were to be made to convert any Moslem to Christianity. After the conquest, a Syrian Monophysite, Abdul Faraj, wrote :

> When our people complained to Heraclius, he gave no answer. Therefore the God of vengeance delivered us out of the hands of the Romans by means of the Arabs. Then although our churches were not restored to us [the Monophysites], since under Arab rule each Christian community retained its actual possessions, still it profited us not a little to be saved from the cruelty of the Romans.[1]

It is clear that any community of empire had disappeared in the East even before the Arab invasions. The Semitic peoples of Egypt and Syria did not feel that they belonged to the Empire, and they did not think that they had lost anything when they ceased to be part of it ; they thought that they had simply exchanged one ruler for another. In Egypt and Syria, the Empire of Heraclius was a chimera like that of Justinian in the West. In these countries the Empire had lost any corporate spirit that it had ever possessed. The Moslems did not have to conquer a ' people ', for there was no Roman people to conquer. All that they had to do was to defeat the imperial armies in the field.

[1] Quoted from A. J. Butler, *The Arab Conquest of Egypt* (1902), p. 159.

Even that task, however, should have been too great for them. The Moslem armies were small and unorganized, and at first had no coherent plan of campaign. They were outnumbered and should have been outgeneralled, for the Emperor Heraclius, who by his daring generalship had defeated Chosroes II, was himself in Syria when the first Moslem attacks were launched. He apparently had no doubt of their true significance, but instead of taking the field himself, departed from Syria for Constantinople. Perhaps he was disillusioned to find that after all the exertions and heroism of the Persian War, fought to recover Egypt and Syria from the heathen, the people of those countries were indifferent to their fate. What was the point in fighting to maintain a Christian Empire where the Empire was hated and the Christians divided ? He left the fighting to his subordinates, who made blunder after blunder and fought without spirit ; in Egypt his lieutenant Cyrus, the persecuting patriarch, insisted on the necessity of surrender as soon as a Moslem army appeared, even though it did not consist of more than 10,000 men. The imperialists were so conscious of their own internal weakness, that blind panic seized them in face of the Moslem armies. Those who did not surrender immediately, blundered forward to defeat.

Resistance to the Moslems only grew stronger as their armies moved away from the countries inhabited by the Semites. In the East they received their first check when they reached the highlands of Persia, and in the West when they reached Tunisia. From Tunisia westwards, the population consisted of Berbers who at first resisted the Moslems fiercely. They only submitted when they found that their interests were identical—that they were both anti-Roman, and both intent on territorial expansion. Then the Berbers flocked to join Islam, and it was they who formed the bulk of the Moslem army that crossed the straits and invaded Spain (711) under the leadership of Tarik who gave his name to Gibraltar (*Gebel-el-Tarik*, the mountain of Tarik). For some five centuries and more the greater part of Spain became a Moslem country, an outpost of the orient in the extreme west. The mosques of Cordova and Seville, though now converted into Christian cathedrals, are amongst the foremost monuments of Moslem art, and many Spanish place-names betray their

Arabic origin (*e.g. El Kantara*, the bridge, and *Guadalquivir*, from *Wadi el Kebir*, the great valley). When at last the country was reconquered by a Christian monarch (and Granada did not fall till 1492), it was found that the only effective way of uprooting Islam was by means of the Spanish Inquisition.

3. THE RESULTS OF THE CONQUESTS

The conquests posed a problem for the leaders of Islam, because the countries conquered had very different traditions and yet had to be governed as a single empire and divine society. It was no easy matter to rule as a single community the Zoroastrians of Persia, the Semitic and Hellenistic peoples of Syria, the Copts of Egypt, the Berbers, and the Spaniards. Indeed, some two centuries after the death of Mohammed the unity of Islam was disrupted, and rival caliphs in Persia, Egypt, and Spain claimed that they, and only they, were the true successors of the Prophet. Even before then, the original idea of Islam had changed, because political power had passed from the religious *élite* to the old governing classes. It passed first to the old Arabic aristocracy that had opposed Mohammed in his early days in Mecca, and then to the Persians.

The history of the Islamic Empire can therefore be divided into three main periods. In the first (632–61), the seat of government was at Medina and the caliphs were chosen from amongst the oldest and most faithful of Mohammed's own followers. Even at this period, however, there were apt to be internal stresses and strains, for Mohammed had left no precise directions for the government of Islam after his death, and no one knew how his successor was to be chosen. The rival parties consisted of the 'Companions of the Prophet' who had accompanied him on his flight from Mecca, the people of Medina, and Mohammed's own family. The first two caliphs were both Companions of the Prophet, Abu Bekr (632–34) and Omar (634–44); Omar engineered Abu Bekr's election, and Abu Bekr nominated Omar as his successor. They received general support because of their seniority, because they were related to the Prophet's family by

marriage, and because it was under them that the greatest conquests were made. But these conquests inevitably produced a
new power in Islam, and a new type of claimant to the caliphate,
the successful governor or general; and in 661 Mcawiya, the
governor of Syria, rebelled, proclaimed himself caliph, and
moved the capital of the empire from Medina to Damascus.

His revolt marks the end of what might be called the ' Moham-
medan ' and the beginning of the Arabic period of Islam. For
Moawiya's family, the Omayyad, was one of the aristocratic
families of Mecca which had been particularly notorious for its
opposition to Mohammed in the period before his final victory.
The caliph whom Moawiya overthrew, on the other hand, was
Ali, who had particularly close ties with the Prophet; he claimed
to have been the first of Mohammed's converts, was certainly
his cousin, and had married his daughter Fātima. (Their descendants are still regarded by the heretical Shi'as as the only true
heirs to the caliphate.) Ali's overthrow by Moawiya, therefore,
marked a victory for the Arab nobility which had been excluded
from the inner circle of Mohammed's religious community.

The period of the Omayyad caliphate (661–750) was remarkable
for the way in which the political interests of the Arabs were given
precedence over the religious interests of Islam. Attempts to
convert the conquered peoples were discouraged, because non-
Moslems had to pay a poll-tax, and the Omayyad caliphs realized
that if their number decreased, the proceeds from the tax would be
less. Non-Arabic Moslems received little or no favour at court,
but Arabs were given positions, whether they were Moslems or
not. El Akhbar, a Christian Arab, was made a sort of ' poet
laureate ', and got drunk at court in the month of Ramadan, in
spite of the official fast and Mohammed's prohibition of wine;
and one of the caliph's treasurers was St. John of Damascus, the
Christian theologian who wrote in defence of the veneration of
images. The tolerant attitude of the Omayyad caliphs is further
illustrated by the fact that, for several years after the conquest of
Syria, the Christians and the Moslems shared the temple-area of
Damascus between them—the Christians retaining their church
at one end of it, while the Moslems used the other as a mosque.

The Omayyads had no intention of destroying the brilliant
civilization that they had conquered. Though they believed in

the supremacy of the Arabs, they believed also in enjoying the culture, art, and luxuries which other peoples could supply. Their mosque at Damascus was built within the walls of the inner enclosure of a Roman temple. It embodied one of the doorways of the old Christian church, and was adorned with all the skill and artistry that was known to the Hellenistic East. Its main feature is a vast courtyard surrounded by arcades, reminiscent of a Roman forum. On the south side is a large building, which looks like a seventh-century Syrian church—it is aisled and cruciform, with a central dome—and on the west side are splendid Byzantine mosaics representing (in spite of Mohammed's prohibition of representational art) the rivers of Damascus. The workmen who built the mosque are said to have been brought by Al-Walid II (705–15) from Persia, India, Maghrib (North Africa), and Rūm (the Arabic word for the Roman or Byzantine Empire), and the work was financed with seven years' proceeds of the Syrian land tax that the Romans had devised. But though it was a mixture of everything, it was none the less a unity. In the same way the Omayyad court was emphatically Arab even though it made free use of alien cultures ; Greek philosophy was freely discussed—St. John of Damascus, for example, disputed with Moslems about the meaning of the terms ' word ' and ' spirit ' which were applied to Christ in the Koran—and Greek science was still understood. But the non-Arabic converts to Islam, the *mawālī*, felt they had a grievance, for though they might be employed in the administration of the Empire, or might even be members of its army, they were not granted equality with the Moslems.

They came to the fore with the third great period of the Islamic Empire, the Abbāsid caliphate (750–1258). In this period a conscious attempt was made to base the policy of the Empire, not on the interests of the Arabs so much as on the religious interests of Islam. The seat of government was moved from Damascus to Baghdad, and there, far from the memory and traditions of the lax Omayyads, there was to be a return to the apostolic custom of Mohammed. But in point of fact the return was not to the custom of Mohammed but to the ceremonial of the pagan Persian Empire. For, in the new order, the *mawālī* of the professional classes were all-powerful, and in Baghdad the chief *mawālī* were

Persian. They transformed the caliphate into an oriental monarchy. In the Arabic periods of Medina and Damascus the
caliphs had lived, like Mohammed himself, as the first among
equals, and it is said that an envoy to the Caliph Omar discovered
him asleep on the steps of the mosque. At Baghdad, however,
as any reader of *The Arabian Nights* will know, the caliphs shut
themselves off from the crowd, and lived in a wonderful and
mysterious palace, elevated above the common rank of humanity
by an elaborate ceremonial. They were fabulously wealthy and
had wide cultural interests; the caliph Ma'mūn, for example,
had the chief books of Greek learning translated into Arabic, with
the result that, in the eleventh century, knowledge of Aristotle's
works in Western Europe was derived mainly from the Arabic
translations which had reached Spain. But the main emphasis
of their policy was that the Islamic Empire was not to be based on
Arab supremacy but on the religion of Islam. In consequence
of this change of policy, Christianity was no longer tolerated so
freely, and conversions to Islam were encouraged. Indeed, once
Arabic supremacy was denied, religious unity was the only conceivable foundation of empire, for the civilization and economic
interests of Persia and Syria, Egypt and Spain, had remained different in spite of the Moslem conquests. The problem facing the
Abbāsids was very similar to that which had faced the Emperor
Heraclius. In both cases there was an empire with no natural
unity except its religion; in both cases an attempt was made to
make that religion the basis of imperial policy; and in both
cases it failed. Every rebellion took on the form of a religious
heresy, and within a hundred years of the establishment of the
Abbāsid caliphate, the Islamic Empire had ceased to exist. Persia,
Spain, Morocco, and Egypt were independent states, each with
its own caliph who claimed that he and he alone was the rightful
successor of the Prophet.

   It is indeed as easy to over-estimate, as it is to under-estimate, the
extent of the changes that the Moslems effected in the countries
they conquered. They did not succeed in creating a unitary
political community which was permanent or a uniform civilization, for in this respect the countries of Islam remain as diverse
as those of Christendom. The Arabs of Mecca and Medina
possessed few of the civilized arts themselves, and consequently

adopted, in each of the countries that they conquered, the arts
and architecture of the subject people ; a Persian mosque is as
different from a Tunisian mosque as Canterbury Cathedral is from
St. Peter's at Rome.   A similar contrast could be drawn in almost
every branch of civilization.   In government, for example,
there was one Moslem system in the provinces that had been
Persian, and another in those that had been Roman.   The reason
for the difference was that the Moslems, unable to create a new
machinery of government for each country as they conquered it,
had had to make use of whatever government they found, for it
would have been a pity if the taxes had not been collected.   In
Egypt some of the highest Roman officials not only retained their
posts under the Moslems, but also embraced the religion of Islam ;
and after sixty years of Moslem rule, the Copts still referred to
the governor of Alexandria as the *augustal(is)* and to his residence
as the *praetorium*.

But though the various countries of Islam retained much of
their individual identity, they all accepted the religion and the
language of their conquerors.   This fact is most striking.   It
might have been thought that on coming into contact with
higher civilizations, the Arabs would have thrown their own poor
culture to the winds.   But in fact, even though they revelled in
Greek philosophy, built palaces in the manner of the Persians
or Byzantines, and wallowed in Roman luxury, they retained
their religion and their language intact.   In this respect the contrast with the Germanic invaders of the Western Empire is most
striking.   The Germans all adopted the religion of the empire
they had conquered and (except in outlying provinces like Britain)
its language too.   The Arabs not only retained theirs, but imposed them on the peoples they had conquered.

A partial explanation for this contrast is to be found in the
way in which the Moslems occupied the conquered countries.
They stood aloof from the subject people, tolerating their
religion and their way of life, but making it clear that their
status was inferior to that of the conquerors.   Mixed marriages
were not permitted, and the conquerors did not usually settle in
any of the existing towns.   In this respect Damascus was an
exception.   Normally, the first act of the Moslems when they
had conquered a new country was to build themselves a new

capital city, like Fustāt (Old Cairo) in Egypt or Kairwan in Tunisia. In effect, the new city was an armed camp or garrison town, with a vast mosque in whose courtyard the whole people (*i.e.* the whole army) could assemble for prayer. It was entirely Moslem. Natives might come to the town to sell their produce or work for the conquerors, but they did so on the Moslems' own terms. In Fustāt the only religion permitted was Islam, and the only language Arabic. Those of the natives who wished to preserve the use of their own religion and their own language had to remain in their old homes, at Alexandria or the ancient fortress of Babylon. The Moslems were segregated from the non-Moslems.

This was in sharp contrast to the pattern of the Germanic settlements in the Western Empire. The Germans did not settle in large communities or in towns of their own making, but in small groups scattered over the countryside. Consequently their influence was diluted, as it were, by the great number of Romanized people around them; though there were Germans everywhere, they were always in a minority. Under the Arabic system of military occupation, however, while the greater part of a country like Egypt was virtually clear of Moslems, in one town, Fustāt, they formed the whole city, and consequently preserved their language, religion, and discipline intact.

It is said that this policy was devised by the Caliph Omar, who did not wish his Arabs to become landowners in the conquered countries, lest they should settle down and desist from further conquests, but it was only made possible because economic conditions were different in the East from what they were in the Western Empire. In the West, the Romans had had to quarter their troops (or settle the barbarians) in the countryside because there was no other way of feeding them, for money was scarce and agricultural labour even scarcer; if the troops had not helped to grow their own food they would have starved. In the East the situation was different. A Moslem community could be established on the edge of the desert, in the sure knowledge that it could levy taxes from the subject population and purchase the necessities of life in an open market. It was the commercial prosperity of the conquered lands that made the policy of Islamic segregation possible.

The way in which the Arabs occupied the conquered countries

accounts for the fact that they retained their own language and religion, but it does not account for the fact that they eventually imposed it on the people they conquered. Doubtless the fact that the poll-tax was levied only on non-Moslems encouraged the mercenary to embrace Islam; and doubtless the ambitions of those who wished to trade in the new Moslem capital or rise to a high position in the State would account for further conversions. The fact that Christianity and Islam had many points in common may well have eased the conscience of the proselyte, but it is none the less difficult, if not humiliating, for the Christian to account for the triumph of Islam in the most Christian parts of the Roman Empire. In Egypt and Syria it was only a small minority of the Christians that remained faithful to the Church; and in north Africa, the home of St. Augustine, the Christian Church eventually died out completely—the last glimpse of it that we have is in the middle of the twelfth century. The success of Islam was won without the assistance of any institution comparable to the Spanish Inquisition, and it was paralleled only by the victory of the Arabic language. It may, however, be observed as a coincidence, if nothing more, that in the beginning of the eighth century the Moslem Empire covered an area which was remarkably similar to that of the two empires that had been the most consistent enemies of Greece and Rome. One, the Persian Empire, has already been referred to. The other was the Empire of Carthage. *Delenda est Carthago* had been the watchword of the Romans. It was now the turn of the Semitic peoples to have their revenge.

Further Reading

ALFRED J. BUTLER. *The Arab Conquest of Egypt.* London. 1902.

SIR THOMAS ARNOLD and ALFRED GUILLAUME (eds.). *The Legacy of Islam.* Oxford. 1931. A good cultural survey.

TOR ANDRAE. *Mohammed, the Man and his Faith* (English translation, London. 1936). An interesting psychological study.

BERNARD LEWIS. *The Arabs in History* (Hutchinson's University Library). London. 1950. The most reliable historical introduction.

ALFRED GUILLAUME. *Islam.* London. 1954. A broad survey from the religious point of view.

ROBERT MANTRAN. *L'Expansion musulmane*, VIIe–XIe siècles. Paris. 1969.

VI

THE FRANKS

THE break-up of the Mediterranean world, the exhaustion of the Byzantine Empire, and the Moslem conquest of the Vandal and Visigothic kingdoms were pre-conditions of the emergence of the Franks as the leading power in Western Europe. The Franks were a branch of the West German people. In the fourth century they had been settled as *foederati* within the Roman Empire and by the beginning of the fifth century they were in possession of the north-east part of modern Belgium (Salian Franks) and the middle Rhine (Ripuarian Franks). In contrast to the East Germans, who included the Vandals, Visigoths, and Ostrogoths and had undertaken vast migrations across the length and breadth of Europe, the Franks were not Christians; but, as we shall see, it was in some ways better in the fifth century to be a pagan than an Arian heretic. They were warriors of formidable appearance. Sidonius Apollinaris has given a vivid description of a small group of them whom he saw on a visit to Lyons in 470. It consisted of a prince and his escort of sworn companions. The prince himself was clothed in silk and was walking behind his richly caparisoned horse.[1]

The appearance of the Kinglets and confederates who accompanied him inspired terror even in peace-time. Their feet were covered entirely, up to their ankles, in boots of bristly hide. Their knees, their legs and their calves were without any covering. Besides this, they wore high, tight, and many-coloured garments which hardly reached down to their bare thighs ; their sleeves only covered their upper arms ; their cloaks were green, embroidered with red. Their swords hung from their shoulders on baldricks, and round their waists they wore a belt of fur adorned with bosses. . . . In

[1] Sidonius Apollinaris, *Letters*, Bk. iv., no. xx.

their right hands they held barbed lances and throwing-axes, and in their left shields, on which the light shone, white on the circuit and red on the boss, displaying both opulence and craftsmanship.

The Franks were renowned for their golden hair. Their kings wore it long as a sign of their royal birth, and if ever they allowed it to be cut they lost their kingship. The names which they bore were Germanic and usually displayed their martial ambitions : Chlodo-wech (*i.e.* Clovis, from which the French name Louis is derived) meant ' battle of glory ', Chlot-hari (Lothar) meant ' celebrated war ', and Sige-bercht (Sigebert) ' brilliant by victory '.

This people had leapt into prominence when its king, Clovis, was baptized to Christianity (*c.* 496–506), for the Church into which he was baptized was the Catholic Church. At that time, all the other peoples of Western Europe were Arians. Most of them, like Theodoric's Ostrogoths in Italy, were far more civilized than the Franks, but their religion prevented them from mixing freely with the Roman population. The Franks, on the other hand, by embracing Catholic Christianity, identified themselves with the cause for which all Romans stood. They were their champions, and received enthusiastic support for their wars. It was with the full backing of the Gallo-Roman Church that Clovis defeated the heretical Burgundians and Visigoths, and made himself master of Gaul (507). (See p. 48.)

The kingdom over which he then ruled is sometimes spoken of as if it were ' France ', but this is incorrect. In the first place his kingdom was not a territory but a people ; it was called the Kingdom of the Franks, and the Franks are claimed as national heroes by the Germans as well as the French. In the second place the territory in which it was situated was not France but Gaul, and Gaul stretched from the Pyrenees to the Rhine, thus including Belgium, part of Holland, and western Germany.

An important factor in the later history of the Franks was the extent of civilization in the land which they conquered. For the ' Romanization ' of Gaul had never been uniform. It was much more complete in the south than in the north. For the south enjoyed a Mediterranean climate ; it was a land of olives, vines, and oranges, where Roman or Hellenistic people might choose to live even for pleasure. The cities were numerous and were provided not only with amphitheatres for blood-sports, but also with theatres, where more sophisticated enjoyment could be had from the production of plays.   The arts flourished, and the forum at Orange or Vienne contained temples that would have done credit to any Hellenistic city.   Men of senatorial rank had vast estates which they farmed by means of slave labour (so long as they could get it), adorned their villas with costly mosaics, and wrote polite verses to each other.   This part of Gaul belonged to *Romania* and even in the sixth century remained in contact with the Mediterranean world as a whole. There were Syrian merchants in the towns, and visitors from Italy or Spain were common.   One of the bishops of Poitiers was Venantius Fortunatus, the poet, who had been born at Treviso in Italy (*c.* 530) and educated at Byzantine Ravenna before moving to Gaul (*c.* 564).   In the south, Roman culture never died entirely.   Sarcophagi were carved in the Roman manner and churches were built with fluted columns and Corinthian capitals till the twelfth century at least, because the civilian population of the towns had a living Roman tradition.   Roman law remained in use till 1789, which was why the lawyers called the south *le pays du droit écrit*.

In the north, however, the Romans had not left a tradition but only a memory.   For the north was a land of oaks, elms, dampness, and mists, and no civilized Roman lived there for pleasure. The senatorial families did not build their villas there, and the towns were mainly garrison towns, with an aqueduct, a bathhouse, a circus for chariot-racing, and an amphitheatre where prisoners could be thrown to the wild beasts.   The civilian population had not the civilization of the south, and when the military population had ceased to be Roman even in name, all that was left was the empty shell of the buildings.   These, however, were immensely impressive in their ruins.   They stood as a monument of the Empire that had once erected them and served as a challenge to the newcomers.   The culture which had created them was dead, and they were but its cenotaph, but their very presence was sufficient to inspire people with a longing to revive the glories of the past.   They were like the monuments of a golden age, in which all men had been wealthy and wise and had lived at peace with each other.   The fact that that age had disappeared only made it the more desirable, and the Franks of northern Gaul were determined to recreate it if they could. Though ignorant of the arts, they tried desperately to imitate the monuments which they saw around them; and the more they tried, the more they travestied the objects of their ambition, so that by attempting to imitate the civilization of the past, they eventually created one that was new.

The point is important, for the difference between the two zones of Gaul was echoed in the two periods of Frankish history. The Merovingians (482–751) derived their wealth very largely from the south, and were able to command the services of aristocratic Gallo-Romans. Their civilization was rich but decadent. The Carolingians (751–891), on the other hand, were northerners through and through; they lacked the arts and graces of the south, they were rude and uncultivated, but at least they were determined to try to be Romans themselves.

1. THE MEROVINGIAN KINGDOM

The history of the Merovingian Kingdom is notoriously difficult, partly because, at crucial points in the story, the evidence is unsatisfactory or lacking, and partly because the Merovingian Kingdom does not fit into our conception of what a kingdom should be. It was regarded not so much as a state as a property, and it was considered natural that it should be divided, on the death of a king, into equal portions among his sons. Thus, when Clovis died in 511 his kingdom was shared out amongst his four sons, and if each of them had in his turn been survived by several sons, the kingdom would eventually have been subdivided even further. That this did not happen was due almost entirely to the skill and ferocity with which the sons and grandsons of Clovis, together with their wives, fought and assassinated each other. By 558 Lothar I had re-united the whole kingdom in his hands, but when he died, three years later, the kingdom was once again divided, for he also had left four sons. It was not re-united again till 613 when Lothar II found that all his rivals had been exterminated. His son and successor, Dagobert (629–39), was the last Merovingian to wield the real power of a king. For during the civil, or fraternal, wars, the power of the

crown had inevitably been weakened, while that of the ' nobility '
had grown enormously, so that the stage was set for the second
period of Merovingian history, that of *les rois fainéants*.

The history of the Merovingian kings, therefore, is not particularly edifying, and any summary of the struggles between the
sons and grandsons of Clovis would be merely confusing.   What
is important is not what this or that king said or did, but what
was happening to the country over which the Merovingians were
ruling.   To what extent did the Franks disrupt the civilization
of Roman Gaul ?   Were they responsible for the growth of a new
state of society called feudalism ?   And to what extent did they
replace Roman institutions by those of the Germanic world ?
These questions have provided a regular battle-ground for historians of all nationalities, but especially for those of France and
Germany, and the whole question is still highly controversial.
But perhaps the best approach is to start by getting a picture of
sixth-century Gaul, when it was being ruled by the sons and
grandsons of Clovis.

Fortunately we are able to get a vivid picture of this period
from the *History of the Franks* by Gregory of Tours.   Gregory
was a Gallo-Roman.   He was born *c.* 539 and was Bishop of
Tours from 573 to 594.   Three-quarters of his history describes
the events that had occurred during his lifetime, and he recounts
them frankly from the view-point of an aristocratic Gallo-Roman
and a Catholic bishop.   His grandfather and great-grandfather
had been bishops of Langres, his uncle Bishop of Clermont,
and his grand-uncle Bishop of Lyons ; he boasted that all but five
of his eighteen predecessors in the bishopric of Tours had in
some way or other been related to his family.

The most striking feature that emerges from his narrative is
that, in Merovingian Gaul, society apparently existed simultaneously on two different planes.   On the one hand, there was the
world of high politics in which most, but not all, of the principal
actors were Frankish, and which was thoroughly brutal and
barbarian.   On the other hand, there was the world of unimportant civilians, merchants, artisans, and townspeople, who
continued to provide a civilized environment for their barbarian
masters, supplying them with luxuries and paying their taxes.
In general, one might say that the Franks were living in, and

ruling over, Roman Gaul, but did not 'belong' to it. Their presence seems to have been casual, accidental, and entirely incongruous, even though the whole country depended on them. Two passages from consecutive chapters of Gregory's *History* may serve as an illustration of the contrast between the Franks and the classical background in front of which they moved. The first describes an incident in the struggle between the sons of Clovis—the murder by kings Childebert and Lothar of their two nephews, the sons of King Chlodomer. Chlodomer had died a year or two previously, and his two boys, aged ten and seven, were staying (*c.* 526–8) with their grandmother, Queen Clotild, when their uncles arranged to meet in Paris.[1]

Childebert spread the rumour among the people that this meeting of two kings had for its object the raising to the throne of the young boys. When they met, they sent to the queen (Clotild) who was residing at the time in Paris, a request that she should let the boys come to them, as they wished to exalt them in the Kingdom. Thereupon she rejoiced, perceiving nothing of their guile, and after giving the boys to eat and drink, sent them forth with these words : 'I shall not feel that I have lost my son [Chlodomer], if I see you raised to his place in the kingdom.' So the children went, but were straightway seized and kept in custody, apart from their attendants and governors (*nutritores*) ; they were in one place, their attendants in another. Then Childebert and Lothar sent to the queen that Arcadius,[2] of whom I have spoken above, with a pair of scissors and a naked sword. Admitted to the queen's presence, he showed her both and said : 'Most glorious queen, our lords thy sons seek to know thy desire with regard to the boys ; is it thy will that they live with shorn locks,[3] or that they both be slain?' But she, terrified at these words and moved to violent wrath, especially when she looked upon the drawn sword and the scissors, distraught by bitterness of grief, and not knowing in her trouble

---

[1] The event occurred before Gregory's birth, and the story may well have improved in the telling, but there is no reason to doubt its substantial veracity. I have followed in this, as in the next passage, O. M. Dalton's translation. (*History of the Franks by Gregory of Tours*, translated by O. M. Dalton. 2 vols. Oxford, 1927. Book iii, c. 18–19.)

[2] He was a Gallo-Roman of senatorial rank from Clermont, who served King Childebert.

[3] Long hair was the badge of a Merovingian king. To cut it was to deprive him of his kingship and reduce him to the rank of other men.

what words came to her lips, said simply : ' If they are not to be
raised to the throne, I had liever see them dead than shorn ! '
But Arcadius took small account of her grief, nor cared to see
what she might afterwards resolve after fuller reflection, but hurried
back with his tale and said : ' The queen approveth ; finish the
task which ye have begun ; she herself desireth the completion
of your design.' They did not wait for more, but Lothar seized
the elder boy by the arm, dashed him to the ground, and driving
his dagger deep under his armpit, did him cruelly to death. At
the sound of his cries his brother flung himself at Childebert's feet,
clasped his knees, and cried amid his tears : ' Help, dearest uncle,
lest I too perish like my brother.' Then Childebert, his face wet
with tears, cried : ' I entreat thee, beloved brother, of thy pity
grant me his life ; only let him be spared, and I will pay whatsoever
thou mayst ask in return.' But the other, giving way to violent
abuse, cried to him : ' Cast him from thee, or thyself shall surely
die in his place. It was thou didst prompt to this business, and
art thou now so swift to recoil from thy pledge ? ' At this rebuke
Childebert pushed the boy from him and drove him to Lothar,
who received him with a dagger-thrust in the side and slew him
as he had done his brother. The attendants and governors of the
young princes were then slain. After all were killed, Lothar took
horse and rode away recking little of the murder of his nephews ;
Childebert withdrew to a suburb of the town. . . . The two
kings divided the realm of Chlodomer between them in equal
shares.

In striking contrast to this passage is the description of Dijon
(*castrum Divionense*), which was, so Gregory tells us, the favourite
residence of his grandfather, the blessed Bishop of Langres :

It is a fortified place (*castrum*) with very strong walls, built in the
middle of a pleasant plain. Its lands are fertile, and so productive
that the fields are sown after a single ploughing, whereupon follows
a great and rich harvest. On the south is the river Ouche, exceed-
ing rich in fish ; on the north another and smaller stream which
enters at one gate, passes under a bridge, and issues through another
gate, surrounding all the fortifications with its tranquil flow : before
the gate it turns mill-wheels with a wondrous speed. Four gates
face the four quarters of the world, and thirty-three towers guard
the circuit of the walls, which are of squared stone to a height of
twenty feet, and above of smaller stones, the total height being
thirty feet with a thickness of fifteen. Why the place is not styled

a city (*civitas*) I cannot say.[1] Round about are excellent springs. On the west side are very fertile hills covered with vines, yielding the inhabitants so noble a Falernian that they scorn the wine of Chalon. The ancients relate that Dijon was built by the Emperor Aurelian.

The contrast between the brutal actions of the Frankish kings and the description of the placid Roman town of Dijon is not merely picturesque. It points to one of the fundamental features of the earlier Frankish monarchy, that there was no necessary connection between it and the land in which it happened to reside. The Frankish Kingdom was mobile because it was not a country but a people. Clovis and his successors were kings not of Gaul, or even of a country called ' Francia ', but of the Franks. Gaul was simply the country which they lived in, and the Gallo-Romans were the people who belonged to it. When the sons or grandsons of Clovis divided Gaul amongst themselves, they divided it as if it was an ' open field ', giving to each a portion of the land in the south and a portion in the north. It did not matter to them if the shares were disjointed and had no territorial unity, or if their frontiers cut across districts which had the appearance of geographical units—a case in point being the ecclesiastical province of Tours, which was at one time divided among three kings. They looked upon the territory of their kingdoms simply as a piece of property. In so far as there was a political or moral unity in any kingdom, it was best seen at the Marchfield (*campus martius*) when the great men of the kingdom assembled in arms before their kings. For the Merovingian kings were more like military chieftains than heads of state in the modern sense of the word. Even at the end of the sixth century they still preserved the spirit of barbarian *foederati*, who were quartered on a country, drew their living from it, and either defended it or fought amongst themselves, as the spirit moved them. They were soldiers of fortune who had won absolute power over the land which they had been employed to

[1] A *civitas*, as previously mentioned (p. 69), was an administrative district of the Roman Empire, but Gregory often uses the word to denote the capital of such a district. A ' city ', therefore, was the residence of a count and a bishop. At this date Dijon had no episcopal see, but was under the jurisdiction of the Bishop of Langres. For archaeological support for Gregory's description, see E. Salin, *La Civilisation merovingienne*, i. pl. xiii.

defend.   Government was not really their business, but as there was nobody to stop them from interfering with it, they took it over as a valuable source of additional revenue.

The administration of the kingdom was centred about the king's person in his ' palace ', which was, like that of the Roman emperors, known as ' the sacred palace ' (*sacrum palatium*).   An identity of name, however, does not necessarily imply an identity of institution.   The Merovingian palace was different from the imperial palace in the same way as the Merovingian Kingdom was different from the Roman conception of a state.   For just as the Merovingians thought of their state as a property, so they thought of their palace or court as a household.   Its chief officials were the steward (*senescalc*) and ' mayor of the palace ' (*major domus*) who was in charge of the royal estates and the officers of the household.   Only less important were the butler (*pincerna*), the chamberlains or servants of the bedchamber (*cubicularii*), the constable or count of the stable (*comes stabuli*), and the grooms or marshals.   The latter were important because the ' palace ' was not a building but an itinerant court.   The king went on progress throughout his kingdom, complete with his entire ' palace '. It was because the seat of government was not stationary that the sons and grandsons of Clovis were able to contemplate dividing Gaul into lesser kingdoms with no natural unity and no natural centre of administration.   They all had their favourite residences in the north of France, at Paris, Orleans, Soissons, Reims, or Metz, but they all moved with their ' palaces ' to the south whenever circumstances demanded.

Besides the household offices there was a writing office in the king's household, controlled by an official known as the referendary.   He supervised the drafting and production of legal and public documents and did his best to see that they were worded in accordance with the best imperial formulae.   Because the documents drawn up were often imitations of the imperial style, some historians, notably Fustel de Coulanges, have been tempted to declare that Merovingian government was to a large extent a continuation of imperial government.   It is likely, however, that the imperial formulae found in Merovingian documents were little more than pompous verbiage, and that the government of the Merovingian kings was very different from that of the Roman emperors.

The local administration, for example, might at first sight appear to have been identical in Roman and Merovingian Gaul, for the administrative unit was in both cases the same. It was the ' city ' (*civitas*) which, after the sixth century, began to be subdivided into *pagi*. Roman Gaul had contained 112 of these ' cities ', and there is little reason to doubt that the ' cities ' mentioned by Gregory of Tours were identical with them. Under the Franks the officers in charge of them were called counts (*comites*), a name which may also have been given to such officers in the last days of the Empire. It is only when we come to consider the duties of the count that the main differences between Roman and Merovingian administration emerge. The first difference was that he did not govern the land according to any single law. He was charged, in the words of his appointment, to judge every man according to his own law, Franks by Frankish law, Romans by Roman law, and Burgundians by Burgundian law, which inevitably led to confusion in mixed cases. Just as the Merovingians were kings not of a country but of a people, so also the count's duties were circumscribed by the different needs of different people. Secondly, whereas in the Roman Empire the military power had been strictly separated from the civil, lest the military should abuse its strength, in the Merovingian Kingdom the count united both in his own person. He was tax-collector and judge, and led the troops of his ' city ' to war. With so many powers united in his hand, it was not surprising that he abused them all. He was responsible only to the king, and the king's main concern was simply that he should preserve the royal rights which were profitable and collect his revenues. In the sixth century the count was usually not a local man, for the king found that it profited him better if his count had no particular interest in his ' city '.

Government, for the Merovingians, was simply another means of making money. It was for this reason that, when they wished to be particularly generous to some favoured subject, they granted him an ' immunity ' (*immunitas*). An ' immunity ' was a legal instrument which declared certain lands to be absolutely free, or immune, from all counts or other royal officials. In such lands the count had no authority whatsoever ; he could not levy taxes, try criminals, or summon men to the royal host. The king had given away his regalian rights over particular lands to one of his subjects, and did so because he regarded his regalian rights simply as so much property. It did not occur to him to ask if such ' immunities ' would benefit the state or commonwealth, for such notions were entirely foreign to him. He ruled the land for what he could get out of it and left the positive side of government to the Christian charity of the Church.

It was for that reason that the bishops were so important in Merovingian Gaul. They were ' Romans ', usually members of the great senatorial families, and had the interests of their territory at heart. They were, moreover, in a very special relation to the government, for just as every ' city ' had its count, so it had its bishop, and the two were expected to collaborate. It therefore followed that though the bishop was elected by ' the people ' (in fact the more important people) of his church, his appointment had to be confirmed by the king. Once he had received the royal confirmation, however, he was virtually irremovable from his see. The count could be dismissed or moved to another district, but the bishop was appointed to his see for life ; and as it still was not the custom to ' promote ' a bishop by translating him from one see to another, he was able to identify himself with the particular interests of his diocese or ' city '. The bishops belonged to their ' cities ' in a way that the counts did not, and were prepared to spend money on them. One way in which they could improve their dioceses was by the building of parish churches in villages, but their interests were not confined to ecclesiastical matters. When a blood-feud between two men in the ' city ' of Tours threatened to grow into a minor civil war, it was Gregory, the bishop, who acted as peacemaker, providing out of the Church's funds the money whereby the more guilty party could pay compensation to the less guilty. The count was quite prepared to see that the two parties had a fair trial, but he was not prepared to let the maintenance of peace cost him money. Similarly the count did not expect to spend any money on public works ; he did not consider it his responsibility to do so, and neither did the king. In such matters it was the bishop who took the initiative and provided most of the money. Injuriosus, Bishop of Tours, founded the two villages of Neuilly and Luzille, Desiderius of Cahors built aqueducts,

and Felix of Nantes altered the course of the Loire. ' You are
the salvation of your country,' wrote Venantius Fortunatus to
Felix, ' . . . you who give to the lands what justice requires and
restore to them the joys of the past. . . . Voice of the principal
citizens, light of the nobility, defender of the people, you are
the port in which shipwreck can be escaped.' A brave bishop
like Gregory of Tours could not only defy his king in matters
ecclesiastical, but also complain successfully to him about the
conduct of secular affairs by the count.

It was the bishops, in fact, who formed the sole link between
the two societies, Frankish and Gallo-Roman, which co-existed
in Merovingian Gaul. The kings respected them because they
were genuinely frightened of invoking the wrath of God or his
saints—St. Martin of Tours being considered a particularly powerful defender of the rights of his church and its bishop. Kings
might break their oaths, murder their nephews, or command
the execution of their own children, but few were brave enough
to violate the Church's right of sanctuary. The moment a man
incurred the wrath of the king, he fled to the nearest church, and
if he succeeded in entering it, he was safe so long as he stayed
there. The king's men might surround the church, or even try
to starve the man out, but they would not dare to seize him in
the sanctuary. Their usual process was to entice the man out
by swearing a solemn oath that the king would forgive him if he
confessed his guilt. Then, once they had him out of the church,
they would break their oath and dispatch him. But though the
breaking of oaths was not uncommon, the violation of sanctuary
was almost unheard of. The Franks were by nature a brave
and ruthless race, but it took a particularly brave and ruthless
Frank to risk the vengeance of God and all his saints.

If it was superstition that made the kings respect the bishops,
it was the interests of the Catholic faith that made the bishops
serve the kings. In the sixth century the Franks were still the
only Germanic people to have embraced the Catholic faith, and
Arianism was still a very real menace. Gregory of Tours went
out of his way to insert in his *History*, accounts of the arguments
which he had used to refute the doctrines of the Arians ; and
the whole theme of his work was that God favoured the cause of
those who confessed the blessed Trinity and punished those that

denied it. The fear that was ever at the back of his mind was that the sons and grandsons of Clovis in their fratricidal wars should incur the wrath of God, and so weaken their kingdom that it might be overcome by one of the Arian kingdoms around it. He did not just tolerate the Franks. He supported them warmly, in spite of their cruelty and their barbarism, because they represented the cause of the Catholic Church. The Catholic Church, which represented the interests of *Romania* and was led by the foremost members of the senatorial aristocracy, was in active alliance with the Frankish monarchy.

While, therefore, it is legitimate to speak of society in Merovingian Gaul as existing on two separate planes, it would be a great mistake to think that the Gallo-Romans and the Franks were opposed or hostile to each other. Many Gallo-Romans took a pride in bearing Frankish names, and Franks delighted in their command of the Latin language—King Chilperic, for example, wanted to add four letters to the alphabet so that he could write Latin ' as it was spoke '. The two peoples ' Roman ' and ' barbarian ' united, as it were, in marriage. The issue of that marriage was, as might be imagined, somewhat diverse in character. It included both Feudalism and the Holy Roman Empire.

2. The Transference of Power from the Merovingians to the Carolingians (639–751)

The period of Frankish history from 639 to 751 was one of momentous change and great confusion. The Merovingian dynasty still reigned over the Kingdom of the Franks, but it had lost its virility. It was represented by *les rois fainéants*, who married in their early teens and died in their early twenties, and who, while alive, were kept in perpetual tutelage by the chief of their nobles, ' the mayor of the palace ' (*major domus*).

It was partly in consequence of this tutelage that the divisions of the kingdom began to take on a new aspect in the seventh century. In the sixth century, as we have already seen, the divisions were made so that each of a king's sons could inherit an equal share of his father's kingdom ; and it was not considered unusual or unfortunate if each son's portion lacked any sort of economic or geographical unity. But in the seventh century the

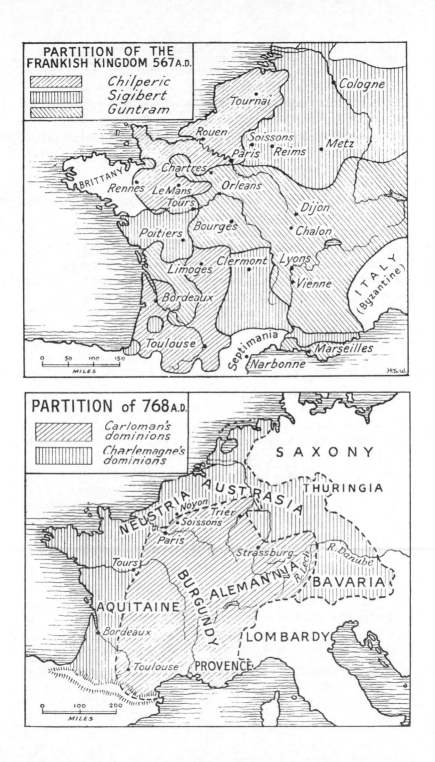

PARTITION OF THE
FRANKISH KINGDOM 567 A.D.

Chilperic
Sigibert
Guntram

Cologne
Tournai
Rouen
Soissons
Paris   Reims   Metz
Chartres
BRITTANY
Rennes   Le Mans   Orleans
Tours   Dijon
Poitiers   Bourges   Chalon
Limoges   Clermont   Lyons
Vienne   ITALY (Byzantine)
Bordeaux
Toulouse   Septimania   Marseilles
Narbonne

0   50   100   150
MILES

H.S.W.

PARTITION of 768 A.D.

Carloman's dominions
Charlemagne's dominions

SAXONY
NEUSTRIA   AUSTRASIA   THURINGIA
Noyon   Trier
Soissons
Paris   Strassburg   R. Danube
R. Lech
BURGUNDY   ALEMANNIA   BAVARIA
AQUITAINE
Bordeaux   LOMBARDY
Toulouse   PROVENCE

0   100   200
MILES

case was different.   The kingdom was continually being divided
into three parts which were geographical units, called Neustria,
Austrasia, and Burgundy ; [1] and the divisions were made, not
so much to satisfy the members of the royal family with a sufficient inheritance, as to satisfy the expressed and reiterated
demands of the ' nobles ' of each district.[2]   In 614, for example,
there was only one king, Lothar II, but his ' nobles ' forced him
to allow that Neustria, Austrasia, and Burgundy should each
have its own ' palace ' (or central administration), complete with
its own mayor of the palace or governor.   A similar tendency
can be seen in local administration, for in the same edict as that
containing the above concession, Lothar II granted that, in
future, counts would be chosen from amongst the people of the
district which they were to administer.   This was an important
concession, because as soon as local men were appointed, they
began to consider the interests of their own ' city ' or *pagus*,
as well as those of the king.

In the seventh century it was the clash of local interests that
dictated the course of Frankish history.   There were perpetual
wars between the ' nobles ' of Neustria, Austrasia, and Burgundy.
They were not ' national ' wars, but wars between associations
of ' nobles '.   The ' nobles of Austrasia ' were those who had
associated themselves with the mayor of the palace of Austrasia,
and the ' nobles of Neustria ' were those who had associated
themselves with his greatest political rival, the mayor of the
palace of Neustria.   In each case the link that bound the
' nobles ' to the mayor of the palace was extremely strong,
since it was based not only on sentiment but also on common
interest ;   the mayor of the palace was able to keep the monarchy in tutelage because of the support he received from the
' nobles ', while they owed their whole livelihood to him.

The reason for this was that the ' nobles ' had not yet succeeded in making their position hereditary—it was not till about
the twelfth century that every count, margrave, or earl was succeeded automatically by his son.   In the seventh century the

---

[1] Aquitaine was also part of the Frankish Kingdom, at any rate in theory.   But
in this period it tended to be autonomous and consequently was not usually included
in the partitions.

[2] The word ' noble ' is placed in inverted commas, because in this period the
' nobility ' was not hereditary.   See below.

' nobles ' were not the holders of titular honours but simply the more important of the king's officials ; and though the son of one of these ' nobles ' would have the advantage of his father's wealth and influence, he had no hereditary right to any office, title, or privilege. The ambitious man, therefore, had to make his own way in the royal service, and the most effective way of doing this was to enlist the support of the mayor of the palace, for almost all offices were, in effect, in his gift. The only question was how to enlist the support of so great a man ; and the stock answer was to ' commend ' oneself to him and become his vassal.

The act of commendation was a formal contract by which both lord and vassal accepted certain definite obligations. The lord promised to ' aid and sustain ' his vassal in food, clothing, and other necessities ; the vassal promised to serve his lord and obey him all his life. No lord would accept as a vassal a man who could not do him any service, and nobody would attempt to become the vassal of a man who was incapable of forwarding his interests. A Frank with a comparatively small property might consider that the most valuable protection he could receive would be that of a richer neighbour, while a lesser bishop who was in need of local support might be prepared to receive into his commendation a man who was only of moderate standing. But almost everyone, no matter how rich or powerful, would have been delighted to ' commend ' himself to the mayor of the palace, and he, in his turn, could afford to refuse all but the most valuable offers. It was to be expected, therefore, that his vassals would be great men with vassals of their own, and that their influence would pervade the greater part of the kingdom. And for this reason his power was formidable, even when compared with that of the king. All the Franks owed obedience to their king as of right, but the most powerful and influential of them had also promised to serve the mayor of the palace all the days of their life, as his vassals.

The institutions of commendation and vassalage obviously played a large part in weakening the authority of the Merovingian kings, but it is important to insist that these institutions would not themselves have grown up so rapidly, if it had not been that Merovingian government had already proved itself to be inefficient, unjust, and unscrupulous. The reason why so many men were ' seeking lords ' was that they required protection from the tyranny of the counts. Such protection could not be provided by the normal working of the king's local government, because the count himself was its representative. The only remedy was to ' seek a lord ' who had, in the first place, influence in the king's ' palace ' and, in the second place, a private army.

Private armies were not exceptional features in the early Middle Ages. Wherever public authority was weak, they were indispensable ; we have already seen that even in Justinian's empire Belisarius had had a large force of private retainers (p. 57). In the Merovingian Kingdom the man who had no armed force at his disposal was lost, because it was a notorious fact that neither kings nor counts obeyed the formal rules of law unless it suited them. Rival kings, even when they were brothers, fought against each other, murdered their nephews, seized their kingdoms, and executed their servants without the semblance of a trial ; and, to judge from the pages of Gregory of Tours, the average count acted in much the same way. It was consequently but common prudence for the ' nobles ' to arrange for their own defence, and this they did by collecting vassals. The vassals promised to serve them, that is to provide them with military support, all the days of their life ; and in return the lord promised to protect them—to come with his private army to the support of any one of them. The contract of vassalage was a sort of insurance against oppression. While the king's subjects owed him service and obedience and received nothing in return, the vassal bound himself to serve and obey his lord in return for protection and maintenance. It was therefore to be expected that a man would serve his lord more willingly than his king.

It was for this reason that armies composed of vassals were more efficient than the official army or ' host ' of the kingdom. The ' host ' consisted of a mass levy, the contingent of each ' city ' or ' pagus ' being led by its own count. It was untrained, undisciplined, and ill-equipped, and consisted of foot-soldiers, for the king could not expect that the great mass of his subjects would have the necessary skill or resources to serve him as cavalry-soldiers. With the vassalic armies it was different. They were trained, disciplined, and well-equipped bodies of cavalry, and provided the decisive striking-force in any battle. Their importance was becoming increasingly apparent throughout the Merovingian period. The demand was always for more cavalry-soldiers, or, to call them by their proper medieval name, knights (Latin *milites*, French *chevaliers*, German *Ritter*).

It used to be held that the military value of knights was not appreciated by the Franks until they had to face the Moslem army which invaded their kingdom from Spain in 732, but it is now recognized that they had been using cavalry, even if on a limited scale, as early as the sixth century. What held up the development of knightly armies was not the failure to realize their military potentialities but the inability to find the means with which to pay for them. For the equipment and maintenance of a knight was, in terms of medieval economy, enormously expensive. It is important to explain why this was so, even at the expense of a somewhat lengthy digression.

The knight's equipment consisted of a shirt of mail, a helmet, a shield, a lance, an axe, and a horse. Of these items the horse was the most important and the most expensive. It had to be strong enough to carry the knight even when fully armed, fast enough to be capable of taking part in a charge at full gallop, and sure enough not to panic or bolt in the middle of a battle. Such horses were rare and extremely costly. They had to be specially bred and trained, while even the simplest requirements, such as stabling and winter-fodder, might tax an ordinary man's resources. To be a knight was a costly business. Quite apart from everything else, one needed a personal servant to help with one's armour, and a groom to look after one's horse, in addition to any ordinary household requirements.

But besides wealth, a knight required skill and training, for fighting on horseback was far more difficult than riding. The knight had to be able to charge his enemy—that is to say he had to be capable of galloping his horse while holding his shield in his left hand and his lance or axe in his right hand, and of hitting his adversary without falling off his horse. If successful, he had to complete the work by following up his charge; if he came to a halt every time he struck an adversary he was no use to anyone in a battle, for he simply got in the way of his fellows and might easily be ' run over ' by the knight behind. It was no ordinary degree of horsemanship that was required.

He also needed discipline, for the most effective charge was one that was made by a whole body of knights—five, ten, twenty, or more—acting in unison. They had to charge straight, so that they did not get in each other's way, and they had to throw their lances or swing their axes without hitting anyone but the enemy. They had to be under the orders of a leader who could tell them not only when to charge, but where. Knights who tried to charge over fields which were heavy with mud or clay could not move at sufficient speed to make their charge effective ; knights who charged down a hill which was too steep might lose control of their horses and be thrown. They had to have complete confidence that their leader had reconnoitred the ground with care. Any concealed object, such as a canal which had not been noticed in advance, could be fatal to a charge ; for the knights would not be able to check themselves in a hurry, and even if they did, would probably be ' run over ' by the line of knights behind them.[1] The whole point of a charge was that it should be at full gallop, so that the opposing infantry should lose its nerve and flee. The knight played much the same part in a medieval battle as a ' tank ' plays in modern warfare. His speed and striking power could be decisive ; but his equipment, training, and maintenance were all extremely expensive.

That was the difficulty that faced anyone who wanted to control an army of knights. There was no particular difficulty in getting the men ; an influential ' noble ' could easily find valiant men who were only too anxious to train as knights, become his vassals, and serve him in all things. The difficulty lay in maintaining his vassals once he had got them, for it was the lord's obligation to supply his vassals with food, lodging, and equipment. How was he to do this ? There was, as we shall presently see (pp. 179 ff.), very little surplus wealth in the form of money, at any rate in the Frankish Kingdom, and no one, king or ' noble ', could possibly have had the resources to

---

[1] This particular mistake was made by the French at the battle of Courtrai (1302), but the English fell into a similar trap at Bannockburn.

pay money-wages to a whole army of knights. There were consequently only two ways by means of which a lord could generally maintain his knights. Either he could maintain them in his own household, providing them with food, clothing and equipment, or he could give them landed estates and tell them to maintain themselves on the produce of the land. The latter method was the more popular, even though it may have been more extravagant, and it is best described as ' feudal '.

This word is important and has often been misunderstood. In its historical sense, at any rate, it is not a term of abuse, and means neither ' reactionary ' nor ' hereditary ' nor ' anarchical '.[1] It is derived from the Latin *feodalis*, which means ' of, or appertaining to a fief (Lat. *feodum*) '. The word *feodum* did not come into general use till about the middle of the eleventh century, but the thing to which it referred was much older. It can be defined as a property held by a vassal as a tenant from his lord in return for the performance of some specified service, usually knight-service. In the eighth century such a property was known as a ' benefice ' (Lat. *beneficium*), but although the word is different, it would be carrying academic precision too far to insist that while the knights of the eleventh century were ' feudal ' those of the eighth were only ' beneficial '.[2] For even though there were differences between the ' feudalism ' of the eighth and eleventh centuries, they were differences not of kind but of degree.

The feudalism of the eighth century, as of the ninth, is usually described as ' Carolingian '. It is an apt description, for the Carolingians were the family who built up so great a power by means of their vassals that they were eventually able to overthrow the Merovingians and make themselves kings of the Franks (751). They were a wealthy Austrasian family, descended from Arnulf, Bishop of Metz (*d.* 641). Although they enjoyed no hereditary right, they had succeeded in gaining for themselves

---

[1] The abusive meaning of the word was developed at the time of the French Revolution. Thus, according to the *Oxford English Dictionary*, Burke wrote in 1790 (*Fr. Rev.*, Wks. v. 395) : ' The leaders teach the people to abhor and reject all feodality as the barbarism of tyranny.' In the seventeenth century the word was still used in its correct legal and historical meaning.

[2] In point of fact, the word *beneficium* continued to be used in Germany till the twelfth century, and clearly meant the same thing as *feodum*.

a firm hold of the office of mayor of the palace in Austrasia, as the accompanying genealogical table will show.[1]

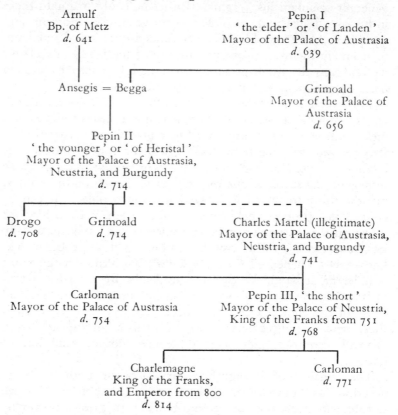

It will be noticed that although it was not always the eldest, or even a legitimate, son who took his father's place, yet, except for a few years after the death of Grimoald, who tried to usurp the throne for his son and failed, some member of the family was mayor of the palace throughout the period from 639 to 751. It was largely by virtue of their possession of this office that the Carolingians had been able to receive all the greater ' nobles ' of Austrasia into their commendation and vassalage.

---

[1] Strictly speaking the family should be known as ' Arnulfing ' (sons of Arnulf) till the time of Charles Martel. It is simply for convenience that I have called it ' Carolingian ' throughout.

Their greatest rivals for power were the ' mayors ' of the other palaces, of Neustria and Burgundy, which, in the sixth century, had been the richest and most important parts of the Kingdom of the Franks, and it was not till 687 that Pepin II was able to defeat them decisively at the battle of Tertry. The reason for his victory, however, is clear. It was simply that by the end of the seventh century the Austrasian mayor of the palace could afford to maintain more vassals than either of his two rivals, because he was richer in land. Austrasia consisted of the whole eastern part of the kingdom, north of the Alps, and in the early Frankish period it was much less densely populated than Neustria, Burgundy, or Aquitaine, containing much forest-land and waste. It was consequently possible for an energetic man to ' open up ' much new land by organizing a regular programme of forest-clearance, building new villages, and attracting peasant-cultivators from the more populous parts of the kingdom. Austrasia, therefore, in the seventh and eighth centuries, was the ' new land ' of the Frankish Kingdom, where fortunes could be made in much the same way as the ' Middle West ' was the ' new land ' of the United States of America in the nineteenth century. While Mediterranean commerce was declining, with the result that the cities of the south and the west were getting poorer, Austrasia was getting richer ; and as it grew richer so the power of its ' mayor of the palace ' increased. He could afford to maintain an ever-increasing number of vassals.

Thus it came about that, in the first half of the eighth century, the Carolingians were masters of the Frankish Kingdom. They controlled the king and his ' palace ', bestowed honours on the ' nobles ', and commanded both the royal ' host ' and their own vassalic army. For six years, from 737 to 743, they even kept the throne vacant. Their power was complete, except that they lacked the name of King.

None the less, their government was very different from that of the Merovingians. Merovingian government has been aptly described as ' despotism tempered by assassination ', for the kings, even when surrounded by their nobles, rarely, if ever, deigned to ask them for their advice. Quite typical is the story which Gregory of· Tours tells of the execution of a count called Magnovald : [1]

---

[1] *History of the Franks* (tr. Dalton), viii. 36.

At the court of Childebert, for some cause unknown, Magnovald was slain by the King's orders in the following way. The King being in his palace at Metz, and looking on at a sport in which a beast was being worried by a pack of dogs on all sides, summoned Magnovald to him. He came, and in ignorance of what was afoot, joined freely in the general laughter as he watched the creature. Then a man who had received his orders, as soon as he saw his victim intent on the sport, swung his axe and cleft his skull. He fell dead, and was thrown out of a window of the house; his own people buried him. His property was seized, and all that was found was taken to the public treasury. Some averred that the reason for his murder was that after his brother died he had done his own wife to death, after cruelly ill-treating her, and then taken his brother's wife to bed.

It is to be noticed that Gregory could not say for certain what was the reason for the execution (or murder), but could only repeat what ' some averred '. There had been no formal trial, and the king had not even thought it necessary to explain to his assembled ' nobles ' the reason for his action.

With the Carolingians, on the other hand, the situation was very different. They hardly moved a step without taking the advice of their ' nobles ', and in their formal documents they were always at pains to stress the fact that what was being done had been determined *concilio procerum suorum*. If a Carolingian made war, it was only after he had taken counsel with his ' nobles '; if he made peace, it was at their request; and if he wished to make new laws his first step would be (' on the advice of the servants of God and of his " nobles " ') to summon a council to discuss them. Since his power rested on the support given by his ' nobles ', it was vital to him that he and they should act in concert. That was an essential feature of a kingdom that was built on vassalage.

There was thus a community of interest between the ruler and his ' nobles ' which gave to the Carolingian state some notion of the ' common weal ' or *respublica*. The Merovingian kings had had no such conception. They had regarded their kingdom as a property and the taxes which they received as booty. When the two sons of King Chilperic were on their deathbeds (580), their mother, Fredegund, ' repented ', as Gregory of Tours put it, and proposed to the king that the tax-registers should be burnt :

> We lay up treasures without knowing for whom we gather them together. . . . And lo ! now we lose our sons ; lo ! now they are slain by the tears of the poor, by the lamentations of widows, by the sighs of orphans. . . . Come, therefore, if thou wilt, let us burn all the unjust tax-lists.[1]

The Carolingians were in a happier state of mind. They knew why they were gathering up treasure. It was so that their government could be sufficiently strong to defend the ' Christian people ' (*populus christianus*) from its enemies. They regarded themselves and their subjects as if they were the chosen people of God, and consequently considered that they had a duty to God in regard to their kingdom. This was not solely because they had to defend their kingdom against the heathen, though they performed this duty efficiently, as when Charles Martel defeated the Moslems near Poitiers in 732, but still more because they considered it was their duty to help the ' Christian people ' to ' secure the salvation of its soul '.

This brings us to what is perhaps the most marked of all the characteristics of Carolingian government. It was inseparable from the Church. The fact was brought out most clearly in 750–1, when Pepin III decided to depose King Childeric III, the last of the Merovingians, and to have himself made king in his place. The revolution might, in one sense, seem trivial since Pepin III was already governing the kingdom in fact, as ' mayor of the palace '. But in another it was fundamental, since it affected the whole conception of kingship.

How did one make a man king ? So far as the Merovingians were concerned, the question was meaningless, for with them kings were not ' made ' but ' born '. A man was a king if he was the acknowledged son of a king, and he was called king even during his father's lifetime, before he was an independent ruler. In the case of normal successions, there was no ceremony of coronation or anointing ; the king would simply make a progress of his kingdom and impose the oath of fealty on his subjects. He did not even ' become ' a king ; he was simply recognized as ' being ' king. For he owed his kingship not to

[1] *History of the Franks* (tr. Dalton), v. 26 (34).

the acclamation of the people but to the myth that the blood of Meroveus flowed in his veins.[1] There was still a quality of primitive magic in Merovingian kingship, and the fact was symbolized by the importance attached to the king's long hair, which could not be cut unless he were to lose his kingship.

It was clear, therefore, that Pepin III could not be made king without the aid of some extraordinary supernatural intervention, and it is interesting to see exactly what authority was considered sufficient. His first step was to send an embassy to the Pope, Zacharias, to ask if it was not right that he who held the power should also have the name of king. The Pope decided that it was, and gave his opinion in writing as a form of authority. Pepin then summoned an assembly of the Franks (*i.e.* the ' nobles ') to meet at Soissons in 751, and there,[2]

> in accordance with the command of the Pope, he was called King of the Franks, and he was anointed to the dignity of this honour . . . by the hand of [St.] Boniface, . . . and, as is the custom of the Franks, was raised on to the throne in the city of Soissons.

The exact order of the events as here related is important. First the nobles gave Pepin the name of king, then St. Boniface anointed him and made him a king, and finally the nobles (by lifting him on to the throne) put him in possession of the Kingdom of the Franks. It was therefore true that Pepin ruled the Franks by right of some sort of election, but he was a king by the grace of God (*Dei gratia*). The phrase was no empty formula, for in anointing Pepin, the Church had consecrated him in much the same way as it might have consecrated a bishop. He received a power which he had not formerly possessed ; he had received not a title but an *ordo* which in some sense transformed him. This can clearly be seen in the passages of the Old Testament from which the Church drew its inspiration in this matter :[3]

> And the Lord said unto Samuel, How long wilt thou mourn for Saul, seeing I have rejected him from being King over Israel? Fill thine horn with oil, and go, I will send thee to Jesse the Bethlehemite : for I have provided me a King among his sons.

*   *   *

[1] The belief in the mythical ancestry of the Merovingians cannot be traced before the seventh century.

[2] *Annales Regni Francorum*, ed. Kurze, p. 9.   [3] 1 Samuel xvi. 1 and 13.

Then Samuel took the horn of oil and anointed him [David] in the midst of his brethren ; and the spirit of the Lord came upon David from that day forward.

It was the 'spirit of the Lord' that transformed Pepin into a king. He was consecrated, or made holy, and his descendants were, as the Pope subsequently expressed it, 'a sacred race and a royal priesthood' (*vos gens sancta estis atque regale estis sacerdotium*).

The Carolingians, therefore, unlike the Merovingians before them, were, in a very special sense, Christian kings, since they owed their kingship to the Pope. So far as is known, the Visigoths of Spain, after their conversion to Catholicism, were the only other 'barbarian' people which had previously been so favoured by the Church. Their kingdom had now been overthrown by the Moslems, and the Franks consequently had a real claim, under Carolingian rule, to call themselves 'the Christian people'. It was to them, in the winter of 753-4, that Pope Stephen II fled from the power of the Lombards ; and in the midsummer of 754, he anointed Pepin afresh, together with his two sons Charles and Carloman. The ceremony took place in the abbey church of St. Denis, near Paris, and the Pope formally forbade the Franks ever to elect as king anyone who was not of the sacred race of Pepin. He also bestowed on Pepin and his sons the title of 'patrician of the Romans'.

In one respect, this alliance between the Papacy and the Carolingian dynasty was surprising, because Pepin's father, Charles Martel, had earned himself an unenviable reputation as a despoiler of church property. He had been mayor of the palace for the whole kingdom (*c*. 717-41) and had found himself in urgent need of more vassals and knights and of more land with which to endow them. He had therefore turned to the Church, which was by far the greatest landowner in the kingdom, and which was also peculiarly defenceless. As mayor of the palace he was able to appoint his own vassals to vacant bishoprics and abbeys. One of these men, Milo, held the sees of Reims and Trèves in plurality for forty years, during which time he was able to distribute an immense amount of ecclesiastical land to Charles's vassals. In the case of the abbey of Fontenelle, Abbot Teutsind was said to have alienated almost one-third of the abbey's property—to one count alone he gave 28 villages (*villae*) in return for a nominal rent of 60 shillings [1]—and the monks remembered his rule as a tyranny.

> For it would have been better on that day, when the aforesaid properties were taken away from the monastery, if there had been a fire and if all the buildings had been burnt down to the ground, for it would have been possible to rebuild them ten times over before such properties could have been acquired. For, where the soldiers of Christ [*i.e.* monks] used to get their sustenance, there one now sees food for dogs, and where the light used to shine before Christ's altar in the church, there one now finds sword-belts and spurs being made, and saddles for horses being adorned with gold and silver. . . . Such rulers [as Abbot Teutsind] are more wicked than pagans, because the pagan, even if he burns the place down, does not take the land away with him.[2]

Pepin III and his brother Carloman, however, had made peace with the Church (742–4), and had come to an agreement with it concerning the property which his father had taken. In theory it was to be restored, but it was agreed that in practice it might be retained by Pepin for the use of his knightly vassals, so long as the kingdom continued to be threatened by external dangers such as the Moslems.[3] This meant that, in effect, the Church recovered hardly any of its lost lands. But it consented to this *fait accompli*, because it knew that without the aid of a powerful defender the whole of Western Christendom might have been submerged beneath another and more terrible wave of barbarian invaders ; and because it knew that unless the ruler had sufficient lands to maintain a really large number of knights, the forces at his disposal would be inadequate for the defence of his kingdom.

The relationship between the Church and the Carolingians was, in reality, as contractual as that which existed between the Carolingians and their vassals. In return for the concession in respect of the church lands, Pepin and Carloman consented to the reform of the Frankish Church. This was effected by St.

---

[1] Theoretically the count was only given the right of usufruct over the land, which he thus held *iure precarii*. Later, such grants of ecclesiastical land made by royal command were known as *precariae verbo regis*.

[2] *Gesta Abbatum Fontenellensium*, ed. Loewenfeld (M.G.H.S.S., 1886), p. 32. This was written about a hundred years later, *c.* 834–45.

[3] Lands thus ' borrowed ' from the Church to form benefices for the vassals of the Carolingians were subsequently known as *precariae verbo regis*.

Boniface, an Englishman who devoted his life to the conversion of the Germans, and who, following in the tradition which Gregory the Great had established in England, was convinced of the necessity of establishing a system of papal government for the Church (see pp. 86–7). Previously, the bishops of the Frankish Kingdom, being nominees of the king or the mayor of the palace, had had more care for the interests and customs of the Franks than for those of the Papacy. They had not normally consulted the Papacy on matters of canon law, nor been subject to metropolitans who had received their *pallia* and their authority from the Pope, and in consequence St. Boniface had had no communion or connection with them. After 742 all that was changed. In 747 the Frankish bishops publicly declared that they would

> maintain the Catholic faith and unity and subjection to the Roman Church till the end of [their] lives, . . . be subjects of St. Peter and his vicar, hold a synod every year, and that the metropolitans would ask for their *pallia* from that see. . . .

The Church had surrendered a great part of its lands, but in return for this concession it had received the freedom to organize itself and recognize the papal authority.

It was the same with the consecration of Pepin as king. The Pope had come to Pepin's aid by making him a king and his descendants a race of kings. But in return for this favour, he asked that Pepin should defend him against Aistulf, King of the Lombards, who was endeavouring to extend his power to the Roman *ducatus*. That was why, in 755, Pepin led his army to Italy. He did not claim the land for himself. On the contrary he had already recognized it as the Pope's by confirming the celebrated, but apocryphal, Donation of Constantine. In that document, which thus makes its first appearance in history, it was alleged that the Emperor Constantine had recognized the Pope as Christ's vicar on earth and made all bishops subject to him ; that he had bestowed on the Pope the rank and ceremonial dress of an emperor, and on the Roman clergy those of the senate ; and that he had made over the imperial palace of the Lateran to the Pope, together with the government of Rome and all Italy.

It is possible that Pepin did not understand the full extent of the papal claims, but it was clear at least that the Pope was asking for a protector who would free him from the Lombards. After the Moslem invasions, the Byzantine Empire had been so pre-occupied with the dangers which threatened it from the east, that it had been unable to spare troops for Ravenna and the remaining imperial possessions in Italy. Pope Gregory the Great and his successors had endeavoured to protect the Patrimony of St. Peter by their own unaided efforts (pp. 83–4) and had hitherto been more successful than might have been expected. But by the middle of the eighth century the power of the Lombards had grown too strong for them. The Papacy had absolute need of a protector; and that protector, if the Popes were to realize the ambitions of independent rule in Italy, had necessarily to come from some other country. It was for this reason that Pope Stephen II turned to the Franks. Theirs was the only Christian and non-Italian kingdom that had sufficient power to give him adequate protection. It was in his interest to see that the Carolingians should be strengthened in their power by being given kingship; and he therefore made an alliance with them, whereby he was to maintain them as consecrated kings, while they, in their turn, were to serve him obediently and restore the rights and properties of the *Respublica Romana*. It was, as much as any vassalic contract, an alliance of mutual interests, and as such it was typical of the Frankish Kingdom as it had been reconstructed by the Carolingians.

3. CHARLEMAGNE (768–814)

Charlemagne, or Charles the Great, the eldest son of Pepin the Short, was by far the most important of all the Frankish kings. He had a new conception of the functions and duties of a Christian king, and wielded such overwhelming military power that he was able to impose it on the greater part of Western Europe. He considered it his duty as a Christian king not only to protect his subjects but also to educate them. Such an idea would have seemed ridiculous to the Merovingians, who had treated their kingdom as nothing more than a property, and had behaved as though they had absolutely no responsibilities to their subjects.

Even to Charles Martel and Pepin the Short, who had accepted the obligation of protecting and providing for their vassals, it would have seemed unnecessary. But to Charlemagne it seemed no more than his duty. He was convinced that he was living in a world which had lost its culture, and he was determined to restore it. He wanted to be worthy of the inheritance of Rome and the Christian Church, and to make his kingdom pleasing to God.

His reign may therefore be regarded as the triumphant result of papal policy towards the Franks. For centuries the Roman Church had been striving to give the Frankish kings a real understanding of the value of civilization and of the duty of a Christian king. It had supported them consistently, had been patient with the brutality of Merovingians, and even tolerated the seizure of church land by Charles Martel, because it believed that eventually it would be able to educate the Franks and make them leaders of the Christian people. With Charlemagne it succeeded. He was devoted to the cause of Christianity and Roman civilization. Acutely aware that all forms of learning and culture were almost dead, he was genuinely anxious to revive them. He wanted to surround himself with learned men, and have a veritable ' palace school ' where the arts might be cultivated ; and since he could not find sufficient men of learning in *Francia* itself, he sought scholars far and wide. Peter of Pisa the grammarian and Paul the deacon, the historian of the Lombards, came from Italy ; Theodulf the Visigoth came from Spain ; and Alcuin, the greatest of them all, was an Englishman from the schools of York.

We know about this group of men from the correspondence which they kept up with Charlemagne and with each other, and it is clear that they were quite remarkably enthusiastic about their work. Charlemagne, for example, is said to have been so keen to learn reading and writing that he slept with writing-materials under his pillow. Perhaps, wrote Alcuin, a new Athens will arise in *Francia* ' only much more excellent ', and as if in anticipation of the event he and his companions adopted, in their more intimate moments, the great names of antiquity. Alcuin, who wrote lyrics about spring and the cuckoo in his spare time, was ' Flaccus ' (*i.e.* Horace). Angilbert, who had seduced one of Charlemagne's daughters before becoming Abbot of St.

Riquier, was ' Homer'. Charlemagne the anointed king was ' David ', while his eldest son, Pepin, was ' Julius '. Aachen, where the court had its favourite residence, was ' the second Rome ', and everything was done to give the impression that the whole of antiquity, Hebrew, Greek, and Roman, was being resuscitated at a breath.

To a real classical scholar, or to the men of the Byzantine Empire, where the classical tradition had never been broken, it would have been tempting to laugh at these serious-minded Franks who strutted about pretending to be Romans, for they were unmistakably Germanic. But, in spite of all their play-acting, Charlemagne and his scholars had grasped one of the fundamental truths which make civilization real—that knowledge had to be loved for its own sake.

> My master [wrote Alcuin] often used to say to me : ' It was the wisest of men who discovered these arts concerning the nature of things, and it would be a disgrace to let them perish in our day.' But many are now so pusillanimous as not to care about knowing the reasons for the things which the Creator has established in nature. You know very well how sweet is arithmetic in its reasoning, how necessary it is for the understanding of Holy Writ ; and how pleasant is a knowledge of the heavenly stars in their courses. And yet how rare it is to find a man who takes the trouble to know these things ! And, what is worse, people despise those who study to gain knowledge ! [1]

Charlemagne put first things first and showed by his own example, king though he was, that learning should be honoured. He thought it his duty, as a Christian king, to issue orders that reading and writing should be taught in all the religious houses of his kingdom, so that the monks and clergy might be not only ' chaste in the lives which they led, but also scholars in the language which they spoke '. He wanted accuracy for its own sake, for slovenliness would have been a disgrace to his generation. A recension of the Vulgate (or Latin Bible) was made, probably by Alcuin, to remedy the errors which had crept into the text through the ignorance or carelessness of former copyists. The liturgical books were revised, to conform with the traditions of the Roman Church, a copy of the *Sacramentarium Gregorianum*

[1] Alcuin, *Epist.* 148.

being obtained from Rome for the purpose—Alcuin's revision of it has become the basis of the present-day Roman mass book. Monasteries were reformed and the Rule of St. Benedict was adopted as the standard Rule for monks.

Equally important was the fact that the revival of learning spread beyond the sphere of religious education. A new style of handwriting, the Carolingian minuscule, which was both beautiful and clear, was introduced and rapidly adopted by scribes throughout Charlemagne's dominions. In this hand scribes in countless monasteries would occupy themselves by copying out not only Bibles, Gospel books, Sacramentaries, and liturgical calendars, but also the works of Virgil and other classical writers. It is no exaggeration to say that it is to the scholars of this period that we owe our knowledge of the classics. That fact is attested in a most impressive way, for when, some seven centuries later, the humanists of the Renaissance were ransacking the monastic libraries of Europe for manuscripts of the classics, the great majority that they found were written in Carolingian minuscule—so much so, that they mistook the handwriting for that of the ancient Romans themselves, called it *scriptura Romana*, and propagated it as the only true classical hand.

In one respect, however, the Carolingian renaissance was markedly different from that of the fifteenth century. It was fundamentally Christian. Charlemagne did not distinguish between the ' classics ' and the ' Fathers ', except to wish that the former had been Christian. To him, Jerome, Augustine, Gregory the Great, and Virgil were all equally Roman. His favourite book, we are told, was St. Augustine's *De Civitate Dei*.

In this work we have a direct link between Charlemagne's literary renaissance and his political ideals, for there can be no doubt that it exercised an enormous influence on his conception of kingship. It was not, however, the precise influence that St. Augustine would have intended, since it was founded on a misunderstanding of his text. For the terms ' city of God ' and ' society of the faithful ', which had been used by St. Augustine to denote the mystical body of the faithful in all eternity, were taken by Charlemagne to denote the community of Christians *on earth*, and he therefore applied them to the Church of Rome and the Kingdom of the Franks. To him it seemed that these two institutions were but one society. Was not Charlemagne the Lord's anointed ('David') and were not the Franks 'the Christian people' (*populus christianus*)?

By the second half of the eighth century, Church and State really did form a single community in the Frankish Kingdom; the Church helped to govern the State and vice versa. The most important officials in local government were the counts and the bishops. The territory for which the count was responsible was his county (*comitatus, pagus, gau*), but it was usually identical with the bishop's diocese since both were derived, as we have already seen (pp. 69 and 117), from the *civitas* of the Roman Empire. Count and bishop therefore worked in the strictest conjunction. The count was supposed to deal with secular affairs and the bishop with spiritual affairs, but in practice it was almost impossible to separate the activities of the one from the other, and they were inspected jointly by the king's envoys. These envoys, known as *missi dominici*, became increasingly important during Charlemagne's reign. They were not permanent officials but were important men of the realm who had received a special commission to spend a few weeks inspecting the working of the government in a group of about six counties. They worked in pairs, one being a layman and the other an ecclesiastic, and were instructed to examine the efficiency and obedience not only of the secular government but also of the Church. Often the ecclesiastical *missus* was an archbishop and the counties which he was inspecting formed the dioceses of his ecclesiastical province.

The most spectacular example of the fusion of Church and State was to be seen in the annual *conventus generalis* or *placitum generale*, which was the general assembly of the whole kingdom. In theory the whole Frankish people was present at these assemblies, but in practice attendance was limited to the greater men of the kingdom. These, however, would certainly have numbered several hundreds, and included ecclesiastics as well as laymen. Even if the ecclesiastics deliberated apart from the laymen, the business which they had to consider was the same. They might all be asked (*a*) what should be done when a vassal deserted his lord and was welcomed by another, and (*b*) whether it was possible to be a monk without observing the Rule of

St. Benedict ; and their answers, even in the case of questions which were purely ecclesiastical, were published by the king and enforced by his authority.[1]

But if the kingdom included both Church and State, it was still essentially an army. The *placitum generale* deliberated wisely, but its main function began when the deliberations were over, when it moved off to war. It was the meeting of the Frankish nation in arms—previous generations had called it the *campus martius*—and it was held not at some central point in the kingdom but on one of the frontiers where the army was to operate. Here, for example, is a translation of a summons sent to the Abbot of St. Quentin, *c.* 806.

Be it known to you that this year our *placitum generale* has been fixed in Saxony, in the eastern district, on the river Bode, at the place called Strassfurt (near Magdeburg-a-der Elbe).[2] Therefore we order you to be at this place with your full contingent, with your men armed and prepared on the 14th of the Kalends of July (18th June), that is to say seven days before the Mass of St. John the Baptist. You must arrive there with your men, complete with supplies, so that you will be able to proceed from there in any direction in which you may be ordered to go, immediately and in full martial array—that is to say with arms, tools, all sorts of instruments of war, food and clothing. Every horseman (*caballarius*) shall have a shield, lance, long-sword, short-sword, bow, quiver and arrows. In your carts you shall have tools of every kind, hatchets, adzes, augers, axes, pick-axes, iron spades, and all other implements which are necessary against an enemy. The food in your carts shall be sufficient for three months, the arms and clothing for one year. And we particularly command that on the journey to Strassfurt you should see that you do not cause any disorder in any part of our kingdom through which you may have to pass on your route ; you are not to commandeer anything except grass [for the horses], wood and water. . . .

It requires no great effort of the imagination to see that in everyday life the military effort required by such a summons

---

[1] The documents in which they were published were known as capitularies, since each contained a number of separate articles or ' chapters ' (*capitulae*).

[2] The distance from St. Quentin to Magdeburg-a-der-Elbe is about 483 miles. The passage is translated from Boretius' *Capitularia Regum Francorum* (M.G.H. 1883), p. 168.

would have loomed larger than the revival of learning and civilization. In almost every one of the forty-two years of his reign Charlemagne summoned his ' host ' to campaigns beyond the borders of *Francia*. If, by any chance, a year went by without a *placitum generale*, the chroniclers carefully recorded the fact, for it was a year to remember. All free men of the Frankish Kingdom were supposed to attend the summons, but towards the end of Charlemagne's reign it was clearly impossible to enforce the rule, for exceptions were always being made ; in some districts it was declared that freemen would not have to perform military service in person unless they held at least four *mansi* of land.[1]

The military demands made by Charlemagne on his subjects were stupendous, but the whole basis of his power depended on the fact that his subjects performed what was demanded of them. The backbone of his army would, of course, have been his mounted vassals, and they had been supplied with estates as benefices so that they could devote the greater part of their lives to military service for the king. But even they might well have been dismayed by the military activities of a king who enlarged his kingdom so that it embraced almost the whole of Latin Christendom, and fought in turn against the Lombards, the Saxons, the Moslems of Spain, the Serbs, the Avars, the Byzantine provinces of southern Italy, the Bretons, the Danes, and the Duchy of Benevento. Charlemagne ruled, by the end of his reign, over territory which included the whole of modern France, Belgium, Holland, and Switzerland, most of western Germany, a great part of Italy, a small part of northern Spain, and Corsica, and in order to defend its frontiers he had to keep his army forever on the move. If he was in Saxony, the Pope would appeal for help in Italy. If he was in Spain, the whole of Saxony would break out in revolt.

For the men of the later Middle Ages, the most famous of Charlemagne's military exploits was his Spanish war. This was not because the conquests made in Spain were particularly extensive—it took more than twenty years of incessant war to

---

[1] A *mansus* was the amount of land considered sufficient for the support of one family. Its size varied, but was usually about 30–35 acres of arable land. Four *mansi* would therefore represent a holding of about 120 acres.

advance the frontier to the River Ebro—but because it was in Spain that the religious character of Charlemagne's wars was most clearly remembered. For the Spanish wars were fought against Moslems. They were the first effective counter-offensive against Islam, and in later centuries were regarded as the proto-type of the Crusade. It is true that many elements of the crusading ideal were absent, for the Pope took no part in it, and Charlemagne was quite prepared to enter into alliance with dissident Moslem emirs. It is also true that the greatest defeat in this theatre of war, the annihilation of Charlemagne's rearguard in 778, was inflicted on the Franks not, as later legends pretended, by the Moslems, but by the Christian Basques.[1] But in spite of these facts, it is abundantly clear that the Franks were convinced that they were fighting on behalf of Christendom. In a capitulary of 815, for example, Charlemagne's son, Louis ' the Pious ', issued detailed instructions for the settlement in Roussillon of Spanish refugees who had fled from ' the wicked oppression and cruel yoke of the Saracens '.[2] It made no difference that the Spanish Christians were not (as yet) deliberately persecuted by the Moslems, since to the Franks the very fact of Moslem rule seemed oppressive. Schooled by St. Benedict of Aniane,[3] the monastic reformer, whose influence on the Spanish March was especially strong, the Franks combined military prowess with religious devotion ; William, Duke of Toulouse, their most successful general, ended his days as a monk in the monastery which he had founded at Gellona.

There was a similar religious background to the Saxon wars, though they lacked the glamour of the wars in Spain. The Saxons were heathen and still worshipped their primitive Germanic gods. They inhabited the North German plain, approximately between the Rhine and the Elbe, their country falling into three parts—Angaria on the River Weser, Westphalia (which

---

[1] This is the defeat celebrated in *La Chanson de Roland*, a magnificent poem of the twelfth century. The French text, together with a fine translation by René Hague, is printed in *The Song of Roland*, London (Faber & Faber), 1937.

[2] As a result of the settlement of these refugees, Catalan displaced Languedoc as the language of Roussillon.

[3] St. Benedict of Aniane (751–821) was by origin a Goth from Septimania, and his real name was Witiza. He took the name Benedict when he became a monk, in honour of the founder of Western monasticism, St. Benedict of Nursia (pp. 74-9).

still retains its name) between the Weser and the Rhine, and Ostphalia between the Weser and the Elbe. The Saxons were the traditional enemies of the Franks, and had never formed part of the Frankish Kingdom. They had little political organization of their own. What unity they possessed, was founded on their heathen religion, the central object of worship being the *Irminsul* or sacred tree-trunk, which was supposed to support the heavens.

In the early years of his reign, it was Charlemagne's policy to attempt either the conquest or the conversion of Saxony. His main preoccupation was with defence. He organized a frontier-province or ' March ' against the southern frontier of Saxony, along the River Lippe, with strong-points at Sigeburg, Eresburg, and Paderborn (*c.* 776); and from this base he conducted occasional military expeditions, demonstrating his power by marching across the length and breadth of Saxony. These demonstrations, however, were of little permanent value. Whenever Charlemagne held a *placitum generale* on the Saxon frontier, and took the field in person with his host, the Saxons submitted. As soon as he had returned home they revolted. A particular example of the way in which they took advantage of Charlemagne's movements was afforded in 778, when he was in Spain. Knowing that the main Frankish army was absent, the Saxons undertook a large-scale raid on the Rhineland. They reached Deutz, on the right bank of the Rhine opposite Cologne, and continued upstream to Coblenz, destroying everything with fire and the sword, before making good their return to Saxony through Hesse.

Henceforward it was clear that a more radical policy towards the Saxons would be necessary. Occasional military victories, especially if they were punctuated by occasional military defeats, did nothing to stabilize the frontier. What was needed was the conquest of the whole country and the subjugation of its people. Permanent subjugation, however, could only be ensured by a change of heart on the part of the Saxons. If ever they were to live in amity with the Franks (' the Christian people ') it was necessary that they should be converted to Christianity. Accordingly, from 785, the Franks began a ' thorough ' policy ; the Saxons were not only to be conquered but also converted, if necessary by force. In the first Saxon capitulary it was declared a capital offence to resist or evade baptism, or to disregard the practices of the Church by cremating the dead or eating meat in Lent. Churches were to be built throughout the country and were to be provided with two *mansi* of land each, and with one serf and one woman-servant from every 120 heads of the population. Burials were to take place only in the cemeteries of churches, and the clergy were to see that the Saxons held no public meetings unless authorized by the officials of the Frankish king. The heathen Saxon was put outside the law. A Saxon who committed homicide was not allowed to atone for his offence with a money-payment like the Frank ; the only way in which he could avoid the death-penalty was by taking sanctuary in one of the churches which the Franks had built in his country, humbling himself before the altar and thus betraying the gods of his ancestors.

It was only to be expected that so stern a policy would meet with armed resistance. The Saxons revolted repeatedly, especially in the years 793–7, but each revolt was suppressed in turn, and resistance was slowly but efficiently ground down. In the later years of his reign, Charlemagne rewarded those Saxons who had proved themselves loyal subjects and Christians by giving them a new code of laws in which most offences were made amendable, as amongst the Franks (797). But even then, little or no mercy was shown to those who remained rebellious or heathen. In the most disaffected areas, such as Wihmode (the low-lying country between the estuaries of the Weser and Elbe), vast numbers of Saxons were deported, together with their wives and children, to various parts of the kingdom. The land from which they had been removed was distributed by the king among his faithful men (*fideles*), ' that is to say ', adds the helpful annalist, ' among the bishops, priests, counts, and other vassals '.

The Church took its share because the pacification and conversion of Saxony was accepted by the whole of Christendom as being in accordance with the will of God. For even though the more enlightened of Charlemagne's advisers (and notably Alcuin) objected that baptism by coercion was a poor way of leading men to God, no one doubted for a moment that the interests of Christianity and the Franks were identical. In Charlemagne's

eyes his kingdom was a sort of Church.   Thus, in a letter written
to the Pope in 796, he expressed himself as follows :

> Our task [i.e. Charlemagne's] is, with the aid of divine piety, to
> defend the holy Church of Christ with arms against the attack of
> pagans and devastation by infidels from without, and to fortify it
> from within with knowledge of the Catholic faith.   Your task,
> most holy father, is to lift up your hands to God, like Moses, so as
> to aid our troops ; so that through your intercession the Christian
> people (*populus christianus*) may, with God as its leader and giver
> [of victory], always and everywhere be victorious over the enemies
> of His Holy Name, and so that the name of Our Lord Jesus Christ
> may be famous throughout the world.[1]

The Church as normally understood, was reduced to a department of state, as a sort of ministry of prayer, and the responsibility
for education and the interpretation of the true Catholic faith
was assumed by Charlemagne in his role of ' David ', the Lord's
anointed.

It is against this background that we must interpret that crucial
but enigmatic event of Christmas Day 800, when Charlemagne
was crowned by the Pope and acclaimed by the people of Rome
as Caesar Augustus, the Christian Emperor of Latin Christendom.
But if we are to understand the imperial coronation correctly, it
is necessary that some consideration should first be given to the
way in which Charlemagne made himself master of the greater
part of Italy.   He conquered it very early in his reign (773-4)
at the invitation of Pope Hadrian I (772-95).   This Pope found
himself in the same dilemma as Stephen II before him (p. 132) ;
the Lombards were perpetually encroaching upon his territory,
and he could get no military aid against them from his nominal
suzerain, the Byzantine emperor.   He therefore turned, like his
predecessor before him, to the Franks.   Reminding Charlemagne of the title ' patrician of the Romans ' which had been
conferred upon him in his youth, he begged him to fall upon the
Lombards and deliver the Papacy from their power.   Charlemagne, after taking counsel with his Franks, accepted the
invitation.   He summoned a *placitum generale* to meet at Geneva
in July 773, crossed the Alps and laid siege to Pavia, the city in

---

[1] Translated from Dümmler, *Epistolae Karolini Aevi* (M.G.H.), ii, no. 93.

which Didier, the King of the Lombards, had taken refuge. After a nine months' siege, Didier surrendered both the city and the kingdom, and Charlemagne became, by the grace of God, King of the Lombards as well as the Franks (June 774). This final development cannot have been entirely welcome to Pope Hadrian I, for all the evidence points to the conclusion that he wanted the Papacy to be free to rule Italy itself. He had probably hoped that, by playing off the Franks and Lombards against each other, he would be able to ' divide and rule ' like the emperors of the fifth century. When, before the fall of Pavia, Charlemagne had visited Rome for the Easter celebrations (774), Hadrian had shown his policy plainly ; it was to give Charlemagne every honour but no power. He went in person to welcome him some thirty miles north of the city, but would not allow him to enter it until he had bound himself to the Papacy with a solemn oath sworn on the shrine of St. Peter. On arrival at Rome, processions of the city's judges, militia, and clergy, gave him the honours due to an exarch (or representative of the Byzantine emperor) ; children carried palms and olive branches before him, and the Pope led him by the hand into St. Peter's basilica to the strains of ' Blessed is he that cometh in the name of the Lord '. But Hadrian would not permit him, patrician though he was, to sleep a single night in the city. He had to lodge outside the walls in ' Nero's meadow ' where the foreigners had their schools.[1] Finally, before returning to the siege of Pavia, Charlemagne was persuaded to renew and expand the ' Donation of Pepin ' (pp. 134–5). In this new donation king and Pope partitioned Italy between themselves. The Pope was to receive Corsica, Istria, and everything south of a line drawn from Luni (near La Spezia) through Parma, Reggio, and Mantua to Monselice (near Venice).

It is probable that Charlemagne was ignorant of the extent and significance of his donation. If it had ever been fulfilled, it would have marked a vast extension of the temporal power of

[1] Nero's meadow was close to St. Peter's basilica, which was outside the walls. The Vatican suburb was not surrounded by walls till the pontificate of Leo IV (847–55) ; hence its name, ' the Leonine city '. It should be noted that throughout the early Middle Ages the Pope's residence was at the Lateran Palace, which was within the city. The move to the Vatican was not made till 1377, after the ' Babylonish captivity '.

the Papacy, for the proposed northern frontier ran through territory which had belonged without dispute to the Lombard Kingdom. When Charlemagne, after the fall of Pavia, had himself become the King of the Lombards, he realized his mistake and refused to fulfil the precise terms of the donation. He was prepared to restore to the Papacy everything that had been taken from it by King Didier, but not to give it territory which it had never possessed before (*e.g.* Corsica, Venetia, and Istria). Though he venerated the Papacy and was genuinely anxious to defend it from its enemies, he considered it an unquestioned fact that he was King of the Lombards by right of conquest, and supreme ruler of ' the Christian people ' by the grace of God.

To the Papacy, therefore, Charlemagne was both a benefactor and a menace. He was a benefactor because he brought order and justice to Italy and protected the Papacy in its established territories. He was a menace because he prevented the Papacy from fulfilling its widest ambitions in Italy and claimed to be the ruler of Western Christendom, regardless of the Pope's own claims in that respect. It was therefore necessary for the Pope to be extremely careful in all his dealings with him. He could not dispense with his protection and could not afford to offend so mighty and benevolent a patron, but he was aware of the danger of accepting his patronage. Charlemagne's conception of his kingdom was so remarkably like a Church, that there was a real danger that, unless the Roman Church absorbed it, it would itself absorb the Roman Church.

It was a particular example of this difficulty that culminated in the imperial coronation of Charlemagne on Christmas Day 800. Pope Hadrian I's successor, Leo III (795–816), was unpopular with an important section of the Roman clergy, which, on 25 April 799, succeeded in ambushing him as he was processing from the Lateran to the church of St Laurence. The conspirators won control of the city, but Leo himself eventually escaped from the prison in which he had been placed, and made his way across the Alps to Paderborn to seek aid from Charlemagne. So did his enemies; they openly accused him of perjury and adultery and asked Charlemagne not to reinstate him.

That was a serious complication, for to Charlemagne it seemed obvious that, before marching an army on Rome, he should establish whether the Pope was innocent or guilty. But could he judge the Pope ? Alcuin insisted that the Apostolic See could be judged by no one, since it judged everyone ; and as a churchman he was right. How then could Charlemagne be satisfied of Leo's innocence ? The only possible solution was a compromise. Charlemagne marched on Rome, reinstated the Pope in his city, and then summoned a synod to consider 'the dispelling of the accusations ' which had been made against him. The synod declared that it did not venture to judge the Apostolic See, which was the head of all churches, but 'allowed' Leo III to take an oath of compurgation to prove his innocence before the world. This he did in St. Peter's basilica on 23 December 800.

Two days later he crowned Charlemagne as Emperor of the Romans. Who had first proposed the coronation and what it signified, are questions which have given rise to endless controversy. Charlemagne's biographer, Eginhard, writing about thirty years after the event, stated that Charlemagne used to say that, if he had known what the Pope was going to do on that day, he would never have entered the church, but historians have been unwilling to accept his statement without reservation. It is therefore proposed to compare in detail the two best accounts of the event. One (*Liber Pontificalis*) is from the papal point of view, the other (*Royal Annals*) from the Frankish :

Liber Pontificalis	*Royal Annals* [1]
After this, on Christmas Day in the aforesaid basilica of the blessed Peter the apostle, all were gathered together again. And then the venerable and beneficent bishop [Pope Leo III], with his own hand crowned him [Charlemagne] with a most precious crown. Then all the faithful Romans, seeing what a pillar of defence he was, and what love he had for the holy Roman	On that very and most holy day of Christmas, when the king, at Mass before the *confessio* of the blessed Peter the apostle, was rising from prayer, Leo the pope put $\{ \begin{smallmatrix} a \\ the \end{smallmatrix} \}$ crown on his head, and acclamation was made by all the people of the Romans : ' To Charles Augustus, crowned by God, great and pacific emperor of the Romans, Life and Victory ! '

[1] The annal quoted is the earliest description of the ceremony that we have, as it was probably written *c*. 801. Its author was perhaps Angilbert the chaplain, but this is conjectural.

Liber Pontificalis—cont.

Church and its vicar, unanimously, at the will of God, and of St. Peter, the doorkeeper of the Kingdom of Heaven, cried out with a great shout : ' To Charles, most pious Augustus, crowned by God, great and pacific emperor, Life and Victory ! ' Before the holy *confessio* [1] of the blessed Peter, the apostle, calling on several saints, they said it three times, and he was made (*constitutus*) emperor of the Romans by all. And there also, on the same day of the birth of Our Lord Jesus Christ, the most holy bishop and pontiff, anointed with holy oil Charles, his [Charlemagne's] most excellent son, as King. . . .

Royal Annals—cont.

And after the ' praises ' (*laudes*), he was ' adored ' by the apostolic [bishop] in the manner of ancient princes, and, discarding the name of patrician, he was called Emperor and Augustus.

To understand the subtle differences between the two accounts, it is necessary to realize what would have been the normal ceremonial for the Frankish king at Christmas.[2] It was one of the two big ' courts ' of the year, the other being at Easter, and can best be described as a solemn ' crown-wearing '—the sort of occasion which would naturally have been chosen by Charlemagne for the anointing of his son as a king. During the Mass, he would, in the normal course of events, have laid aside his crown, sceptre, mantle, and sword, in order to prostrate himself before the altar. When he rose from prayer and resumed his *regalia*, it would be normal for the people to ' praise ' him, by formally reciting his titles and uttering pious exclamations.

It is clear that, in his account of the ceremony of Christmas Day 800, the Frankish royal annalist was deliberately trying to make the whole thing appear a normal court ceremonial. He

[1] The *confessio* was the small crypt containing the shrine of St. Peter, immediately beneath the high altar.
[2] The following interpretation is very largely based on the work of P. Schramm, ' Die Anerkennung Karls des grossen als Kaiser '. *Historische Zeitschrift*, clxxii. 449–516 (1951).

gives the impression that the only unusual circumstances were, that after the prostration it was not Charles himself but the Pope who replaced the crown on his head, and that in the ' praises ' (he uses the word *laudes*, the correct technical term) a new title, that of Emperor, was employed. Finally the ' adoration ' of the Pope (whereby he prostrated himself before Charles) is carefully, and correctly, described as the normal way in which the Pope should humble himself before an emperor on a solemn occasion.

In the papal account, on the other hand, we find that the ceremony is described as something quite out of the ordinary. It does not, like the Frankish annalist, merely say that the Pope ' placed ' (*imposuit*) the crown on Charles's head; it states that he ' crowned him ' (*coronavit eum*). And, so far from allowing that the triple acclamation was part of the normal royal ' praises ', it states specifically that it was by means of this that Charles was ' made ' (*constitutus*) Emperor. To make the fact clear beyond all doubt, it adds that this was done according to the will of God and St. Peter, because Charles loved and defended the Roman Church and its Vicar. It would seem, therefore, that the Pope meant the ceremony to have more significance than Charles would have liked to admit. By crowning him Emperor, Leo III had reaffirmed the superiority of the Papacy, and had regularized the anomalous position in which he found himself, by giving his *de facto* patron an official position within the Roman Church. Henceforward Charlemagne was to be regarded as protector of the Papacy, not because he was a conqueror, but because the office had been conferred on him by the Church.

That was the suggestion to which Charlemagne took exception. He had no objection to being called an emperor, for his whole career had been an attempt to emulate the emperors of old, as the civilized ruler of the civilized state. He considered himself to be responsible not only for the defence of his kingdom but also for its culture and religion. He ruled over the greater part of Western Europe. He was the protector of Latin Christianity and of the Roman Church. He was received in Rome itself. In all these ways he was as good as an emperor long before his imperial coronation. He had even imitated the manners of an emperor. He had worn the purple *chlamys*, the official clothing of an emperor; he had had books written for him in purple ink ; he had described his court as ' holy ' and had modelled his palace at Aachen on the plan of the *chrysotriklinos* of the imperial palace at Constantinople. He was pleased to be recognized for what he was—not a barbarian king but an emperor—but he was angry that the Pope should have claimed the responsibility for his elevation. When, towards the end of his life, he wanted his son Louis to become co-emperor, he crowned him himself (813) and not at Rome but at Aachen. Thereby he showed most clearly that though he considered he was an undoubted emperor, he owed his position not to the coronation by the Pope, nor to the acclamation by the Roman people, but to himself.

Nevertheless, the coronation had taken place, and the impression which it had made was ineffaceable. The Pope had apparently renewed the Roman Empire in the West by crowning Charlemagne as Emperor. The significance of his act was not simply that he had rejected the claims of the Byzantine emperor —for he had ceased to recognize that emperor's rights in Western Christendom as long ago as 775 [1]—but that he had at one and the same moment accepted Charlemagne's conception of his kingdom as ' the Christian people ' and had subordinated it to the authority of the Roman Church. Leo III had given perfect symbolic expression to the new mode of political thought, and his conception of it is best illustrated in the mosaic which he erected in the Lateran Palace. In it, St. Peter is represented with Leo III and Charlemagne kneeling before him. With his right hand he gives the *pallium*, representing spiritual authority, to the Pope. With his left he gives the banner, representing temporal authority, to Charlemagne. Both powers, spiritual and temporal, were thus seen to derive from St. Peter, the rock on whom the Church was founded; and they were to be exercised over a single community which might be called either Church or State, ' Christian people ', or Holy Roman Empire (Plate II).

That was the ultimate significance of Charlemagne's coronation. No matter what may have been intended in that historic ceremony of Christmas Day, the event was subsequently regarded as the beginning of a new epoch. It was not that people thought that they had advanced one step farther on the road of human

---

[1] Schramm, *op. cit.*, 449–79.

progress. On the contrary, they thought that they had moved one step backward towards the more perfect world which had existed before the break-up of the Roman world. In the Lateran mosaic this was made extremely clear, for alongside the scene which we have just described was another which depicted Christ himself giving the keys of heaven and hell to Pope Sylvester and a banner surmounted by a cross to the Emperor Constantine. The one event prefigured the other. That was why Charlemagne claimed to have renewed the Roman Empire; he was to be the new Constantine, the Christian ruler of a Christian Empire.

Further Reading

(See also the list for Chapter II)

N. D. FUSTEL DE COULANGES. *Histoire des Institutions Politiques de l'Ancienne France*, iii. *La Monarchie franque* (Paris. 1888); vi. *Les Transformations de la Royauté pendant l'époque Carolingienne* (Paris. 1892). Both these volumes are of the first importance, though they have to be used with caution.

J. M. WALLACE-HADRILL. *The Long-Haired Kings*. London. 1961.

H. W. C. DAVIS. *Charlemagne* (Heroes of the Nations series). London. 1900.

L. HALPHEN. *Etudes Critiques sur l'histoire de Charlemagne*. Paris. 1921. This has a valuable discussion of the sources.

DONALD BULLOUGH. *The Age of Charlemagne*. London. 1965.

L. HALPHEN. *Charlemagne et l'Empire Carolingien* (L'Evolution de l'Humanité series). New ed., Paris. 1949.

P. SCHRAMM. Die Anerkennung Karls des grossen als Kaiser (*Historische Zeitschrift*, 172 (1951), pp. 449–519).

F. L. GANSHOF. *Feudalism* (tr. P. Grierson). London. 1952.

W. ULLMANN. *The Growth of Papal Government in the Middle Ages*. London. 1955. Chapter III concerns Charlemagne.

O. M. DALTON (tr.). *The History of the Franks by Gregory of Tours*. 2 vols. Oxford. 1927. The first volume consists of an Introduction which is not of great importance, but the translation of the text is good.

L. HALPHEN (ed.). *Eginhard. Vie de Charlemagne*. Paris. 1923. Latin text with a French translation.

VII

THE BREAK-UP OF THE CAROLINGIAN EMPIRE

1. The Sons and Grandsons of Charlemagne

THE idea of a Christian Empire did not die with Charlemagne. On the contrary, it grew. For there were many who thought that he had not gone nearly far enough in his attempt to bring about the rule of God on Earth, and foremost amongst these critics was his only surviving son, and immediate successor, Louis the Pious (814–40). His great friend and adviser in the early years of his reign was a monk, St. Benedict of Aniane (751–821). Louis built him a monastery at a little distance from the imperial palace of Aachen, so that he could keep in touch with him, and his influence was to be observed in every department of state. Under his guidance Louis set himself the task of reforming the empire on Christian principles. Bishops were to abandon their military finery (though they were still expected to lead their contingents to the army) and to behave with the outward decorum that befitted the leaders of the Church. Strict regulations were framed to improve the standard of moral virtue at the imperial palace; all women of doubtful morals were to be expelled—they were lucky if they escaped without a public whipping in the market place—and Charlemagne's daughters, the delectable ' doves ' of his court, who had been the objects of so much admiration and delight, were required to withdraw themselves to nunneries.

But the reform went deeper than mere puritanism. Under St. Benedict's influence, Louis believed that his empire should partake of the perfect unity which Christ had destined for His Church. He thought that the subjects of the Empire should be regarded not as an aggregation of Franks, Lombards, and

154

numberless other different peoples, but as one single body; and that in place of the legal labyrinth created by the system of ' personal law ', whereby everyone retained as his birthright the law of his own people, there should be a single and universal code.   As Agobard, Archbishop of Lyons, put it in a famous letter :

> There is now neither Gentile nor Jew, Scythian nor Aquitanian, nor Lombard, nor Burgundian, nor Alaman, nor bond, nor free.   All are one in Christ. . . .   Can it be accepted that, opposed to this unity which is the work of God, there should be an obstacle in the diversity of laws [used] in one and the same country, in one and the same city, and in one and the same house ?   It constantly happens that of five men walking or sitting side by side, no two have the same terrestrial law, although at root—on the eternal plan—they belong to Christ.[1]

In accordance with these sentiments, Louis the Pious changed the formulae of his official documents.   His father, Charlemagne, had always employed multiple titles, as if he had governed the different parts of his empire by separate authority.   He had been *Carolus serenissimus augustus a Deo coronatus magnus pacificus imperator, Romanum gubernans imperium, qui et per misericordiam Dei rex Francorum atque Langobardorum*, and lest the significance of the separate titles should be missed, it had been re-emphasized in the dating clause, the year 812, for example, being described as ' the 12th of our Empire, the 44th of our reign in *Francia*, and the 38th in Italy '.   Louis swept all such distinctions away.   In his protocol he described himself simply as *Hludowicus divina ordinante providentia Imperator Augustus*, and the year 814 was ' the first year of the Empire of the lord Louis, most pious Augustus '.

Such changes make it clear that what Louis wanted was an empire which was an entity in itself, with one ruler, one people, and one law.   But the difficulty was that it would have been impossible to abolish all the separate ' national ' laws at a stroke.   No king or emperor could have done so, because every ' nation ' regarded its law as its birthright and would have fought to

---

[1] M.G.H. *Epist.*, v. 159.   Agobard was in fact exaggerating.   There were still many different codes of law, but attempts were being made to regionalize them.   See for example, M.G.H. *Cap. Reg. Franc.*, i. 323, para. 5, where it is stated that (in 824) ' the whole Roman people ' was to make up its mind as to what law it wished to live by.   In 862 we find Charles the Bald referring to those *regions* in which judgments were given by Roman law.   *Ibid.*, ii. 315, para. 13.

preserve it. The most that could be done was to issue capitularies which added new regulations to the existing laws in such a way as to remove the worst anomalies, and in the early years of his reign Louis did his best in this respect. An example of a chapter that was thus ' added to the law ' reads as follows :

> That every payment or composition contained in the Salic Law should be paid in Francia with shillings of twelve pence, except when the dispute has arisen with Saxons and Frisians. In that case we desire that the shilling, which the Saxon or Frisian must pay to the Salian Frank with whom he is litigating, should contain forty pence.[1]

It did not have the effect of making all men equal before the law, but it was at least a step in the right direction towards an orderly body of imperial law.

The sphere in which the greatest uniformity was possible was that of the Church, and here Louis did not hesitate to act. For he considered that Church and State were one, and though he treated the clergy with greater respect than his father had done—he allowed the Pope to re-crown him in 816—and though he was always asking their advice, yet he did not hesitate to legislate on their behalf. Under the influence of St. Benedict of Aniane it was decreed that cathedral canons should live a quasi-monastic life, becoming ' regular ' as opposed to ' secular ', and the monasteries of the Empire were systematically reformed. All monks were to live according to the Rule of St. Benedict, which they were instructed to learn by heart, and further regulations were added to ensure the utmost uniformity ; nothing was to be taken in Lent except bread and water, for example, and the length of cowls was to be two cubits.

With such a desire for uniformity, it was hardly surprising that the subject of greatest concern was that the territorial unity of the Empire should be preserved. But this was the greatest stumbling-block of all, for the Franks had hitherto clung to the custom of their forefathers, and had accepted it as natural and right that, on the death of a king, the kingdom should be divided amongst his sons in equal portions. The practice had proved the ruin of the Merovingian monarchy, but it had not been

---

[1] *Cap. Reg. Franc.*, i, 268, para. 3.

abandoned by the Carolingians, because it was an integral part of Frankish law. On Pepin's death, in 768, his kingdom had been divided between Charlemagne and his younger brother Carloman (who had fortunately died soon after), and it was universally assumed that a similar division would have to be made of Charlemagne's own empire. In 806, when three of his sons were still alive, he had drawn up a formal scheme of partition, and though the death of the young Pepin and the young Charles (in 810 and 811) had for the moment preserved the unity of the succession, it was only a temporary respite. For Louis the Pious had four sons, three by his first wife and one (born in 823) by his second. Was he to observe Frankish law at the expense of dividing his empire? Or was he to preserve the unity of the Christian people even at the expense of flouting the immemorial custom of his ancestors? In 817 he was specifically asked at the general *conventus* how he was going to provide for his sons in the manner of his ancestors, and his reply was as follows:

> Although this request was made faithfully and devoutly, it seemed to Us and to those who know what is wise, that the unity of the empire which God has entrusted to Us should not be rent by any human division, not even out of love or favour for Our sons, lest haply this should give rise to a scandalous state of affairs in Holy Church, and lest We should incur the displeasure of Him upon whose power the laws of all kingdoms depend.

He was prepared to give the younger sons dependent kingdoms —Pepin was to have Aquitaine on much the same terms as Louis himself had held it during his father's lifetime—but they were to be the subordinates of the elder brother, Lothar, who alone was to enjoy the prerogatives of empire.

In one sense such a scheme might have seemed a reasonable compromise, but to a great body of the Franks it seemed completely unjust, because it disinherited the younger sons although they had committed no offence. Consequently the major part of Louis' reign was occupied with fratricidal strife very similar to that of the sons and grandsons of Clovis, except that while in that case every son fought to win his brother's portion, in this case all the brothers thought they were fighting simply for

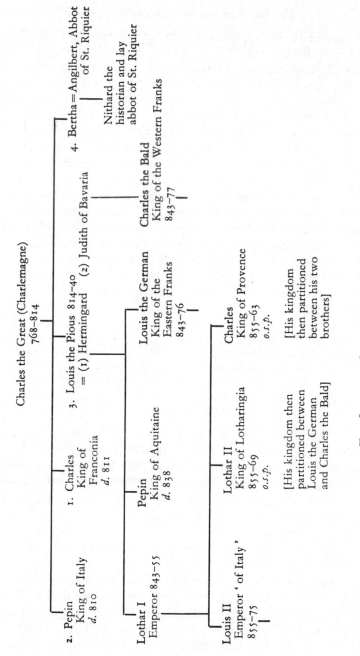

THE SONS AND GRANDSONS OF CHARLEMAGNE

Charles the Great (Charlemagne)
768–814

1. Charles
King of
Franconia
d. 811

2. Pepin
King of Italy
d. 810

3. Louis the Pious 814–40
= (1) Hermingard   (2) Judith of Bavaria

4. Bertha = Angilbert, Abbot
of St. Riquier

Nithard the
historian and lay
abbot of St. Riquier

Lothar I
Emperor 843–55

Pepin
King of Aquitaine
d. 838

Louis the German
King of the
Eastern Franks
843–76

Charles the Bald
King of the Western Franks
843–77

Louis II
Emperor 'of Italy'
855–75

Lothar II
King of Lotharingia
855–69
o.s.p.

Charles
King of Provence
855–63
o.s.p.

[His kingdom then
partitioned between
Louis the German
and Charles the Bald]

[His kingdom
then partitioned
between his two
brothers]

their rights. Lothar was fighting for the Empire which he had been given and his brothers were fighting for their birthright.

The details of these wars, with all the humiliations and public penances which they involved for Louis, need not detain us. What triumphed was the principle of the divisible inheritance, for even Louis himself ended by supporting it. His religious adviser, St. Benedict of Aniane, died in 821, and for the rest of his reign the most important person in his counsels was his second wife, Judith of Bavaria. In 823 she bore him a son, Charles, later known as ' the Bald ', and thenceforward she bent all her efforts to the single aim of ensuring that he was treated on a parity with his three half-brothers. Partition-schemes followed rapidly on each other, but their aim was now no longer that the unity of the Empire should be preserved, but that it should be divided into four portions rather than three.

The details of the proposed partitions are not of importance to us here, because they all turned out to be useless. No sooner had a division into four been agreed, than one of the four sons (Pepin) died, and the work had to be begun all over again. And when Louis the Pious finally died (840) civil war broke out. The two younger brothers, Louis the German and Charles the Bald, united against Lothar, and though they did not destroy him they forced him to agree to the principle of division. Their first success was at the battle of Fontenoy (841) which was fought in a strangely religious atmosphere as if it were an appeal to the judgment of God, and their final victory was marked by the Partition of Verdun (843). Lothar was to retain the title of emperor, but the Empire was to be divided into what, in effect, were three independent kingdoms.

The partition itself is usually criticized as a geographical monstrosity, since the kingdom which it awarded to Lothar stretched from the north coast of Frisia to the Duchy of Benevento, so that he might retain the two imperial centres of Rome and Aachen. But if it is compared with the partitions effected or proposed by previous Frankish kings it will be found a distinct improvement. None of the kingdoms was completely surrounded by the others. None of them possessed enclaves in the others. And two of them, those of Charles the Bald and

Louis the German, bore some resemblance to the modern conceptions of France and Germany.

Nothing would be a greater mistake than to imagine that the
partition was in any way haphazard. Immense pains were taken
to establish the most suitable frontiers. The final treaty was
drawn up by 120 commissioners—forty from each of the interested parties—and they toured the territories concerned before
making their recommendations. As the historian Nithard states
(and he himself had served on a preliminary commission), ' less
account was taken of the fertility or equality of area in each
kingdom, than of the affinity and convenience of everyone '.

' Affinity and convenience ' meant in practice the relation between vassals and their lords. For it had been accepted as a
principle of all the partitions proposed, from 806 onwards, that
no king should be allowed to have vassals in the territory of one
of his brother kings. The reason for this was that, since the
bond between lord and vassal was at least as strong as that
between a king and his subjects, any king with a large number of
vassals in his brother's kingdom would have been able to overthrow his brother with ease. The complications that resulted
from the principle, however, were immense, especially for those
who held lands on or near the proposed frontiers. If a frontier
cut through the middle of a man's benefices, he might have to
sacrifice a part of them, and consolidate his lands as best he
could, in one kingdom or the other. That was why ' affinity
and convenience ' were preferred to the ruthless logic of geography. Special arrangements could be made to suit the needs
of particular lords ; the whole of the county of Chalon, for
instance, was included within the kingdom of Charles the Bald,
although its territory lay on both sides of the River Saône which
would normally have been taken as the frontier.

The final division of Charlemagne's empire, therefore, took
due account of the feudal geography of the ninth century, and
that in itself was an achievement of some importance. For
feudal geography was not as haphazard as is sometimes imagined.
Every lord was anxious to acquire vassals primarily in the districts
from which his own lands might be threatened, while anyone
who was commending himself to a lord would be careful to
choose one who had the power to defend him in his own locality.

CHARLEMAGNE'S
EMPIRE

— Frontiers of the Empire

--- Boundaries laid down
by the Partition of
Verdun, 843

It therefore followed that feudal domains, since they had grown up from small beginnings, were likely to be defensible units, and therefore to conform with the natural geographical divisions of the land. The vassals of Louis the German, the centre of whose power was in Bavaria, came from the neighbouring parts of the Empire and were German, while those of Charles the Bald, whose kingdom was in the west, were French.

This fact is attested by the famous oaths of Strasbourg, for they show what was the common language of Louis' army and what of Charles's. Louis and Charles were anxious to bind themselves to a treaty in the most solemn manner possible, and consequently they each took a solemn oath before the army of the other, in a language which it could understand. Louis, addressing Charles's army, spoke in Old French (*lingua romana*); Charles, addressing Louis' army, spoke in Old High German (*lingua teudisca*). The ceremony was performed on 14 February 842 and the actual words used have been preserved by the historian Nithard. They are as follows :

The oath of Louis in Old French	*The oath of Charles in Old High German*	*English translation*
Pro Deo amur et pro christian poblo et nostro commun salvament, d'ist di in avant, in quant Deus savir et podir me dunat, si salvarai eo cist meon fradre Karlo et in aiudha et in cadhuna cosa, si cum om per dreit son fradra salva dift, in o quid il mi altresi fazet, et ab Ludher nul plaid nunquam prindrai, qui, meon vol, cist meon fradre Karle in damno sit.	In Godes minna ind in thes christianes folches ind unser bedhero gehaltnissi, fon thesemo dage frammordes, so fram so mir Got geuuizci indi mahd furgibit, so haldih thesan minan bruodher . . . . soso man mit rehtu sinan bruodher scal, in thiu thaz er mig so sama duo, indi mit Ludheren im nohheiniu thing ne gegango the, minan uuillon, imo ce scadhen uuerdhen.	For the love of God and for the Christian people and for our common salvation, from this day forward, so long as God give me knowledge and power, I will help this my brother [Charles both with my aid and in everything] as by right one ought to help one's brother, on condition that he does the same for me, and I will not hold any court with Lothar, which, of my own will, might cause [my brother Charles] harm.

The people (*populus*) of both armies then took oaths of guarantee, each in its own language (Charles's army in French and Louis' in German), which can be translated as follows :

If Louis [*or Charles*] observes the oath which he has sworn to his brother Charles [*or Louis*], and if Charles [*or Louis*], my lord [1]

---

[1] The words used are *meos sendra* and *min herro*.

on his part does not keep it, if I cannot turn him away (from his wickedness), neither I, nor any of those whom I will have been able to turn away, will give him any help against Louis [*or Charles*].

The text of these oaths is worthy of detailed study by historians as well as by linguists, for it shows with utmost clarity that the only real basis of political power in the middle of the ninth century was the relationship between lord and vassal. Empire and kingdom were ideals which might receive the enthusiastic support of the religious; 'the Christian people' and 'our common salvation' might be convenient catchwords on the lips of all men; but the fact remained that the armies which took the oaths (and won the war) were vassalic armies. They obeyed the commands of Charles the Bald and Louis the German not because they were their lawful kings (for the question of their constitutional position was what the war was about), nor because they were 'all French' or 'all German' (for Charles himself was half-German), but because they were their feudal lords (*meos sendra* or *min herro*). The only way in which Charles or Louis could guarantee that his brother would observe the treaty was by gaining the co-operation of his brother's vassals. No one could wage a successful war unless his vassals were prepared to follow him—that was the foremost political reality of the ninth century.

But in addition to that fact there is the interest of the languages. Historians will surely be pardoned if they point to the ceremony at Strasbourg as the first symbolic appearance of the French and German nations. But it must be stressed that it was only symbolic. The Emperor Lothar also had an army, but no one knows what, if anything, its common language would have been. So far as we know, it contained men of many different 'nations', but that did not make it any the weaker as a fighting force. Lothar was able to rule his Middle Kingdom with some success, and it only came to an end when he died, in 855. Then it had to be partitioned, in accordance with Frankish law, among his three sons, Louis II (855–75) to whom was given Italy and the title of emperor, Charles (855–63) to whom was given a newly-created kingdom of Provence, and Lothar II (855–69) to whom was given the northern part, between the Alps, the Rhine, and the Scheldt, which was henceforth known as Lotharingia (*Germ*. Lothringen, *Fr*. Lorraine).

Indeed, the history of the Carolingian Empire ends, like that of the Merovingian Kingdom, by becoming family history. Everything depended on a king having sons, but not too many of them. Lothar I had had too many, but Lothar II, alas ! had none. He made desperate efforts to divorce his wife in order to try again. But Pope Nicholas I refused to condone any matrimonial irregularity, and Charles the Bald and Louis the German supported the Pope for all they were worth, knowing that if Lothar II died childless they would have an opportunity of dividing his kingdom amongst themselves. Events turned out as they had hoped. Lothar II died in 869 without legitimate issue, and in the following year his kingdom was divided at the Partition of Mersen. To Louis the German were given Aachen, Cologne, Trier, Thionville, Metz, Mainz, Alsace, and the Jura, and to Charles the Bald the districts farther west. The Middle Kingdom disappeared, and the political map of Europe took on an appearance which is more familiar to our eyes, even though the kingdoms were still little more than family affairs, and were not France and Germany but the kingdoms of the West and East Franks.

2. Vikings, Saracens, and Hungarians

Even if the sons and grandsons of Charlemagne had not been distracted by their family affairs, they would have found it extremely difficult to put up an effective defence against the raiders who beset their kingdom on all sides. The Vikings (or Danes, or Northmen) attacked it from the north and west, the Saracens from the south, and the Hungarians from the east, and it is probably true to say they caused more devastation between them than did the Germanic invaders of the fifth century. Abbeys and churches were sacked and left abandoned, towns were burnt to the ground. There was no part of Western Europe which completely escaped the attention of one or other of these raiders ; they were irresistible and ubiquitous. Their raids penetrated so deeply into Europe that the abbey of Luxeuil, in Burgundy, suffered from all three of them in turn.

No satisfactory explanation has yet been offered for the dramatic outburst of the Vikings from Scandinavia. Given the geography of their country it is not difficult to appreciate why they should have taken to the sea, and it is quite probable that in conquering the Frisians, Charlemagne had destroyed the only naval power which might have deterred them from attacking the mainland of Europe. But the great difficulty is to explain how and why the population of Scandinavia had become sufficiently vast to account for all the fleets and armies of which we read. Quite apart from the Vikings who raided Western Europe, there were those other Vikings, the Varangians, who raided the East. One group of them, known as the Rūs, made a settlement at Novgorod, worked down the Dnieper to Kiev, and made that city the capital of a kingdom which, by an adaptation of their name, became known as Russia. Some even proceeded southward to the Black Sea and launched two attacks on Byzantium (865 and 907); and in the second of these, which the Greeks bought off with a ransom, we are told that the Rūs disposed of 2,000 ships. One cannot help wondering where they all came from. (See Appendix II.)

In the west, the first Viking expeditions of which we have definite information took place at the end of the eighth century. There was an attack on the south coast of England in 787, and another on Lindisfarne in 793, and in the summer of 800 Charlemagne found it necessary to make a tour of the coastal defences between the Seine and the Loire. But the chief target of Viking raids in the early years of the ninth century was Ireland; by c. 834 they had raided the greater part of the country, destroyed its ancient civilization, and established bases on its coasts from which they could conveniently send expeditions to other parts of the British Isles and Europe. By 840 they had raided Noirmoutier, Rhé, Duurstede (four times), Utrecht, and Antwerp. In 843 they wintered for the first time in Gaul (at Noirmoutier), captured Nantes, ravaged the valleys of the Loire and Garonne, and even threatened the Moslem cities of Lisbon and Cadiz. In 845 they sailed up the Seine with 120 ships and destroyed Paris, and in the following thirty years they raided up the Rhine, the Meuse, the Scheldt, the Somme, the Seine, the Marne, the Loire, the Charente, the Dordogne, the Lot, and the Garonne. One particularly spectacular expedition (859–62) sailed through the Straits of Gibraltar and raided in turn Nekur in Morocco, the Murcian coast of Spain, the Balearic Islands, and Roussillon, wintered in the Rhone delta, whence it raided upstream as far as Valence, and finally proceeded to the Italian coast where it sacked Pisa and Luna (which it apparently mistook for Rome), before returning through the straits of Gibraltar to its base in Brittany. In 866 the main force of Vikings, the Danish 'great army', made a concentrated attack on England. It quickly overran East Anglia, Northumbria, and Mercia, but met with bitter resistance from the West Saxons under their king, Alfred the Great. In 878 Alfred defeated one Danish leader decisively at the battle of Edington, and in view of this reverse the main Viking forces moved back to the Continent. In 879 they were at Ghent, in 880 both at Courtrai and in Saxony, in 881 at Elsloo and at Aachen, where they sacked Charlemagne's palace, in 882 at Condé on the Scheldt, in 883 at Amiens, and in 884 at Louvain. In 885-6 they were outside Paris, besieging it with a force which is said to have numbered 700 ships and 40,000 men; and, though they failed to take the city, the Emperor Charles the Fat paid them a ransom of 700 pounds of silver and gave them permission to spend the winter plundering in Burgundy (which was when they sacked Luxeuil). In 891 they were back in the Netherlands, where they were defeated by Arnulf, King of the East Franks, at the battle of the Dyle. But they were still powerful enough to establish settlements in the district round the lower Seine, which in 911 was formally conceded to them as the Duchy of the Northmen (Normandy).

The Saracen attacks were less spectacular. They developed in two ways. One of these was the invasion of Sicily and South Italy, which was undertaken by discontented emirs from Aghlabite Tunisia and began in 827. Palermo was captured in 831, and the Saracens got their first footing on the mainland in 837 when they were employed as mercenaries by the Duke of Naples. They derived their strength mainly from their fleets, thanks to which they were able to capture Bari in 840 and to make a raid up the Tiber in 846—they failed to get into the city of Rome, but sacked the basilica of St. Peter which was outside the walls and still unprotected[1] —and later they attacked St. Benedict's

---

[1] It was in consequence of this disaster that Pope Leo IV surrounded it with walls, to form the ' Leonine city ' in the year following.

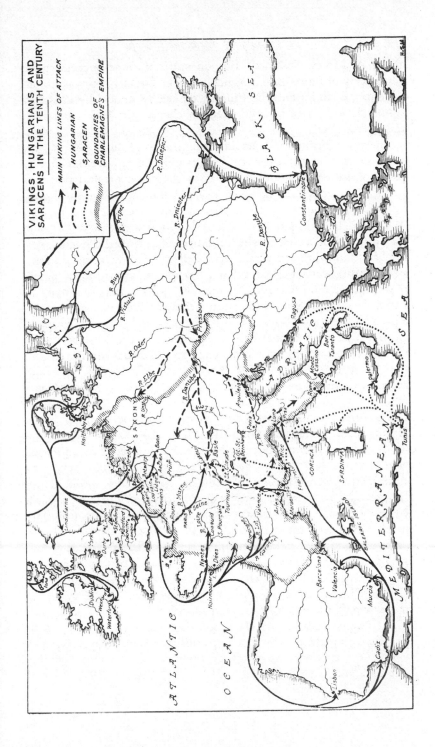

VIKINGS, HUNGARIANS AND
SARACENS IN THE TENTH CENTURY

MAIN VIKING LINES OF ATTACK

HUNGARIAN

SARACEN

BOUNDARIES OF
CHARLEMAGNE'S EMPIRE

abbey of Monte Cassino. But, in spite of these successes, the geography of Italy made it difficult for the Saracens to make rapid advances inland ; and the Franks, especially under the Emperor Louis II, were able to hold them in check. In 871 Louis even recaptured Bari.

A second form of Saracen attack consisted of rapid plundering-raids on the south coast of Gaul, and these were less easily resisted since they covered much of the same ground that was being attacked simultaneously by the Vikings. Saracen pirates, sailing from the ports of Moslem Spain, sacked Nice in 813, Marseilles in 838 and 848, and Arles in 842 and 850. In 860 they established a base on the Camargue, captured the Archbishop of Arles, and directed a raid up the Rhone to Valence. Subsequently their activities extended as far north as Burgundy, where they sacked Saint-Claude, Baume-les-Dames, and the luckless Luxeuil. By the end of the ninth century they had established a base on the south coast of Gaul at Fraxinetum (near St. Tropez), from which their robber-bands terrorized all the western passes of the Alps, their most famous exploit—and also the last before they were extirpated—being the capture of Maiolus, the holy Abbot of Cluny, on his way through the Great St. Bernard pass in 972.

The third danger which beset Western Europe was that of the Hungarians. They did not make their appearance till the end of the ninth century, but they were great horsemen and they were soon able to make their power felt. In 892 they were employed by Arnulf, King of the East Franks and subsequently Emperor, on an expedition against Moravia, and seven years later they made the first expedition on their own account. By way of Aquileia, they advanced to Pavia and wintered in Lombardy, which they held at their mercy. In the next year (900) they moved to Bavaria, and in the next (901) to Carinthia. In 906 they raided Saxony twice, in 907 Bavaria, in 908 Saxony and Thuringia, and in 909 Swabia. After 917 they had sufficiently recovered from certain local setbacks to raid Basle, Alsace, and French Burgundy (it was then that they sacked Luxeuil) and in 924 their expeditions operated in Saxony, Lombardy, and Provence. From that date onwards, their power began to decline, but they remained a menace to Christian Europe till 955 when they were decisively defeated by Otto the Great at the battle of Lechfeld.

The conjunction of all these different raids, Viking, Saracen, and Hungarian, proved fatal to the Carolingian kingdoms, because they were incapable of organizing an adequate defence. The first reaction to the invaders was usually to buy them off with a ransom (*danegeld*) or to flee from the neighbourhood of coast or rivers. The monks of St. Cuthbert, for example, moved from Durham to Chester-le-Street, and the shrine of St. Edmund was transported on a cart from Bury St. Edmunds to London. Most spectacular of all were the wanderings of the monks of St. Philibert. Their monastery had been founded in the seventh century on the island of Noirmoutier, which was off the west coast of France, near the mouth of the Loire. There they were desperately exposed to the sea-raiders, and so they normally took refuge during the summer months at a place called Deas which was a few miles inland. By 836 they had abandoned Noirmoutier completely and moved their monastery permanently to Deas, which consequently took the name of St. Philibert de Grandlieu. Much of the church which they built there is still standing, but by 857 they had decided that it was too dangerously near the coast and moved to Cunauld, near Saumur, about a hundred miles up the Loire. In 862 they retreated still farther to Messay in Poitou, in 872–3 to St. Pourçain-sur-Sioule (near Moulins), and finally in 875 to Tournus on the Saône. They had trekked almost six hundred miles in the course of forty years, but seemed at last to have found a safe retreat, for Tournus was well inland and was strongly fortified. Nevertheless, in 937 or 939 they were raided by the Hungarians. It must have seemed that there was no safety anywhere.

It would be a mistake to imagine that these disasters were due solely to the absorption of the Carolingians in their own family affairs, for several of them showed the most praiseworthy activity in the defence of their kingdoms. The trouble was that their efforts were necessarily spasmodic; even if there had been no family disputes to distract their attention, the Carolingians could not have maintained a systematic defence, simply because their kingdoms were too large.

Imagine, for example, the position in which the King of the

West Franks found himself. All his subjects expected him to
defend them at once. If the Vikings sailed up the Seine, a
messenger would be sent post-haste to inform the king. The
king's ' palace ' was still itinerant, so the messenger would first
have to discover where the king was. Then he would have to
reach him ; he might easily have to ride a distance of two or
three hundred miles. This accomplished, he would tell the king
his story, and the king would send out messengers summoning
his counts and vassals to levy their forces. All that took time,
and it might easily be three weeks or more before the royal army
arrived at the place where the Vikings had been reported ; and
by then they would most probably have disappeared.

The difficulty was that the Vikings moved too quickly. In
their ships they could move faster than any land forces could
pursue them, and they could sail from the north coast to the
south and take their pick of all the rivers of France. When
they had sailed some distance upstream, they would leave their
ships and take to their horses—sometimes they used captured
horses, sometimes transported their own—and being more lightly
equipped than the Franks would move faster, with little to fear
from pursuit. They might continue land operations for several
weeks before rejoining their ships, perhaps on an entirely different
river ; and then at last they would sail away, disappearing as
swiftly as they had first appeared.

The first essential of any effective defence against such raiders
was to destroy their mobility. The ideal solution would have
been to build a fleet and win control of the seas, but this was not
practicable ; King Alfred of Wessex bravely attempted it, but
with indifferent success, because he could not get sufficient
sailors who could equal the skill of the Vikings. More feasible
was the scheme of building fortified towns or castles at strategic
points, in order to block the routes which the Vikings would
most naturally use. If they wanted to ensure the means of
a safe retreat, the Vikings would not dare to pass such fortified
towns without destroying them. They would have to besiege
them, and if the defence was sufficiently obstinate the Vikings
might be detained for several weeks. Such a delay would give
the royal army its chance ; cumbersome though it was, it might
arrive in time to fight a battle before the enemy disappeared.

This system of defence by means of fortified towns or castles was very widely employed, for it was equally effective whether the enemy came by land or by sea, and whether he was Hungarian, Saracen, or Viking. We know that Charles the Bald arranged for the construction of castles along the Seine, the Loire, and the Oise, the most famous of them being at Paris, where the Ile de la Cité was fortified, so that the bridges connecting it with either bank could effectively prevent navigation farther upstream. Similarly, Alfred the Great surrounded his kingdom of Wessex with *burhs* or boroughs, Pope Gregory IV constructed a fortress at the mouth of the Tiber (though it did not prevent the Saracens from landing on the other bank), and Henry the Fowler built fortified towns, such as Quedlinburg and Pöhlde, to defend his duchy of Saxony from the Hungarians.

But fortresses in themselves were not enough; they were worse than useless unless they were garrisoned permanently. This raised a major problem, because the number of men required for an effective garrison was very large indeed. In Wessex the official estimate was that eight men were needed for the defence of eleven yards of wall, which meant that 27,671 men were needed to garrison the thirty *burhs* that existed in the first decade of the tenth century, in addition to the mobile forces which constituted the king's army.

To maintain the garrisons permanently it was necessary to have good organization and good morale. In Wessex a specific district was attributed to each *burh* and made responsible for its upkeep, but a rather more famous system is that which was adopted by Henry the Fowler for his fortress-towns in Saxony. He disposed all his soldiers in groups of nine, and decreed that from each group one man was to live in a fortress-town and build houses for himself and the other eight, while they cultivated his land for him. One-third of all agricultural produce was to be sent to the fortress-towns, where it was to be put in store in readiness for a siege, and the work of building went on, so we are told, night and day, ' so that men might learn in peace what they ought to do against an enemy in time of necessity '.[1]

Such plans were more easily conceived than executed, for the great difficulty was for the rulers to persuade their subjects to carry them out. The work of building the fortresses was unpopular, especially if the local people did not see the need for

[1] Widukind, *Rerum Gestarum Saxonicarum*, i. 35 (ed. Waitz, M.G.H.S.S., p. 28).

some particular fortress, and the garrison-duty could become particularly tedious. It was only to be expected that men would complain at the necessity of waiting in the *burhs* while their crops were rotting in the fields and there was not an enemy in sight. It could easily happen that they performed their duty both grudgingly and inefficiently, so that the fortress was only half-built and occupied by a handful of peasants when the unexpected happened and the Danish army attacked it.

It was therefore extremely important that the ruler who devised a scheme of defence should also be capable of sustaining the morale of his men. A king could only command his subjects to perform those services to which they had always been liable, and a lord could only expect customary services from his vassals. He had no right to invent new duties, and his subjects or vassals would not perform them, unless they had voluntarily given their consent. A king who wanted to increase taxation, lengthen army-service, or impose additional duties such as the building and garrisoning of fortresses, had therefore to convince his subjects that it was worth their while to perform those services, since, given the means, he would be capable of defeating the enemy. He had both to have a good reputation as a warrior and to convince his subjects that he would be at the right place in the time of need. Consequently everything favoured the rulers of small territories as against the rulers of vast empires. A man whose responsibilities were limited to Wessex, the Paris region, or Saxony, could make himself personally known to his subjects, inspect their preparations with care, and remain at the point of danger. But a man like Charles the Fat (881–7), who re-united the whole Empire in his own person, was necessarily regarded askance. Even if he had proved himself to be energetic, the likelihood was that when the Danes were in the north he would be fighting the Moslems in the south, and vice versa.

Thus it was that the conception of a united Latin Christendom ruled by a single monarch ceased to have the practical appeal which it had formerly possessed. It was still supported by the Church, and especially by the Pope, but the ordinary layman was too intent on his own security to accept it as anything more than a distant ideal. He preferred to accept as king the man who could defend him against his immediate dangers, and consequently the Carolingians gave way to the Capetian counts of Paris in the west, to the ducal house of Saxony in the east, and to a host of lesser nobles in Provence and Italy. One lord with a castle, completed, garrisoned, and victualled, was worth twenty emperors who spent their time marching and counter-marching from the Rhine to the Pyrenees or from the Danube to the Scheldt. It was agreed that it was God's will that His people should unite, but when the Vikings, the Moslems, and the Hungarians were abroad, the urgent necessity was a safe stronghold and a lord whose protection would be at hand.

APPENDIX

The Battle of the Dyle. 891

(Translated from the Chronicle of Regino of Prüm, ed. Kurze, 1890, pp. 136 ff.)

In the year of Our Lord's incarnation 891, the Northmen, having suffered severe losses in two successive battles in Britain, brought their fleet across [the channel], built fortified camps and went plundering in the kingdom of Lothar.[1] King Arnulf sent an army against them,[2] and he ordered it to pitch its tents on the Meuse and to stop the enemy from crossing the river. But before the army had assembled at the place which had been appointed near the castle of Maastricht, the Northmen, keeping to the upper reaches, crossed the Meuse in the neighbourhood of Liège, and spread out over the marshes near the palace of Aachen. They killed everybody whom they came across, and captured very many waggons and carts in which supplies were being brought up for the army. When the news of this reached the army, which on that very day of the nativity of St. John the Baptist [June 24] had almost completely assembled, it was not so much fear as amazement which seized the minds of all. The leaders (*principes*) called a meeting and consulted together not so much about the danger as about the difficulty of the situation, for they were uncertain whether the Northmen would enter the region of the Ripuarian Franks and make for Cologne, or whether they would go across by Prüm and make for Trier, or whether they would take fright

---

[1] *i.e.* Lotharingia. The Vikings approached by way of the Seine and Oise.

[2] The sequel shows that he did not lead it in person, as he was in Bavaria at the time.

when they heard that a whole multitude [1] had assembled against them, cross the Meuse and hurry back to their ships. They were still discussing these questions when night fell and the meeting broke up. On the next day, when the sun showed the rays of its light, they armed themselves, raised their standards, and, setting off downstream, marched to battle. When they had crossed the stream called the Geule [about 5 miles from Maastricht], they drew up in line of battle. Then, so as not to tire the whole army to no purpose, they decided that each one of the nobles [*procerum*] should send twelve of his men to form a single troop and scout out the enemy. While they were discussing these arrangements, the scouts of the Northmen suddenly appeared. When the whole multitude saw them it pursued them, without consulting its leaders and in confused order, and blundered into the Northmen's infantry squadrons in a certain little village. The Northmen gathered together in a circle and easily repelled the scattered attackers and forced them to turn back. Then making a great noise with their quivers, according to their custom, they raised a shout to heaven, and joined battle. Hearing the very great shout, the Northmen's cavalry came flying up in haste, and the army of the Christians was borne down by the battle, and, alas for its sins ! turned tail and fled. In this battle Sunzo [arch]bishop of the city of Mainz and Count Arnulf fell, together with an innumerable multitude of noble men. The Northmen, having won the victory, broke into the camp, which was full of all sorts of riches, and, having killed the prisoners whom they had taken in the battle, returned to their fleet, heavily laden with their booty. This slaughter took place on June 26th.

While these things were happening, King Arnulf was at the Bavarian frontier, repressing the insolence of the Slavs. When he was informed of the slaughter of his men and of the enemy's victory, he first of all grieved for the loss of his faithful men (*fidelibus*) and made lamentation that the Franks who had hitherto been invincible should have shown their backs to their adversary ; then reflecting on the shame of it, he was incensed against the enemy, collected an army from the eastern kingdoms,[2] and soon, having crossed the Rhine, ordered camps to be set up on the banks of the Meuse. After a few days, the Northmen, elated by the previous battle, set

---

[1] The word used is *multitudo*. Though it always refers to an army, it has been translated as ' multitude ' so as to preserve the impression of confusion given in the text.

[2] The Annals of Fulda (M.G.H. Scriptorum, i. 407) say that he collected an army from Swabia too, but the Swabians, ' as if sick ', dropped away from the king and returned home.

out in full strength on a plundering raid, and the king advanced against them with his army. The Northmen seeing him approach in battle array over the river which is known as the Dyle, constructed a fortification of wood and piled-up earth in their usual manner,[1] assailed the [Frankish] line of march with jeers and insults, and scoffingly shouted to them in derision that they should remember the slaughter and shameful flight that had taken place at the Geule, the like of which they were shortly to suffer themselves. At this the king [Arnulf] was moved to wrath (*felle commotus*) and ordered his army to dismount and to launch its attack on foot against the enemy.[2] As quick as a word the Franks dismounted from their horses, raised a shout of encouragement and burst into the enemy's entrenchment; and with the help of God they slew them and beat them down to the earth, so that out of an innumerable multitude (of Northmen), there was hardly a man left to report the news to the fleet.[3] After this happy conclusion, Arnulf returned to Bavaria.

Further Reading

L. HALPHEN. *Charlemagne et l'Empire Carolingien* (L'Evolution de l'Humanité series). Paris. 1949.

MARC BLOCH. *La Société Féodale* (L'Evolution de l'Humanité series). 2 vols. Paris. 1939–40.

PH. LAUER (ed.). *Nithard. Histoire des Fils de Louis le Pieux* (Les Classiques de l'histoire de France series). Paris. 1926. Latin text with French translation.

H. WAQUET (ed.). *Abbon. Le Siège de Paris par les Normands* (885–6) (Les Classiques de l'histoire de France series). Paris. 1942. Latin text with French translation.

[1] The Annals of Fulda add that the place was near Louvain (about 50 miles west of Maastricht).

[2] The Annals of Fulda explain that the Franks had come upon the Northmen's army unexpectedly, and found themselves in a difficult situation with a marsh on one side and the river on the other, so that there was no possibility of launching a cavalry attack. Therefore, in spite of grave doubts that were expressed ' because the Franks were not used to fighting on foot ', Arnulf decided to dismount, and holding his standard in his hand, advanced to the attack on foot. The passage is of interest since it shows that, in contrast to the Anglo-Saxons, the Franks relied on cavalry almost exclusively.

[3] None the less those Northmen who had remained with their ships during the battle were sufficiently numerous to cross the Meuse again in the following year and to raid the territory of the Ripuarian Franks, reaching as far as Bonn and Prüm, from which the majority of the monks only just had time to escape.

HAAKON SHETELIG (ed.). *Viking Antiquities in Great Britain and Ireland : Pt. i, An Introduction to the Viking History of Western Europe.* Oslo. 1940 ; *Part vi, Civilisation of the Vikings in relation to their old and new countries.* Oslo. 1954.

A. W. BRØGGER and HAAKON SHETELIG. *The Viking Ships, their ancestry and evolution.* Oslo. 1953.

P. H. SAWYER. *The Age of the Vikings.* London. 1962.

LUCIEN MUSSET. *Les Invasions. Le Second Assaut contre l'Europe Chrétienne (VIIe–XIe siècles).* Paris. 1965.

VIII

EUROPE AT THE END OF THE NINTH CENTURY: ECONOMIC SURVEY

1. TRADE AND COMMERCE

THE first and most obvious fact to be observed about the economy of Europe at the end of the ninth century is the contrast between East and West. Though the Latin West was poor, the Byzantine and Islamic empires were rich.

The prosperity of the Byzantine Empire was in part a comment on its political conditions, for the government was far stronger than any government in the West. It had an army and a civil service, and was even capable of organizing mass movements of population in order to repopulate devastated provinces or to ' colonize ' districts which had not previously been developed— thus 70,000 Slav prisoners were settled in Eastern Macedonia in the eighth century. The government controlled economic activity by making itself responsible for the corporations into which the main trades and industries were organized, controlling prices and profits, granting import and export licences, and even regulating the membership of the corporations and their dependent guilds. Under its direction the market was adequately supplied, but not flooded, with all the luxury goods for which the Byzantine Empire was famous—silk fabrics, heavy brocades, fine cloths, goldsmithery, enamel plates, fine glass, and ivories. Byzantine copes and reliquaries were amongst the most precious objects that a church in the Latin West could possess, and every barbarian king who wanted to establish a correct ceremonial for his court would go to endless expense to procure Byzantine furnishings. Even the seventh-century king who was commemorated in the ship-burial at Sutton Hoo in Essex had a silver bowl which had been manufactured in Constantinople. That city was indeed the central entrepôt of medieval Europe. Its population is said to have numbered about 700,000, and its gold coins, the *nomisma* or *besant*, maintained their intrinsic value and were used as the international currency of the early Middle Ages.

Second only to Byzantium was the Islamic Empire. In the ninth century its capital and the centre of its commerce was Baghdad. The contrasts of wealth and poverty which existed in that city in the time of Harun ar-Raschid (786–809) [1] were as extreme as in *The Arabian Nights*, and it is a fact that when watermelons were out of season they were imported in ice across the desert from Khorasan. Other Moslem cities were, in their different ways, almost equally rich. At Cordoba, in Spain, we are told that in the tenth century there were seventy libraries and nine hundred public baths, while in Cairo at the end of the ninth century there was a ruler who endeavoured to cure his insomnia by lying on an aircushion moored with silken ropes on a lake of quicksilver.

Moslem merchants travelled as far as India, Ceylon, the East Indies (whence they brought spices for re-export to the West), China (whence they brought porcelain), Africa, Spain, and the Baltic (which they reached by means of the Caspian Sea and the Volga). In the early ninth century trade with the Latin West was maintained by Jewish merchants who, according to a contemporary Moslem, came from the south of France and :

> speak Arabic, Persian, Greek, Frankish, Spanish and Slavonic. They travel from west to east and from east to west, by land and sea. From the west they bring eunuchs, slave-girls, boys, brocade castor-skins, marten and other furs, and swords. They take ship from Frankland in the western Mediterranean Sea and land at Farama [the ancient Pelusium, near Port Said], whence they take their merchandise on camel-back to Qulzum, a distance of twenty-five parasangs. Then they sail on the eastern [Red] Sea from Qulzum to Al-Jar and Jedda, and onward to Sind, India and China. From China they bring back musk, aloes, camphor, cinnamon, and other products of those parts, and return to Qulzum. Then they

---

[1] Charlemagne entered into diplomatic relations with him, and Harun sent him an elephant which became a pet of the Frankish court ; it was called Abul Abaz and died an honourable death campaigning in Denmark.

transport them to Farama and sail again on the western sea. Some sail with their goods to Constantinople, and sell them to the Greeks, and some take them to the King of the Franks and sell them there.[1]

But the greatest testimony to the extent of trade in the Islamic Empire is afforded by the development of banking which, since usury was forbidden to Moslems, had to be undertaken by Christians and Jews. Already by the ninth century there were banks in the capital which had branches in most of the important cities of the Empire, and according to Professor Lewis ' it was possible to draw a cheque in Baghdad and cash it in Morocco '.[2]

As well as serving as an entrepôt between the Far East and the West, the Islamic Empire had industries of its own, which, as in the case of the Byzantine industries, were state-controlled either wholly or in part. Most important was the textile industry, producing silk (which included damask from Damascus), cotton (which included muslin from Mosul), linen (which was a speciality of Egypt), carpets, and ceremonial clothing for rulers, generals, and other high officials. Another industry, eventually to be of great importance, was paper-making. In the ninth century this was still confined to the eastern provinces of the Empire, where the industry had been established after the capture of some Chinese paper-makers in 751, but in the tenth century it was to spread to Iraq, Syria, and Egypt, and took the place of papyrus as the ordinary writing material.

While the Byzantine and Islamic empires were flourishing, the economy of the Latin West was stagnant. Indeed, the question which has caused most controversy is whether there was any regular commerce at all in the Latin West of the ninth century.

> Buying and selling did not form the regular occupation of anyone ; they were simply expedients to which one had recourse in case of necessity ! [3]

That was the considered judgment of Henri Pirenne, whose thesis concerning the breakdown of the Western economy, so

---

[1] The passage is from Ibn Khurradādhbeh, an early ninth-century geographer, as quoted by Bernard Lewis in *The Arabs in History* (2nd ed., 1954), p. 90 (Hutchinson's University Library).

[2] *Ibid.*, p. 91.   [3] Pirenne in Glotz, *Histoire Générale*, viii. 14.

seductively entitled *Mahommed and Charlemagne*, has formed the basis of all subsequent discussions of the economic history of the period. His views have not been generally accepted, at least not without serious reservations, but it is important to understand what they were.[1]

They derive from a consideration of the economy of the ancient world, which depended, as Pirenne was quite right to insist, on the existence of commercial navigation in the Mediterranean. As long as it was unmolested by pirates, trade could pass from east to west and north to south, and the population of Rome, to take but one example, could be fed on African corn. But if, for any reason, the Mediterranean were to become unsafe for navigation, commerce would inevitably decline. If commerce declined, so would the towns and cities ; they might retain a certain importance as centres of secular or ecclesiastical government, but they would lose their economic significance, and with it the flourishing life which expressed itself in municipal institutions. If the towns declined, their population would fall and the landed proprietors who had formerly made a business of supplying them with food would find that there were fewer and fewer potential purchasers for their produce. The agricultural wealth of the country would be bottled up, because there would be no outlets for it ; those who worked the land would have to consume its produce themselves, because there would be no one else to buy it. In these circumstances money would cease to have any importance. The greater landowners would have their own workshops for making tools or weaving cloth, and they would pay their workmen in kind, with land or food.

That is what Pirenne called an ' economy of no outlets '. He claimed that it was typical of the eighth and ninth centuries and that it was not only the concomitant but also the cause of feudal society :

> Commerce has so completely ceased to be one of the branches of social activity, that each domain endeavours to provide for all its

[1] H. Pirenne, *Mahommed and Charlemagne* (ed. F. Vercauteren), tr. B. Miall (London, 1939), which was published posthumously, is the most convenient exposition of his views. For criticisms of the thesis, see in particular, F. L. Ganshof, ' Notes sur les ports de Provence du viiie au xe siècles ', *Revue Historique*, vol. 183 (1938), pp. 28–37, and R. S. Lopez, ' Mohammed and Charlemagne—a Revision ', *Speculum*, xviii, 14–38 (1943), and A. F. Havighurst, *The Pirenne Thesis* (' Problems in European Civilization series '. Boston, U.S., 2nd ed., 1969).

needs from its own resources. That is why one sees the abbeys of regions which lack vineyards, like the Low Countries for example, contriving to obtain donations of vine-land, whether in the Seine basin or in the valleys of the Rhine and Moselle, so as to be able to secure their annual provision of wine.[1]

The land was the only real source of wealth, and nobody had any use for money because it could not be spent. That was why the Carolingians had to endow their vassals with lands as benefices. Feudalism was the inevitable result of an ' economy of no outlets ', and the consequence of feudalism, as Pirenne graphically put it, was Charlemagne.

But if the ' economy of no outlets ' was the precondition of Charlemagne's rise to power, what was the cause of the economy itself ? According to the strict logic of Pirenne's theory it was obvious that the free navigation of the Mediterranean must have come to an end, and the only problem was to discover when that cataclysmic event took place. He therefore sought evidence within the Frankish Kingdom for the use of goods which could only have been produced on the eastern or southern shores of the Mediterranean. Of these the most important were gold, olive oil (from North Africa), oriental silk, papyrus (from Egypt), and spices. Pirenne found (though his findings have been disputed) that they were all used in Gaul up to the last quarter of the seventh century, and that they had all disappeared by the first quarter of the eighth century. Gold coinage was replaced by silver, olive oil by butter and candles—for it had been used for illumination as well as food—oriental silk by Frisian cloth, and papyrus by parchment. (It was noteworthy that paper was not introduced into the Latin West till the twelfth or thirteenth century, although it could have been procured from Islam as early as the tenth.) For spices, last recorded in Gaul in 716, there was no substitute; they just disappeared. It would seem, therefore, that Mediterranean commerce had come to an end. One could even witness the disappearance of money, the indispensable means of trade. In 695 the Frankish king gave the villa of Massigny to the Abbot of St. Denis in exchange for the surrender of a perpetual annuity of 300 *solidi* ; apparently he could no longer

---

[1] Pirenne in Glotz, *op. cit.*, viii. 14.

afford to pay in money the annuity which his predecessors had paid, because money had disappeared.

Having thus established that Mediterranean commerce came to an end, so far as the Latin West was concerned, in the last quarter of the seventh century, it was only necessary for Pirenne to see if there was any major political event which occurred at about the same time and which could possibly have disrupted the navigation of the Mediterranean. It was then that the importance of the Moslem invasions leapt to the eye. The Moslems had conquered Palestine and Syria in 636–40, Egypt in 639–42, Tunisia in 670–95, and Spain in 711–20 (see above, page 94). So far as Pirenne was concerned the most important of these conquests was that of Tunisia, which happened, be it noted, at exactly the right date for his theory. For Tunisia had a position of particular strategic importance. It was situated at the narrow waist of the Mediterranean, and from its ports it would have been possible, even before the conquest of Sicily in the ninth century, for Moslem pirates to disrupt communications between the eastern and western halves of the Mediterranean. Admittedly Venice, whose ships sailed down the Adriatic and consequently evaded the dangers of the Mediterranean waist, might continue to trade with Byzantium, but Pisa, Genoa, and the ports of Provence were cut off from the navigation on which their commerce depended. As Pirenne put it, ' a vacuum is created in the great port of Marseilles, which had formerly been the principal mart connecting the West with the East '. The cities of Southern Gaul would inevitably decline (in fact it is just in the period from *c.* 675 to *c.* 780 that even the succession of their bishops cannot be established) and the ' economy of no outlets ' would be imposed on the Latin West by the Moslems. That was why Pirenne gave his thesis the title *Mahommed and Charlemagne*, for, in his view, a chain of economic causes and effects united the careers of the two men and made them the central figures of medieval history.

Seductive though this theory may be, it must be admitted that it is open to several objections. The first is that its validity depends on the assumption that because certain Mediterranean goods had not entirely disappeared from the Frankish Kingdom before the last quarter of the eighth century, Mediterranean trade must necessarily have been maintained at full strength. Could it not have been that Mediterranean trade had been declining gradually for three or four centuries, but that the final stages of its decline were not reached till the end of the seventh century ? If so, that gradual decline must itself have had a cause, and since it would have started before the Moslem invasions it could not have been caused by them.

Secondly, even if we were to grant a stoppage of Mediterranean trade at the turn of the eighth century, we could still legitimately ask if there was any real evidence for the supposition that it had been caused by the Moslems. Pirenne quoted the dictum of Ibn Khaldūn, that the Christians could no longer ' float a plank ' on the Mediterranean, but Ibn Khaldun lived six centuries too late to be an eye-witness (he died in 1406). Pirenne, it would seem, had relied simply on the *probability* that, once installed in Tunisia, the Moslems would automatically disrupt the commerce of the Mediterranean ; and that probability was not so great as he imagined. In the fifth century the Vandals had had a fleet based on Tunisia, had controlled Sardinia, Corsica, and (at times) parts of the coast of Sicily, and had earned themselves a great reputation as pirates. But according to Pirenne they had failed to deal the death-blow to Mediterranean commerce. Why, then, was it inevitable that the Moslems should have succeeded ?

Thirdly, it has been shown that the stoppage of navigation and commerce in the Western Mediterranean was not so complete as Pirenne thought. In addition to the evidence of the Jewish merchants of the ninth century (page 178) it has now been shown by Professor Ganshof that sea-communications between Rome and Marseilles were never entirely closed during the eighth and ninth centuries, and Professor Lopez has demonstrated that the evidence of the disappearing goods is less convincing than had once been thought. Papyrus, for example, though its last recorded use by the Merovingian chancery was *c*. 660-70, continued to be used by the Papacy till the eleventh century, Oriental silk was still imported into the Latin West in the ninth and tenth centuries, and the change-over from gold to a silver coinage under the Carolingians was less complete than Pirenne supposed.

In this connection the surprising discovery has been made that the silver coinage of the Carolingians was linked to the relative value of silver and gold in the Islamic Empire. When the extraction of silver from the mines in the Hindu Kush was at its greatest (*c.* 850), the value of silver in relation to gold dropped, and the content of silver in the Carolingian *denarius* was increased so that it should maintain its intrinsic value. But when the Moslem conquest of Nubia led to a great increase in the supply of gold (*c.* 900), the relative value of silver rose again, and the silver content of the Carolingian *denarius* was accordingly reduced.[1] Could these adjustments have been made if there had been no commercial contact between the Frankish Kingdom and Islam ?

None the less, even though Pirenne's picture of a sudden cessation of commerce in the Latin West was a gross exaggeration, it was useful because it focused attention on the fact that the known commercial dealings of the eighth and ninth centuries were pitifully small when compared with those of earlier and later centuries. In 748 we hear of a man in Trevano (Como) who borrowed one gold *solidus* on the security of a small piece of meadow. In 768 there is record of a moneyer who bought a plot of land for the equivalent of 28 gold *solidi* ; but as the vendor apparently had no use for so large a sum of money he accepted a horse in lieu of a part of the price (13 *solidi*). Similarly, it is possible to find instances of money-lending which, in spite of the Church's prohibition of usury, was sometimes practised by Christians as well as by Jews. But the striking feature of all such instances is that the sums of money involved were comparatively trivial.

Two main reasons would seem to have been responsible for this state of affairs. The first was that the Latin West could not get all the imports which it would have liked from the East, because it could not pay for them. The balance of trade had for centuries been in favour of the East and against the West ; the main exports from *Francia* to the East were, as we have already seen (page 178), slaves and furs, and the slave-trade was declining as the Church induced the kings of the West to prohibit it. In the sixth and seventh centuries the adverse balance of trade had to some extent been offset by the subsidies which the Byzantine court had occasionally granted to the barbarian kingdoms in return for military aid—it had paid 50,000 *solidi* to King Childebert of the Franks for an alliance against the Lombards (*c.* 582). But

[1] These facts, established by E. Bolin, are reported by E. Perroy in ‘Encore Mahomet et Charlemagne’ (*Revue Historique*, vol. 212 (1954), pp. 232-8). See also Appendix III.

by the eighth century even that temporary source of relief had dried up, for the Byzantine emperors were so fully occupied defending their eastern frontiers against the Moslems, that they had neither time nor money to spare for the West. Thus the adverse balance of trade became ever more acute, and westerners were forced from sheer poverty to dispense with many of the luxuries of the East.

Secondly, there was the general insecurity of communications. In part, of course, it is true that this was caused by the Moslems, but the Vikings, and ultimately the Hungarians too, were equally responsible. They disrupted communications not only in the Mediterranean but also in northern Europe, and did so the more easily because the natural trade-routes were also the natural routes for pirates. Merchants would, in normal times, have found it simplest to transport their goods by water whenever possible, and would have found the most convenient markets situated on navigable rivers. But the river-valleys were, as the monks of St. Philibert had found (page 169), the districts which were most exposed to the ravages of the Vikings.

It is perhaps for this reason that the most prominent towns of the ninth and tenth centuries—and they were in reality very small—were not those whose geographical situation led them to become the great centres of commerce in the later Middle Ages. Instead of Milan, Florence, Siena, and Pisa, we read of Pavia and Amalfi, the one protected by its royal fortress and the other by its inaccessibility from the land, while in the north the great names were not Antwerp, Ghent, Bruges, or St. Omer, but Reims and Verdun, which were relatively secure because they were farther from the coast.

Except in one or two exceptional towns like Venice (which still retained its allegiance to the Byzantine Empire), trade was at a very low ebb in the Latin West, during the ninth and tenth centuries. The fact is shown by the very looseness with which the word merchant (*mercator*) is used. We read, for example, of an abbey's ' merchants ' who were declared exempt from toll provided that they could certify that their goods were for the consumption of the monks ; and we suspect that these so-called ' merchants ' were nothing more than peasants, carting the produce of the abbey's outlying estates to the monastery itself. Even in the cases when the 'merchants' seem to have been genuine traders, like those who served Charlemagne's court, we find them being employed as 'maids-of-all-work', for they had to allow the officials of the royal estates to load supplies for the court on their wagons.

Everything points to the fact that, though trade had not come to a standstill, and though money had not ceased to be used, the ninth and tenth centuries formed the period at which the commerical activity of Europe was smaller than at any other time since the fall of the Roman Empire in the West. And this is not surprising, for governmental authority also reached its lowest ebb at the same time. The Carolingian Empire was disintegrating rapidly, and only in one or two localized areas had any alternative form of effective authority been found. 'Everywhere the country is infested with brigandage', wrote Nithard, and he expressed his amazement that in 841 the crown jewels should have been transported from Aquitaine to the Seine valley without mishap.

Such conditions were clearly not conducive to trade, for merchants rely on security of travel, and when that security is lacking their number will decline. A few intrepid men might brave the perils of the road, but the risks would be such that they would raise their prices to prohibitive levels, so that only the exceptionally rich could afford to buy their wares. Such an economy might not in the strictest sense be an 'economy of *no* outlets', for a few outlets might remain. But the markets would probably have been for local trade, and long-range commerce was not likely to revive until political stability returned and the Latin West was made safe for travellers and trade.

2. AGRARIAN ECONOMY

The best way to get a picture of agrarian economy in the ninth century is to study one of the polyptychs (or surveys of landed property) which were made by some of the greater religious houses of the Carolingian Empire. The most famous is that of the abbey of St. Germain-des-Prés at Paris. It was made in the time of Abbot Irmino (*c.* 811–*c.* 829) and it describes most of the abbey's estates. Originally it described them all, but unfortunately the manuscript is no longer complete, the most serious loss being the section dealing with the lands which had been given out as benefices.   But even though the lands surveyed may have formed no more than half the total owned by the abbey, their extent is impressive.   The exact size cannot be determined with accuracy, since the measures used were variable from place to place, but the editors of the manuscript have offered the following statistics as a rough indication of the abbey's wealth.[1]

I. Demesne Land (*Mansi dominicati*)			II. Tributary Lands		
Arable land .	6,041	hectares	Arable land .	16,088	hectares
Vine land. .	196	,,	Vine land. .	231	,,
Meadowland .	176	,,	Meadowland .	327	,,
Pasturage . .	6½	,,	Pasturage . .	86	,,
Marshland .	1½	,,	Marshland .	—	,,
Woodland. .	10,922	,,	Woodland. .	177	,,
TOTAL . .	17,343	hectares	TOTAL . .	16,909	hectares
or	42,855	English statute acres	or	41,782	English statute acres

The figures have been drawn up in two columns to show the great and overriding distinction between demesne land and tributary land.   Demesne land (*dominicata terra*) means the land of the lord (*dominus*), and its produce belonged entirely to him ; in this instance the theory was that the produce of the demesne would be sent to the abbey of St. Germain-des-Prés, where the monks would consume it.   Tributary land was the land which provided labour for the cultivation of the demesne.   Its tenants were not paid wages, but were simply given the use of certain lands on condition that they should do the necessary ploughing, reaping, cartage, and other services required by the lord.   For this purpose they were under the authority of an officer chosen from amongst themselves and known as the *maior, villicus,* or reeve.

The advantage of this system was that it made the use of money unnecessary ; it might be explained in theoretical terms as a

---

[1] The statistics used throughout are taken from the edition by Auguste Longnon (Paris, 1895).   He reprints, with corrections and observations, the most important parts of the prolegomena of the previous edition by B. Guérard (Paris, 1844).

perfect example of an ' economy of no outlets '. But it is important not to exaggerate nor to overlook the fact that the tenants
of tributary land owed other dues besides labour-services. Taking the 41,782 acres of the tributary land as a whole, these dues
consisted of money rents totalling £115 9s. 4d., and 4 horses,
55¼ oxen (the quarter being one ox due every fourth year), 5
heifers, 1,158 sheep (wethers), 288⅓ ewes, 96 lambs, 96⅓ pigs,
2,139 modii of wine,[1] 165 sesters of malt, 97½ modii of corn,
1,047 modii and 10 sesters of bearded wheat, 77 modii of oats,
58 sesters of mustard, 20½ modii and 97 sesters of hops, 2 cartloads and 11 pedales of firewood, 105 pedales of laths, 46,903
shingles (wooden roofing tiles) and 25,458 small planks (axiculi)
on which to fix them, 1,017 staves, 508 hoops and 350 bundles
of osiers for the making of barrels, 5,818 chicken, 30,965 eggs,
2,600 pounds of iron, and 440 torches. This list, it must be
stressed, is simply what was due from the tributary land and
does not include anything from the demesne. Can it seriously
be maintained that the monks, who in Abbot Irmino's time numbered 210, consumed all these dues and their demesne-produce
in their own monastery? On the face of it, even allowing for
the fact that the abbey would have had a great many dependent
servants and would have had to offer hospitality on a large
scale (for the more important visitors would come with considerable retinues), it would be simpler to assume that there was
at any rate a small marketable surplus of agricultural produce.

Returning to the estates themselves, some comment must be
made upon their size, 84,637 acres without counting the lands
given out as benefices. St. Germain-des-Prés was admittedly
a wealthy monastery but it was by no means unique. In the
ninth century, abbeys with great estates were numerous—we may
mention St. Denis, St. Bertin, St. Riquier, St. Rémi of Reims,
St. Martin of Tours, Fontenelle (St. Wandrille), Luxeuil, Prüm,
Fulda, Tegernsee, St. Gall, Lorsch, Gandersheim, and Bobbio—
and many bishoprics were even more wealthy still, for large
estates were typical of the time. Outside a few exceptional
districts like south-west France and the plain of Saxony, the
general tendency everywhere was for the free peasants to surrender themselves and their lands to lords. It happened even

---

[1] The modius was something between 52 and 68 litres.

in the Byzantine Empire, in spite of the strenuous efforts made by the emperors of the Macedonian dynasty to prevent it, for there were social and economic forces at work which favoured, and even impelled, the formation of large estates.

The most important of these was that peasant proprietors of allodial land (*i.e.* of land which they held in absolute and hereditary right) found the burdens of freedom too heavy. They had to attend the count's *placitum* and do military service which was, as we have already seen (pp. 140–1), particularly onerous, while at the same time trying to make a living out of some 30 acres of land. In a good year the difficulty of making all ends meet might not be too great, but in a bad year it might be hopeless, for the peasant who could not find the equipment necessary for his military service would be at the mercy of the king's officers. In such circumstances it often happened that the only way in which a peasant could save himself from ruin would be by surrendering his land to a lord. The lord would then grant him a lease of the land and assume ultimate responsibility for the military service, while in return the peasant would pay him regular dues. Thus, a tenth-century addition to the polyptych of Abbot Irmino records that fourteen tenants in Neauphlette (near Mantes) had once been freemen (*liberi et ingenui*), ' but as they had not the means for performing their service in the King's army, they handed over their allods to [the abbey of] St. Germain '.

The second observation to be made is that about one-third of the abbey's lands were woodland. This was certainly not an exceptionally high proportion, for the main bulk of the abbey's land was within 25 or 30 miles of Paris, a district which, in spite of the forests of Fontainebleau and Rambouillet, was not more than normally well wooded.[1] Some historians have even estimated that two-thirds of the Carolingian Empire north of the Alps was forest-land, for quite apart from the Ardennes, the Eifel, the Vosges, the Black Forest, the Thuringian Forest, and the Bohemian Forest, there were vast areas of woodland in Saxony, Picardy, and lower Poitou ; even in the Netherlands and Flanders,

---

[1] The principal estates not in the Paris region were Nogent l'Artaud, nr. Chateau-Thierry (Aisne) ; Neuilly-les-Bois, nr. Chateauroux (Indre) ; Corbon and Boisy Maugis, both nr. Mortagne (Orne) ; and Quillebeuf (Eure), then known as Villa Super Mare.

which are now so bare of trees, there were forest-districts or *houtlands*. The work of clearing these forests was one of the major achievements of the Middle Ages, but in the ninth century it had only just begun. Whole tracts of land which were later to be among the richest in Europe were virtually uninhabited except by the wild beasts which then included wolves, boars, deer, stags, and bears. One has only to recollect the typical background of Grimm's *Fairy Tales*—genuine folk-tales which the brothers Grimm collected with scholarly care—to appreciate the extent to which the forest dominated the life of the peasant.

Turning from these preliminary observations, we may now proceed to the study of one particular estate. But here a difficulty arises. If we translate the words of the polyptych into English, we shall find that we have inevitably begged the question, for the precise details of ninth-century agrarian history are controversial not because we lack the technical terms that were used at the time but because we cannot be sure what they meant. Are we to translate the word *servus* as ' slave ' or ' serf '? How are we to translate *colonus* and how *mansus* ? And above all, how are we to interpret the measurements of land or quantity when everything points to the fact that the measures varied, although their names were constant, from village to village ? In consequence of these difficulties, the text will be given in Latin, and the English translation which is given alongside must be taken as nothing more than tentative.[1]

The following extracts are from Abbot Irmino's survey of Gagny near Pontoise, which was a conveniently small estate. The survey was drawn up from the evidence provided by a sworn inquest of tenants (in some cases, though not in that of Gagny, we are given the names of those who testified under the heading of *isti juraverunt*), and it begins as follows :

BREVE DE WANIACO

1. Habet in Waniaco mansum dominicatum cum casa et aliis casticiis sufficienter. Habet de terra arabili culturas iiii, quae

ACCOUNT OF GAGNY

In Gagny there is a demesne manse with a house and other buildings in sufficiency. There are four fields of arable land

---

[1] The text is taken from *Polyptyque de l'Abbaye de Saint-Germain-des-Pres rédigé au temps de l'abbé Irminon*, ed. Auguste Longnon (Paris, 1895), pp. 41 ff.

habent bunuaria xlviii, ubi possunt seminari de frumento modios cxcii, de vinea aripennos lxvi, ubi possunt colligi de vino modios cccc. Habet ibi de siiva per totum in giro leuvas ii, quae possunt saginari porci cl. Habet ibi de prato aripennos xiiii, ubi potest colligi de feno carra xxx.

containing 48 *bunuaria* (163 acres ?) where 192 *modios* (12,240 litres ?) of corn can be sown, there are 66 *aripennos* (13½ acres ?) of vine which can provide 400 *modios* (25,500 litres ?) of wine. The woodland measures as a whole 2 leagues (4½ kilometres ?) in circumference and can fatten 150 pigs. There are 14 *aripennos* (2⅘ acres ?) of meadow, from which 30 cartloads of hay can be got.

2. Ansegarus colonus et uxor ejus colona, nomine Ingalteus, habent secum infantes ii his nominibus, Ansegildis, Ingrisma. Tenet mansum ingenuilem, habentem de terra arabili bunuaria iii et quartam partem de bunuario, de vinea aripennos iii. Solvit ad hostem in uno anno de argento solidos iiii, ad alium annum solidos ii, in pascione de vino modios ii; arat ad hibernaticum perticas iiii, ad tramissum ii, curvadas, carroperas, manoperas, caplim, ubi ei injungitur; pullos iiii, ova xv, scindulas l.

Ansegarus, a *colonus*, and his wife, Ingalteus by name, a *colona*, have with them 2 children called Ansegildis and Ingrisma. He holds a free manse consisting of 3¼ *bunuaria* (11 acres ?) of arable land and 3 *aripennos* (⅗ acre ?) of vine. He pays as army-tax four silver shillings in one year, and two in the next; in return for [rights of] pasture [he pays] 2 *modios* (127½ litres ?) of wine; he ploughs 4 'perches' of land (1,650 sq. yds. ?) for winter wheat, for spring wheat 2 'perches' (825 sq. yds. ?). He owes *corvées*, cartage-work, manual work and tree-felling when ordered, and 4 hens, 15 eggs and 50 roofing-tiles.

21. Aregius colonus et uxor ejus colona, nomine Blitgildis, homines sancti Germani; Ingelhaus colonus et uxor ejus colona, nomine Erlindis, habent secum infantes ii, his nominibus, Rectrudis, Aclevolda; Amalgaudus servus et uxor ejus colona, nomine Frotbolda, habent secum infantes ii, his nominibus, Frotberga, Lotberta; Lontgaus,

Aregius, a *colonus*, and his wife, a *colona*, called Blitgildis, vassals of [the abbey of] St. Germain; Ingelhaus, a *colonus*, and his wife, a *colona* called Erlindis, have with them 2 children called Rectrudis and Aclevolda; Amalgaudus, a serf, and his wife, a *colona* called Frotbolda, have with them 2 children called Frotberga and Lotberta; Lontgaus,

BREVE DE WANIACO—*cont.*

colonus sancti Germani. Isti quattuor tenent mansum ingenuilem i, habentem de terra arabili bunuaria iiii, de vinea aripennos ii. Cetera similiter.

ACCOUNT OF GAGNY—*cont.*

a *colonus* [of the abbey] of St. Germain. These four hold one free manse consisting of 4 *bunuaria* ($13\frac{3}{5}$ acres ?) of arable land, and 2 *aripennos* ($\frac{2}{5}$ acre ?) of vine. The rest [*i.e.* their dues] are similar [to those paid by Ansegarus, as listed above].

Altogether $23\frac{1}{2}$ 'free estates' (*mansus ingenuiles*) are listed, containing $82\frac{1}{3}$ *bunuaria* (or about 280 acres ?) of arable land. There follows a second section which starts as follows:

DE SERVIS

26. Alaricus colonus tenet mansum servilem i, habentem de terra arabili bunuaria iii, de vinea aripennos ii, de prato dimidium aripennum. Solvit in pascione de vino modios iii; facit in vinea aripennos iiii^{or}; arat ad hibernaticum perticas ii; corvadas, carroperas, manoperas, caplim, ubi ei injungitur; faculas vii de sinapi sestarium i, pullos iiii, ova xv.

THE SERFS

Alaric, a *colonus*, holds one servile manse, consisting of 3 *bunuaria* (10 acres ?) of arable land, 2 *aripennos* ($\frac{2}{5}$ acre ?) of vine, and $\frac{1}{2}$ *aripennus* ($\frac{1}{10}$ acre) of meadow. In return for [rights of] pasture he pays 3 *modios* ($191\frac{1}{4}$ litres ?) of wine; he does 4 *aripennos* ($\frac{4}{5}$ acre) of vine [land], he ploughs 2 'perches' of land (825 sq. yds.) for winter corn, and owes *corvées*, cartage-work, manual work and tree-felling when ordered; and 7 torches, 1 sester ($3\frac{1}{4}$ litres ?) of mustard, 4 hens and 15 eggs.

The above entry is typical of all those for the 7 servile mansi (*mansi serviles*) which include 24 *bunuaria* (about $81\frac{3}{5}$ acres ?) of arable land.

After this there follow a list of 20 people who apparently held no manses from the abbey but who paid a poll tax (*capaticum, chevage*) of fourpence each, and a further list of 28 *votivi homines* who had given themselves and their land to the abbey on condi-

tion of enjoying the usufruct of the land and the protection of
the abbey. Finally, the following summary is given :

35. Sunt mansi ingenuiles xxiii
et dimidium, serviles vii. Exit
inde in hostilicio ad unum annum
de argento libras iiii et solidos x ;
ad alium annum, propter carna-
ticum, libras ii et solidos v ;
de vino in pascione modios lxvi
pullos cxviii cum ova. De capa-
tico solidos vi et denarios iiii.

There are 23½ free manses, and
7 servile estates. Outgoings are
in army-tax every other year 4
silver pounds and 10 shillings,
and in the alternate years 2
pounds and 5 shillings in lieu of
provisions [for the army] ; 66
modios (4207½ litres ?) of wine for
[rights of] pasture ; 118 hens
with . . . eggs. From the poll
tax 6 shillings and fourpence.

In the above passages several problems call for comment.
The most important is the meaning of the word *mansus*. It has
been translated as ' manse ' although that word has acquired a
specialized meaning in Scotland as the house of a clergyman. In
the ninth century it did include, amongst other things, a house ;
but just as a farm is a group of buildings with the fields that
belong to them, so the manse was a house and the agricultural
holding that went with it. The holding was not necessarily a
compact block of land. Indeed, it was far more likely to consist
of a number of strips scattered about the open fields, but it was
none the less a unit. Its size might vary, and sometimes it
varied very considerably, but in theory it was what was sufficient
and necessary for the support of one household. A lord, since
he had a big household, would have a big and lordly manse
(*mansus dominicatus*), but the manses of the peasants would be
very much smaller. Their size varied from vill to vill and within
each vill, but, taking the statistics of the polyptych as a whole,
the average for free manses (*mansi ingenuiles*) was 26¾ acres, and
for servile manses 18¼ acres. Elsewhere in the Carolingian
Empire a more common size for the manse was between 30 and
35 acres.

What is absolutely clear is that the manse was not a measure
of land but an institution. For one thing it was indivisible.
In one of the excerpts which have been quoted, there was a
manse shared by four households. But though it was shared,
it was not divided. It was inscribed as one manse, and the rents

and services were due not from this partner or that but from the land. This was an important point for the landlord, for if he had allowed the division of the manse into four or more portions, the business of collecting rents and enforcing services would have been enormously complicated. As it was, it was simplicity itself. Each manse had to provide one man for the *corvées*, and the lord did not mind which man it was ; that was a problem for the partners or *socii* to decide amongst themselves.

Some manses, in fact the great majority, were called free (*ingenuiles*), and some were called servile (*serviles*) ; at one of the abbey's estates there was even a third class of *mansi lidiles* or freedmen's manses.[1] But it is clear that by the ninth century such distinctions of title had become more or less antiquarian ; for men who were apparently slaves (*servi*) held free manses, while others who were apparently free cultivators (*coloni*) held servile manses. How could a freeman remain free if he held a servile manse and owed the dues which had once been expected of a slave ? And how could a manse be described as free (*ingenuilis*) when its dues were similar in kind to those of the servile manses, including ploughing-service and ' *corvées*, cartage-work, manual-work, and tree-felling when ordered ' ?

The truth of the matter is that in the ninth century agrarian society was in a state of transition. The institutions of serfdom had not yet been fully developed, and those of the ancient world had not yet been completely discarded. There were still servile manses which had once been held by real slaves and free manses which had once been held by free tenants, but now the distinction between them was blurred. The so-called free tenants (*coloni*) and the so-called slaves (*servi*) were both becoming more like serfs or villeins, with more rights than were consonant with slavery and fewer than were necessary for freedom.

The simplest way of seeing how this situation had developed is to consider the difficulties which faced the greater landowners of the third, fourth and fifth centuries, when there was an acute shortage of labour (*cf.* p. 28). It made little difference to the landlords whether they cultivated their lands with gangs of slaves or whether they let out their lands to free tenants, for in

---

[1] The polyptych records 1,430 *mansi ingenuiles*, 191 *mansi serviles*, and 25 *mansi-lidiles*, the last-named being all at Boisy-Maugis (Orne).

either case the problem with which they were faced was a shortage of man-power.   Slave owners had always to be buying new slaves as ' replacements ' (for though the children of slaves belonged as of right to the master, the birthrate among slaves has always been notoriously low), and slaves, though they were bought and sold at least as late as the tenth century, were becoming increasingly rare and costly, both because of the general decline in population and because the Church forbade the enslavement of Christians. It was therefore important to make the most economical use of those slaves already in one's possession, and it was found that the best thing to do was to turn them into servile tenants.   Instead of having to work in a gang each slave would be given his own hut (*casa*) and his own land, which he would till for his own profit in return for certain rents and labour services.   He would be called a ' hutted slave ' or *servus casatus*, and his holding would be a servile manse.   He would still belong to his master and could be bought or sold or given away with the land.   But having a tenément of his own he would work with a will, and having a hut of his own he might live a normal family life.

It might be thought that those Roman landowners who let out their land to peasant cultivators (*coloni*) would have nothing to fear from a labour shortage, but this was not the case.   For the landlords were responsible for paying the taxes due from their land, whether it was cultivated or not, and consequently it was a very serious matter for them if any of their land was untenanted.

What were they to do if, in a bad year when the crops failed, some of their tenants deserted their land and went off to the towns to enjoy the bread and circuses ?   They urged the imperial government to circumscribe the free cultivators with regulations similar to those made for the workers in other essential trades and industries.   The ship-owners, corn-traders, oil-merchants, bakers, and pork-butchers were organized, as we have already seen (p. 28), into hereditary guilds or *collegia* which were granted the monopoly of their business and compelled to continue it from generation to generation, and it was only logical that the free cultivators or *coloni*, who were equally essential to the imperial economy, should be treated similarly.   Consequently it was decreed that every *colonus* had to remain on his tenement and cultivate it.   No one was allowed to dispossess him of it, but neither was he allowed to leave it of his own free will. If he ran away he was to be pursued and forced to return to his tenement. He and his progeny were ' tied to the soil '. He was still called a ' free cultivator ' (*colonus*) and his tenement a ' free manse ' (*mansus ingenuilis*), but he was in fact more like a medieval serf. He had certain rights, however. He could (and did) refuse to perform services that were not customary, and if he could prove that his status was really that of a ' free *colonus* ', he could make a complaint against his lord to the king. But he belonged none the less to his lord, and, as we have already seen in Abbot Irmino's polyptych, the number and names of his children were carefully recorded, because they were the lord's property.

The process which we have been describing is, of course, the growth of the manorial system. For the manor was primarily a matter of lordship ; in French it is called *seigneurie* and in German *Landherrschaft*. It concerned the ownership of the land and the status of the peasant-cultivators, but not the lay-out of the village or its fields. The land had already been cultivated for generations, and the manorial system was simply superimposed on the agricultural settlements which already existed. Because some magnate had made himself lord of a village, it was not to be expected that he would pull it down and rebuild it on some novel plan. Nor would he change the pattern of the fields, for in a primitive society, in which accurate maps and plans were unknown, the whole security of property depended upon the immutability of boundaries. If boundaries were changed, who could possibly define ' the three acres called Northgrim ' or ' the land called Blackland ' ? Such plots of land were recognizable units simply because they always had been the same and the whole village knew them. Once concede that their boundaries might be moved, and no one would feel certain about the precise extent of his lands ; there would be claims and counter-claims, and boundaries would be moved by stealth.

The different field-systems and patterns of settlement to be found in medieval Europe, therefore, have no necessary connection with the introduction of a manorial system. They are far older than that. But because they imply different degrees of communal life, even within the context of the manor, it will be useful to end this chapter with a brief account of the two main systems involved—' open-field ' and ' enclosure '.

The essential feature of the ' open-field ' system was that it could only be operated by a closely-knit village community. It was designed pre-eminently so that the fields might be tilled with a heavy plough (Latin *carruca*, French *charrue*, German *pflug*). Since none of the villagers individually could have afforded to maintain the full plough-team of eight oxen which was needed to draw it, the ploughing was done in common, each villager contributing one or two oxen to a plough-team. Therefore it was convenient that there should be no hedges separating the different holdings from each other, and that the whole village would be organized as if it were a single farm, with two or three enormous fields, in which every villager had his share. In the case of the three-field system, one field would be devoted to winter corn and one to spring corn, while the third would lie fallow. Every year the crops would rotate, the field which had lain fallow one year being sown with winter corn the next, and so on. Consequently it was necessary for every villager to have some land in each of the three fields, for if his land had been in one field only, he would have starved when that field lay fallow. If he held a manse of thirty acres, he would probably hold ten acres in each of the three great fields. But those ten acres would not form a compact block of land ; they would consist of ten one-acre strips scattered about in different parts of the field, some on the better land, some on the worse, some amongst the first to be ploughed and some amongst the last.

Districts laid out in ' open fields ' were known as ' champion ' country (French, *champagne*). They were most common in northern Europe, being general in north-eastern France, and in the plains of northern Germany, Poland, and western Russia. (In England they were normal in a belt of territory which stretched from Yorkshire in the north to Hampshire in the south, but excluding East Anglia and Kent on the one hand, and Lancashire, Cheshire, Devon, Cornwall, and Wales on the other.) There were variations of the open-field system farther south, as in southern France and in Italy, where the communal element was present though less strong, the fields having been designed for a lighter plough (*aratrum*, *araire*) which needed a smaller plough-team and consequently less communal organization. But wherever the need for communal organization was present the peasants were automatically villagers and lived in the village street or square, their houses being both dwellings and farm buildings, since they provided shelter not only for the villager's family but also for his cart, his ox, and his other livestock. Early in the morning a long procession of men and beasts would be seen emerging from the village—cattle being taken to pasture and villagers going to their work (perhaps a mile or two away) in the remoter parts of the village fields; and in the evening a similar procession would return.

In sharp contrast was the ' bosky ' land (Fr. *bocage*) or woodland, where hedges and enclosures were the rule. Here there was no village life. The peasants lived in scattered hamlets or farmsteads, each isolated farm being surrounded by its own fields, and the only attempt at any communal organization was made by the ecclesiastical parish. At church the parishioners might assemble together, and a few houses might be built round it to form a ' bourg '. But parish-life apart, the villagers had no communal responsibilities; they would owe their lord services and dues as rent for the land which they held from him, but they had no obligation to help in the ploughing of their neighbours' land. Rugged individualism was more in evidence than the community spirit.

In the British Isles ' bosky ' land was to be found in Devon, Cornwall, and Wales, in which districts, it will be observed, the place-names most often refer not to a town or ' home ', but to a church, as at St. Levan or Llanbedr (the church of Peter). On the Continent the best examples are to be found in Brittany, the Massif Centrale, the Cotentin, Perche, Gex, and Bugey. But the problem why the field-systems vary from district to district remains insoluble. It used to be thought that they were due to racial differences between the Germanic peoples and the Celts, but this theory is no longer tenable. The most popular explanations now are those which involve geographical factors. It is clear, for example, that the enclosed field system would have been impracticable either on calcareous plateaux where the sources of water are rare, or where the natural contours do not allow for a sufficient expanse of arable land. But no single explanation

that has yet been offered has been proved to be universally applicable, for both geographical and historical factors are necessarily
involved. The conformation of the land was important, but so
was the agricultural skill of its first cultivators ; it must have
made a big difference whether they knew of the heavy wheeled
plough (*carruca*), or only of the light plough (*aratrum*), or indeed
of no plough at all. Before a more confident answer can be given,
a lot of detailed work will have to be done, not only by historians
but also by geographers and archaeologists.

Further Reading

*The Cambridge Economic History of Europe : vol. i, The Agrarian Life of
the Middle Ages* (2nd ed., Cambridge, 1962), vol. ii, *Trade and
Industry in the Middle Ages* (Cambridge, 1952).

H. PIRENNE. *Mahomet and Charlemagne* (ed. F. Vercauteren) (tr. B.
Miall). London. 1939.

R. S. LOPEZ. ' Mohammed and Charlemagne : a revision '. *Speculum*,
xviii. 14–38 (1943). This also contains bibliographical references to previous criticisms of Pirenne's work.

R. S. LOPEZ and I. W. RAYMOND, *Medieval Trade in the Mediterranean
World* (Records of Civilization series). Columbia University
Press and London. 1955. Illustrative documents translated
with commentary.

AUGUSTE LONGNON (ed.), *Polyptyque... de l'Abbé Irminon.* 2 vols.
1895. This edition also reprints the prolegomena of B. Guérard
(1844), which remain the best introduction to the agricultural
economy of the period.

MARC BLOCH. *Feudal Society* (trans. L. A. Manyon). London.
1961.

MARC BLOCH. *French Rural History : an essay on its basic characteristics* (trans. Janet Sondheimer). London. 1966.

ROBERT LATOUCHE. *The Birth of the Western Economy* (trans. E. M.
Wilkinson). London. 1961.

GEORGES DUBY. *Rural Economy and Country Life in the Medieval West*
(trans. Cynthia Postan). London. 1968.

Part II

THE HIGH MIDDLE AGES

900–1250

INTRODUCTION

THE first period of the Middle Ages, from the fourth century to the ninth, was a time of despair—the ' Dark Ages '—which witnessed the disintegration of the Mediterranean world and the collapse of its political, cultural, and economic unity. But even more important than the actual destruction was the fact that people realized that they were living in an age of decline. It was what made St. Augustine and Gregory the Great think that the end of the world was at hand. It was what gave the sense of urgency to the work of Cassiodorus and Alcuin, striving to salvage the culture of the ancient world before it was too late. It was the motive-force behind the great political developments of the period.

But in the High Middle Ages (900–1250), it was no longer despair and the recognition of failure that were to the fore, but hope and the realization of success.[1] The hope was often to restore the glories of the past, but it was none the less confident. Pessimism gave way to optimism; the change was so marked that historians have tried to explain it by reference to the sudden removal of an all-pervasive fear. They claimed that everyone had been expecting the world to come to an end with the year 1000, and that the new optimism was a result of the *joie de vivre* which was experienced when the millennium was safely passed. But in fact the change to optimism had occurred a generation or two before, and was more probably caused by the cessation of the Viking, Saracen, and Hungarian raids. It was visible in every aspect of life, political, economic, religious, and cultural, and particularly in an outburst of church-building which an eleventh-century monk described as follows :

One would have thought that the world was shaking itself to cast off its old age and was clothing itself everywhere in a white robe

[1] The term ' High Middle Ages ' originated in the German, *das Hochmittelalter*, which would perhaps have been better translated as the ' exalted ' or ' sublime ' Middle Ages.

of churches. Then nearly all the churches of episcopal sees, and all the other minsters of divers saints, and even the little village-oratories, were reconstructed more beautifully than before.

The author of this passage, Ralph Glaber, was apparently referring to the years 1002–3, and was therefore guilty of the wildest exaggeration; but the statement would be valid if it were applied to the whole period from 900 to 1250. During those three-and-a-half centuries the vast majority of the cathedrals and churches of the Latin West were built in their present form, at least in so far as their main fabric was concerned.[1] For while the monuments that have survived from the Dark Ages (*c.* 400–900) consist of only a very few churches, fragments of churches, or crypts, those that have survived from the central period of the Middle Ages are innumerable. They are to be seen in almost every town and village of Western Europe, and still amaze us by their grandeur.

Even more impressive than the number of the monuments is their variety. This also is in contrast with what had gone before. Under Roman rule the general style of monumental architecture had been recognizably uniform in all the provinces of the Empire, from Britain to Africa and from Spain to Syria. In the Dark Ages something of that uniformity had been maintained, for though the architecture of the Islamic countries was beginning to follow a divergent course, the buildings of the Ostrogoths, Visigoths, Lombards, and Franks were built as imitations (though sometimes poor imitations) of the Roman or Byzantine style. But in the period from 900 to 1250 this uniformity ceased completely; the Byzantine style was gradually confined to the Eastern Empire, the various Islamic styles became more and more distinctive, and in the Latin West there was a whole medley of different styles.

This lack of uniformity, even in the West, may at first sight seem surprising, for it is often thought that Romanesque architecture was uniform, and gave way to Gothic in all the countries of Western Europe. To rid oneself of such a misconception, it

---

[1] It is of course true that additions and alterations were made to most churches during the later Middle Ages, but it was only on comparatively rare occasions that the work of the High Middle Ages was entirely swept away as at Bath Abbey, Abbeville Church, Ulm Minster, and Milan Cathedral.

is only necessary to travel across Europe, watching one type of church-tower give place to another as one passes from province to province, or sometimes even from valley to valley. In Saxony the western towers of a church rise from a *Westwerk* which looks like (and in origin was) a castle designed to protect the monks from the heathen. In the Rhineland the greater churches sometimes have as many as six cylindrical towers which look like overgrown pinnacles and give the whole building the air of some monster out of Germanic legend. In the brick towers of Lombardy, each storey has more windows than the one below. In those of Rome every storey looks identical. In France there are different types of tower for almost every region. They are not merely architectural curiosities. They stand as monuments to the intense localism of the High Middle Ages, when every man's ' country ' (*patria*) was not the kingdom, duchy, or county in which he lived, but his town or village. An echo of this sentiment may still be caught by the French peasant who refers to his village as *mon pays*, but in the Middle Ages it was all-pervading. Even the law might change from village to village ; a thirteenth-century judge pointed out that in the various counties, cities, boroughs, and townships of England he had always to ask what was the local customary law and how it was employed before he could successfully try a case. The legal uniformity of the Roman Empire had disappeared completely, and law, like the architectural style of the church-towers, varied from parish to parish.

That was why medieval civilization was so firmly rooted. It grew out of the earth, as it were. It was not until the middle of the thirteenth century that the diversities which had previously distinguished each valley or village were absorbed into a more generalized cultural pattern, and even then the civilization of Latin Christendom was by no means uniform. On the contrary, there were at least two distinct cultural traditions, one in the north and west, the other in central Europe. The first was primarily French and is typified by the great Gothic cathedrals. The finest of these—Amiens, Beauvais, Laon, Reims, Soissons, Paris, Sens, Chartres and Bourges—were already in course of construction, if not completed, by 1250, and are commonly regarded as the most typical expression of medieval civilization. It is not always recognized, however, that in this period of the High Middle

Ages, the art which they represented was confined to part of
northern France and England.[1] It was only in the later Middle
Ages that Gothic art spread to the greater part of the Latin West.
Before the middle of the thirteenth century it was still pre-
eminently French and as novel as the newly-found strength of
the French monarchy or the speculations of the philosophers
at Paris University.

In Germany and Italy there was a different culture and a different
political background. The Germans, indeed, might have been
described (from a French point of view) as ' backward '. They
were slow in developing feudalism beyond its Carolingian stage,
being in this respect at least a century behind France and
England, and they retained till the middle of the thirteenth century
the political ideal of reviving the Roman Empire in the West.
Consequently, it was not surprising that, as would-be Romans,
they long adhered to the Romanesque style of architecture in
preference to Gothic. It was only after the death of Frederick II
and the collapse of the medieval Empire (1250) that they laid
themselves open to French influences in both politics and culture,
and turned from Romanesque to Gothic architecture.

In Italy, however, the Roman tradition was so strong that it
was never completely overcome. Even in churches where the
pointed arch was used, there was, except on very rare occasions,
little or nothing of the true Gothic spirit. An occasional church,
like Milan Cathedral, might be genuinely Northern in spirit,
but normally there was a calm insistence on horizontal rather
than vertical lines, on wall-space for frescoes rather than large
windows, on coloured marble inlays rather than sculpture, and
on correct proportions rather than overwhelming height. The
tradition of the Roman basilica was never entirely forgotten.
It persisted throughout the Middle Ages, and as was only to be
expected, was especially strong in Rome itself. Compare, for
example, the nave of the basilica of St. Laurence-without-the-
walls (1216–27) with that of Amiens Cathedral (1220–36).
(Pl. III.) The one, though a church of some importance, is a
simple structure, with Ionic colonnades and a wooden roof. The
other, with its stone vault poised 138 ft. 9 in. above floor-level,

---

[1] Gothic art was in many ways the badge of the French monarchy, but it was
also popular in a slightly modified form in England, Normandy, and Anjou.

is a miracle of engineering skill. The Roman church shows conservatism and a determination to preserve the classical tradition, while the Gothic reflects the fact that in the north men did not know how to build in the classical manner, and consequently had to experiment, hoping by sheer boldness and grandeur to atone for their lack of *Romanitas*.

Italy and France, indeed, were the two cultural poles of the Latin West. In the one, culture was formal, since it was based on the classical tradition which constituted, as it were, a body of rules for what was ' done ' and what was ' not done ', so that a poem, painting, or even a way of life was considered good only if it was ' correct '. In the other, formal rules were subordinated to the excitement of bold experiment and the spirit of inquiry ; the aim was not to conform to the standards of the ancients but to surpass them. It was therefore typical that while Bologna, the foremost Italian university, specialized in Roman law, Paris specialized in philosophy and theology ; and that while the Church was governed and organized from Rome, the enthusiasm which created the great monastic movements of the eleventh and twelfth centuries came from France.

The distinction between Italy and Germany on the one hand, and France and England on the other, was fundamental for the whole period from 900 to 1250. It was not merely cultural in the narrow sense of the word, but was political also. Italy and Germany were the home of the Papacy and Empire, France and England of feudal monarchies and (ultimately) of nation-states. Papacy and Empire were the two aspects of a universal society which was held to have been founded by God and which had been consecrated by the tradition of St. Peter and Gregory the Great, or of Constantine and Charlemagne. It might, in the same sense as classical art, have been described as ' correct ', since it was based on absolute principles. But in France and England the conception of this universal society, though not denied, was pushed into the background since, correct though it might be, it hindered the development of feudal monarchy. Feudal monarchy was supported, not because it was in conformity with any theoretical right-ordering of Christian society, but because it worked. Like Gothic architecture, it was a triumph not of abstract reasoning but of empirical skill.

The essential difference between the two political systems can best be seen if we turn to the beginning of the tenth century and examine the chaos out of which they arose. By then the Vikings, Hungarians, and Saracens had almost completely disrupted the political organization of Europe. Though from time to time there was an emperor he had no empire, and though there were a number of kings it was never certain what they were kings of. All political divisions were in a state of flux. There were kingdoms ' in ' Burgundy and Provence, and kingdoms ' of ' the Lombards, Italians, Lotharingians, Franks (both eastern and western), and Teutons. But these were not institutions so much as titles, and even as titles they were not indispensable. In their formal documents, the kings of this period did not usually trouble to name or describe their kingdoms, but simply styled themselves by a formula such as *divina clementia favente rex*. What was important to them was that God and the Church had given them authority to be kings, or licence to rule if they could.

When a man was made king, he was not given a complete machinery of government, but simply power to rule. He was not instituted into an office but made a special sort of person. The old idea of a state or *respublica* had vanished because the political institutions of the ancient world had ceased to have any reality. The only way in which effective power could be established was by means of the bond between vassal and lord. Consequently, the king who was to be successful in ruling his kingdom, had to inspire such confidence and loyalty that his subjects chose him voluntarily as their lord. He had to build up his power by his own exertions.

There were two ways in which this might be done. The first was that of the Capetian kings of France and was exceedingly cautious. It consisted of the consolidation of the royal demesne, or king's private estate—in this case a narrow belt of territory which stretched, approximately, from Paris to Orleans. The earlier Capetians devoted almost all their attention to it. It was there that they wanted obedient vassals, and there that they hoped to make their power real. With some exaggeration, it might be said that they put the interest of their demesne above that of the kingdom at large. In their view it would have been useless for a king to try to make himself obeyed by mighty subjects such as the dukes of Normandy, Aquitaine, or Burgundy, unless he could first establish in the royal demesne a power that was at least as great as theirs. Consequently they endeavoured not to dissipate their strength by undertaking futile expeditions across the length and breadth of France, but to concentrate it round Paris. It was important, in the Capetian view, that before a king tried to rule he should be strong enough to enforce obedience to his command.

The disadvantage of this policy was that, though it was eventually successful, it was painfully slow and ran counter to the accepted conception of Kingship. *Rex a regendo*, said the learned : kings were kings because they ruled, and if they abandoned the attempt, they were not worthy of the name. It was not surprising therefore, that monarchs who were influenced by the classical tradition, rejected the Capetian policy as unworthy, and adopted instead, as in Italy and Germany, the policy of the ' large view '. According to this, the interests of the whole kingdom, perhaps even of Latin Christendom itself, were to be put above all considerations of mere expediency. The king or emperor was to govern in God's name, establish peace and justice, and protect the Church. If he found difficulties in his way, he was not to wash his hands of them, but to overcome them. If his subjects defied him, he had to march against them and establish his authority by force, or perish in the attempt.

It was a heroic policy, and one that called forth some of the best qualities in a ruler. For close on three-and-a-half centuries, a series of German kings and emperors attempted to fulfil it, and, though they eventually failed, the story of their attempt to build the society which they considered to be right is still worthy of consideration.

I

THE SAXON EMPIRE

THE Empire which was revived by Saxon rulers in the tenth century, was thought to be a continuation of that of Charlemagne and ancient Rome, but in fact there were several ways in which it was different. Territorially it was smaller, for though it included the greater part of Germany and Italy it did not contain any French or Spanish territory. Indeed it was predominantly German and is regarded by German historians as the first of their three empires or *Reichs* (the second being from 1871 to 1918 and the third being Hitler's, from 1933 to 1945).

None the less, though we may well find it convenient to call it German, it is important to realize that we do so only for want of a better word. For in the tenth century the Germans did not recognize themselves as such. They might conceivably have recognized that all the Germanic peoples, including the Swedes, Norwegians, Danes, and Anglo-Saxons, were akin, but till the twelfth century, they had no conception at all of what we would now describe as Germany. When Otto the Great referred to the German parts of his kingdom, he called it *Francia*, and its people were described as Saxons, Franks, Bavarians, or Swabians. For just as England had once been divided into seven kingdoms, so Germany was divided into four duchies, each of which claimed to have a tribal origin.

The distinct identity of each of these four peoples is indeed an undoubted historic fact. The Bavarians are not mentioned by that name before the sixth century, but the Saxons, Franks, and Swabians (*Alemanni*) were well known to the writers of imperial Rome. Each people had its own laws which, in spite of their general resemblance, often differed from each other on important points of detail, and each people had its own historic traditions. The Saxons, who, as we have already seen, remained heathen till the time of Charlemagne, were the least Romanized of the tribes and the fiercest warriors ; they were the hereditary enemies

of the Franks, and their emblem was the dagger (*Sachs*). The Bavarians, on the other hand, though they also had a tradition of hostility to the Franks, were the softest of the tribes, and, owing to their geographical position, the most Romanized.

The tribal or 'national' element in each of the four duchies is important since, throughout the central period of the Middle Ages, it was a potential force to which every aspiring rebel could

appeal.   At the same time, it must not be exaggerated, for at
the beginning of the tenth century the duchies were ruled not
by tribal kings but by dukes who were, in origin, generals of the
Frankish king, who might be ' foreigners ' to their duchy, and
who had not yet succeeded in making their office hereditary.
There can be little doubt that they would have liked to identify
themselves with the tribal interests and to have made themselves
' kings ' of their duchies, but as yet they had not succeeded in
doing so ; and during the tenth century they were effectively
checked in their ambitions, as we shall presently see.

There was also a fifth duchy, which was different.   This was
Lotharingia.   Unlike the other four duchies, it had no tribal
origin (at the present day we would call it half-French and half-
German) and no geographical unity.   It owed its origin, as its
name denotes, to Lothar II, the great-grandson of Charlemagne,
whose kingdom it had been.   Yet, although it had been brought
into existence by the fortune of a family-partition, it retained its
individuality throughout the central period of the Middle Ages,
and its people did not hesitate to call themselves Lotharingians.
Even today its memory is kept alive in one pitiful remnant of its
former territory, the French province of Lorraine (German
Lothringen)—a survival which forces the historian to ask whether
some of the more imposing political divisions in Europe may not
have originated in some equally fortuitous event.

Germany was a land of both tribal and artificial divisions in
911, the year in which its history is said to have begun.   The
event was marked by the death of Louis the Child, the last of the
descendants of Charlemagne through Louis the German, after
which the German tribes, instead of transferring their allegiance
to Charles the Simple, King of the West Franks (or ' French '),
elected a king of their own who was not of the Carolingian
dynasty, Conrad, Duke of Franconia.   He, as he himself is said
to have recognized, was a luckless king and was unable to defend
the tribes against their common enemies, and in consequence
the royal power did not become effective until the accession of
Henry I, the Fowler, in 918.

He was the first non-Frankish king of Germany.   He came
from Saxony, of which he was duke, and was nominated to the
kingdom by Conrad I on his death-bed.   Conrad, it seems, had

recognized that Henry was the only man capable of defeating the Hungarians, whose raids were then at their height, and he instructed his brother Everard to take the regalia of the East Frankish Kingdom (the holy lance, golden bracelets, chlamys, sword of the old kings, and crown) to Henry.[1] After this, he was designated king by the army of the Franks in the presence of 'the whole people' of the Franks and Saxons. The Archbishop of Mainz offered to anoint him as king, but Henry refused, declaring himself unworthy of the honour. This refusal is usually taken to mean that he did not intend to be controlled by the Church, but it is just as likely that it was due to the pride of a Saxon, in not wanting to submit to what was primarily a Frankish custom.

Once elected king, Henry had to establish his power, and this could only be done by enforcing his royal rights over the dukes. These rights were the relics of the Frankish system of government, but had too often been allowed to lapse during the previous twenty years. They can be summarized under three heads. First, there was military aid, for the dukes were the king's generals (Latin, *duces*) and were responsible for levying the army in their duchies and for leading it to whatever place the king might command (*cf.* pp. 140–1). Secondly, there was the nomination of counts and bishops who, since the time of the Merovingians, had been the twin pillars of local government (*cf.* pp. 117–18). Henry's insistence on his right in this matter was of the utmost importance, since the dukes had often, in recent years, succeeded in usurping this royal prerogative, hoping that if they installed their own nominees they would be able to control the entire government of their duchies. Thirdly, there was the royal demesne, or *fisc*. This was not concentrated in any single part of the kingdom but was scattered over its whole length and breadth, so that when the king went on progress he was always within reasonable distance of a royal estate from which to draw supplies for his court. In the past the dukes had often appropriated these royal estates for themselves and it was only to

---

[1] When the embassy arrived, Henry was out fowling. Hence his nickname, 'the fowler'. The list of the regalia is from Widukind's *Rerum Gestarum Saxonicarum*, i. 25, but Liudprand of Cremona (*Antapodosis*, iv. 25) says that the holy lance was not acquired till later (926) from Rudolf of Burgundy.

be expected that they would oppose any attempt to reclaim them.

Most of the dukes refused to comply with the king's demands, and consequently Henry had to fight in order to enforce his supremacy. Franconia, whose duke, Everard, had played so large a part in Henry's election as king, was the only duchy with which he had no trouble. In Swabia and Lotharingia he intervened decisively, appointing a Franconian to succeed Burchard, Duke of Swabia, who died in 926, and annexing Lotharingia from the kingdom of the West Franks. In Bavaria, however, his success was only moderate. He began a war against its duke, but found it prudent to accept a vague submission. The duke, Arnulf, swore fealty to him, but otherwise continued to enjoy virtual independence, dating his official documents by the years of his own reign, and probably appointing his own counts and bishops.

Thus civil wars occupied the first six years of Henry's reign. They were only brought to an end by the Hungarian invasions, which recommenced on a large scale in 924. The question then was whether or not Henry was capable of fulfilling his royal function by defending the kingdom. At first it seemed that he was not, for he had to devote himself entirely to the defence of his own duchy of Saxony, leaving the rest of the kingdom to fend for itself. Then, owing to the fortunate capture of a Hungarian chieftain, he was able to purchase a nine-year truce for Saxony, during which he turned his attention not to the defence of the kingdom at large but to the fortification of Saxony itself. We have already, in a different context, seen how he set about this work (p. 172). The point to be stressed now is simply that he considered his obligations as Duke of Saxony to be more important than his duty as king. When, for example, Swabia was being devastated by the Hungarians (928), he did not go to its rescue ; he was busy capturing Brandenburg so as to strengthen the defensive position on his own eastern frontier.

This purely Saxon phase of his policy, however, was only temporary. In 933, when the defences of Saxony were complete, and when he had trained an army of knights, he refused to pay further tribute to the Hungarians. As a result they launched a massive expedition against him, but he defeated it completely at the battle of the Unstrut (933). In the following year he fought the Danes and pushed them back to the River Eider. These victories established him in the eyes of the German peoples as a worthy king. His army hailed him as *pater patriae, rerum dominus imperator.*[1] His prestige was enormous, and it was said that he even contemplated a visit to Rome, where he might have revived the Empire in all its glory. But before any such ambitions could be realized, he died (936).

Some idea of the nature of the kingdom which he had established can be gained from the detailed account of his son's accession. The throne was not hereditary, though Henry had designated his eldest son, Otto I, the Great, as his successor, at any rate in his capacity of Duke of Saxony. But it was still necessary for him to be formally elected by ' the whole people ' of the Saxons and Franks as their prince, and even this election did not give him the kingdom. For that, it was necessary to have a ' universal election '. It was held, significantly enough, in Charlemagne's palace-chapel at Aachen, and consisted of a double ceremony. The first part took place in the narthex of the church, where the dukes, principal counts, and other knights lifted him on to the throne and swore fealty to him, thus making him king after their manner. The second occurred in the main body of the church (an octagon surrounded by a triforium-gallery) where the clergy were awaiting him. The Archbishop of Mainz took him by the hand, and leading him to the central space, addressed the people as follows :

> Behold, I bring before you Otto, chosen (*electum*) by God, designated by Henry, formerly lord of the kingdom (*domino rerum*), and now made king by all the princes. If this choice (*electio*) pleases you, you should signify the fact by raising your right hands.

When this had been done, the people acclaimed him, and the archbishop invested him with the regalia (the tight tunic of the Franks, the sword, baldric, chlamys, bracelet, orb, sceptre, and crown) with the words :

> Accept this sword with which you are to eject all the enemies of Christ, barbarians and bad Christians. For all power over the

---

[1] What was he ' lord emperor of ' ? There was no satisfactory word for ' Germany ' or ' the German peoples '. Hence the use of the vague word ' rerum ', which might perhaps be translated as the ' thingumabobs '.

whole empire of the Franks has been given to you by divine authority, so as to assure the peace of all Christians.[1]

Finally he anointed Otto, and installed him on the throne which
was in the gallery of the church, where Otto displayed himself
to the people.   The whole ceremony suggests a conscious revival
of the memory of Charlemagne.

Afterwards there was a banquet, at which the dukes demonstrated their subservience to the king by acting as the officials
of his household.   Gilbert, Duke of Lotharingia, in whose
duchy Aachen was situated, took general charge of the proceedings as chamberlain.   Everard, Duke of Franconia, acted as
steward (in charge of the food), Hermann, Duke of Swabia, as
cup-bearer (in charge of the drink), and Arnulf, Duke of Bavaria,
as marshal (in charge of billets and stables.)   This demonstration
of submission gave a spectacular start to the new reign.   But it
was only a demonstration.   The real test came when Otto began
to use the powers which had been conferred upon him.   For then
the dukes rebelled, and Otto had to fight a whole series of campaigns in order to subdue them.

Though he was victorious he could not afford an endless succession of such civil wars.   It was clearly necessary to devise
some permanent method of pacification, and in some way to
curb the power of the dukes.   It might be thought that the
simplest way would have been to abolish the duchies altogether,
but this would have been impossible, both because of the strength
of their historical traditions, and because they were necessary
for the defence of the kingdom.   For a glance at the map will
show that the duchies resembled frontier-commands, with
Lotharingia on the north-west, Swabia on the south-west, Bavaria
on the south-east and Saxony on the north-east.   The only
duchy which had no strong traditions and no defensive function
was Franconia, and Otto did virtually abolish it, after the revolt
of its duke in 939, by uniting it permanently to the crown.   The
other duchies were necessities and therefore had to be retained.
The problem was how to control them.

The first essential was to ensure that they were treated as royal

---

[1] The passages quoted and all the details given are from Widukind's *Rerum
Gestarum Saxonicarum, Libri Tres* (ed. Waitz, M.G.H.S.S., 1882), bk. ii, c. 1.

offices rather than as hereditary possessions. No ducal dynasties had been firmly established by the beginning of the tenth century, but it was clearly the intention of every duke to make his office hereditary, if he possibly could. Otto's first aim, therefore, was to check this tendency by deposing all existing dukes, replacing them with men of a different family, preferably his own. Thus, by 947, he had given the duchy of Bavaria to his brother, Henry the Quarrelsome, Swabia to his eldest son, Liudolf, and Lotharingia to a Franconian called Conrad the Red, whom he gave in marriage to his sister. As Saxony and Franconia were in his own hands, it followed that all the duchies were under the control of men who were bound to him not only by the bonds of loyalty but also by the bonds of kindred.

But no king could trust even his own family implicitly—not, at any rate, in the tenth century, when the revolts of brothers and sons were amongst the more common dangers to which kings were exposed. It was therefore essential to maintain a balance of power between the various duchies, so that none of the dukes should be tempted into thinking that rebellion was easy. Here the main difficulty concerned the southern duchies of Swabia and Bavaria, the only two which bordered on a country which was both weak and rich. For while the duchy of Lotharingia looked on to the kingdom of the West Franks, and the duchy of Saxony on to the Slavs, those of Bavaria and Swabia controlled the Alpine passes which looked down on to the plain of Lombardy whose cities were wealthy, and whose government was one of the most unstable in Europe. A duke who succeeded in laying his hands on so rich a province might easily upset the balance of power in Germany.

The danger was evident and came to a head in 950 when, as the result of a series of marriage alliances and unexpected deaths, the kingdom of Italy fell to the inheritance of a woman, Adelaide. In the Middle Ages, such circumstances always brought out the worst in human nature. In 949 Henry, Duke of Bavaria, anticipating the crisis, had seized the province of Aquileia; in 950 a prominent Italian, Berengar, Marquess of Ivrea, had himself elected King of the Lombards, captured Adelaide and tried to make her marry his son; and in 951 Liudolf, Duke of Swabia, crossed the Alps to rescue her. The affairs of Italy were obviously getting out of hand, and Otto decided that he had no option but to invade Italy himself, take the lady as his wife, and subject the Italian kingdom to his own rule (951). This was his first expedition to Italy and was in many ways the turning-point of his reign, for it could not but reinforce the memories and traditions of Charlemagne which had already been so much to the fore at his coronation.

In the event, however, the Italian expedition created more problems than it solved, because it caused the revolt of Otto's son, Liudolf, Duke of Swabia. He had been thwarted in his own Italian ambitions ; he feared (and rightly) that as a result of his father's second marriage, he and his line would be excluded from the succession to the kingdom ; and he was furious that while he had not been allowed to hold an inch of Italian territory, his uncle, Henry, Duke of Bavaria, had been awarded the marches of Verona, Friuli, and Istria. Consequently he plotted with all the discontented elements that he could find—Conrad the Red, Duke of Lotharingia, who was in disgrace for having made terms with the king's enemies in Italy, Arnulf, the Count Palatine, a member of the former ducal family of Bavaria, and Frederick, Archbishop of Mainz, to whom rebellion came as second nature. The revolt, as was to be expected, since it was led by the heir to the throne and the head of the German Church, was serious. Though the rebels were driven out of Lotharingia they established themselves firmly on the middle Rhine and in Swabia, and had considerable success in Bavaria. Their final submission was only brought about by the general reaction caused by a new invasion of Hungarians.

The Hungarians, as we have already seen, were the scourge of Europe. They were heathen and barbaric, and destroyed everything that lay in their path. The peoples of the German duchies were prepared to drop all their internal disputes in order to unite against them. They rallied round their king, and after a great struggle in which one of the heroes, characteristically enough, was a former rebel, Conrad the Red, they defeated the Hungarians decisively at the battle of the Lechfeld, near Augsburg (955). As a result of the victory the power of the Hungarians was crushed in Western Europe ; their raids ceased, not only in Germany but also in Italy, Burgundy, and France. Otto, who was thenceforward called ' the Great ', was hailed as the saviour of Christendom. Indeed, his victory could be compared with that of Charles Martel over the Moslems in 732. Widukind, the Saxon monk who wrote the history of his reign, enthusiastically called him ' emperor ' from that day forward, and though he may have used the word metaphorically it had its symbolical meaning, for the victory of the Lechfeld showed that Otto was worthy to be a great ruler. In subsequent years, when Otto was formally styled Emperor, the basis of his fame was still that he had saved Christendom from the Hungarians.

But though the victory gave him immense prestige, he was still left with the problem of how to govern the various parts of his kingdom without fear of revolt. It was one thing to depose Liudolf and Conrad from their duchies, but another to replace them with men who were more reliable. Personal loyalty was not enough. What was needed was the bond of a common ideal. That was why Otto made a bold experiment in the government of Lotharingia. Instead of making a conventional appointment of a new duke (as he had done in Swabia), he put the duchy in charge of his younger brother, Bruno, who was a cleric and Archbishop of Cologne. The combination of an archbishopric and a duchy did not seem in any way incongruous to him, for he did not consider that there was any essential division between ' Church ' and ' State ' ; they were merely different aspects of the same society. The magistrate, as St. Paul had put it, was ' God's servant for the infliction of vengeance upon evildoers ' (Romans xiii. 4).

> Dearest brother [wrote Otto], it is impossible to say how happy I am that we have always felt one and the same thing, and that our aims have never differed on any matter of policy. It is this that gives me the greatest consolation in the midst of my bitter trouble [*i.e.* Liudolf's revolt], when I see that through the grace of Almighty God, a royal priesthood has come to our empire. For you have both priestly religion and royal strength, so that you know how to give every man his due, which is justice, and are able to withstand the terror and deceit of your enemies, which is strength and justice.[1]

But in addition to these ideal considerations, it must be admitted that there was a further advantage to be gained from appointing

[1] Ruotger, *Vita Brunonis*, c. 20 (ed. Ott, M.G.H.S.S., 1951, p. 19).

a cleric to an important office of state, for, unlike a layman, he could not marry and therefore could not found a dynasty.   This was a matter of first importance in the tenth century, when the general tendency was for all offices, all lands, and all duties to become hereditary.   The king might wish to check the tendency, but he would normally find it very difficult to do so, since in practice he would usually be at some distance from the place in question when a duke or count died.   He would have, quite suddenly, to appoint someone who was suitably trained, knew the district, and would be accepted without trouble in it ; and in such circumstances the obvious candidate would nearly always be the son of the previous holder of the office.   The king could not afford to antagonize the dukes and counts of his kingdom by refusing them the hereditary right which they considered to be their due, and which he was endeavouring to establish for himself ; but on the other hand he could not view with equanimity the prospect that, after two or three generations, a family might consider ' its ' duchy or county to be its inalienable right.

It was therefore a double consideration, both ideal and practical, which led to what is known as the Ottonian System of government.   In broad outline this was that the king should govern his kingdom through the clergy, and that he should appoint them himself.   The details of the system were most ingenious, for what Otto did was to endow the churches of royal foundation with enormous expanses of land, and to grant them the privilege of ' immunity '.   ' Immunity ', as we have already seen (p. 117), meant exemption from the control of royal officers, such as dukes and counts, and what the king *seemed* to be giving away was the rights of his kingdom.   Royal judges were not to hear pleas in the Church's territory or summon the Church's men to the count's court.   No royal officials were to enter the land or levy toll or tribute from it.   The church in question was regarded as being free from all earthly obligations, so that its canons, monks, or nuns could contemplate the Kingdom of Heaven undisturbed.

But there was another side to the picture.   No one imagined that every abbey which had an ' immunity ' should be handed over to the forces of anarchy.   The king had not abolished government within the immune territory ; he had simply handed it over to the abbot, who was to administer it for him. Justice was still done, but in the abbot's name. Taxes were still collected, but went in the first place to the abbey. What an abbey gained by such an immunity, therefore, was not less but more worldly responsibility. That indeed was the point of the Ottonian System. For the royal rights which Otto bestowed so liberally on these abbeys were not rights which he would otherwise have exercised in person. They were the rights which would have been exercised in his name by the counts. It was their power, and not his own, that he was reducing.

According to the Ottonian System, therefore, a new basis of administration was established within the existing duchies and counties. But it must not be thought that the system was merely a cynical abuse of ecclesiastical organization. The bishops and abbots concerned believed that, in doing their duty to the kingdom, they were serving the best interests of God and His Church. They were a remarkable body of men and, besides being efficient government officials, brought about a revival of art and letters which is rightly known as ' the Ottonian Renaissance '. Bruno, the ' royal priest ', was Archbishop of Cologne, ' Archduke ' of Lotharingia, arch-chaplain and chancellor to the king, and a scholar as well. He was a collector of classical manuscripts, knew Greek, having learnt it from Greek monks at Reichenau, and was genuinely interested in monastic reform. He devoted much of his energy to the school in which he trained the future bishops of the Empire, instructing them not only in grammar, rhetoric, dialectic, arithmetic, geometry, music, and astronomy, but also in the art of fortifying cities and controlling markets. To him the study of the classics was prompted not by the otherworldly delights of an academic discipline but by the ambition to ' get on ' in the world. To the barbarians, amongst whom the Germans were still to be numbered, Rome represented civilization ; from it flowed all riches and luxury, knowledge and grandeur, order and power. The only art which they con-sidered civilized was classical, the only education Latin, and the only empire Roman. Consequently they did not consider that a learned career was incompatible with governmental responsibility. Bruno, indeed, did not even consider the profession of arms to be unbecoming in a bishop. ' We have seen him ', wrote his biographer, 'not only reading aloud, counselling and in disputation, but also in the line of battle, " providing things honest " not only before God but also before men.' [1]

The best example of the attitude which he represented is seen in the conquest and conversion of the Wends (or Slavs) who lived to the north and east of the Elbe. Every successive stage in the conquest was marked by the foundation of new bishoprics, each one situated in a fortress and dominating the country which was to be subdued and converted to Christianity. To the years 946–8 belong the foundation of Aarhus, Schleswig, Riba, Havelberg, Brandenburg, and Oldenburg, which were lavishly endowed with lands and immunities. For the war against the Slavs was regarded as a holy war. As in the case of Charlemagne's war against the Saxons, almost two centuries before, baptism was regarded as the test of submission to the king (*cf.* p. 144). 'State' and 'Church' formed a single society, and the heathen Slavs were the enemies of both. Consequently the bishops governed the conquered territory with an easy conscience, for they were serving God as well as their king ; they were both missionaries and government officials. [2]

So far as the king was concerned, however, the essential point was that the bishops and abbots in question should be his own nominees. Consequently, he only gave 'immunities' to imperial churches (*Reichskirchen*) or those to which he stood in the position of founder or founder's heir. [3] In these churches he had rights—in a later century to be disputed by the Church—which amounted to a sort of proprietary interest. For in a primitive society it was only natural that a founder should consider that, having built a church on his own land and endowed it from his own resources, it was ' his ' (*i.e.* a ' proprietary church '

---

[1] Ruotger, *op. cit.*, c. 37 (p. 39).

[2] Boso, Bishop of Merseburg (968–70), was a great missionary and translated the *Kyrie eleison* into Slavonic, so that the Slavs could sing it. ' But they, being sacrilegious, derisively changed it to *ukrivolsa* which was bad, since in our language it means " There is an alder-tree in the copse." And they said " Those were the words which Boso spoke " though he had really said something quite different.' (*Chronicon Thietmari Merseburgensis episcopi*, ed. Holtzmann, M.G.H.S.S., 1935, pp. 84 ff.)

[3] By the beginning of Otto's reign, all bishoprics counted as ' imperial churches ', the king having a founder's rights in them, no matter who their true founder had been.

or *Eigenkirche*). He and his heirs would have the duty of protecting it, and the right of nominating (or sometimes even of appointing) its bishop or abbot. In the tenth century the principle was virtually unquestioned; it was simply a matter of proprietary law.

The king, therefore, could be sure that the bishops or abbots of churches with ' immunities ' would be men of his own choice. But his rights over these churches went even further than that. In some ways he continued to treat their lands as his own. They could not be alienated or exchanged without his consent, and the Church had to pay an annual tribute for them. He demanded the right of hospitality for himself and his court, which at times might be so numerous that it consumed in a single day 1,000 swine and sheep, 2,700 gallons of wine, 2,700 gallons of beer, 1,000 measures of grain, and 8 oxen. He demanded that the bishops and abbots should lead their own contingents to the royal army. The sees of Mainz, Cologne, Strasbourg, and Augsburg apparently owed 100 knights apiece, and the abbeys of Fulda and Reichenau 60, and in one Italian expedition (that of Otto II in 981) it is known that about three-quarters of all the knights of his army came from ecclesiastical fiefs. Thus it might be said that whereas, in the eighth century, Charles Martel had despoiled the Church in order to provide himself with knights, Otto enriched the Church for the same purpose. Of the 435 charters which survive from his reign, 122 concern donations to the Church. The figures make him look generous, but the generosity was largely to himself.

There were some difficulties which could arise in the system, however, and of these the most immediate was that Otto might fall out with some of his bishops. A case in point was Frederick, Archbishop of Mainz, the Primate of Germany (937–54). At the end of his life he took a leading part in Liudolf's revolt, but even before then his opposition had been marked. It was caused partly by his personal sympathies and antipathies, and partly by his resentment at the king's interference in the affairs of his ecclesiastical province. To Otto its chief importance was that it demonstrated a danger which was inherent in his whole system of government, for though he could appoint bishops, he could not dismiss them. Consequently, just as it had been necessary to create a balance of power between the duchies, so it was necessary now to create a balance of power among his churchmen. And just as in the one case he had to interfere in the affairs of northern Italy, so in the other he had to go to Rome, for the collaboration of the Papacy was essential to the success of his system.

The reason for this will be clear if it is considered how the ecclesiastical balance of power was constructed. First there was the prevention of territorial expansion. This was particularly important in the case of the province of Mainz, which was easily the largest in Germany, stretching from the source of the Rhine almost to the mouth of the Elbe. The danger was that it would grow even larger by absorbing all the territories which the Germans were conquering from the Slavs to the east of the Elbe ; and the only way of preventing such expansion was to create a new archbishopric. In this connection, Magdeburg was the church which Otto specially favoured, but unfortunately he had not the power to create a new archbishopric and a new ecclesiastical province. That, even in the days of *Eigenkirchen*, was beyond the reach of any layman and was controlled, in the last resort, by the Pope.

It was the same with the second method of balancing the power of the bishops, which was that of privilege and exemption. The Pope would take an abbey under his special protection and exempt it from all episcopal and archiepiscopal control. Normally these privileges, the equivalent of royal ' immunities ' in the ecclesiastical sphere, had been reserved for monasteries whose founders or abbots had deserved some signal mark of gratitude from the Papacy. (The earliest example in Germany was that of Fulda (751), which had been founded by St. Boniface, the man who had first brought the Frankish Church under papal control (p. 134).) But now Otto had hopes that he would be able to persuade the Pope to be more generous with his grants. What he wanted, and eventually got, was papal exemptions for abbeys such as Hersfeld, Quedlinburg, and Gernrode, which were to be the perfect examples of the Ottonian System. Their royal ' immunities ' would exclude the power of counts and dukes, and their papal exemptions that of bishops and archbishops. In them the abbot would preside over all things ; and over the abbot would stand the king.

For such a system the support of the Pope was essential. It

was not surprising therefore that Otto wanted to follow in the footsteps of Charlemagne, to be crowned Emperor, and receive a special position as the protector of the Papacy. As early as 951, on his first expedition to Italy, he had sent an embassy to the Pope, asking to be crowned in Rome ; and though on that occasion his request had been refused, his opportunity came later and in a manner very similar to Charlemagne's. In 959 Pope John XII, a young man who owed his elevation to the fact that his father had been leader of the Roman nobility, found himself in conflict with Berengar of Friuli, the old enemy of Otto I. His position was extremely precarious and he was forced to appeal to Otto for help. Otto answered the appeal and led his second expedition to Italy (961). He defeated the Pope's enemies and then asked for his reward. On 2 February 962, Pope John XII crowned him Emperor in St. Peter's basilica.

Ten days later a pact between Pope and Emperor was sealed in two documents. The first was a bull issued by John XII authorizing the erection of an archbishopric at Magdeburg.[1] The second was a document known as the *Ottonianum* in which the Emperor confirmed the Donations of Pepin and Charlemagne, recognized the independence of the Papal State, defined its frontiers, and formally became its protector (*defensor*). But in these latter clauses there was misunderstanding from the start. Otto was so used to the idea of giving his bishops ' immunities ', which none the less formed part of his kingdom, that he found it hard to grasp the notion of independence in the Papal State. This made itself clear as soon as he set out to capture the last castles held by Berengar, for in the course of his campaign he demanded that the inhabitants of the Papal State should take an oath not to the Pope but to himself. John XII immediately complained, but got no satisfaction : ' How can We restore this territory to the Pope [asked Otto] unless We first wrest it from the hands of violent men and bring it under Our control ?'[2] He thought, apparently, that the Pope would be pleased to hold the patrimony of St. Peter as an imperial dependency. But John

---

[1] It is an interesting comment on papal power at the time that Otto was unable to bring the archbishopric of Magdeburg into being until 968, by which time death had conveniently removed Bernard Bishop of Halberstadt and William Archbishop of Mainz, the principal opponents of the scheme.

[2] *The Works of Liudprand of Cremona*, tr. F. A. Wright (Broadway Medieval Library), London, 1930, p. 219.

XII thought otherwise. Regretting the rash invitation which he had extended to Otto, he decided to change sides, transferred his support to Berengar of Friuli, welcomed his son Adalbert in Rome, and sought help not only from the Byzsntine Empire but also from the Hungarians.

It was not surprising that Otto should have regarded such conduct as the very worst form of treason, for the Pope had not only broken the oath which he had sworn to him on the body of St. Peter, but had also invoked the aid of the enemies of Christendom. In such circumstances Otto had no doubt that the Pope should be deposed, and consequently he summoned a synod of bishops to Rome. John XII fled to Tivoli, but the charges against him were made in his absence. John's life had not been lacking in the picturesque, and he was accused, *inter alia*, of ordaining a deacon in a stable at an improper season, of turning his palace into a brothel and resort of harlots, of castrating a cardinal, of wearing armour in public, of hunting, and of invoking the aid of Jupiter and Venus while playing at dice. But it was clear that a blind eye would have been turned to these particular failings if there had not also been the more serious charge of treason. That last charge was decisive, and the synod, over which Otto himself presided, deposed John XII (4 December 963), and elected in his place a layman, the Chief Notary of the Roman Church, as Leo VIII. With him Otto renewed the pact which he had made with his predecessor, but on this occasion he inserted a clause to the effect that in future no Pope was to be consecrated until he had taken an oath of loyalty to the Emperor. The Papacy itself was thus brought into line with the general principles of the Ottonian System. The Pope was to be at once the nominee and the lieutenant of the Emperor ; and the Emperor was to be the ruler of Christendom.

It was a reversion, once again, to the ideal of Charlemagne, but the revolution was not accomplished without difficulty. For one thing, John XII was still at large, and as soon as Otto had left Rome he returned to it and summoned a counter-synod which annulled all the acts of the previous synod. The Romans rose to his support, and Leo VIII had to flee for his life. Even when John unexpectedly died (May 964), the Romans still would not accept Leo in his place, but elected a new Pope. This time they chose a man who was both virtuous and learned, Benedict V, but since the election was in defiance of the oath which they had sworn not to elect or ordain a Pope without the consent of the Emperor, Otto returned to the city to reinforce his authority. He reinstalled his own nominee on the papal throne, and witnessed the trial of his rival, who was reduced to the rank of deacon and banished to Germany. His control over the city was complete, and the opposition of its clergy and nobles broken :

Woe to thee, Rome, that thou art crushed and trodden down by so many peoples ; who hast been seized by a Saxon king, and thy folk slaughtered and thy strength brought to naught !

That lament, written by a monk in the city, found an echo in Byzantium, for the New Rome could not remain unmoved by the fate of the Old. Otto's treatment of the Romans in general and of the Papacy in particular was viewed with horror, while his assumption of the imperial title was regarded as a vulgar usurpation. It was only the Byzantine emperors who were the lawful heirs of Augustus, and they had not the slightest intention of recognizing a barbarian king such as Otto as their ' brother-ruler '. Moreover, they had the opportunity to stir up opposition against him, for they still retained the provinces of Apulia and Calabria in southern Italy. Otto therefore found it a matter of importance either to drive them out of Italy or, when his attempt to do that had failed, at least to make them recognize his imperial title. In this he was at length successful, but only in the penultimate year of his reign. The Byzantine Emperor then recognized him as an emperor, and sent an imperial princess, Theophano, to be the bride of his son, Otto II. In April 972 the marriage was celebrated in Rome. It was a fitting demonstration to the clergy and people of Rome that Otto was not to be regarded as a mere Saxon usurper. His *Romanitas* was approved by the Byzantine Emperor himself.

Otto I died in 973, and it might have been thought that his Empire would die with him, as Charlemagne's had done. In fact it survived him, and with some modifications became a permanent feature of medieval Europe. The system of government which Otto had devised was so strong that it was able to withstand the rudest of shocks. The closing years of the reign of his son, Otto II, were disastrous. In a renewed attempt to reconquer the whole of southern Italy from the Byzantines he encountered the hostility of the Moslems of Sicily and suffered a crushing defeat at their hands (982). The news of the disaster caused such a stir that it encouraged the Slavs to take up arms again. They reconquered all the lands between the Oder and the Elbe, destroyed the churches, and restored the worship of their heathen gods (983). This, for an emperor who considered that his prime duty was the defence of Christendom against the heathen, was the greatest of catastrophes, and Otto II did not long survive it. He died in the same year, leaving an only son of three years old. In the circumstances it might have been thought that since the hereditary principle had not yet been recognized this infant's claims to the crown might have been waived. But such was the reputation of the dynasty, and such the strength of the government which it had erected, that the infant was elected to succeed his father as Otto III. Even more remarkable was the fact that the regents chosen for his minority were two women, his mother and his grandmother. In medieval Europe the accession of a female was usually the signal for an outbreak of civil war, but in this case the regency of the two empresses was successful. It was a tribute to the cohesion of the Empire.

Otto III himself, during the period of his personal rule (994–1002), typified the more idealistic aspects of the Empire. He acceded to full power at the age of fourteen and died before he was twenty-two, with the result that all his actions were coloured with the romanticism of youth. In religion, his imagination was fired by ascetics such as St. Adalbert of Prague, St. Romuald of Ravenna, and St. Nilus of Calabria, and he would often abandon the work of practical government in order to practise austerities or go on pilgrimage. He appointed as Pope the most learned man in Latin Christendom, Gerbert of Aurillac, who was already his tutor and who, moved by his pupil's enthusiasm, styled himself Silvester II (999–1003). It was a significant name, because the first Silvester was the Pope who, according to legend, was supposed to have baptized the Emperor Constantine. A second Silvester implied a second Constantine, and just as Constantine had styled himself ' the equal of the apostles ', so Otto III invented titles of a religious nature for himself. In imitation of the papal title (*servus servorum dei*), he sometimes styled himself *servus apostolorum*, and in such extravagances he was apparently encouraged by Gerbert. Christ, declared the latter, had been crucified ' so that our Caesar might rule more freely '; and as an echo of this fantastic pronouncement we duly find the Emperor styling himself *Otto tercius, servus Jesu Christi, et Romanorum imperator augustus, secundum voluntatem Dei salvatoris nostrique liberatoris.*

But even in the exultation of Christian enthusiasm Otto III was insistent that his empire was Roman. His mother, it will be recalled, was the Byzantine princess Theophano, and he himself was immensely conscious of the fact that, having been born in the double-purple as it were, he was more Roman than either his father or grandfather.

> You are our Caesar, emperor of the Romans and Augustus [wrote Gerbert]. You are of the highest birth among the Greeks. You surpass the Greeks in empire, you rule the Romans by hereditary right, and you surpass them both in mind and eloquence.[1]

Otto himself asked Gerbert to rid him of his ' Saxon rusticity ' and to encourage the growth of his ' Greek subtlety '. In Rome he lived in a palace on the Aventine, robed in silk and dining alone at a semicircular table placed on a dais. His officials were called *logothetes* and *protospathars*, and occasionally their names were written in Greek characters, for Otto was determined to be learned, civilized, and no wit inferior to the cultured Byzantines. On the obverse of his seal was portrayed a female figure with shield and lance, representing Rome, and round it was the inscription RENOVATIO IMPERII ROMANORUM.

The reverse of his seal was equally significant, for it represented yet another aspect of the imperial ideal : it portrayed the head of an emperor, not that of Otto himself, but of Charlemagne. In Charlemagne indeed were fused the Frankish, Christian, and Roman concepts of the Empire, and Otto III revered his memory. The most famous of his pilgrimages was in the year 1000, when

---

[1] *Epistolae Gerberti*, ed. J. Havet (1889), p. 237.

he went to Aachen and opened up the tomb of Charlemagne. He is said, by an eye-witness, to have found Charlemagne,

> not lying down, as is the manner with the bodies of other dead men, but seated in a certain chair as though he lived. He was crowned with a golden crown, and held a sceptre in his hands, the same being covered with gloves, through which the nails had grown and pierced. . . . So we did worship to him with bended thighs and knees ; and straightway Otto the Emperor clad him with white raiment, and pared his nails, and made good all that was lacking about him.[1]

It was from the memory and legend of Charlemagne that the Ottonian Empire derived its strength. For the ' Germans ' thought it was their historic mission to fulfil the work which Charlemagne had begun. That was why the Empire lasted so long. It was not, like the passing conquests of warrior-kings, a fortuitous source of wealth and glory. It endured, in spite of the fact that both Otto III and his successor Henry II died childless, because the peoples of ' Germany ' were prepared to make sacrifices and elect successors who would continue the work of building an empire to continue the tradition of Charlemagne, Christianity, and Rome.

APPENDIX

A Bishop Reproved

(Translated from ' The Bishops of Eichstädt ' by an anonymous writer of Herrieden, *c.* 25 (M.G.H. *Scriptorum,* vii. 260.)

The most Christian Emperor Henry [II] was unable to give the bishopric of Bamberg [which he had founded], a royal endowment unless he could purchase the boundaries of its district [*parrochia*] from the dioceses around it.[2] Alone our Agonistes [Megingaudus, Bishop of Eichstädt], relying on his character and [royal] descent,

---

[1] The story is recorded in the *Chronicon Novaliciense* which was written half a century later. The chronicler claimed, however, to have it from Otto, Count of Lomello, who was an eye-witness. I have quoted, with adaptations, the translation in *C.M.H.*, iii. 213–14.

[2] Henry II had founded a bishopric at Bamberg, but as it was in central Germany it was necessary, in order to create a diocese for it, to remove territory from the surrounding bishoprics.

resisted him manfully, refusing, even to the end of his life, to acquiesce in the wicked exchange [of territory]. But happily he died, and the ingenious Emperor gave the bishopric of Eichstädt, which from its origin till then had been held by nobles and men of high birth, to a person of servile origin. Then the Caesar, hastening his project, wanted the aforesaid exchange hurried through, but this new bishop, relying on the advice of his chaplains and chief knights, resisted him constantly. The Caesar then got very angry, and is alleged to have said : ' Gunzo, what's this I hear about you ? Don't you know that I made you bishop of this place because I was not able to get my way with the previous bishop as I would have expected with a kinsman, and in order that with you, being what you are, I might achieve it without delay. Take care that I never hear any such thing of you, if you want to keep either the name of bishop or my favour.'

[Needless to say, the bishop gave way.]

Further Reading

H. A. L. FISHER. *The Medieval Empire*. 2 vols. London. 1898.

G. BARRACLOUGH. *Mediaeval Germany*. 2 vols. Oxford. 1938. The second volume contains translations of important articles by German historians.

G. BARRACLOUGH. *The Origins of Modern Germany*. Oxford. 1946.

G. TELLENBACH. *Die Entstehung des deutschen Reichs*. 3rd ed. Munich. 1943. A good introduction.

R. HOLTZMANN. *Geschichte der Sächsischen Kaiserzeit*, 900–1024. Munich. 1943. The best detailed narrative.

H. MITTEIS. *Der Staat des Hohen Mittelalters*. 3rd ed. Munich. 1943. A study in comparative constitutional history, and very suggestive.

W. ULLMANN. *The Growth of Papal Government in the Middle Ages*. London. 1955. Chapter viii is especially relevant.

KARL LEYSER. ' The battle of the Lech, 955 ; a study in tenth century warfare' in *History* 1 (1965), 1–25 ; ' Henry I and the beginning of the Saxon Empire ' in *E.H.R.* lxxxiii (1968), 1–32 ; and ' The German Aristocracy from the Ninth to the early Twelfth Century ' in *Past and Present* 41 (1968), 25–53.

II

THE REFORM OF THE PAPACY

1. Before Gregory VII

THE weakness of the Saxon Empire was that though it depended on the co-operation of both the Pope and the bishops it could not rely on their willing support. An increasing number of clergy viewed its power with alarm and thought it portended the secularization of the Church. They believed that when a man was ordained priest he was transformed and set apart from the world, and they considered it sacrilege for the successor of St. Peter to receive his orders from the Emperor. To their way of thinking, it made no difference how virtuous or devout the Emperor might be, since even if he were a saint, the objection would remain that he was a layman. They wanted a sacerdotal government for the Church, because they believed that it would enable them to build the Kingdom of God on Earth. But they also saw that such a government could not be attained until the Papacy had been reformed.

During the first half of the eleventh century, as during the greater part of the tenth, the state of the Papacy was low, since it was dominated by the Roman nobility. The Popes were supposed to be elected by the people and clergy of Rome, with the Emperor's consent; but the clergy could be terrorized and the people 'managed', while the Emperor was normally too far away to exercise an effective control. The nobles of the Roman Campagna therefore had everything their own way. They had castles in the city and could exercise continuous pressure to ensure that members of their family were given all the most lucrative positions in the Roman Church. One outstandingly successful family was the house of Tusculum, which produced

Benedict VIII (1012–24), John XIX (1024–32), and Benedict IX (1032–46); but a rival family was that of the Crescentii who in 1045 started a rebellion and set up a rival pope in the person of Silvester III. Silvester was not able to maintain himself in Rome for more than fifty days, but even when he had fled he continued to call himself Pope, so that there was a division in the Papacy. Worse still was to come, however, when Benedict IX resigned 'his' Papacy in favour of his godfather, and then changed his mind and tried to reclaim it; for then there were three popes. Benedict's godfather, Gregory VI, was undoubtedly the best of them, being an ardent reformer, but it was alleged that he had committed the sin of simony, having bought the Papacy by promising to pay Benedict the income derived from Peter's Pence in England, as a sort of pension.[1]

It was at this stage that the Emperor Henry III intervened. He was a deeply religious man and considered it his duty as leader of 'the Christian people' to put an end to the scandal in the Papacy. He marched on Rome, summoned the Synod of Sutri (1046) which deposed all three popes, and installed a worthy German in their place, as Clement II (1046–7). In this he was opposed, first by the Roman nobles (whom he subdued by force) and secondly by the 'high sacerdotalists'. Wazo, Bishop of Liège, though devoted to the interests of the Emperor, wrote to complain of the injustice which he had done since, 'according to both divine and human law the highest bishop can be judged by no one, unless by God alone'.

There was, however, a strong body of common-sense support for the Emperor, including two men who were among the foremost apostles of reform, Peter Damian and Cardinal Humbert. The former wrote a Book of Gratitude, and declared that after God it was Henry III who had 'snatched us from the jaws of the insatiable dragon'. Indeed, it was in consequence of Henry's intervention that the Papacy turned to the work of reforming both itself and the Church at large. Especially successful was the appointment of Bruno, Bishop of Toul, as Pope Leo IX (1048–54). He made it his task to extirpate the sin of simony,

---

[1] It is possible, however, that the charge against Gregory VI was trumped up by his enemies. He was a relative of Hildebrand (Gregory VII) who made no secret of his respect for him.

which was prevalent in all the provinces of the Church; and since the severest acts of discipline were necessary, he worked to establish an effective control over the Church, so that all transgressors might be punished.

In order to achieve this end it was necessary for him, not to reside in splendour at Rome, but to demonstrate his authority in other parts of Europe. He had, like a medieval monarch, to make a solemn progress round his dominions. Accordingly, in March 1049, he left Rome for the north and, passing through Florence and Pavia to Cologne, proceeded to Reims. While still Bishop of Toul he had pledged himself to be present at the consecration of the new church which had been built in honour of St. Remigius, the 'apostle of the Franks' who had baptized Clovis, and now he prepared to make the ceremony the occasion for an ecclesiastical council. Owing to the opposition of the French king, however, only twenty bishops and forty abbots attended—a fact which in itself demonstrated the weakness of papal authority. On 1 October 1049 the consecration took place. The shrine of the saint was removed from its old site, and, after a solemn procession round the town, it was taken into the new church (of which the nave still stands). But instead of placing the shrine on the new site which had been prepared for it, Leo placed it on the high altar, so that the saint might be a silent witness to the council. He then asked all the bishops and abbots to get up, one by one, and declare that they had not paid any money for their offices. The demand caused consternation. Some, including the Archbishop of Reims, asked for a day's grace. The Bishop of Langres fled, and the Archbishop of Besançon was struck dumb when he rose to defend him. 'St. Remigius lives,' cried the Pope, as he went to the high altar where the *Te Deum* was sung. For the awful presence of St. Remigius had indeed established the papal authority. Confessions of simony abounded, and were carefully examined, so that the correct degree of punishment could be meted out; the worst offenders, among whom were included all bishops who had disobeyed the summons to the council, were deposed.

By such means the Pope became the leader of Christendom and the effective head of the Church. But there was as yet no suspicion that the Papacy would endeavour to break free from the

Empire. Peter Damian, for example, regarded the relationship between Emperor and Pope as a perfect partnership.

> The heads of the world [he wrote] shall live in union of perfect charity, and shall prevent all discord among their lower members ; these institutions, the kingdom and the priesthood, which are two for men, but one for God, shall be enflamed by the divine mysteries ; the two persons, who represent them, shall be so closely united by the grace of mutual charity, that it will be possible to find the king in the Roman pontiff, and the Roman pontiff in the king.

None the less, there were powerful influences which wished to make the Papacy independent of the Empire, and they got their opportunity to act after the death of Henry III in 1056. While he had lived the opposition had not dared to move, but when he died, his son, who was elected to succeed him, was only six years old, and the regency was given to his mother, the Empress Agnes.

In the Middle Ages the rule of a woman was always taken as a sign of weakness, and when, in 1057, the last of Henry III's Popes died, the ' clergy and people ' of Rome decided that it was safe to act on their own initiative, by electing a Pope without consulting the Regent first. The man whom they chose was a noted reformer, Frederick of Lotharingia, who, in addition to his religious qualifications, happened to be the brother of Godfrey the Bearded, an arch-rebel of the Empire who, having been deposed from the duchy of Lotharingia (1049), had re-established his fortunes by marrying Beatrice of Tuscany (1054). His dominions, or more strictly speaking hers, lay across the main routes from Rome to the north, and his alliance was therefore of the utmost value to the Papacy. Indeed, it was probably decisive. When Frederick sent an embassy to the Regent to request consent to his election as Pope Stephen IX, she weakly gave way, thus waiving the imperial prerogative, established by Otto I and jealously guarded by Henry III, of nominating to the Papacy. It was a dangerous precedent, and its effect was simply to encourage the reformers, as was to become apparent in the next pontificate, that of Nicholas II (1058–61).

The first development for which Nicholas was responsible was the election decree of 1059. This declared that, in future, Popes were to be elected not by the ' clergy and people of Rome ' but by the cardinal bishops. The expressed intention was to prevent the interference of the Roman nobles who were so adept at ' managing ' mobs, but the unexpressed intention was to prevent any imperial control. There was no mention of nomination by, or consultation with, the Emperor—nothing but a vague phrase ' saving his rightful honour and reverence ', which was correctly interpreted at the imperial court as signifying nothing. When Nicholas II sent a cardinal north of the Alps with the decree, the Regent refused to accept it, and summoned a council of German bishops to quash it.

Since the election decree was accepted as an act of open hostility, Nicholas II found himself in urgent need of allies who would, if necessary, defend him from the Emperor. He therefore initiated a papal ' foreign policy ', which eventually became one of the permanent features of medieval Europe. He came to an understanding with the French king, Philip I, who for all his shortcomings was the most obvious counterpoise to imperial power in the north ; he clung to the alliance with Godfrey the Bearded of Tuscany ; and most important of all, he made an alliance with the Normans of southern Italy.

This last alliance requires some explanation, for the history of southern Italy was particularly involved in the Middle Ages. It was a country where a little of everything had survived, every age and every barbarian invasion having left its mark on the political framework. There were provinces of the Byzantine Empire, Lombard duchies, a Moslem state (in Sicily), a claim to overlordship by the western Emperor (which was generally resisted), and lastly the Normans. They had been invited to the country in 1016 by one of the Lombard rulers, who met some of them as pilgrims at Monte Gargano and asked them to enter his service as mercenaries. They had accepted with alacrity, and rapidly proved themselves to be expert pillagers and dangerous servants. They turned on their employers, played them off against each other, and began to conquer the country for themselves. By 1030 they had created a principality of their own at Aversa, by 1046 they had conquered the greater part of Apulia and Calabria, and in 1053 they had the honour of defeating a papal army and capturing Leo IX himself.

But now Nicholas II intended to make these terrible warriors

and former scourges of Christendom the allies of the Apostolic
See. On 23 August 1059 he met their leader, Robert Guiscard,
at Melfi, and accepted him as his vassal. Robert pledged his
oath that if the Pope died before him he would assist the cardinals
of the Roman Church, so that they could elect a new Pope
according to the election decree. He was, in short, to defend them
from any interference by the Roman nobility or Emperor, and in
return the Pope bestowed upon him the title of Duke, with
possession of Calabria and Apulia. The act was an open defiance
of the Emperor, who claimed all Italy as his own, and considered
that the Pope had no right to dispose of lands which were not his
own, and no authority to confer a ducal title on anyone. Was he
not merely usurping the imperial prerogative in order to purchase an ally to help him fight the Emperor?

The pontificate of Nicholas II, therefore, marked the open
rupture between Empire and Papacy. Though hostilities were
not to break out for another sixteen years, it was clear beyond
all doubt that there was no longer the 'bond of perfect charity'
between the 'two heads of the world'. The basic question at
issue was the Emperor's rights in papal elections, and during the
pontificate of Nicholas II's successor, Alexander II (1061–73),
both sides were jockeying for position. Alexander was elected
by the cardinals, under Norman protection, but had to face the
opposition of an imperial anti-pope, Cadalus, Bishop of Parma,
until he consented to appear before a council of bishops at Mantua,
which (under the presidency of the new imperial Regent, Anno,
Archbishop of Cologne) finally recognized him as lawful Pope
(1064). The decision might be regarded as a victory either
for the reformers, whose candidate had been accepted, or for the
imperialists, to whom the Pope had submitted his case. But the
issue was in no way decided, and the real testing-time was to
come with the elevation to the Papacy of the archdeacon Hildebrand, as Gregory VII (1073–85).

2. GREGORY VII AND THE BREAK WITH THE EMPIRE

Hildebrand is one of the most fascinating and mysterious figures
of the Middle Ages, the centre of endless historical controversy.
It is debated whether his family was descended from a Jewish

convert called Benedict the Christian (*d.* 1051), whether he was
the 'grey eminence' behind Leo IX, Stephen IX, Nicholas II,
and Alexander II, whether he ever really believed that the
Empire and the Papacy could live in harmony with each other,
and whether he was sincerely religious or merely in love with
power. The difficulty is not that the evidence is lacking, for
we possess more than 350 of his letters and numberless tracts
which were written in his lifetime in order to attack or to defend
him ; it lies rather in the problem of deciding what to believe,
and what to discredit as empty propaganda.

Hildebrand was elected Pope on 22 April 1073, in circumstances
which were surprising for a reformer. The election was made,
not by the cardinal bishops in accordance with the election decree
of 1059, but by an apparently spontaneous gathering of the Roman
clergy and people. His own account of it was as follows :

> We doubt not that rumour has outrun our letter and informed you
> and many others of the death of our lord Pope Alexander. His
> death was a great blow to me, and all my inward parts were shaken
> to their depths. For at first the Roman populace, contrary to their
> custom, placed the control of affairs in our hands so quietly that it
> was evidently done by the special providence of God.[1] Wherefore,
> having taken advice, we came to this decision : that after a three
> days' fast and after the public funeral services and the prayers of
> many persons, accompanied by works of charity, we would declare
> by God's help what should seem best to be done about the choice
> of a Roman pontiff. But then, suddenly, while our late master
> the Pope was being borne to his burial in the church of Our
> Saviour,[2] a great tumult and shouting of the people arose and they
> rushed upon me like madmen, leaving me neither time nor oppor-
> tunity to speak or to take counsel, and dragged me by force to the
> place of apostolic rule, to which I am far from being equal. So
> that I may say with the prophet : 'I am come into deep waters
> where the floods overflow me. I am weary with my crying ; my
> throat is dried.' And again : 'Fearfulness and trembling are come
> upon me, and horror hath overwhelmed me.'[3]

---

[1] Hildebrand was Archdeacon of Rome and therefore responsible for the burial
of Alexander II and the election of a new Pope.

[2] The original dedication of St. John-in-the-Lateran.

[3] Letter to Wibert of Ravenna, tr. E. Emerton, *The Correspondence of Pope
Gregory VII*, Columbia. 1932, p. 3.

The personality of the man who had thus been elected Pope made such an impact on the Latin West that eventually the whole movement of church-reform was attributed to his energy and vision. We read of the ' Hildebrandine ' or ' Gregorian ' reform, or quite simply of ' Hildebrandinism '. In fact, however, his own contribution to the movement was not a set of revolutionary ideas, but simply an unflinching determination to carry out the reforms which had already been advocated. Before he had been Pope three months, he was writing to the people of Lombardy in the following terms :

> I desire you to know, beloved brethren, as many of you do not know already, that we are so placed that, whether we will or no, we are bound to proclaim truth and righteousness [*justitiam*] to all peoples, especially to Christians, according to the word of the Lord : ' Cry aloud ; spare not, lift up thy voice like a trumpet and declare unto my people their transgressions ! ' And elsewhere : ' If thou shalt not declare his wickedness unto the wicked, I will require his soul at thy hand.' Also saith the prophet : ' Cursed be he that keepeth back his sword from blood ! ', that is he that keepeth back the word of preaching from reproving the carnally minded.[1]

What were the transgressions which he was so loudly to proclaim ? First, there was the sin of ' nicholaism ', or clerical marriage. The rule of clerical celibacy was not new, having been accepted by the Roman (though not by the Greek) Church as early as the fourth century, but in spite of the spasmodic effort of reformers, such as St. Benedict of Aniane in the ninth century, it had not been vigorously enforced. In Italy in particular, the custom of marriage among the lower clergy was prevalent, and in the province of Milan it was justified by an appeal to the authority of St. Ambrose. There was, indeed, no scriptural authority for clerical celibacy (the marriage of priests being explicitly recognized in the Old Testament), but the reformers based their argument on the doctrine that no man could serve two masters. He who was bound to the world by permanent ties would become enslaved to the world.

The argument was not only theoretical. It was strongly supported by experience. The great danger, in the eleventh

[1] Tr. Emerton, *op. cit.*, p. 11.

century, was that the offices of the Church would become hereditary in the same way as lay offices. For though the wives of the clergy were known as concubines, and though their offspring were technically illegitimate, it was not uncommon in the eleventh century to find sons succeeding their fathers, not only in parishes but also in higher preferments, though in the case of bishops it was considered more polite to refer to the sons as ' nephews '. Even when the sons of the clergy did not themselves proceed to a career in the Church, there were difficulties to be encountered ; for their loving fathers might be tempted to alienate ecclesiastical endowments to them, thus robbing the Church of its property because of their enslavement to the world.

The second evil which the reformers attacked was simony, which often went hand in hand with nicholaism. Simony, as we have already seen, was the purchase of an ecclesiastical office, whether with money or any other worldly favour. It did not matter whether the purchase was effected by oneself, one's father, one's uncle, or the king. For the principle at stake was that there should be no trafficking in spiritual gifts. Simony could only enslave the Church to the world, and would only ensure that the bishops or abbots thus elected were more outstanding for their social or political accomplishments than for their holiness. The sort of case which the reformers loved to quote was that of Megingaud, Bishop of Eichstädt, who owed his preferment to the fact that he was a relative of the Emperor Henry II (1002–24).

> In every divine service he was a lover of brevity, preferring a short mass to a short meal. Thus, there was one occasion when he was publicly singing Mass on Easter Day. He had at last got to the point at which the sequence [1] should be sung, and the precentor solemnly started it in the usual way. Angrily the bishop called to the archdeacon and ordered him to read the gospel as quickly as possible. ' These fellows ', he said, ' are mad, and by singing for such a dreadfully long time they are making me die of hunger and thirst. Fool ! Before sequences were invented, plenty of masses were sung that were pleasing to God.' [2]

[1] A sequence is a long-drawn melody, sung on feast-days to the final syllable of the *Alleluia* which preceded the gospel.
[2] Anon. Haserensis, *De episcopis Eichstetensibus* (M.G.H. *Scriptorum*, vii. 258).

Was that proper conduct for a bishop ? Was not the abolition of a system which put such men in control of God's Church bound to be the first essential of any programme of ecclesiastical reform ? The difficulty, however, was that there were not only clerics who bought spiritual offices, but also laymen who sold them. The Emperor, for example, disposed of all the bishoprics in Germany, and of many in Italy too, and he normally bestowed them on clerics who had either paid for them or won his favour as efficient servants in the imperial administration. We have already seen how, according to the Ottonian System, the whole foundation of the Emperor's rule rested on his control over the Church. But by what authority could he, or any other layman, distribute ecclesiastical functions and dispose of the pontifical and pastoral grace ? The question was asked by one of the greatest of the Lotharingian reformers, Cardinal Humbert, whose three books against simoniacs (*Adversus simoniacos*) put the whole question of church-reform in a new light. To him it seemed that the control of the Church by laymen was at the root of all evil ; and it was symbolized by the ' lay investiture ' of ecclesiastics. ' Investiture ' was the installation of someone in an office by conferring on him its outward symbols, in the case of a bishop the ring and staff (crosier) ; and ' lay investiture ' was the term used when an ecclesiastic received these symbols not from his immediate superior in the Church but from a layman.

The question at issue was not merely formal, for it was natural that, in an age when the vast majority of people were illiterate, the only way of informing people as to who was the lawful holder of any particular office was to make his investiture a matter of public ceremony. A king, for example, was invested with regalia at his coronation, and the ceremony was performed by ecclesiastics, with the utmost possible splendour, so as to show that he derived his power from God (*cf.* p. 215). Dukes and counts, on the other hand, were invested by the king, since they were his officials, and he would make a point of performing the ceremony himself, so as to demonstrate that the officials in question derived their power from him and were under his authority. When, therefore, a king invested a bishop with his ring and staff, was not the same conclusion to be drawn ? And was not this unwarranted dominance of the laity the source of simony, nicholaism, and all other evils of the Church ?

To the more radical reformers it seemed that there could be no question of the fact, and their view was shared (at any rate from the end of 1074 onwards) by Pope Gregory VII. For the Emperor, however, no matter how holy he might be, acquiescence in such a view was quite impossible.   Since his government was constructed on the Ottonian System he could not lose control of the Church without losing control of his Empire too.   He was bound to resist the pretensions of the reformers on this matter, and there was little doubt that in such circumstances many of the bishops whom he himself had appointed would remain loyal to him.   The reformers, therefore, if they persisted in forbidding lay investiture, were likely to cause a schism in the Church unless they could establish an authority which even the imperial bishops would recognize as superior to that of the Emperor.

It was for this reason that the question of papal supremacy was fundamental.   The reformers were always looking back to the precedents of the early Church, to see how it had been organized before it had been contaminated by the vice of lay control.   They read histories, the works of the Fathers, and all the documents that they could find—decrees of Councils, letters of Popes, and so on—and were greatly impressed by the leadership which the Papacy had once given to Christendom as a whole.   Looking back, beyond the period of discreditable episodes such as the dominance of the house of Tusculum, it seemed that the Apostolic See had once supervised the various provinces of the Church in a manner which had subsequently been forgotten.   There was Gregory the Great, for example, who had defended Rome from the Lombards, supervised the bishops of Italy, converted the English, reproved the Patriarch of Constantinople, and declared that ' every bishop was subject to the Apostolic See when a fault had been committed '.   Why was it that the powers which he had wielded had fallen out of use ?

So far as the reformers were concerned, it was axiomatic that the reason lay in the fact that the Church had become corrupted by its contact with the world and had forgotten its ancient discipline, Canon Law. Canon Law consisted of a whole series of regulations for ecclesiastical discipline, concerning the collection of tithes, the distribution of alms, the correction of im-moral clergy, the election of bishops, and so on, but a good deal of work was required before it could be made intelligible. It consisted of a mass of ill-organized material, consisting of excerpts from the Bible, writings of the Fathers, papal letters, approved penitentials, the canons of the councils of the Church, and Roman Law. Before the eleventh century anyone who wanted to ascertain the Canon Law on any given subject, such as the rights of a lay patron or the procedure to be followed when a diocesan bishop was in dispute with his metropolitan, had to search through all this material himself. The labour involved was immense, and so the reformers set to work producing ' col-lections ' or handbooks of Canon Law which would arrange the relevant material according to subject matter. One of the earliest examples, the *Decretum* of Burchard (*c.* 1000), was com-posed in Germany, but in the second half of the eleventh century three more collections were made in Rome (those of ' The Seventy-four Titles ', *c.* 1050, of Anselm of Lucca, *c.* 1083, and of Cardinal Deusdedit, *c.* 1083–7), and they were notable for the emphasis they placed on the rights of the Papacy. The spirit in which they were compiled is illustrated by Peter Damian's remark that Hildebrand had often asked him, when reading the decretals or histories of the Roman pontiffs, to make a note of anything that concerned the authority of the Apostolic See, since it was his ambition to have all the relevant information collected into one small volume, so that the potentiality of papal power could be readily explored.

When he became Pope he made use of the information he had acquired in two main ways. First he used it to centralize the government of the Church and to supervise the discipline of all its provinces. He insisted on the old rule, which derived, as we have already seen, from Gregory the Great (p. 86), that all metro-politans should receive their *pallium*, the sign of their authority, from the Pope himself; and he made them take an oath of obedi-ence to the Apostolic See, which established his right of inter-vening in the disciplinary affairs of their province. From time to time he sent papal legates to almost all the provinces of the Church and accorded them the fullest powers, so that they could even depose diocesan and metropolitan bishops; ' he that receiveth you, receiveth me ; and he that rejecteth you, rejecteth me,' he said.   If an archbishop objected that the Pope was trespassing on his metropolitan rights, he was speedily told that the rights claimed by the Pope were no novelty, even though, ' through the negligence of our predecessors ', they might not have been exercised for a very considerable time ; and Gregory was ready to support his claims with chapter and verse.   To Siegfried, Archbishop of Mainz, he wrote :

> As it is evident that your advisers neither know nor care very much about the rights of the apostolic authority, we invite you to go over with us the canonical traditions and the decrees of the fathers, so that, recognizing the enormity of your presumption, you may perceive at once your faults of negligence and presumption.[1]

The second way in which he used Canon Law was even more drastic, to establish the place of the Papacy in regard to the secular power.   As in all things, he looked for his inspiration not in the practice of recent centuries, but in the usages of the early Church. He looked beyond the control of the Papacy by Henry III or Otto I to the part which Pope Zacharias had played in deposing the last of the Merovingians (*cf.* p. 131), to St. Ambrose who had excommunicated the Emperor Theodosius, and to Gregory the Great who had, as Hildebrand understood it, ' not merely excommunicated kings and dukes who opposed him, but declared them deprived of the royal dignity '.   When, therefore, on 3 or 4 March 1075 he dictated, in twenty-seven sentences (the *Dictatus Papae*), a list of the most important papal prerogatives, they included the following :

I   That the Roman Church was founded by God alone [*i.e.* it was more than apostolic].

XVI   That no council held without his [the Pope's] authority can be called general [a statement aimed at the Greek Church].

XXII   That the Roman Church has never erred, and never will err, as scripture testifies.

XIX   That he [the Pope] can be judged by no one [*i.e.* that the synod of Sutri was uncanonical, *cf.* p. 233].

III   That he alone can depose or reconcile bishops.

XII   That he can depose emperors.

[1] Emerton, *op. cit.*, p. 27.

Gregory VII was not the man to rest content with statements of theory. He considered it his duty to cry aloud and lift his voice ' like a trumpet '. In the winter of 1075–6, two-and-a-half years after his accession to the Papacy, his breach with the Emperor, Henry IV, was complete. In the Lenten Council held at Rome in 1075 he had issued a decree forbidding any cleric to receive the investiture of a bishopric, abbey, or other church from the hand of a layman. He had instructed the Germans not to obey those of their bishops who had failed to enforce the rule of clerical celibacy, and had asked the Dukes of Swabia and Carinthia to prevent simoniac or married priests, ' even by force if that be necessary ', from administering the sacraments. Finally, he had been forced to extreme measures in the long-standing dispute over the archbishopric of Milan.

The origin of that dispute was that owing to the activities of a popular, and revolutionary, party known as the *pataria*, the Emperor had lost control of Milan, and with it the nomination to its archbishopric. This loss was a matter of extreme importance to him. Milan was one of the strategic centres of his power, since it controlled the central passes of the Alps, and as soon as he felt strong enough he gathered supporters in the city, expelled the papalist archbishop, and intruded a candidate of his own. Such interference in the affairs of the Church could not be tolerated by any reformer. Gregory wrote to him firmly, enjoining him to obey the Apostolic See as he would obey God, and in a verbal message threatened him with excommunication and deposition.

In these circumstances Henry IV decided to act first. He summoned an assembly of German bishops to Worms (24 Jan. 1076) to make complaint of the Pope's conduct. They did not attempt to argue what the proper relationship between Empire and Papacy should be, nor to attack the institution of the Papacy as such. Their complaint was simply against that ' false monk ' Hildebrand, who had forsaken his cloister, made himself Pope, assumed unheard-of powers over the episcopate, and destroyed the peace of the Church. Each of the twenty-four bishops and two archbishops present signed a declaration which ran as follows :

I, N . . . bishop of N . . . , give notice to Hildebrand, that from this moment I refuse submission and obedience to him, that I will no longer recognize him as Pope, and will no longer give him that title.

These declarations were sent to Rome with a covering letter from the Emperor. The messenger appeared before the Pope at the first session of his Lenten Synod, at which 100 bishops were present, and before the whole assembly ordered Gregory to rise from his place and to abdicate the Papacy, which he had un-canonically usurped. There was an immediate tumult, and the messenger's life was saved only by the intervention of Gregory himself. Two days later, Gregory excommunicated the Emperor, and deposed him :

> Blessed Peter, prince of the apostles, mercifully incline thine ear, we pray, and hear me, thy servant, whom thou hast cherished from infancy and hast delivered until now from the hand of the wicked who have hated and still hate me for my loyalty to thee. . . . Therefore by thy favour, not by any works of mine, I believe that it is and has been thy will, that the Christian people (*populus christianus*) especially committed to thee should render obedience to me, thy especially constituted representative. To me is given by thy grace the power of binding and loosing in Heaven and upon earth.
>
> Wherefore, relying upon this commission, and for the honour and defence of thy Church, in the name of Almighty God, Father, Son and Holy Spirit, through thy power and authority, I deprive King Henry, son of the Emperor Henry, who has rebelled against thy Church with unheard-of audacity, of the government of the whole kingdom of Germany and Italy, and I release all Christian men from the allegiance which they have sworn or may swear to him, and I forbid anyone to serve him as king. . . . And since he has refused to obey as a Christian should, or to return to God whom he has abandoned by taking part with excommunicated persons, has spurned my warnings which I gave him for his soul's welfare (as thou knowest), and has separated himself from thy Church and tried to rend it asunder, I bind him in the bonds of anathema in thy stead. I bind him thus as commissioned by thee, that the nations may know and be convinced that thou art Peter and that upon thy rock the Son of the living God has built his Church, and the gates of hell shall not prevail against it.[1]

This sentence of excommunication and deposition caused consternation on all sides, for everyone within the imperial frontiers

---

[1] Emerton, *op. cit.*, pp. 90–1, with minor alterations.

had to decide which of the two 'heads of the world' to obey. To follow the Pope was to break one's oath of allegiance to the king or emperor; to follow the king involved oneself in excommunication.[1] It was not surprising, therefore, that a large number of controversial pamphlets were written, in order to justify the positions adopted by both sides. What may surprise the modern reader is that the imperialists did not attempt to erect a theory of the supremacy of the 'State' against the 'Church'. The reason for this was that, in the eleventh century, the Church was regarded as being far more than the spiritual power. It denoted the body of Christ, or whole community of Christendom, of which the Papacy and Empire were but the two executive arms. Consequently, the quarrel between Gregory VII and Henry IV was considered not as a struggle between two independent institutions but as a schism in the Church, and the aim of the pamphleteers was merely to demonstrate that this schism had been caused by the opposing party. Thus, one of the most effective attacks on Gregory VII bore the title *De Unitate Ecclesiae Conservanda* ('On preserving the unity of the Church').

The claim of the imperialists, indeed, was that Hildebrand was not a rightful Pope, but a usurper and a trouble-maker; and setting the invective and abuse aside, the essence of their case was that Hildebrand had proved himself to be a wrongful Pope by attempting to make so many innovations. His insistence on clerical celibacy, his interference in the internal affairs of the various provinces of the Church, and his condemnation of lay investiture, could only be regarded as revolutionary, since they were contrary to established tradition, and had the undoubted effect of disrupting the peace and harmony of the Church.

Gregory VII and his supporters, on the other hand, claimed that the question at issue was not one of peace but of righteousness (*justitiam*), the relevant text being, 'Cursed be he that keepeth back his sword from blood.' At the same time, however, he maintained that he had excommunicated Henry IV only because that king had publicly, and in spite of the most solemn warnings,

---

[1] In 1076 Henry IV had been crowned king, but not emperor. He did not assume the title of emperor till 1084, when he was crowned by his own anti-pope, but the papalists continued to refer to him only as 'king'.

consorted with excommunicated heretics (simoniacs) and had 'dared to divide the body of Christ, that is the unity of the Church', by inciting the German bishops to renounce their allegiance to the Pope. He himself, he insisted, had introduced no novelties or inventions. On the contrary, having found that the ordering of the Christian religion had fallen to a very low state, he had simply renounced the wicked practices which had grown up during the last few centuries, and had returned to the 'teaching of the holy fathers' and the 'well-trodden way of the saints'. He claimed, in short, that by reverting to the practices of primitive Christianity he was adhering to the true tradition of the Church, while the imperialists insisted that any attempt to 'put the clock back' by about five centuries was nothing short of a revolution.

3. WAR

As usually happens in bitter controversies, the original question at issue was soon obscured by extraneous factors. Thus in Germany there were already in existence two groups of potential rebels. The first consisted of magnates, led by Rudolf, Duke of Swabia, and Otto of Nordheim (sometime Duke of Bavaria), who had made use of the king's minority in order to further their private interests. They resented the fact that since the king had come of age they had lost the influence which they had previously wielded at court; and they were alarmed by the forceful manner in which he was determined to re-assert every royal right that had been exercised by his father. To them, therefore, the papal excommunication came as a heaven-sent justification for a revolt which they had already been meditating.

More serious, however, was the second group of rebels, the Saxons, for their rebellion was aimed at the very foundations of royal power. Since the second quarter of the eleventh century, the emperors, realizing the potential weaknesses of the Ottonian System, had begun to construct an alternative basis of power by attempting to create a powerful royal demesne. Instead of continuing the policy of making lavish grants of land to the Church, Conrad II (1024–39) and Henry III (1039–56) had done all they could to increase the extent of the crown lands, and the duchy in which they had had the greatest success was Saxony. The reason for this was that in Saxony the great majority of the peasants were free, that is to say, they had no lord but the king. They had not yet been appropriated to any manorial system, but simply owed certain royal dues and services, such as payments for forest- and water-rights. These dues, however, if ruthlessly exploited, could easily be converted into manorial customs, and Henry IV continued the policy of his predecessors in this direction with the utmost vigour. He despatched commissioners to discover, by means of sworn inquests, what were, or ever had been, the royal rights in every particular place. He built castles and garrisoned them with Swabians so as to enforce the payment of all the dues in full, and in general treated the land as if it was his own, and the peasants as if they were already his serfs. It was at this point that the nobles intervened. Otto of Nordheim, in particular, was quick to realize how easy it would be to exploit the Saxons' very real grievances and raise the whole duchy in revolt. He had already done so once, in 1073, before Henry's excommunication, and his manifesto to the rebels had then, according to a sympathetic chronicler, run somewhat as follows :

> The injuries and insults which our king has now for a long time done to you severally are great and intolerable. But those which he now proposes to do (if Almighty God permits him) are much greater and more serious. He has built, as you know, strong castles in places which are naturally strong, and there he has collected no small multitude of his henchmen (*fideles*), equipped with arms of all sorts. These castles could not possibly have been built as a defence against the heathen [Slavs], who have in the past devastated our whole country which is adjacent to theirs ; for it is in the very middle of our land (where no heathen have ever tried to carry on war) that they have been built with such vigour. What they portend—and there are already many of you who know it from experience—you are all about to experience shortly, unless God's mercy and your valour prevent it. Your goods and those who live with you will be carried off into those castles against your will ; they will use your daughters and wives for their desire as much as they want. They will take command of your serfs and your beasts of burden—yes and you yourselves they will force to carry all sorts of burdens on your backs, even dung. But when I contemplate what is to come, I think that what you now tolerate is

tolerable indeed. For, when he has built castles to his heart's desire, all over our land, and filled them with armed soldiers and such-like—then he will no longer snatch at your belongings piecemeal, but will grab absolutely everything you possess at one swoop. He will distribute your goods to foreigners (*hominibus advenis*), and you yourselves, the free and the native, he will make the serfs of unknown men.[1]

The situation in Saxony, in short, was highly inflammable. The first revolt (1073–5) had only been put down with the greatest of difficulty, and the Saxons needed little encouragement to take up arms again. In 1076, as soon as they heard the news of their king's excommunication, they joined in a revolt with the magnates of southern Germany, and by the autumn they had Henry at their mercy. At the Diet of Tribur (October 1076), the magnates made preparations to depose him, hesitating only because they could not decide whom to elect in his place. They therefore adopted delaying tactics and summoned Henry to appear before a Diet of the kingdom, over which the Pope was to preside, at Augsburg on 2 February 1077. They declared that, if he had not been reconciled to the Apostolic See within a year of his excommunication (*i.e.* by 15 February 1077), they would cease to treat him as king; and they did their best to make such a reconciliation impossible. They kept a close watch on the Alpine passes so as to intercept any messengers to the Pope, and guarded Henry as if he was their prisoner. Henry, however, realizing that he had no hope except in the division of his enemies, succeeded in escaping from them. Taking a circuitous route through Burgundy and along the Mediterranean coast, he made his way to Italy, determined to seek out the Pope and gain his forgiveness.

Gregory VII was already on his way to the proposed Diet of Augsburg—but for the difficulties experienced in getting an escort, he might already have been in Germany—and Henry found him in the castle of Canossa, in the Apennines (25 January 1077).

There [wrote Gregory VII] on three successive days, standing before the castle gate, laying aside all royal insignia, barefooted and in coarse attire, he [Henry] ceased not with many tears to

[1] Translated from Bruno's *Liber Saxonici Belli* (ed. Lohmann, M.G.H.S.S., 1937), pp. 28–9.

beseech the apostolic help and comfort, until all who were present or who had heard the story were so moved by pity and compassion that they pleaded his cause with tears and prayers. All marvelled at our unwonted severity, and some even cried out that we were showing, not the seriousness of apostolic authority, but rather the cruelty of a savage tyrant. At last, overcome by his persistent show of penitence and the urgency of all present, we released him from the bonds of anathema, and received him into the grace of the Holy Mother Church.[1]

Gregory was far too astute to be deceived by Henry IV's penitence. He realized only too well that Henry was simply forcing him to betray his allies. The magnates and the Saxons had risen in arms at the Pope's behest, and now he was making peace with the king without even consulting them. But what else could he do? Though his political sense might tell him on no account to relent, it was his duty as a priest to forgive the repentant sinner, not once or twice, but seventy times seven. If he had been an unscrupulous politician he would have spurned the king's advances and would thus have assured the victory of the rebels. But he did his duty as a priest, and thus made certain of his own defeat.

The reader of Gregory's letters is left in no doubt that he was bitterly aware of the dreadful predicament in which he had been placed. He continually remarks that if only the absence of the promised escort had not prevented him from crossing the Alps, the king would never have found him, and the painful decision would have been avoided. Again and again he repeats the hope that perhaps all has not been lost, so far as the rebels were concerned. He insists that he had given Henry no decision about his kingdom, and that the proposed Diet of Augsburg was still to be held. But on the crucial point of whether or not he had relieved Henry of his sentence of deposition, he could not, apparently, make up his own mind.[2] Three years later, he was to claim categorically that he had only absolved him from the excommunication and not from the sentence of deposition, but

---

[1] Emerton, *op. cit.*, pp. 111–12.

[2] That, at least, is the simplest explanation of his contradictory statements. For a different explanation, see A. Fliche, *La Réforme grégorienne et la reconquête chrétienne*. (Fliche and Martin, *Histoire de l'Eglise*, vol. 8, 1946), p. 142, n. 3.

at the time he continued to give him the title of king. Thus the very oath which Henry took at Canossa was ambiguous :

> I, Henry, King, within the term that our lord Pope Gregory shall fix, will either give satisfaction according to his decision, in regard to the discontent and discord for which the archbishops, bishops, dukes, counts and other princes of the kingdom of Germany are accusing me, or I will make an agreement according to his advice —unless some positive hindrance shall prevent him or myself— and when this is done I will be prepared to carry it out.[1]

The affair of the kingdom was still *sub judice*, but Henry was described as king. Was it a mistake, or was there some reason for the apparent contradiction ? No one can tell, for the proposed Diet of Augsburg never took place. The rebels, disgusted at their betrayal by the Pope, took action without him. They declared that Henry IV was deposed, though they no longer had him in their power, and elected Rudolf of Swabia in his place. Germany was given over to civil war, and Gregory VII, now politically isolated, attempted to preserve an attitude of neutrality, hoping that he would be invited to make peace and give judgment between the ' two kings ' so as to determine which party was ' the better qualified for the government of the kingdom '.

Eventually, in 1079, he sent two papal legates north of the Alps to hold a conference, inquire into the justice of the rival claims for the kingdom, and decide between them. Henry and Rudolf both agreed to the conference and were warned that any attempt to prevent it from being held would involve them in excommunication. None the less, an empty victory over the Saxons at Flarchheim (27 January 1080) induced Henry to change his mind. He thought, apparently, that his triumph was now assured and he hesitated to risk the fruits of his victory by trusting himself to the judgment of the Pope. He took steps to prevent the conference, and in consequence was excommunicated and deposed by Gregory VII a second time (7 March 1080).

This time the papal deposition was intended to be final and irrevocable, for Gregory immediately recognized Rudolf as rightful king in his place. With no further hope of forgiveness, therefore, Henry IV had no alternative but to depose the Pope.

---

[1] Emerton, *op. cit.*, p. 112.

He summoned an assembly of bishops to Brixen, had Gregory VII deposed, and elected Wibert, Archbishop of Ravenna, as Pope in his place. These proceedings, however, did not meet with general approval. Since the Synod of Sutri (1046), the general climate of ecclesiastical opinion had changed, and it was widely held, even among many of Henry IV's supporters, that the Pope could be judged by no one, and certainly not be deposed by an emperor. Though the Lombard bishops, fanatical as ever, did not shrink from any act against Gregory VII, the number of German bishops who obeyed the summons to Brixen was only eight, and even of these there was one who successfully avoided putting his name to the act of deposition.[1]

This failure of Henry IV to command the support of ecclesiastical opinion for his father's policy of caesaro-papism, was ultimately the most significant feature of the whole Investitures Struggle. But at the time, it probably seemed less important than the military victories of the king. On 15 October 1080 Rudolf of Swabia was killed in battle, and Henry was temporarily left without a rival in Germany. In May of the following year he crossed the Alps and advanced on Rome. At first he may have hoped that Rudolf's death would lead to a second reconciliation with Gregory VII, but finding this impossible he determined to capture the city. By March 1084 the greater part of the city was in his hands, and thirteen cardinals had deserted to his cause. On Palm Sunday (24 March) Clement III (' Our Pope ', as Henry IV described him) was solemnly enthroned in St. Peter's basilica, and on Easter Day he crowned Henry IV as Emperor.

Gregory VII was meanwhile still resisting, a few hundred yards away from the basilica, in the Castel Sant' Angelo (then known as ' the house of Cencius '). He appealed to the Normans for help, and on 27 May they entered the city, under the leadership of Robert Guiscard. Though they rescued the Pope and escorted him to safety, they added the last touch of bitterness to his defeat by pillaging the city and putting a large part of it to flames. From his refuge at Salerno it might have seemed to Gregory VII that all was lost, since even Rome had been destroyed. In the following year he died (25 May 1085) and his last words were said

[1] See Appendix, *The Eye of Prudence*.

to have been, ' I have loved justice and hated iniquity, and therefore I die in exile.'

Though Gregory died in exile, he had not been defeated.   The
fact emerged when, after a lot of hesitation and delay, a Pope was
elected to succeed him.   Desiderius, Abbot of Monte Cassino,
who took the title of Victor III, was not one of the great leaders
of the reforming party—indeed he seems to have owed his elevation to the influence of the Normans—but the very fact of his
election showed that no amount of superior force would induce
the reformers to give their allegiance to Clement III.   That
man might retain possession of Rome and be solemnly enthroned
in St. Peter's basilica, but the fact that he was the Emperor's
nominee and a rebel against the authority of Gregory VII put
him beyond the pale.

More important still was the fact that on Victor III's death the
reforming cardinals elected Odo of Châtillon to succeed him, as
Urban II (1088–99), for he was one of the three persons whom
Gregory VII himself had suggested as his successor.   He was a
Frenchman from Châtillon-sur-Marne, and after having been
Archdeacon of Reims, had become a monk at Cluny, Bishop
of Ostia (1078), and papal legate in Germany (1084–5).   He
was just the man to rally the Gregorian party in the Church
and to re-establish its fortunes.   While adhering firmly to all
the major principles at stake, he showed considerable flexibility
in the early part of his pontificate, and thus regained the support
of many bishops and cardinals who had deserted Gregory VII
in his last years.

But the real measure of his success is to be seen in the fact that
it was he who preached the First Crusade, at the Council of
Clermont (1095), and thus mobilized the greater part of Western
Europe to recover Jerusalem from the Moslems.   The details
of the campaign do not concern us here.   What is important
in the present context is that, by means of the Crusade, he became
the effective leader of Christendom in matters temporal as well
as spiritual.   For according to the view which Charlemagne
had expressed, and which had hitherto been accepted without
question, it was the Emperor's duty ' to defend the holy Church
of Christ with arms against the attack of pagans and devastation

by infidels from without '. But if the Emperor was in fact so
busy fighting the Pope that he had no time to spare for the chastise-
ment of infidels, it was necessary for the Pope to step in and perform the Emperor's function himself. He launched the appeal
for an army and assumed command of it himself, appointing a
papal legate to command it in the field. And his leadership was
accepted. That was the truly significant fact. The Frenchmen
and Normans who took the Cross (they were in the majority,
since the Germans and Lombards were preoccupied with their
civil war), never questioned the Pope's right to lead the army
of the faithful. They had apparently forgotten what had once
been the Emperor's right and duty in this respect. To them,
Henry IV was the ruler (or pretended ruler) of an empire which
consisted of Germany and Italy. They no longer regarded his
powers as in any way œcumenical. If they had been asked
who was head of the Church and leader of the Christian people,
their answer would have been emphatic, that it was the Pope.

That was the most important fact which emerged from the
Investitures Struggle. It was not a sudden development—
for Gregory VII himself had hoped to lead a Crusade in 1074,
though on that occasion he had intended to leave the Roman
Church, during his absence, to the Emperor's care—but it marked
the completion of one stage in the development of the Christian
Church. The Papacy was supreme, and the hope which Gregory
VII had expressed had at last been realized :

> Throughout the world all who own the Christian name and truly
> understand the Christian faith know and confess : that St Peter,
> chief of the Apostles, is the father of all Christians, and under Christ
> their chief pastor : and that the Holy Roman Church is the mother
> and mistress of all churches.[1]

But what had been the price paid for this supremacy ? The
difficulties which ensued from the Crusades will be seen in a
later chapter. For the present, it must be sufficient to point
out that the Investitures Struggle had proved disastrous for
the Emperor's power in Germany and Italy. This was not, as
might have been expected, because the Emperor lost the right of
lay investiture and the ability to control the greater churchmen

---

[1] Emerton, *op. cit.*, p. 195.

as his civil servants, for Henry IV and his son Henry V (1106-25) succeeded in saving their most important rights in this respect. By the Concordat of Worms (1122) Pope Calixtus II agreed that, while elections to bishoprics and abbeys in the German kingdom were to be free of simony or violence, they were to be made in the Emperor's presence and therefore under his influence; and that while the Emperor was to renounce the right to invest bishops with the ring and staff, which were the symbols of their spiritual office, he would still be entitled to invest them with the sceptre, which symbolized the regalian rights which they were to exercise in his name.

But though the Emperor thus retained some power over the imperial churches, the factor which damaged his power irreparably was that he had lost the religious authority which normally belonged to the office of a king. In France, England, or the Christian states in Spain, the king was able to overcome rebellions of his magnates and to establish the power of his royal demesne, because he could rely on the backing of the Church, which was prepared (and even anxious) to give him a mystical authority. From time to time a king might quarrel with the Church and fall under the ban of excommunication, but sooner or later he would declare himself penitent and be received once again into communion. Henry IV, alone of medieval monarchs, remained excommunicate for twenty-six years (1080-1106), being unrepentant to the end. In consequence a whole generation of people grew up in Germany and Italy in an atmosphere of civil war, doubt, and scepticism. During those years the papalists had been so busy propounding arguments to show that the royal power was not of divine origin and that there were circumstances in which it should not be obeyed, that they had succeeded in undermining its moral foundations. Just as in modern times the fundamental issues raised by the French Revolution of 1789 have continued to cause serious divisions in France to the present day, so in medieval Germany and Italy the Investitures Struggle destroyed the moral unity of the kingdom completely. It was not just that the Emperor was no longer regarded as the oecumenical ruler of ' the Christian people '. The trouble was more far-reaching than that. It was probably responsible for the fact that neither Germany nor Italy became a nation-state till the nineteenth century. For the eleventh century was one of the formative periods of European history, and the other countries of Western Europe trace their unity from it. In Germany and Italy, that century saw the origin not of unity but of long-standing feuds, and of an unresolved conflict of ideals which was to keep them in turmoil throughout the Middle Ages.

APPENDIX

The Eye of Prudence

[The following story concerns Benno, Bishop of Osnabrück, who had been given his bishopric by Henry IV as a reward for being his chief military architect. Despite his imperialist sympathies, however, he was opposed to the extreme policy of deposing Gregory VII and electing an anti-pope in his place.]

And so a multitude of bishops was assembled at Ticinum (*recte* Brixen), a city of Italy. These bishops favoured the king's side and were said to be enemies of the pope [Gregory VII] because he was said by them to be too indiscreet, (and their true wickedness is often talked about). On their counsel and at their instigation, the king was planning to raise another pope to the apostolic see. Bishop Benno also was present at that assembly although unwillingly, but he had the eye of prudence which he always carried about with him. For he saw that on both sides most things were being done out of spite rather than from reason ; and as he was always faithful to the king, but never wanted to be disobedient to the pope ; and since he did not see what sort of an ending so great a quarrel could have, [he was anxious] that, so far as he could honestly do so, he should not be guilty at law with either party. It so happened that in the church, where everything was happening, there was an altar with a hole at the back, into which he could just get, and which was covered by a cloth that hung over it—afterwards, as if to give thanks to the insensible material, he had our altar [at Osnabrück] built just like it. He was sitting close to this altar, alone and abstracted as is usual while the psalms are being sung, and going closer to it thought that it would make an excellent hiding-place ; and by degrees, while no one was looking, he tried to see if he could get into it. He got through the mouth of the hole with some difficulty, but found that inside it was a very cave sufficiently large for the reception of his little body. So he gave great thanks for the divine dispensation and carefully stretched out the cloth which hung over the opening, and spent a whole day hiding there with no one any the wiser. And the more he said his prayers the more he knew himself to be nearer to God because of the opportunity given to him by the place itself, and the more scarcely he noticed the [passage of] time, in which the state of the whole Church was shaking. At the hour at which everyone had assembled and the business was beginning it was noticed that Benno, bishop of Osnabrück, was not there. Messengers were sent by the king and rushed about everywhere looking for him—especially in the house where he had his lodging, which almost collapsed under the rush of people looking for him. But he was nowhere to be found. Some said he had run away, others that he was detained by illness, others that he had kept away from the meeting from some special lack of fidelity. But already towards evening, when they had renounced the pope and put the bishop of Ravenna in his place (who even to this day presides over the Roman church under the name of Clement) and had done lots of other things to which our bishop, if he had been present, would not have given our consent,—then Benno came out of his hiding place, and once again no one saw him. Suddenly he was noticed sitting near the altar where he was sitting earlier [in the day]. They were all astounded and amazed and were most particular in their questions as to where he had been. He promised to swear by the saints that he had not gone away all day. He was promptly taken to the king and fully purged himself of all infidelity, and the king preferred to encourage him to stand fast in his pristine faith by means of kind words instead of constraining him by fear. Hence it came about that, by astonishing good luck or forethought, he had the friendship of both popes (a thing that was possible to very few people in that time of tempest), and in nowise incurred the royal displeasure, hearing most efficaciously the words of the apostle—'If it be possible, as much as lieth in you, live peaceably with all men.'

Translated from *Vita Bennonis II Episcopi Osnabrugensis*, ed. Bresslau, M.G.H.S.S., 1902, pp. 23–5.

Further Reading

A. FLICHE. *La Réforme Grégorienne.* 3 vols. Louvain. 1924–37.
J. P. WHITNEY. *Hildebrandine Essays.* Cambridge. 1932.
H.-X. ARQUILLÈRE. *St. Grégoire VII.* Paris. 1934. Useful for political theory.

G. TELLENBACH. *Church, State and Christian Society at the time of the Investiture Contest* (tr. R. F. Bennett). Oxford. 1940.

E. EMERTON (trans.). *The Correspondence of Pope Gregory VII* (Records of Civilization series). Columbia. 1932. Selections from Gregory's *Register* translated.

JAMES WESTFALL THOMPSON. *Feudal Germany.* Chicago. 1928.

KARL HAMPE. *Deutsche Kaisergeschichte in der Zeit der Salier und Staufe.* 10th edition by F. Baethgen. Heidelberg. 1949. The standard text-book for German history in this period.

THEODOR E. MOMMSEN and KARL F. MORRISON (trans.) *Imperial Lives and Letters of the Eleventh Century* (Records of Civilization series). Columbia. 1962. Includes the *Life* of Henry IV together with his letters, several of which were intended as propaganda.

See also works by Fisher and Barraclough listed on p. 231.

III

MONASTICISM IN THE ELEVENTH AND TWELFTH CENTURIES

RELIGION in the Middle Ages was usually taken to be synonymous with monasticism. If a man was said to have been ' converted to religion ' the meaning was not that he had been baptized but that he had become a monk ; and the amazing thing is that in this sense one might almost talk of the ' conversion ' of Europe in the eleventh and twelfth centuries. Hundreds and thousands of new monasteries were founded, and there was a whole series of monastic reforms, amongst the most important being those that originated from Cluny (910), Grandmont (1076), Hirsau (1079), La Chartreuse (1084), Cîteaux (1098), Fontévrault (1101), Savigny (1105), Prémontré (1120), and Sempringham (1131).

The various reforms had their own peculiar characteristics, but none the less it is possible to generalize about them as a group. All of them except the Carthusian Order, which was more closely in harmony with the earlier semi-eremetical monasticism of Syria, Palestine, and Egypt (p. 75), drew their inspiration directly from the Rule of St. Benedict. This, as we have already seen (pp. 74-9), was designed for a closely-knit community in which the life was to be austere without being excessively harsh. On entering Religion a Benedictine monk renounced the world. He vowed to surrender all his private property, to obey the abbot in all things, and not to leave the monastery until he died. The aim of his life was to practise Christian humility by humbling himself before his superiors, by working in the fields, and by giving the glory to God. The most important of his duties was the *opus Dei* or ' work of God '—the proper performance of the church services for which St. Benedict had offered such precise liturgical instructions.

But though St. Benedict had envisaged a simple, rustic, and largely uneducated community, the reformers of the eleventh and twelfth centuries tended to regard monks as a sort of spiritual *élite*. They considered themselves to be not so much ' the slaves of God ' as ' the soldiers of Christ '. It is true that the new ideal could be traced back to St. Benedict's own words, since in the very first lines of the Rule he urged every new monk to give up his own will and ' take the all-powerful and excellent arms of obedience to fight under the Lord Christ, the true King '. But in the eleventh century this aspect of the monastic ideal became ever more important. Even Orderic Vitalis, whose monasticism was a matter of habit rather than ardour, considered it a truism that monks ' should fight for the King of Kings ', while in the twelfth century the letters of St Bernard, the great Cistercian, are riddled with the metaphors of the battlefield.

> Arise, soldier of Christ, arise ! [he wrote to a monk who had run away from his monastery]. Get up off the ground and return to the battle from which you have fled ! Fight more boldly after your flight, and triumph in glory ! [1]

Did this monk think that because he had run away the enemy would not pursue him ? Did he feel safer now that he had thrown his armour away ? Did he not think that he would have been more secure if ' surrounded by his friends, guarded by angels, and led by Christ ' ? Such passages, which could be multiplied, show that St. Bernard, along with almost all the monastic reformers, thought of the monk as a spiritual warrior whose enemy was the devil. The devil was as real as he would be to us if we were to imagine him as a monstrous force which controlled all the elements of germ-warfare and which was for ever striking people down. To guard against him, one had to be ever watchful, ever praying.

The only hope against the devil was Christ. Christ had overcome the world. So convinced of this was St. Bernard that he expected the very elements to aid him in God's work. When, for example, he was dictating the letter just quoted, he was in

---

[1] Epistola I, Migne, *P.L.* 182, col. 78.

an open courtyard and it began to rain. His secretary wanted to go indoors so as to keep the parchment dry. But Bernard said, 'It is the work of God! Write on and fear nothing.' So the letter was completed in the rain, and the parchment remained dry.[1]

Nothing was allowed to hinder the work of God, for monks were his soldiers and had to obey Him. The prime purpose of monks was not to educate other monks, nor to copy out the classics, nor to write history, nor to give hospitality, nor to tend the sick, nor to preach to the world, though some of these might well be by-products of their vocation. Their purpose was to live a Christian life themselves. Seven times a day, and at midnight too, the praises of God were sung. At least forty-two psalms were chanted every day and the whole life of the monastery centred on the church-services. Those who were converted to Religion were not social workers looking for a job. They were inspired with the desire, not to reform the world (for that was impossible), but to reform themselves.

Despite the fact that monks set out to reform themselves, the eleventh and twelfth centuries witnessed an 'unregulated passion for monasticism' among the laity. Turning over the pages of Dugdale's *Monasticon* one gets the impression that there was hardly a single lord in twelfth-century England who did not have some share in the endowment of a monastery. Some were prompted by particular motives, a terrible illness, repentance for some crime, or even a weak title to land which (it was felt) God might be able to help in defending. But the invariable formula which a founder propounded was that he had founded the monastery 'for the safety of his soul'.

I hope [said one founder] that I will profit [by this gift] in the future life, if what I have done in this present life should please God. I bear it always in mind that 'as you shall sow, so shall you reap' and that word which was spoken unto God, 'Thou renderest to every man according to his work.' (Ps. lxii.) [2]

Monasteries were founded 'to maintain an unbroken chain of intercession for particular people in a particular place'. Intercession for the dead was regarded not as a quaint theory but as a reality; so was intercession for the living. Men would travel

---

[1] Sancti Bernardi Vita Prima, lib. i, c. xi : Migne, *P.L.* 185, col. 255.
[2] Alcester, 1140. *Monasticon*, iv, 175.

hundreds of miles to pray at the tomb of a saint; they would pay vast sums of money even for a small relic, for then the saint might intercede for the soul of the guilty suppliant.   But if dead saints were venerated, might not living saints be venerated also, so that even while on this earth they might pray for the souls of the wicked?   Many lords gave land and protection to a single hermit; for perchance the hermit might become a saint.

Medieval people had difficulty in distinguishing between the concrete and the abstract.   The moment they saw holiness, they wanted to possess it.   They collected holy men and women as a Renaissance prince collected artists, or as a scholar collects books and calls it ' learning '.   Their aim was not to subscribe to a Central Fund for the Promotion of Monasticism, nor to further missionary work in distant parts.   They wanted holy monks to come and live near them on their own lands..   In the eighth century, pious Englishwomen had gone to Rome to ' find at the shrine of St. Peter the quiet life which [they] had long sought in vain '.   In the eleventh and twelfth centuries many people hoped for similar benefits by persuading future saints to live (and die) on their doorsteps.   William of Warenne and his wife Gundrada visited, almost by chance, the abbey of Cluny in France.   And because they found there ' such great holiness and religion and charity ' they could not bear not to take some of it home with them.

> And so we sent and asked the Abbot Hugh and all the holy body to give us two, or three, or four holy monks from their holy flock to whom we might give the church, which we had converted from wood to stone, below our castle at Lewes.[1]

This passion for collecting holiness may seem strangely vicarious, for founders of monasteries did not usually become monks themselves, unless it was on their deathbed.   But we must not be too harsh.   Today we do not expect the man who endows a library to read the books in it; nor do we expect the founder of a university to become a student or teacher in it himself.   We praise such benefactors for having enabled scholars to continue in their search for knowledge.   In the same way we

---

[1] Foundation charter of Lewes Priory (*The Chartulary of the Priory of St. Pancras of Lewes*, ed .L. F. Salzman, *Sussex Record Society*, vol. 38, p. 3 (1932)).

might praise the feudal lords who enabled monks to search for God, to obey Him, and to fight the perpetual battle against the devil.

The main novelty of the tenth, eleventh, and twelfth centuries was the introduction of monastic Orders, or organized groups of monasteries which functioned as veritable armies of Christ. Previously every monastery had been an independent community. It might be ' visited ' (*i.e.* inspected) by the diocesan bishop, who had the right to enforce such reforms as he thought necessary, and it might, to a greater or lesser extent, be subject to the control of its lay patron, who was the founder or the founder's heir, but it would not have been subject to any external monastic organization. Though the abbey of Monte Cassino was the senior house of Benedictine monks, neither it, nor any other monastery, could exercise any control over the way in which the Rule was observed elsewhere.

That was the deficiency which the monastic Orders were to repair. The first of them, and in many ways the model for them all, was the Cluniac. As with most great institutions, it is difficult to say when it began, for it came into existence very gradually and in a way that was apparently unpremeditated. Its centre the abbey of Cluny was founded in 910 not as the mainspring of an elaborate organization but as a simple Benedictine monastery. It was founded for a monk called St. Berno who was renowned for the strictness with which he observed the Rule, and who was already Abbot of Gigny. His austerity had won him such fame that new recruits flocked to his monastery, and it was in order to provide for this increase of numbers that Cluny was founded. It was from the start intended as a model of monastic virtue, and its founder, William the Pious, Duke of Aquitaine and Count of Mâcon, gave it the privilege of complete exemption from lay control. Neither the founder, nor his kindred, nor any other layman was to interfere with the monks in any way ; and to insure that this privilege was respected, William called on the apostles Peter and Paul, together with the Pope himself, to be the guardians and defenders of the abbey.

This papal protection was ultimately to play a very large part in the history of Cluny, but at the beginning of the tenth century it was not so important as the reputation which the monastery acquired for strict monasticism. The lay patrons of other monasteries soon began to call on its abbots for advice and assistance in monastic reform. Thus St. Berno, the first abbot (910–26), was called in to reform three other monasteries, while his successor, St. Odo (926–42), reformed an enormous number, amongst the more famous being Tulle, Sarlat, St. Martial de Limoges, St. Jean d'Angely, St. Pierre-le-vif of Sens, Saint-Benoît-sur-Loire (Fleury), and four monasteries at Rome, *viz*. St. Agnes, St. Laurence, and St. Paul-without-the-walls, and St. Mary on the Aventine. The number was large, because St. Odo regarded himself as an apostle of monastic reform. He did not shut himself up in his monastery at Cluny, but travelled the length and breadth of France and Italy in an endeavour to spread the stricter monastic life. He concentrated his attention in the first place on influential laymen, for they were the patrons of monasteries and could, quite literally, hand them over to him for reform. Thus his Roman successes were due to the fact that Alberic, the self-styled 'Prince of Rome', had made him 'Archimandrite' of all his monasteries in or near Rome. Odo would go with a small body of monks to the monastery in question and, armed with the patron's authority, would seek admission. He might at times be refused, as at Farfa or (for a few days) at Fleury, but usually the monks would submit, even if with a bad grace, and accept him as their Superior. He would then try to win them over to the idea of reform. With his own companions he would show them how the life was led at Cluny, and every day in the chapter house he would expound the Rule of St. Benedict. But he would not stay in the monastery for long. As soon as the policy of reform had commended itself to a small party of the monks, he would leave the monastery in charge of some of his companions and proceed to his next mission. He would return to 'visit' (*i.e.* inspect) the monastery from time to time, but his role was more or less that of a consultant specialist in monastic reform.

It was only to be expected that some of the reforms which he effected were more permanent than others, for the success of his work depended, in the long run, on the quality of the reforming monks whom he left behind him in each house. Consequently it could easily happen that anxious lay-patrons might hope to ensure the continuity of the reforming-spirit by linking their monasteries to Cluny in perpetuity. Thus Adelaide, Duchess of Burgundy, in giving Romainmoutier to Cluny (929), stipulated that its monks should form a single congregation with those of Cluny, and that they should always have the same abbot. It was a method of ensuring that the apostles of reform should not lose interest in her particular monastery, and the first step towards the foundation of the Cluniac Order.

Eventually the abbots of Cluny were the masters of about 1,450 dependent priories whose monks, as in the case of Romainmoutier, formed a single congregation. They were monks not of this priory or that, but of Cluny; that was why they were called Cluniacs. Nobody could become the monk of a Cluniac priory, even if it were in England or Asia Minor, unless he was professed by the Abbot of Cluny and took the vow of spiritual and temporal obedience to him in person. No Cluniac priory could elect its own prior, for the prior was but the deputy of the Abbot of Cluny and was therefore appointed by him. By the eleventh century, indeed, no bishop or archbishop had any control over the Cluniac monasteries in his diocese or province, for Pope John XIX had in 1025 granted the monks of Cluny immunity from the see of Mâcon and all other dioceses. The Abbot of Cluny was the only person who was entitled to ' visit ' or reform his monasteries, and he was dependent on no one but the Pope. His ' Order ' might be compared to an army with its own commander-in-chief and its own martial law. The comparison was made even in the eleventh century, for Adalbero, Archbishop of Reims, wrote a bitter satire in which he put the following words into the mouth of a Cluniac monk :

> I am a soldier now, and if a monk, a monk with a difference. Indeed I am no longer a monk but fight at the command of my master Odilo [Abbot of Cluny, 994–1049].

In general, however, the idea of a monastic ' Order ' was given an enthusiastic welcome, since it established a fixed standard and uniform system of government. The discipline was similar everywhere. Cluniac monks, wherever they might be, processed into the church or chapter house at exactly the same time and in exactly the same way, and this, in an age when local ustom differed immensely from place to place, was a rare virtue. From the point of view of religious idealists, diversity was not desirable. To them it seemed that there must be one perfect way of being a monk, and that the sooner it was enforced, the better it would be for the world.

In the Middle Ages that point of view was maintained, even though there was a whole succession of different monastic reforms. Though the ideals of the various reformers might be different, they all thought that their monasteries should be linked together in such a way as to ensure the maintenance of discipline and uniformity. They did not think that individual monasteries should be left to develop their own individual pattern of life, for they were painfully aware that the natural tendency was for monasteries to become rich and for monks to become lazy. Monasticism involved a sustained endeavour to mortify the flesh, and if it was to be practised successfully it was necessary to take every precaution to defend the weakness of human nature from the wiles of the devil. Every reform started from the desire, not to alter St. Benedict's *Rule*, but to observe it more strictly.

Thus the Cistercian Order owed its origin to circumstances very similar to those which had led to the foundation of Cluny. In 1098 a group of monks, led by their abbot, Robert, left the abbey of Molesmes in order to live a stricter life in the ' desert ' (*i.e.* forest) of Burgundy. They had, in the first place, no thought of founding a new Order. They wished merely to found a monastery which would not be burdened with riches, as was that of Molesmes, and where they could restore the Rule to its primitive simplicity. According to their later tradition,

> they resolved unanimously to establish themselves [at Cîteaux] and to observe the *Rule* of St. Benedict, rejecting everything that was contrary to it, such as [the use of] coats, capes, worsted cloth, hoods, pants, combs, counterpanes and bedclothes, together with a variety of dishes in the refectory, fat, and everything else that was contrary to the purity of the *Rule*.[1] Thus they arranged the whole conduct of their life in exact conformity with the *Rule*, in ecclesiastical matters as well as in other observances. Having put off the old man, they joyfully put on the new. And because they did not

[1] This catalogue of forbidden articles, and especially the inclusion in it of pants, which other monks wore beneath their robes, was the object of much ribald criticism, as readers of Orderic Vitalis or Walter Map will know.

read, either in the *Rule* or in the *Life* of St. Benedict, that this same master had possessed churches, altars, oblations, burial rights or the tithes of other men, nor [that he had owned] bakehouses, mills, villages or peasants, nor that he had buried any nuns there, saving only his sister, they rejected all these things, saying : ' Since the blessed father Benedict teaches that the monk should make himself a stranger to the customs of the men of this world, it is clear that his testimony is that these things should not be found either in the actions or in the hearts of monks, who, by fleeing from them, should justify the meaning of their name.' [1]

The natural consequence of this decision was that Cistercian monks had no choice but to obey St. Benedict's injunction to devote a portion of each day to manual labour. ' Idleness is the enemy of the soul ', he had written, ' and therefore the brethren ought at certain times to be occupied with manual labour.' But in any case it was necessary for the monks to work if they were not to accept tithes, rents, or manorial dues, or have control of any villeins or serfs. They allowed themselves the institution of lay-brothers (*conversi*) who, while not being monks or clerks, since they were illiterate, lived a quasi-monastic life in the abbey —their quarters occupied the west range of the claustral build-ings—and worked not for money but for the love of God. But, none the less, the monks themselves worked also, and conse-quently had not time for all the elaborate church-services which were celebrated in Cluniac monasteries.

This, perhaps, was the greatest novelty of the Cistercians, even though it was a return to the literal interpretation of St. Benedict's *Rule*. For the normal tendency of monastic reformers, as of St. Benedict of Aniane in the ninth century and the Cluniacs in the tenth, had been to multiply the church-services. The more time a monk had spent at the *opus Dei* in the choir, the holier he was thought to be. Thus at Canterbury, at the end of the eleventh century, the services on a normal winter's day would include about 120 psalms (55 of them before daybreak), while at Cluny the timetable of services in church was so full that when the Office of the Blessed Virgin Mary was added, the only place where it could be celebrated was the infirmary.

The work of psalmody was strenuous, especially as the monks

---

[1] *Exordium Parvum* (*c.* 1151), as quoted in Fliche and Martin, *op. cit.*, viii. 452–3.

had to remain standing when they were in the choir, and it had a particular appeal to the laity, who were always impressed by the maintenance of an unbroken chain of intercession and prayer. But the Cistercians justified their break with tradition by appealing to the authority of St. Benedict. He had wanted monks to work in the fields as well as in the choir, and had devised his timetable accordingly; and the Cistercians were determined to do what he had commanded. They would celebrate the services which he had laid down in precisely the manner which he had stipulated. They would add nothing to the *Rule*, and take nothing away from it, for they believed that it was to be obeyed literally.

In order to ensure that the *Rule* should not be corrupted, all Cistercian houses had to have their copy of it transcribed from the manuscript at Cîteaux and none other. Similar precautions were taken with the texts of other important books, such as the Missal, Epistles, Bible, Collects, Gradual, Antiphonary, Psalter, Lectionary, and Calendar. But mere uniformity was not enough. To men who believed in the verbal inspiration of the scriptures, and who were determined to submit to the letter of the *Rule*, it was essential to establish the correct reading of every text. In the case of the Bible, we know that they experienced some difficulty, for Stephen Harding, one of the founder-members of Cîteaux and its third abbot, has recorded how they borrowed manuscripts from various monasteries, compared them, and finally copied the one which contained the fullest text. But then they reflected, and were puzzled by the fact that it contained many passages which were not found in other manuscripts. And so, to quote his own words,

> We went to find certain Jews who were expert in their own writings. We questioned them very carefully in the vulgar tongue about all those passages in our work which we did not find in other Latin histories. They opened several of their books before us, and explained the Hebraic or Chaldaean writing in the vulgar tongue. They did not find the verses or paragraphs about which we were worried and had questioned them.[1]

[1] As quoted by C. Oursel, *La Miniature du XIIe siècle à l'abbaye de Cîteaux* (Dijon, 1926), who describes the great Bible of Cîteaux in detail. It was written between 1098 and 1109. Stephen Harding was an Englishman from Sherborne and was Abbot of Cîteaux from 1109 to 1133.

As a result, Stephen Harding deleted the passages in question from the Cistercian Bible. ' The places where these errors occurred appear plainly ', he added, ' for the erasure of the parchment can be seen.' They mostly occurred in the two Books of Kings, as an inspection of the manuscript, now in the library at Dijon, will show.

The incident shows not only the scholarly care with which the Cistercians established their texts but also their historical perspective. They consulted Jews about the Old Testament, because they realized that what was common to the Hebraic and Latin texts must, of necessity, date back to the first century of the Christian era. And it was primitive Christianity which they wished to revive. Every departure from the customs which had then been observed was, in their view, one step farther away from the tradition of the historic Christ. The more recent a custom, the worse they thought it must be. That was why they wanted to strip St. Benedict's *Rule* of all its later accretions, and why they paid so much attention to an even earlier tradition, that of the Desert Fathers.

In the first years of their history they used to refer to their monastery at Cîteaux as ' the desert ', and they always laid great stress on the hardships that a monk should endure. Their emphasis lay not so much on the fact that St Benedict had ordained ' nothing harsh or burdensome ' as on the fact that he had called his *Rule* ' a school for beginners '. He had, in his very first chapter, spoken of ' the long probation of the monastery ' as the only satisfactory training for hermits and anchorites, and the Cistercians consequently thought, as many later Benedictines have done, that the *Rule* established only the minimum requirements of a monastic life. They themselves were anxious to advance farther, so as to attain that same indifference to, and separation from, the world that the Desert Fathers had attained. Many of the first Cistercians had formerly been hermits themselves, and determined on a communal life, as St. Benedict had done before them, not in order to diminish their ardour but to increase it.

Their monasteries were built on sites that hermits might have chosen. They were far from towns and other habitations, and were usually not on cultivated land but in virgin forest or wasteland.   In England, for example, one of their sites was Fountains in Yorkshire, which was then ' thick-set with thorns, lying between the slopes of mountains and among rocks jutting out on both sides, fit rather to be the lair of wild beasts than the home of human beings '.[1]   The buildings themselves were plain and austere.   It was laid down that their churches were not to be grandiose like those of the Cluniacs, but modest and devoid of ornament.   There were to be no bell-towers, and in their churches crucifixes were to be of wood, candelabra of iron, and thuribles of copper.   Albs were not to be of silk, but of linen, and copes, dalmatics, and tunicles were abolished.   In carving and painting there was to be no representation of fabulous, frivolous, or grotesque subjects, and manuscripts were to be written in ink of one colour, without illumination.

Some of these severe rules, certainly the one about illuminated manuscripts, would seem to have originated not with the founders of Cîteaux but with their more famous disciple, St. Bernard.   He joined the community in 1112, and by the impact of his personality rapidly made it famous.   He was a great preacher, a great letter-writer, and an eloquent controversialist ; and, among other things, he was able to direct the full light of publicity to the differences which divided him and his fellows from the Cluniacs.

> Tell me, O poor [he wrote] if you are poor, what is gold doing in the sanctuary ?   There is one reason for bishops, indeed, but it will not do for monks.   We know that bishops, since they have to serve both the wise and the foolish, and cannot excite the devotion of the lewd populace with spiritual ornaments, do so with material ornaments.   But we have left the people.   We have judged all the glamour of beauty, the sweetness of song, the fragrance of scent, the sweetness of knowledge, and the pleasure of touch—we have judged all such pleasures to be filth, in order that we might attain Christ.[2]

It was, as a runaway Cistercian once said, ' forcing a man to go beyond the bounds of human nature '.   But that, in St. Bernard's

---

[1] *Narratio Fundacionis*, in *Memorials of Fountains*, i, ed. J. R. Walbran (Surtees Soc., 1863), p. 32.
[2] *Apologia ad Guillelmum*.   Migne, *Patrologia Latina*, vol. 182, cols. 914–15.

view, was the purpose of monasticism—to overcome human
nature, to conquer the flesh, and to converse with God.

Such asceticism made an enormous appeal to the people of the
twelfth century, especially when it was coupled with the eloquence
of St. Bernard. Consequently the rise of the Cistercian Order
was meteoric. In 1112, the year in which St. Bernard was
admitted, Cîteaux had no daughter-houses ; yet in 1153, the
year of his death, it had three hundred. It was probably the
most spectacular development in the whole history of monasticism, and it created the problem of how to control and organize
the Order so that, with the increase of numbers, there should be
no diminution of the strictness with which the *Rule* was observed.
A first constitution was drawn up by Stephen Harding and was
confirmed by Pope Calixtus II in 1119. But changes were
made throughout the age of expansion, and it was not until the
middle of the twelfth century that the *Carta Caritatis* (charter
of charity) took its final shape.

It was a remarkable document, which outlined a whole scheme
of government, with admirable lucidity, in about 1,680 words.
It presupposed that the Cistercian Order would, like that of
Cluny, be under papal protection and exempt from diocesan
control. It assumed also that it would want to act as a united
body. But the means taken to secure that end were very different
from those of Cluny. The Abbot of Cîteaux, though described
as ' the universal father of the Order ', was not allowed the
dictatorial powers of the Abbot of Cluny, and could, if necessary,
be removed for misconduct. The sovereign authority rested
not with him but with the ' chapter-general ' which met annually
and consisted of the abbots of all the houses of the Order. It
alone could authorize alterations to the constitution, and it
alone had the power to compel the resignation of unworthy
abbots.

The most striking feature of the Cistercian Order was its
decentralization, which was made possible by the ' family
relationship ' of all its houses. No new Cistercian abbey could be
founded unless there was a ' mother-house ' to provide it with a
colony of at least twenty-five monks. Each ' mother-house '
watched over its ' daughters ', its abbot visiting them annually.
But every ' daughter ' might in its turn become a ' mother ', with

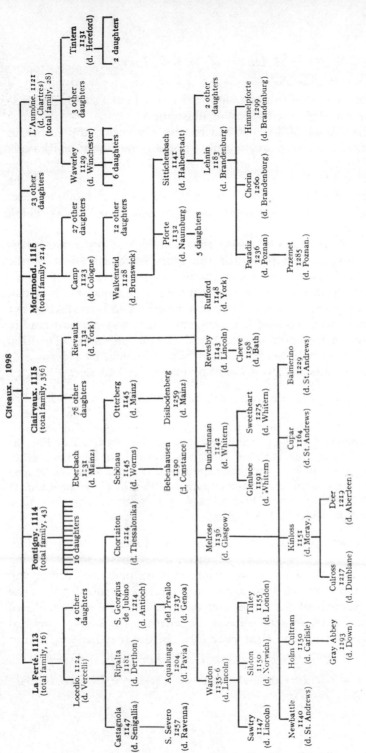

(Note: d. = diocese)

Compiled, with corrections, from P. L. Janauschek. *Originum Cisterciensium*, vol. i. (Vienna 1877)

the result that the houses of the Cistercian order could be arranged in the form of a family tree, of which a small portion is given on page 273 by way of illustration.

The Abbot of Cîteaux had to visit Clairvaux, the Abbot of Clairvaux had to visit Rievaulx (Yorks.), the Abbot of Rievaulx had to visit Melrose, and the Abbot of Melrose had to visit Newbattle. The only question was who should visit the abbey of Cîteaux itself, since it alone had no mother-house. It was visited jointly by the abbots of its four ' eldest daughters '.

The Cistercian Order was thus a model of organized other-worldliness. It represented the most sustained effort of the Middle Ages to ensure that, in spite of the weakness of human nature, strict monastic poverty should be maintained in certain specific places for ever. It was a superhuman undertaking, but the men who initiated it considered that it was the only way in which the Kingdom of God could be built on earth. The ideal which they held before them is best explained by reference to St. Augustine's *City of God*. Mankind, he had said,

> is divided into two sorts, such as live according to man, and such as live according to God. These we mystically call two cities or societies, the one predestined to reign eternally with God, the other condemned to perpetual torment with the devil. . . . For the city of the saints is above, though it have citizens here upon earth, wherein it lives as a pilgrim until the time of the kingdom comes ; and then it gathers all the citizens together in the resurrection of the body, and gives them a kingdom to reign in with their King for ever and ever.[1]

But was the Cistercian Order more successful than its predecessors ? The history of medieval monasticism is a long record of perpetual reforms followed by perpetual decay, and even the Cistercians make no exception to its general rule. The very success of the Order was dangerous. The first monks of a new foundation could live a life worthy of hermits ; they had to uproot trees and clear away rocks before they had any land to cultivate, and might even sleep under an oak tree before the

[1] *City of God*, xv. 1 (Healey's translation as printed in Everyman's Library. 1945).

building of the monastery was complete. But once the first years of colonization were over life became easier. Only too often the monks found that the site which they had chosen was wild only because it was overgrown, and that the soil was fertile, suitable not only for briars and thorn-bushes but also for the lilies of the field.

The very enthusiasm with which the world welcomed ascetic monks tended to make the Cistercians wealthy, for the poorer and holier they were, the more men and women wanted to give them gifts. Even the number of new recruits might prove an embarrassment. So many men flocked to Clairvaux to become the monks of St. Bernard that not only the buildings but also the site proved too small for them. St. Bernard himself was naturally unwilling to leave his restricted site for one which, by its very size and convenience, would make the monastic life less arduous. But the prior was a practical man and saw the necessity of a move.

> If [he said to the saint] the Lord had ceased to send us people to live with us, then your view might have been right, and it would have been reasonable to stop building. But now, when God multiplies his flock daily, we must either drive away those whom he sends, or else provide a house in which they can be received. It is not a question of who provides the guest, but of who prepares the house for them.[1]

The move to a more spacious site was made, and the admiring laity, led by Theobald, Count of Champagne, gave all the funds that were necessary for the new buildings. How could the laity have failed to support a monastery that was so holy as Clairvaux? And how could Clairvaux fail to become rich?

Thus, even the greatest efforts to achieve a permanent state of poverty and holiness eventually ended in failure. Monastic Order followed on monastic Order without avail in a desperate attempt to discipline holiness and enclose it within the walls of a Rule. Men continued to think that, if only the organization were perfect, a perfect monasticism might be found, but they wound their ideal so high that they were bound eventually to be

---

[1] *Sancti Bernardi Vita Prima, Auctore Ernaldo,* lib. ii, c. v. Migne, *Patrologia Latina,* vol. 185, col. 285.

disillusioned. St. Bernard might, by sheer force of personality, force a man to go ' beyond the bounds of human nature '. But could the flaming zeal be maintained even after he was dead ?

APPENDIX

A Miracle of St. Bernard

(S. Bernardi. Vita Prima. Lib. VII (ex. exordio magno Cisterc), cap. XXI.)

A certain monk, departing from his monastery and his discipline, threw off his habit, and returned to the world at the persuasion of the Devil. And he took a certain parish living ; for he was a priest. Because sin is punished with sin, the deserter from his Order lapsed into the vice of lechery. He took a concubine to live with him, as in fact is done by many, and by her he had children.

But as God is merciful and does not wish anyone to perish, it happened that many years after, the blessed abbot [Bernard] was passing through the village in which this same monk was living, and went to stay at his house. The renegade monk recognized him, and received him very reverently, and waited on him devoutly and provided him with every necessity both for himself and his beasts ; but as yet the abbot did not recognize him.

On the morrow, the holy man said Matins and prepared to be off. But as he could not speak to the priest, since he had got up and gone to the church for Matins, he said to the priest's son ' Go, give this message to your master.' Now the boy had been born dumb. He obeyed the command and feeling in himself the power of him who had given it, he ran to his father and uttered the words of the Holy Father clearly and exactly. His father, on hearing his son's voice for the first time, wept for joy, and made him repeat the same words a second and yet a third time ; and he asked what the abbot had done to him. ' He did nothing to me ', said the boy, ' except to say " Go and say this to your father ".'

At so evident a miracle the priest repented, and hastened after the holy man and fell at his feet saying ' My Lord, and Father, I was your monk so-and-so, and at such-and-such a time I ran away from your monastery. I ask your Paternity to allow me to return with you to the monastery, for in your coming God has visited my heart.' The saint replied unto him, ' Wait for me here, and I will come back quickly when I have done my business, and I will take you with me.' But the priest, fearing death (which he had not done before), answered ' Lord, I am afraid of dying before then.' But the saint replied, ' Know this for certain, that if you die in this condition, and in this resolve, you will find yourself a monk before God.'

The saint [eventually] returned and heard that the priest had recently died and been buried. He ordered the tomb to be opened. And when they asked him what he wanted to do, he said ' I want to see if he is lying as a monk or a clerk in his tomb.' ' As a clerk ', they said ; ' we buried him in his secular habit.' But when they had dug up the earth, they found that he was not in the clothes in which they had buried him ; but he appeared in all points, tonsure and habit, as a monk. And they all praised God.

Further Reading

C. OURSEL. *La Miniature du XIIe siècle à l'abbaye de Cîteaux.* Dijon. 1926. Though primarily concerned with art-history, it has considerable interest for the development of the Cistercian ideal.

G. DE VALOUS. *Le Monachisme Clunisien des origines au XVe siècle.* Vienne. 1935.

A. FLICHE and V. MARTIN (ed.). *Histoire de l'Eglise.*

Vol. 7. *L'Eglise au pouvoir des laiques* (888–1057) by E. Amann and A. Dumas (1940).

Vol. 8. *La réforme grégorienne et la reconquête chrétienne* by A. Fliche (1940).

B. S. JAMES (trans.). *The Letters of St. Bernard of Clairvaux.* London. 1953.

DAVID KNOWLES. *Great Historical Enterprises.* Cambridge. 1962. The article on ' The primitive documents of the Cistercian Order ' is the best critical survey of the work of J. A. Lefèvre.

DOREEN HUNT. *Cluny under St. Hugh (1049–1109).* London. 1967.

IV

JERUSALEM REGAINED AND LOST:
THE FIRST THREE CRUSADES

THE first three Crusades cover a period of almost exactly one hundred years (1095–1192), during which medieval religious enthusiasm was at its height. It was the century which saw the greatest expansion of monasticism in the Latin West, when even princes of the blood might take the cowl and wash dishes for the love of God and his saints, and it was only natural that the laity, and above all the military aristocracy, should want themselves to perform some special service for the Christian community. 'What then must we do?' is a question which has usually proved as difficult as it is urgent, but in 1095, at the Council of Clermont, Pope Urban II gave a short and specific answer. He appealed to the laity to use their arms for the reconquest of Jerusalem. While their brethren in the monasteries were fighting the devil with spiritual weapons, they, the laity, were to fight the heathen in the flesh. They accepted the proffered task with alacrity, and their efforts were at first crowned with the most astounding success. Jerusalem was regained. But alas! within a hundred years it was lost again, and the cause of its loss was widely held to be the mutual jealousies which had divided the crusaders against themselves. Expectant hope gave way to disillusion.

It might well be asked why no Crusade had been preached before the eleventh century, since Jerusalem had been lost to the Moslems more than four-and-a-half centuries earlier (p. 94). The religious reformers assumed that the reason was to be found in the state of apathy into which the Church had fallen, but this was not nearly so important as the fact that the Byzantine Empire would previously have resented, and resisted, any attempt by the barbarians of the Latin West to interfere in Palestine or Syria. From *c.* 650 to *c.* 1050, the Byzantines had stabilized their frontier with the Moslems, and they looked on the Franks, Saxons, and other Germanic peoples not as potential allies but as usurpers of imperial rights and territories in Italy and the West. It was not until the advent of a new and more formidable Moslem power that their attitude changed. In 1071, still reeling from defeats at the hands of the Croats, the Serbs, the Pechenegs, and the Normans of Italy, the Byzantines were overwhelmed by the Seljūk Turks at the battle of Manzikert ('l'urk = *Malesgird*) and lost almost the whole of Anatolia. The Emperor Alexius Comnenus, succeeding to an empire bounded almost by the walls of his capital, was in despair and appealed to the Pope for assistance from the West. He received, as we have already seen, a sympathetic response from Gregory VII, who hoped that an opportunity would thus be provided for the reconciliation of the Greek and Latin Churches, which had been divided since 1054. But the Investitures Struggle intervened and diverted his attention, with the result that it was left to Urban II to preach the call to arms.

The enthusiasm with which it was greeted would seem to have astounded the Pope himself. He had no practical plan of campaign before him, and had not troubled to discover what sort of help the Byzantine Emperor really wanted. He simply preached the special sanctity of Jerusalem, alluded to the victorious advance of the Seljūk Turks, who treated pilgrims more harshly than their (Egyptian) Fātimid predecessors, insisted that the work of reconquest was God's work, promised a plenary indulgence for those who partook in it, and made an appeal to everyone to abandon iniquitous combats and fight the war of righteousness. He declared that the Christian army was to set out on the Day of the Assumption in the year following (1096), under the command of a papal legate, Adhemar, Bishop of Le Puy ; but beyond that he made no detailed plans. God was to be the leader of the Crusades, and apparently all preparations were left to His providence.

Urban II had expected the crusaders to form a single army, but in fact they set out in separate contingents. One, from southern France, was led (as arranged) by the papal legate and Raymond,

Count of Toulouse ; a second, from northern France, by Hugh
of Vermandois (brother of the French king), Robert, Count of
Flanders, Stephen-Henry, Count of Blois, and Robert, Duke of
Normandy ; a third, from the borders of France and Germany,
by Godfrey de Bouillon, Duke of Lower Lorraine (and a strong
supporter of the Emperor Henry IV), and his brother Baldwin ;
and a fourth, from southern Italy, by the Norman Bohemund,
son of Robert Guiscard, and his nephew Tancred. They set
out for Constantinople independently and arrived there by
various routes, in the late spring of 1097.

The Emperor, Alexius Comnenus, did not give them the warm
welcome which they had expected. Indeed, he was dismayed
at their approach. He had asked for military assistance, but had
not envisaged the arrival of whole armies of crusaders. He
was particularly alarmed by the presence of Bohemund's contingent of Normans from southern Italy, for Bohemund and his
father were old enemies of the Byzantine Empire. They had
invaded it on several occasions before, and their valour and
treachery were both well-known. Were their intentions really
disinterested ? Unpleasant incidents were reported from along
the routes of all the crusading armies—towns and villages were
destroyed if they were unwilling or unable to provide the crusaders with provisions—and it was little wonder that Alexius
was apprehensive. He decided that, before transporting the
crusaders across the Bosphorus, he would demand from their
leaders an oath of fealty. This they at first refused to give.
But eventually, by coercion or bribery, they were persuaded to
comply. It was agreed that the Emperor should furnish the
crusaders with supplies, and that in return they would restore
to him any provinces of his Empire which they should reconquer
from the Moslems. This was the first cause of misunderstanding
between them, for though the crusaders thought that the agreement referred only to those provinces which had belonged to
the Empire within the last thirty years or so, the officials of the
Byzantine court were never able to forget that, once upon a time,
their Empire had embraced the whole of Syria and Palestine.

The situation was not improved by the fact that the Latins
and the Greeks took an instant dislike to each other. The
Latins were immensely impressed by the riches of Constantinople,

but thought its people effeminate. They thought the Greek Church schismatic, and hated the Emperor because he had not welcomed them cordially, because he was a puny little man, and because they thought him and his fellow-countrymen deceitful. The Greeks, on the other hand, viewed the Latins as conceited and undisciplined barbarians. They were appalled both by their manners and by their ignorance, and admired nothing but their bravery.

That indeed was astounding. On the march across Asia Minor they endured almost perpetual famine and lack of water—sometimes simply because of their own stupidity, for it was a long time before they thought of carrying water-bottles with them—and yet they emerged victorious, defeated the Turks, and eventually arrived at Antioch. They captured the city (though not the citadel), but, succumbing to the ill-effects of the local climate and its fruits, were smitten by a plague of dysentery. In that condition they were themselves besieged by a relieving army of Turks, and after agonies of starvation (which was probably the best thing for their dysentery) they discovered a holy lance, sallied out to fight a decisive battle, and aided by St. George and other saints (who fought on white horses) defeated the Turks.[1] By sheer stupid bravery, together with an unshakable belief in their own destiny, they had succeeded where the Byzantine armies had failed (28 June 1098).

It is true, however, that they had the most incredible good luck, for when they arrived on the scene the two major Moslem powers of the Near East were at war with each other. These were, on the one hand, the Seljūk Turks who, having won control of the Abbāsid caliphate at Baghdad, were advancing westwards ; and, on the other hand, the Fātimid caliphs of Egypt. Palestine lay between them and was consequently their major theatre of war. The Seljūks had captured Jerusalem in 1070, though apparently their control of the surrounding country was exceedingly tenuous, and in 1099 the Fātimids had just succeeded in recovering it. Into this confusion came the crusaders. They marched down the coast from Antioch, and the main Fātimid forces, fearing an attack on their own country, retreated to the Egyptian frontier,

---

[1] The miracle of the invention of the holy lance and the appearance of the saints was, however, strongly disputed by one part of the crusaders.

so that when the crusaders turned aside to take Jerusalem the opposition was not serious. Jerusalem fell into their hands on 15 July 1099, and they massacred its inhabitants.

A great deal of the country remained to be subdued, but the crusaders could now, having accomplished their primary aim, consider how to organize and defend their conquest. Many problems had already solved themselves, though in an unsatisfactory way. Bohemund had claimed Antioch and had preferred to secure the conquest of its surrounding territory rather than to advance on Jerusalem; Baldwin, brother of Godfrey de Bouillon, had likewise left the main army, having been invited to Edessa (Urfa) by the Armenian ruler of that city in order to marry his daughter and become his heir; and many other crusaders were showing unmistakable signs of ambition either for themselves or their protégés—the chaplain of Robert, Duke of Normandy, Arnulf of Rohez, succeeded in being elected patriarch of Jerusalem. But the main problem remained the organization of the conquered territory as a whole.

At one time it had seemed possible that it would be offered to the Byzantine Empire, if the Emperor could provide for its defence, but a more likely eventuality seemed to be that it would become a fief of the Holy See. In the West, in both Spain and Sicily, the Pope had maintained (successfully) that all territories conquered from the Moslems should be held as papal fiefs, and signs were not lacking that he had the same intentions in Palestine. At the time of the fall of Jerusalem, however, there was no papal legate in Palestine, since Adhemar of Le Puy had died at Antioch, and so the nobles took matters into their own hands. They elected Godfrey de Bouillon as their ruler. The title which he took—'Advocate (or lay-protector) of the Church of the Holy Sepulchre'—might, perhaps, have reserved to the Papacy its ultimate rights over the territory. But when, in the following year, Godfrey died, his brother Baldwin I was elected in his place and had no hesitation in taking the title of king (1100–18).

The task which confronted him, however, was by no means easy, for although a number of individual crusaders had decided to settle in the country and build themselves lordships or principalities, the great mass of the army had returned home as soon as Jerusalem had been captured ; it had undertaken the Crusade as a pilgrimage, and having accomplished it, had no cause to remain. Consequently Baldwin was left with only about 300 knights for the defence of Jerusalem, Jaffa, Haifa, and Ramleh. The position was the more serious since many of the coastal towns remained in the hands of the Moslems and had still to be captured. The first necessity, therefore, was to purchase as much temporary assistance as possible. Thus the help of the Genoese fleet was enlisted against Caesarea (1101), Tartous (1102), Acre and Jubail (1104), and Tripoli (1109), the price of its assistance being one-third of the booty and a trading-quarter in every town which it helped to take. Venice, being Genoa's principal trading-rival, was equally anxious to purchase concessions, and consequently lent its fleet, in 1110, against Beyrouth and Sidon (in the capture of which a Viking king, Sigurd of Norway, also gave assistance), and in 1124 against Tyre. Pisa, on the other hand, gave its assistance to Bohemund of Antioch against Laodicea.

But even when the country was conquered there was the problem of defending it and governing it. Its defence might have been made a comparatively simple matter if only the line of the desert could have been secured as the frontier, but the crusaders never succeeded in capturing Aleppo, Hama, Homs, or Damascus, and consequently their frontier had to be in the mountains of Lebanon or along the River Jordan. Fortunately there were comparatively few passes and river-crossings, and these could all be defended by castles. The valleys of the Orontes and Litany were comparatively unimportant since they could easily be protected by Iron Bridge in the one case and Belfort and Toron on the other. The main routes which were open to an invading army were the Eleutheros valley and the plain of Esdraelon. The first of these gave easy access from Homs to Tripoli. Its defence was the responsibility of the Count of Tripoli (Raymond of St. Gilles and his descendants) and was secured by a network of castles, the most important of which were Krak des Chevaliers, Safad (Chastel blanc), and Aarka. The plain of Esdraelon, on the other hand, could only be defended by holding the line of the Jordan, which an invader coming from Damascus would have to cross either at Jacob's Ford (south of Lake Huleh) or at Samakh (south of Lake Tiberias). The

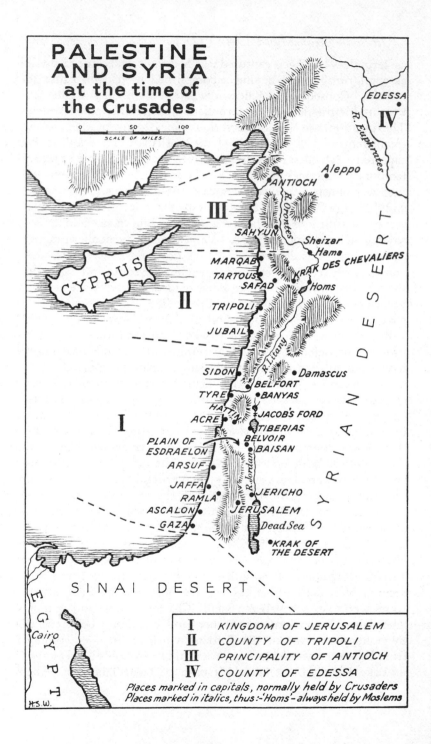

PALESTINE
AND SYRIA
at the time of
the Crusades

SCALE OF MILES
0   50   100

EDESSA
IV

R. Euphrates

ANTIOCH
R. Orontes
Aleppo

SAHYUN

Sheizar
Hama
KRAK DES CHEVALIERS

MARQAB
TARTOUS
SAFAD
Homs

TRIPOLI

JUBAIL

CYPRUS

R. Litany

SIDON
Damascus
BELFORT
TYRE
BANYAS
HATTIN
JACOB'S FORD
ACRE
TIBERIAS
PLAIN OF
ESDRAELON
BELVOIR
BAISAN
ARSUF

R. Jordan

JAFFA
RAMLA
JERICHO
ASCALON
JERUSALEM
GAZA
Dead Sea

KRAK OF
THE DESERT

S Y R I A N   D E S E R T

S I N A I   D E S E R T

E
G
Y
P
T

Cairo

I   KINGDOM OF JERUSALEM
II   COUNTY OF TRIPOLI
III PRINCIPALITY OF ANTIOCH
IV   COUNTY OF EDESSA

Places marked in capitals, normally held by Crusaders
Places marked in italics, thus :- 'Homs'- always held by Moslems

H.S.W.

key to both these crossings lay, in the last resort, in Tiberias, which belonged, after 1174, like the Eleutheros valley, to Raymond III, Count of Tripoli. It was not surprising that he was to be consistent in urging that the hostility of the rulers of Damascus and Homs should not lightly be provoked.

The weak points of the frontier were, as we have already stated, defended by castles, but the size and the elaboration of their defences have to be seen to be believed. Krak des Chevaliers, for example, has in recent times housed a whole village. It commands the pass at the top of the Eleutheros valley, but is situated high above it, on the spur of a mountain, so that to reach it by road a detour of ten miles is required. From the pass one sees it fitfully through the clouds which shroud the black mountainside, and when one eventually reaches it, one is astounded by its enormous proportions. No English castle can compare with it in size ; the thickness of its walls and its rock-cut tunnels would withstand a bombardment with modern weapons. In the Middle Ages it was virtually impregnable, its only disadvantage being that it was remote from the pass which it was supposed to guard (Plate IV).

The crusaders, however, always preferred impregnability to convenience, for the reason that they had not sufficient forces to operate in open warfare. There were the military Orders, the Knights Hospitallers (founded 1113) and the Knights Templars (founded *c.* 1119), who lived a quasi-monastic and military life and made themselves responsible for the defence of a great deal of the country—Krak des Chevaliers for example belonged to the Hospitallers—but, even so, the numbers involved were never large. An encounter of five or six knights with a Moslem force was quite a little battle, and when in 1187 a force of 130 knights (mainly Templars) was overwhelmed, the loss to the crusaders' fighting-strength was disastrous.

The crusaders' policy, therefore, was dictated by their shortage of numbers. Though they organized the kingdom on a feudal basis, and though they retained their own civilization, building cathedrals in the style of architecture which belonged to southern France, they were always in the minority. The great majority of the townsfolk and peasantry were Moslems, and the crusaders made little effort to convert them to Christianity. In many of the coastal towns one can still see the remains of the ' Frankish ' or crusaders' quarter. It consisted of a church and a citadel, dominating the town but slightly remote from it, so that in the event of a riot or revolt the crusaders would not be completely surrounded. The main town would usually be governed by Moslem officials in much the same way as before. In Acre, we know that there was a mosque even as late as 1184, and that though the customs-clerks were Christians, they kept their records in Arabic.

The condition of the Moslems who lived in the Latin kingdom of Jerusalem has been described by a Moslem from Spain, Ibn Jubayr, who set out from Granada on a pilgrimage to Mecca in February 1183 and returned by way of Baghdad, Mosul, Aleppo, and Damascus in 1184. He left Damascus on 9 September, and subsequently spent the best part of a month in Acre (8 October–6 November) waiting for a ship back to Spain. (He was back in Granada on 3 May 1185.) He referred (as the Moslems always did) to the crusaders as ' Franks ',[1] and wrote as follows :

We moved from Tibnin—may God destroy it—at daybreak on Monday. Our way lay through continuous farms and ordered settlements whose inhabitants were all Muslims, living comfortably with the Franks. God protect us from such temptation ! They surrender half their crops to the Franks at harvest-time, and pay as well a poll-tax of one dinar and five qirat for each person. Other than that, they are not interfered with, save for a light tax on the fruits of trees. Their houses and all their effects are left to their full possession. All the coastal cities occupied by the Franks are managed in this fashion, their rural districts, the villages and farms, belonging to the Muslims. But their hearts have been seduced, for they observe how unlike them in ease and comfort are their brethren in the Muslim regions under their [Muslim] governors. This is one of the misfortunes afflicting the Muslims. The Muslim community bewails the injustice of a landlord of its own faith, and applauds the conduct of its opponent and enemy, the Frankish landlord, and is accustomed to justice from him. He who laments this state of affairs must turn to God.[2]

[1] In Syria the Moslems still refer to all westerners, whether European or American, as ' Franji ' (' Franks ').
[2] *The Travels of Ibn Jubayr*, tr. R. J. C. Broadhurst (1952), pp. 316–17.

Even more surprising, to Ibn Jubayr, was the fact that trade continued between the Moslem and Christian kingdoms, even in times of active warfare.

> The Christians impose a tax on the Muslims in their land which gives them full security ; and likewise the Christian merchants pay a tax upon their goods in Muslim lands. Agreement exists between them, and there is equal treatment in all cases. The soldiers engage themselves in their war, while the people are at peace and the world goes to him who conquers.[1]

In Palestine and Syria such a state of affairs was simply a matter of tradition. Those countries had lived under foreign domination literally for thousands of years, and the merchants of the cities had discovered that the only hope of survival lay in their ability to dissociate themselves from both war and politics, and to confine their interests to trade.

There was also a certain amount of intercourse between the nobles on both sides. Usāmah ibn Munqidh, the Moslem lord of Shaizar, who lived from 1095 to 1188, was a frequent visitor to Frankish territory, and has preserved the following story, which gives a vivid picture of conditions in Jerusalem :

> I saw one of the Franks come up to al-Amir Mu'in al-Din (may Allah's mercy rest upon his soul) when he was in the Dome of the Rock and say to him ' Dost thou want to see God as a child ? ' Mu'in-al-Din said, ' Yes '.. The Frank walked ahead of us until he showed us the picture of Mary with Christ (may peace be upon him) as an infant in her lap. He then said, ' This is God as a child '. But Allah is exalted far above what the infidels say about him.[2]

The crusaders and Moslems might thus meet in one of the principal churches (which had originally been a mosque) and converse with the outward forms of courtesy, but there was no real intellectual contact between them. Usāmah was, as usual, amused at the intellectual simplicity of the Franks, whom he compared to animals ' possessing the virtues of courage and fighting, but nothing else '.[3] He thought them cruel, superstitious (as in their use of trial by ordeal), ignorant (especially in

[1] *Ibid.*, pp. 300–1.
[2] Philip K. Hitti, *Usāmah ibn Muniqdh, an Arab-Syrian Gentleman and Warrior* (1929), p. 164.
[3] *Ibid.*, p. 161.

medical and scientific matters), and immodest (in their sexual behaviour). But what astonished him most was the fact that they did not appreciate that their civilization was infinitely barbaric in comparison with that of the East. They did not realize what treasures of Greek learning or science the Moslems might possess, because they were not the sort of men who were interested. Though in Spain and Sicily it was possible to have a real cultural interchange between Christians and Moslems, in Palestine the crusaders were too proud to learn. The only concessions which they would occasionally make to the native culture were when they relapsed into oriental luxury ; Usāmah quotes the case of an exceptional old knight at Antioch who employed Egyptian cooks, had a clean kitchen, and ate no pork.

He also pointed out, however, that there was a great difference between those crusaders who had recently arrived from Frankish lands and the ' old-stagers ' who had become acclimatized by long association with the Moslems. The new arrivals simply could not understand the spirit of toleration that prevailed. They were amazed to find that their brethren did not force their Moslem subjects to become Christian. A holy war, as they understood it, would have been more like Charlemagne's Saxon war in which the conquered heathen had been given the alternative of conversion or death (pp. 143-4). They thought that the mosques should have been destroyed like the Golden Calf or the pagan Irminsul, and were astounded to find that Moslem emirs might walk at liberty in their churches.

Consequently, relations between the new arrivals and the ' old-stagers ' (*pulliani*) were often strained. The fact was not surprising, since the only way in which reinforcements could be obtained in times of crisis was by an appeal to the religious conscience of the Latin West. Thus, after the fall of Edessa (1144), which exposed the crusaders' northern flank, there was an immediate call for a Second Crusade, and it was preached by St. Bernard :

> The earth trembles and is shaken because the King of Heaven has lost his land, the land where once he walked. . . . The great eye of Providence observes these acts in silence ; it wishes to see if anyone who seeks God, who suffers with him in his sorrow, will render him his heritage. . . . I tell you, the Lord is testing you.

III. TWO TRADITIONS
COMPARED

(See p. 206)

(*a*) Amiens Cathedral,
Nave (1220–36)

(*b*) Rome. St. Laurence-without-the-walls, Nave (1216–27)

IV. A CRUSADER CASTLE

Krak des Chevaliers from the East

To kill a pagan, he said, was not homicide, but malicide, and made for the glory of Christ. To die in battle for the cause of Christ, was to gain the bliss of eternal reward. It was all most inspiring and caused men by the thousand to take the Cross. But it was not surprising that when they reached the Holy Land and saw the easy-going ways of the crusaders, they were both shocked and disillusioned.

There was worse to follow, however, for the Crusade ended in total failure, owing to the divisions which existed among the resident crusader-princes. Some wanted to march on Aleppo and crush the rising power of Nūr-ad-Dīn, whose forces had been responsible for the crusaders' loss of Edessa, while others, partly from ignorance and partly from selfish motives, urged that an attack should be made on Damascus. The emir of that city, being an enemy of Nūr-ad-Dīn, was traditionally an ally of the Franks, and the resident crusaders did everything in their power to prevent an attack on him. They knew that in normal years, when no special Crusade was preached in the West, they would have to hold the country with minute forces and would need every ally they could get. But to the overseas crusaders the very idea of an alliance with the Moslems was treason. They marched against Damascus and, having failed to take the city, put the blame for their failure on the resident crusaders. In the West the consternation was great.

> It seems [wrote St. Bernard] that the Lord, provoked by our sins, has forgotten his pity and has come to judge the earth before the appointed time. He has not spared his people ; He has not spared even His own name, and the gentiles say ' Where is their God ? ' We promised success, and behold desolation !

Subsequently, even worse disasters were to befall the Christians, and suspicions of far deeper treachery were to be aroused.

But the basic reason for the ultimate discomfiture of the crusaders was that the Moslem powers, which had been dis-united at the end of the eleventh century, were being re-united in the twelfth century. Previously the Moslem rulers of Aleppo had welcomed the Christian Principality of Edessa as a buffer-state against the Zengids, and those of Damascus had rejoiced at the crusaders' attacks on their old enemy, Egypt. But in the second half of the twelfth century all that was changed. In 1154 Nūr-ad-Dīn had, as a direct result of the failure of the Second Crusade, extended his power southward from Aleppo to Damascus, and in 1168 had succeeded in gaining control of Egypt from the last of the Fātimids. The general who was responsible for this latter victory, Shirkuh, became the viceroy of Egypt, and on his death in the following year, was succeeded by his nephew, Saladin. It was he who was destined to unite the greater part of Islam against the Franks. In 1174, on the death of Nūr-ad-Dīn, he returned from Egypt to Damascus, and by means of a *coup de main* succeeded in having himself proclaimed King of both Egypt and Syria, so that the Latin states were surrounded by his power. For the first time the crusaders had to face a united Moslem opposition.

Saladin himself was a very remarkable man. He was untiring in his zeal to preach the *Jihad* or holy war against the Christians, yet he was a patient statesman and extremely chivalrous warrior. Even the Christians admired him, for at a time when massacres were considered one of the normal incidentals of warfare Saladin was outstandingly humane : ' Abstain from the shedding of blood ', he said, ' for blood that is spilt never slumbers.' It was declared by the Christians that he had actually been knighted by one of the crusaders, Humphrey de Toron, and it is certainly true that in the conduct of his wars, he displayed more chivalry than any of his opponents.

It was probably because of his qualities of gentleness and kindness that many of the resident crusaders were prepared to come to terms with him. To them it seemed that they were at last confronted with a reasonable Moslem ruler, whose word they could trust and whom they thought they understood, and they therefore advocated a policy of appeasement. On grounds of general strategy there were two main arguments which could be urged in favour of this policy. First, Saladin was stronger than any Moslem ruler they had previously had to face ; his power encircled them, since he could attack them simultaneously from the east and south and could blockade their seaports with his Egyptian fleet. Common prudence dictated that the crusaders should not provoke hostilities until they had had time to build up their own forces. Secondly, there was everything to be gained by delay. Saladin had difficulty in keeping his own kingdom united, and there was always a chance that, given time, his lieutenants in Egypt or northern Mesopotamia might rebel against him. Saladin himself was well aware of this danger, and thought that the most effective way of keeping his subjects united was by preaching the *Jihad* against the Christians. So far as the Moslems were concerned, this call for united action in the cause of religion met, at first, with only moderate success, and the crusaders who favoured appeasement thought that they could ignore it.

Their leader was Raymond, Count of Tripoli, and from 1174 to 1185 he controlled the affairs of the kingdom of Jerusalem as Regent for Baldwin the Leper. But there was considerable opposition to his policy, and it came to the fore on Baldwin's death (1185). Since Baldwin had no son his successor had to be elected, and the barons chose not Raymond but his rival Guy of Lusignan. Guy himself was a nonentity who owed his position to his wife, but the party which supported him was unmistakably the party of war, and Raymond was therefore doubly affronted. The question which contemporaries asked, and historians still ask, was whether he retaliated by entering into an offensive and defensive alliance with Saladin, in order to gain the crown for himself.

That he had some sort of understanding with Saladin cannot be denied. The only doubt concerns the precise terms which were understood. It is certain, however, that Raymond gave Saladin's forces permission to raid across the Jordan in the district of Tiberias. He claimed that the intention had been that only the Moslem peasantry should suffer, since the crusaders had strict orders to remain within their castles or towns, which were not to be attacked, and he asserted that it was purely an accident that the order was ignored by his personal enemy, the Master of the Temple, who happened to be in the area with a force of 130 knights (1187). But whatever Raymond's responsibility may have been, the virtual annihilation of the Templar force was the beginning of the end of the Latin kingdom of Jerusalem.

Saladin, claiming that the truce had been broken, laid siege to Tiberias, and the crusaders were forced into action. But their divisions still prevented them from acting in a spirit of unity. Raymond of Tripoli urged, although his wife was in the beleaguered city, that the crusaders should not march to the relief of Tiberias, since they would thereby expose themselves to ambush in waterless country. They should wait, he said, for Saladin to move, and then fight him on ground of their own choosing. The advice happened to be sound, but it was (quite understandably) rejected, because of doubts as to Raymond's loyalty. The crusaders marched towards Tiberias and were surrounded, as Raymond had warned them, at Hattin. They lacked water, and the terrain, which has been compared to calcarized ice-packs, was totally unsuitable for cavalry warfare. The crusaders suffered a decisive defeat, and Guy himself was captured. One of the few contingents to make its escape in good order was that of Raymond of Tripoli, which fought its way out. Some said that the Moslem forces did not try to oppose it, but opened their ranks in order to facilitate its escape.

The battle of Hattin took place on 4 July 1187, and by the end of the year Saladin had overrun almost the whole of the kingdom of Jerusalem. He had captured Jerusalem on 2 October (allowing its defenders to ransom themselves and giving them a safe passage back to the nearest Christian territory) and had secured his communications with Egypt by the capture of Ascalon. There remained to the crusaders only Tyre (defended by Conrad of Montferrat), the county of Tripoli, and the principality of Antioch.

A Third Crusade was preached in the West, and it was hoped that the disasters of the year might be retrieved. The Emperor Frederick Barbarossa set out with a vast army from Germany (1189), but as he took the overland route his army was decimated in Asia Minor, and he himself was drowned in the River Saleph before reaching Antioch. The kings of England and France, Richard Cœur de Lion and Philip Augustus, set out by sea and arrived with their armies intact, but were so consumed by mutual jealousies that they only added to the divisions of the crusaders. They did, indeed, succeed in recapturing Acre in 1191 (largely because Richard had, in the course of his journey, secured a naval base by conquering Cyprus from the Byzantine Empire); and subsequently the crusaders took Jaffa and had advanced to a point within sight of Jerusalem. But that was the limit of their successes and it was more than offset by the disastrous failure on the moral plane.

The quarrels of the crusaders had become an open scandal. Richard Cœur de Lion and Philip Augustus could not agree in anything. Richard, in his capacity as Duke of Normandy and Aquitaine, was the vassal of the French king, and Philip Augustus accordingly expected him to accept his leadership. Richard, on the other hand, made no secret of the fact that he thought nothing of Philip's qualities as warrior or king, and that he had no intention of submitting to him or anyone else. When Richard wanted to attack Acre, Philip would complain of a headache ; when Philip wanted to lead an assault, Richard would ostentatiously announce that he was at dinner. They quarrelled over everything, from the division of the booty to the question of who should be King of Jerusalem ; Richard supported Guy of Lusignan who had been released by Saladin, but Philip Augustus and the Palestinian barons preferred Conrad of Montferrat. When Conrad was murdered by one of the Assassins of northern Syria, the French accused Richard of complicity ; and when Philip Augustus abandoned the Crusade (October 1191), he returned to France and made use of the opportunity to attack Richard's territory with impunity. Finally, when Richard himself decided to return home (October 1192) he fell into the hands of Leopold, Duke of Austria, whose banners he had insulted at the siege of Acre. Leopold gave him up to his overlord, the Emperor Henry VI, who would only consent to release Richard on condition that he became his vassal and paid a ransom of 150,000 silver marks.

That last incident showed how cynical men had become about the whole ideal of the Crusade. Every crusader was supposed to be protected by the Church from the moment when he took the Cross until his return home from the Holy Land. But now, one crusader did not hesitate to attack the land of another, and the Emperor, the temporal head of Christendom, did not scruple to hold a crusader to ransom. The whole conduct of the Third Crusade had belied the intentions of idealists such as Urban II or St. Bernard. They had promised the crusaders a plenary indulgence for their sins, because they had regarded a Crusade as a religious exercise or pilgrimage in arms. They had thought that those who took the Cross would, like those who took the cowl, renounce their worldly jealousies and former enmities for the sake of Christ. In fact they had merely transferred them from Europe to Palestine, and had defiled the Holy Land with their iniquities. Younger sons who had no land in Europe would make a career of crusading, and would, if they were lucky, end up with a lordship or principality. Italian cities which lent their fleets, did so in return for concessions which would assist their trade. Crusading, so far from being a religious exercise, had become an enterprising way of making one's fortune.

It was a pitiful end for a brave ideal. The enthusiasm had all been spent, and the advantages of taking the Cross were weighed in pounds, shillings, and pence. The religious enthusiasm which had passed like a flame over Europe was spent, and Jerusalem, once triumphantly regained, was lost.

Further Reading

STEVEN RUNCIMAN. *A History of the Crusades.* 3 vols. Cambridge. 1951–4.

R. C. SMAIL. *Crusading Warfare* (1097–1193). Cambridge. 1956.

S. LANE POOLE. *Saladin and the Fall of the Kingdom of Jerusalem* (Heroes of the Nations series). London. 1898.

ELIZABETH S. DAWES (tr.). *The Alexiad of the Princess Anna Comnena.* London. 1928.

PHILIP K. HITTI (tr.). *An Arab-Syrian Gentleman and Warrior* (Usāmah ibn Munqidh). Columbia. 1929.

R. J. C. BROADHURST (tr.). *The Travels of Ibn Jubayr.* London. 1952.

KENNETH M. SETTON. *A History of the Crusades* : vol. i (ed. Marshall H. Baldwin) *The First Hundred Years;* vol. ii (ed. R. L. Wolff and H. W. Hazard) *The Later Crusades, 1189–1311.* Pennsylvania, 1955 and 1962.

V

FEUDAL MONARCHY AND THE FRENCH
KINGDOM (1066–1223)

BENEATH all the religious excitement and imperial dreams of the eleventh and twelfth centuries was the solid reality of feudalism, the social order which was rapidly being established in almost all the countries of Western Europe. Emperors might oppose it and temporarily even hold it in check, but in the long run its progress was irresistible. Local interests and the needs of warfare demanded more knights, more fiefs, and more castles, and a whole body of custom grew up to regularize the relations between lord and vassal—feudal law. The strongest kings were those who, instead of opposing the new order, made use of it. That was why feudal monarchy was important, for a feudal monarch was one who, in addition to being king, was also the feudal lord of his kingdom. It is important that the point should be grasped, for it is very easy to slip into the mistake of thinking that feudal monarchy was simply ' medieval '. In fact it was a New Leviathan, the medieval equivalent of a socialist state. In a socialist state, the community owns, or should own, the means of production. In a feudal monarchy, the king did own all the land—which in the terms of medieval economy might fairly be equated with the means of production.

The best and simplest example of a feudal monarchy is to be found in England after the Norman Conquest. When William the Conqueror defeated Harold Godwinsson at the battle of Hastings (1066), he claimed to have established his legitimate right to succeed Edward the Confessor as King of England, but, owing to Harold's resistance, he was also able to claim that he had won the whole country by right of conquest. Henceforward, every inch of land was to be his, and he would dispose of it as he thought fit. As is well known, he distributed most of it to his Norman followers, but he did not give it to them in absolute right. They were simply his tenants and held the land from him. A revolution had thus been effected, and its nature can be clearly seen in the case of the few Englishmen who retained William's favour. They had to surrender their land to him, in order that they might receive it back from him as his tenants. Thus, in Norman England, the word *allodium* was unknown ; on the continent of Europe it denoted land which was a man's absolute and inalienable property, but in England there was no such thing. All land was the king's, and the best a subject could do was to hold land freely from him.

The Conqueror's ownership of the land was firmly established in Domesday Book, which was a survey of the king's landed property in England. It describes practically the whole kingdom,[1] county by county, and shows that all land was held either by the king in his own hand or of him by his tenants-in-chief. The names of these tenants are carefully listed at the beginning of the description of each county, and their lands are grouped together. The lands of Robert Malet, for example, occupy several pages in the survey of Suffolk, but it is repeatedly emphasized that they were held of the king. That was why the king wanted to know all about them—the number of plough-lands and ploughs in each manor, the number of villeins, bordars, cottagers, slaves, freemen, or sokemen, the extent of the woodland and meadowland, the amount of tax payable, and the total annual value. This last item was naturally the one that interested the king most, and it was usually given in three different ways—as it was on the day when King Edward the Confessor was alive and dead (5 January 1066), as it was when the survey was made (1086), and as it could be, if the land were fully exploited.

The information thus collected was needed, not for fixing the amount of knight-service owed by each tenant (*servitium debitum*), for that had already been arbitrarily fixed before the survey was made, but in order that the king might make the most of the 'incidents' of feudal tenure. These 'incidents' were a regular

---

[1] There are a few omissions, the most important being the counties of Northumberland, Cumberland, Durham, and most of Lancashire.

feature of feudal law from the eleventh century onwards, and had been developed as a means of safeguarding the overlord's rights, while permitting the tenant to make his fief hereditary. Thus a son was allowed to succeed to his father's tenancy if he paid his overlord a ' relief '. This was a money-payment fixed arbitrarily by the overlord. In England the king's tenants-in-chief usually complained that the sum he demanded was far too high ; they were prepared to concede that one year's income from the land would be a fair price for a relief, but the king often asked, and got, more. With all the information at his disposal in Domesday Book, he knew exactly how ˙much each of his tenants could afford.

Even more valuable were the ' incidents ' which fell to the king when one of his tenants died without leaving a son of full age. If there were young children, the king had their wardship. This meant that, provided he educated the children according to their station in life, he enjoyed all the profits of their father's land till they came of age. He could instruct the sheriff of the county to take possession of the land (and he could tell from a glance at Domesday Book what its annual value should be), or, if offered a sufficiently attractive price, he would sell the wardship to one of his barons and let him make a profit if he could. If the children were girls, he would sell them in marriage to the highest bidder. It was all simply a matter of feudal law. Every lord reckoned to make a handsome profit when one of his feudal tenants died, and if, by any chance, the tenant was the last of his line and had no heirs at all, the land would ' escheat ' or revert to the lord in its entirety.

That was why, at the beginning of this chapter, a comparison was drawn between a feudal monarchy and a socialist state, for in the former the land, if not nationalized, was at least ' monarchized '. So far as monarchs were concerned, feudal monarchy was highly desirable. The only difficulty was to establish one, for it could hardly be expected that the subjects of a king would voluntarily surrender their lands to him, while a lucky stroke, like William's conquest of England, was an opportunity the like of which would not occur again. How then was an ambitious king to proceed ? The answer to that question must be sought in the history of the Capetian kings of France, for they did succeed, in the period between 1100 and 1223, in making themselves feudal monarchs.

In order to appreciate the magnitude of their achievement, it is necessary to see how tenuous their powers were at the beginning of that period. The Capetians were kings of the Franks; that is to say that, so far as the kingdom of the West Franks was concerned, they were legally the successors of Charlemagne. But the monarchy to which they succeeded was but a shadow of his. They were still recognized, in theory at least, as the leaders of the western Franks in arms, but they did not attempt to summon their army annually and did not usually expect to receive contingents from many parts of the kingdom. The counts were no longer their officials, but were virtually independent potentates. The fisc, or crown-lands of the Carolingians, had been alienated. All that remained to the king was the prestige which was given to him by the moral authority of the Church. The Church realized that without law and order there could be no Christian life, and so it supported the monarchy to the utmost of its powers. It did not form a mighty civil service for the king, as the imperial Church did for the Emperor, but it relied on the king for protection, and in return gave him authority. It even sanctified his person and gave support to the claim that by his royal touch he could miraculously cure the scrofula. (A similar claim was made for the kings of England and was exercised till the reign of Queen Anne, one of the last people to be ' cured ' in that way being Dr. Johnson.) It allowed that the miraculous gift might pass from father to son, and helped the Capetians to make the crown hereditary in their line by consenting to crown the king's eldest son during his father's lifetime. And it taught the French that it was God's will that they should obey their king.

This was the main asset belonging to the French crown in the second half of the eleventh century. It had the support of the Church, but very little else. The king did not attempt to govern the kingdom outside his royal demesne, a narrow strip of territory stretching approximately from Paris to Orleans. Outside it, he was merely *primus inter pares*. The Duke of Normandy was also King of England, and though he occasionally obeyed the French king he was more usually at war with him. A similar mixture of independence and occasional conformity was shown by the Dukes of Burgundy, Brittany, and Aquitaine, and by the Counts of Flanders, Toulouse, Anjou, Champagne, and Blois. Though they recognized the authority of the king, they did not expect him to employ it in their territory. They thought that the king should normally confine his attention to his own demesne, and only exercise his authority outside it when asked to do so.

From the time of Philip I (1060–1108) the Capetian kings were themselves prepared to fall in with this view, because they realized that it was only in their demesne that they could establish a power which was real. The royal crown gave prestige and glory, the moral support of the Church and the lip-service of the greater nobility ; but to be an effective king it was necessary also to have money and men, and these were most easily to be procured by an efficient exploitation of feudal resources. Consequently the king had to concentrate first and foremost on his own demesne. It was there that he was a feudal lord, and there that the resources necessary for the exercise of his royal power were to be gained.

But even a feudal lord could not afford to sit at home and expect all rents to be paid and services to be punctually performed. He had to exercise his rights in person. It is for that reason that Philip I's son, Louis VI (the Fat) (1108–37), was so famous. He spent the greater part of his reign on horseback, riding from end to end of the royal demesne, and enforcing the royal rights ruthlessly. He had to defeat innumerable petty vassals, such as Thomas de Marle, lord of the castle of Montlhéry, who had defied his feudal authority, and he fought engagements even in the immediate neighbourhood of Paris, at Livry, Gournay, Lagny, Montmorency, Luzarches, and Meaux. And so it continued all over his demesne. He was determined that his feudal authority should be respected.

The nature of the task which he thus set himself will best be appreciated if we examine the precise nature of his demesne. It is always tempting to think of it as a compact block of territory which he simply owned. In one sense that is true, but it is important to realize that his ownership was reflected in many different ways. A manor might have been given by him to a knight as a fief, in which case the appropriate military service had to be enforced. Alternatively, the serfs of a village might owe the king a proportion of their produce (*champipart*), a money-rent (*census*), or labour services (which went under the generic name of *la corvée*). The king had to know exactly what were his rights in every single village, and exercise them every year. For if he did not exercise them he would lose them. In the Middle Ages, ' twice made a custom ' and custom had the force of law.

It was the same with the various royal rights and revenues which he exercised in his demesne. No coinage might be minted without the king's authority, but if a moneyer succeeded in establishing an unlawful mint, and worked it for several years without let or hindrance, he would have established a custom. Similarly, no fairs or markets could be held without the king's permission, but the king would lose this privilege in any place where he did not forcibly close a fair which had come into existence unlawfully. He had the right of demanding hospitality (*hospitium, la gîte*) for himself and his court at certain places, but if he did not demand it regularly he might discover that the custom had lapsed. It was the same with a number of other rights, such as the holding of a court of justice, the collection of toll, purveyance, and the right to receive the tithe of some particular crop or the chattels of a villein who died without heirs. No right was secure unless it was exercised ceaselessly.

The same was true in regard to larger issues such as the control of the greater churches of his demesne. The king expected, in spite of occasional opposition from the Pope, to have the last word in the appointment of bishops and abbots in his demesne, but he was well aware that the first essential for a successful intervention in the affairs of the Church was speed. If he was at Orleans when the Bishop of Beauvais died, he could not afford to delay. He had to take to his horse and make his intervention in person. If he was too slow, the canons of Beauvais might proceed to an election before the king's views were known, and then there would be trouble ; for though the Pope might turn a blind eye to friendly interventions by the king, he could not willingly allow him to overturn a canonical election which had already been made. If such an event were to occur twice running, ' twice made a custom ' and the king had lost all hope of control. He had to be ready, therefore, to intervene without

delay, and to ride from Paris to Bourges or from St. Denis to
St. Benoît-sur-Loire, exercising his rights punctually.

It was for this reason that Louis VI paid such ceaseless attention to the affairs of his demesne. The reward of his labour was
that, by the end of his reign, his authority as feudal lord of his
demesne was secure. He was not yet a feudal monarch, because
he was not yet the feudal lord of his whole kingdom. But at
least he had made a start. In his own demesne nobody dared to
disobey him, and in this respect he was already more fortunate
than many of the greater nobles of his kingdom. The Dukes
of Burgundy and Aquitaine, for example, could not boast nearly
so much authority in their demesnes, and consequently their
respect for the king increased. As soon as they saw that he was a
really powerful man they became more mindful of their obligations to him.

Thus in the second half of his reign Louis VI was able to look
beyond the immediate concerns of his kingdom. In 1122 he led
an army to the Auvergne to reinstate the Bishop of Clermont
who had been expelled from his see, and in 1127 he made a
similar expedition to Bruges to avenge the murder of Charles,
Count of Flanders. The latter expedition was only partially
successful, since he failed, probably owing to the influence of
English gold, to establish his own nominee, William Clito, as
the new count, but at least it showed his determination to intervene in Flemish affairs whenever he thought it necessary.

The great triumph of his reign, however, occurred in 1124.
In that year the Emperor Henry V invaded France from the east,
and Louis VI summoned the whole army of his kingdom to
assemble at Reims. Contingents came from Reims, Chalons-
sur-Marne, Laon, Soissons, Orleans, Etampes, Paris, St. Denis,
St. Quentin, Ponthieu, Amiens, and Beauvais, and amongst the
nobles who obeyed the summons were the Counts of Flanders,
Anjou, Brittany, Chartres, Troyes, Vermandois, and Nevers,
and the Dukes of Burgundy and Aquitaine. Even though the
Duke of Normandy was absent, since he was in alliance with the
Emperor against the King, the army was a most splendid display
of the military power of *Francia*. The Emperor did not challenge
it in battle, but beat a hasty retreat, and Louis VI had the immense
satisfaction of having successfully exercised a royal prerogative

which had been dormant for more than a century. When even the Dukes of Aquitaine and Burgundy obeyed his summons, he could begin to think that some day he might revive the glories of Charlemagne. A similar thought may well have been in his mind when, at Reims in 1131, he himself crowned his son Louis as his associate in the kingdom, in the presence of Pope Innocent II.

But the essential aim which he and his chief minister, Suger, Abbot of St. Denis, kept in mind was always that the royal demesne had to be consolidated and enlarged. In 1137, just before his death, he succeeded in marrying his son, Louis VII, to Eleanor, the only daughter and heir of William X, Duke of Aquitaine. It was a glorious match, and one that gave promise of an expansion of the royal demesne beyond all bounds. Unfortunately the young Louis could not abide his wife. He restrained himself during Abbot Suger's lifetime, but almost as soon as that great minister was dead he divorced her. It was the most unfortunate action of his career, for it meant that he lost Aquitaine, which had seemed within his grasp, and that he allowed it to pass to an enemy. Within two months of her divorce, Eleanor married Henry Plantagenet, subsequently to be King Henry II of England (1154–89). In his own right he was Duke of Normandy and Count of Anjou and Maine, so that the acquisition of Aquitaine gave him control of the whole of western France, from the English Channel to the Pyrenees, a territory which, in comparison with the royal demesne of Louis VII, was enormous. Louis VII had to make a virtue of necessity by priding himself on his poverty :

> As for your prince [he said to one of Henry's subjects] he lacks for nothing : valuable horses, gold and silver, silken fabrics, precious stones, he has them all in abundance. At the court of France we have only bread, wine and gaiety.

In spite of all his apparent modesty, however, and in spite of the disaster of Eleanor's second marriage, Louis VII continued to promote the cause of feudal monarchy. In this he was greatly assisted by the growth of the legend of Charlemagne and the glamour which it gave to the conception of the Kingdom of the Franks. (It was probably during the period of his reign that

THE FRENCH KINGDOM c.1170

━━━━━ Dominions of King Henry II of England

━━━━━ Royal Demesne

▨▨▨ Counties of Champagne, Blois and Chartres

▥▥▥ County of Flanders

-·-·-·- Frontier of the French Kingdom

0   50   100   150
SCALE OF MILES

H.S.W.

The Song of Roland was written.) But more important still was the fact that the magnates often needed his assistance. They were weary of their mutual quarrels and lawsuits, and discovered that the surest way of bringing them to an end would be to submit them, as did the Duke of Burgundy and the Bishop of Langres in 1153, to the judgment of the king's court. This court was a feudal court, and submission to its judgment necessitated the recognition of the king as one's feudal lord. But the price was worth paying, for a judgment given by the king was enforced by his authority. If either party in the dispute failed to obey it, the king would send an army against him and overpower him.

Feudal monarchy therefore was not unpopular. If the king could show, by the way in which he kept his own demesne in order, that he was worthy of his position, there would be many nobles even in the remoter parts of his kingdom who would be willing, and even anxious, to become his men. Louis VII, for example, received homage from the Count of Forez, the Lord of Beaujeu, the Bishop of Mende, and the Viscount of Narbonne, and their voluntary submission need not surprise us. For though it is often imagined that the prime aim of a count, viscount, or petty lord was to make himself independent of all authority, he was usually far more preoccupied with the problem of his security. He wanted a feudal lord because he needed protection against his neighbours, and he thought that the obligation of feudal services and dues was a reasonable price to pay for such a boon.

So far as the French monarchy was concerned, the main danger to be feared was that many barons would consider the protection of Henry II of England more efficacious than that of Louis VII of France. Popular sentiment, however, was on the side of the French king, the English kings being considered foreigners and interlopers in spite of their French ancestry. Abbot Suger in his *Life of Louis VI* declared that it was ' neither right nor natural for Frenchmen [*Francos*] to be subjected to Englishmen, nor Englishmen to Frenchmen ', and in *The Song of Roland* there is a distinct tendency to glorify both the French (or Frankish) people and the country of ' sweet France ', a phrase which (in this context) seems to have referred to all the territory that belonged to, or actually obeyed, the French king. The most graphic illustration of nascent nationalism, however, is to be found in a story told by Gerald of Wales of the rejoicing which attended the birth of Louis VII's only son, who was later to reign as Philip II, ' Augustus ' (1180–1223). Gerald was then a student at Paris, and he relates how he was woken in the night by the clanging of bells and the blaze of lighted candles. Fearing that the city was on fire, he looked out of the window and saw in the square outside :

> Two old hags who, in spite of their poverty were carrying candles, and showing great joy in their faces, voices and gestures, running precipitately to meet each other as if they were charging. And when [Gerald] asked them the cause of such commotion and exultation, one of them looked up at him and said : ' We have a king given us now by God, an heir to the kingdom, who by God's grace shall be a man of great might. Through him your king shall suffer dishonour and defeat, punishment and shame, confusion and misery.' . . . For the woman knew that he [Gerald] and his companions were from the realm of England.[1]

The story, whether true or apocryphal—for Gerald of Wales was quite capable of inventing realistic stories—has a symbolic value, since there can be little doubt that the main aim of Philip's policy throughout his reign was the expulsion of the English from his kingdom. With this end in view he often contemplated an invasion of England, a project which at times amounted almost to an obsession, and which on one occasion led him into the most absurd of personal entanglements. After the death of his first wife, Isabella of Hainault, he was anxious to form an alliance with King Canute VI of Denmark, in the hope that he could induce him both to resign in his favour the claims which he had to the English throne, and also to lend him a fleet with which to enforce them. The project came to nothing, except that Philip married Canute's daughter, Ingeborg (1193), and then discovered that he felt a positive repugnance to her. He attempted to have the marriage annulled, but though the French bishops were prepared to do their best for him, the Pope

[1] Giraldus Cambrensis, *De Principum Instructione*, iii, xxv (R.S. viii, 292–3). Translation based, with alterations, on that of H. E. Butler, *The Autobiography of Gerald of Wales* (Cape, 1937), pp. 37–8.

resolutely supported Ingeborg, and Philip was saddled with her for the rest of his days. (She survived him by several years.) He normally refused to live with her and kept her as a virtual prisoner, but when he attempted to make an illicit marriage with Agnes of Meran, he was foiled by Pope Innocent III, who put all his lands under interdict (1200) until he submitted to the judgment of the Church.[1]

Most of Philip's plans against the English were more fortunate in their outcome. He was adroit at exploiting the quarrels of Henry II's sons, and supported, in turn, Richard against his father, John against Richard, and Arthur against John. Any member of the Angevin family who felt aggrieved with his father or brothers was sure of a warm and sympathetic welcome at the court of France. He had only to pour his grievances into Philip's ear, and Philip would gravely accept his homage and go to war in order to see, as he put it, that justice was done. In this way he was able to establish his claim to be overlord of the continental possessions of the English monarchy. For every time his aid was invoked he made his claims more explicit and more precise.

Thus, on John's accession to the English throne (1199), he was able to exploit the difficulties caused by the rival claims of John's nephew, Arthur of Britanny, who was supported by many of the barons of Anjou, Maine, and Touraine. John needed Philip's support, and Philip was prepared to grant it, at a price. He gave a formal judgment in his court in favour of John (1200), but gave it as feudal lord and demanded a ' relief ' of 20,000 marks. John, of course, was unwilling to regard his own relationship to Philip in the same light as that of any other vassal to any other lord. He considered that the position of the duchy of Normandy was a special one, and that by long custom its dukes were exempt from the ordinary feudal services and dues. But Philip was insistent. If John wanted the benefit of a judg-ment in his court, which was equivalent to feudal protection, he had to pay for it by accepting the normal feudal obligations.

---

[1] Innocent III did, however, legitimize the children born of the illicit union. They were (1) Mary, who was betrothed to Arthur of Brittany, and who married, after his death, first Philip the Margrave of Namur, and secondly Henry of Brabant, and (2) Philip Hurepel, subsequently Lord of Boulogne.

He was soon to be provided with a test case. John, in the course of his matrimonial exploits, had fallen foul of the family of Lusignan, which held an important position in Aquitaine. He summoned them to his court to prove the justice of their case in trial by battle, he himself having enlisted professional champions to defend his cause. The Lusignans, however, demanded a trial by their peers, and appealed to Philip as John's overlord. Philip summoned John to his court, and John refused to obey the summons. Such disobedience could only, according to feudal law, be punished by the lord's ' defiance '. Thus :

> The court of France met and judged that the king of England should be deprived of all the lands which he had held of the king of France up to that time, because they (the kings of England) had, for a long time past, neglected to do services for those lands, and had on practically no occasion been willing to comply with their lord's summons.[1]

It remained only to put the judgment into force, to march against Normandy and conquer it. In the reign of Henry II or Richard I of England such a task would have been beyond the French king's means, for the Norman frontier was heavily fortified, the most famous of its castles being Château Gaillard (' saucy castle ') which had been built near Les Andelys by Richard I on his return from the Third Crusade. But with John at the head of the English army no amount of scientific fortification could save Normandy, for though he was able to form bold plans he always hesitated in the execution of them. He did not inspire confidence in his troops, but rather defeat, and in two years (1202-4) he lost the whole of Normandy.

Since, in the last resort, the acquisition of Normandy by the French crown was a matter of military conquest, it may be asked why so much importance had been attached to the legal preliminaries. It should be remembered, however, that for Philip it was essential to have the reputation of being just towards his vassals. If it was thought that he neglected his duties as a feudal lord and, instead of protecting the lands of his vassals, seized them for himself, no one would voluntarily become his man. Feudal relationships could only be based on mutual confidence,

[1] Ralph of Coggeshall, *Chronicon Anglicanum*, ed. J. Stevenson (R.S. 1875), p. 136.

and if Philip wanted his subjects to become his vassals it was essential that, even in the case of Normandy, he should have his quarrel just. Feudal monarchs who, like John of England, acquired a reputation for injustice, invariably found themselves confronted with feudal rebellion.

Normandy was not the only addition which Philip Augustus made to the royal demesne. He also expanded it northwards, in the direction of Flanders. By his first marriage, to Isabella of Hainault, he acquired the district of Artois, and in 1182, on the death of Isabella of Vermandois and Valois, he put forward a claim to her inheritance which, in spite of its inherent weaknesses, enabled him, by agreement with the other claimants, to acquire first Amiens and Montdidier (1185), then Péronne (1192), and finally the whole of Valois and St. Quentin (1213). His power, therefore, extended northwards to the English Channel, and it was still further strengthened in 1210, when, on discovering that Renaud of Dammartin was in alliance with King John, he seized (amongst other lands) his lordship of Boulogne.

The main object of Philip's northern expansion, however, was to control Flanders. That country was of very exceptional importance since it was the richest part of northern Europe. It was the centre of the cloth trade, and the towns of Ypres, Douai, Bruges, and Ghent were fabulously wealthy. Each town was, in effect, a little city-state, but paid the count large sums of money for the enjoyment of its liberties, and it was only natural that the King of France should be anxious to exploit his over-lordship in such a way that he also benefited from the wealth of the district. Like every medieval king he was perpetually short of money—his military expenditure for the first year of his Norman campaign (1202–3) had totalled £95,000 *parisis*— and the prospect of increasing his revenue by control of the commercial and industrial centre of northern Europe was peculiarly tempting. He was anxious to show himself a good lord to merchants and, near the Flemish frontier, was liberal in his treatment of the trading towns of his demesne. At Montdidier, Beauvais, Soissons, Noyon, Roye, Bapaume, St. Quentin, Amiens, St. Riquier, Montreuil, Hesdin, Arras, and Tournai, he granted the townsmen charters that made them communes. In return for royal protection and certain specific liberties they were to have communal responsibilities to the king, paying him fixed sums of money and owing him definite services ; Tournai owed him 300 well-equipped foot-soldiers, and Philip Augustus saw to it that, in every case, he struck a profitable bargain.

In Flanders itself, however, Philip was always meeting with opposition from King John of England. For John also was aware of the importance of the district, and had a special interest in its affairs, since the Flemish cloth-manufacturers obtained almost all their wool from England. He had agents in the more important cities, and allowed them considerable sums of money with which, apparently, they purchased the goodwill of the most important citizens. He also made ceaseless attempts to gain the alliance of Ferrand, Count of Flanders, who, in spite of his original attachment to Philip Augustus, was eventually won over by the trading-interests of his principal cities. The English cause made headway and Philip Augustus found it necessary, once again, to resort to arms.

His first plan was to revive the project for an invasion of England. King John had quarrelled bitterly with the Papacy, and Pope Innocent III had placed the Kingdom under interdict. Philip and his barons, hoping that the resultant breach would provide them with a heaven-sent opportunity, prepared a fleet for the invasion, but at the last moment their plans were thwarted by two events. John submitted to the Pope and surrendered his kingdom to him, so that on 22 May 1213, Philip received papal instructions to abandon the invasion. And eight days later the English destroyed the French invasion-fleet at the battle of Damme.

Philip was suddenly thrown on to the defensive. John had already formed alliances with Raymond, Count of Toulouse, and the Emperor Otto IV, and now he was openly joined by Ferrand, Count of Flanders. Philip was to be attacked simultaneously from the south and the north, by a coalition which seemed to consist of all the other important powers of Western Europe. It was the great crisis of his reign, and he emerged from it triumphant. Leaving his son, Louis, to ward off the southern attack—which, since it was led by King John himself, eventually proved ineffectual—he concentrated all his remaining forces against Otto and Ferrand. He eventually joined battle with them at Bouvines, near Tournai (1214), and though greatly outnumbered won an overwhelming victory.

The battle of Bouvines was one of the decisive battles of medieval Europe. It ensured that the county of Flanders should be under the effective control of the French monarchy for about a century. It so weakened the position of the Emperor Otto IV in Germany that he lost his crown to his rival, Frederick II. And in England it was taken as the final proof of King John's incompetence and wickedness, with the result that his barons revolted and forced him to grant them *Magna Carta* (1215). By contrast, the reputation of Philip Augustus was assured. By force of arms he had proved himself the arbiter of Europe. The description given by his chaplain, William the Breton, of the popular rejoicing after the battle, makes it clear that his subjects considered his cause as their own. In all the towns and cities through which he passed on his return from the battle, he was given a triumphal entry; the houses were hung with curtains and silks, and the streets strewn with flowers and greenery. In the country, where it was harvest-time, the peasants dropped their work in the fields and rushed to the road to see Count Ferrand in chains (*ferratus*), being taken to captivity in a litter drawn by two iron-grey (*ferrandi*) horses. At Paris, the citizens and university students kept up their celebrations night and day for a week.

The enthusiasm was all the greater, since the victory in arms had its parallel in the cultural ascendancy of the French kingdom. Paris seemed to be the heart and soul of Latin Christendom. It was the Athens of the North, where the works of Aristotle were studied with the zeal and excitement reserved for revolutionary discoveries, and where the university, which in the reign of Philip Augustus was taking shape as a corporate institution, drew scholars from Germany, Spain, England and Italy; Pope Innocent III himself had studied there. It was the centre of what might have been called the *new* culture of the Middle Ages; Aristotle displaced Augustine in philosophy, and in art the Gothic triumphed over Romanesque.

Gothic art, in spite of its English connection, was the style *par excellence* of the French kingdom, and it spread with the expansion of the royal demesne. The great Gothic cathedrals were a sign of the new era inaugurated by the feudal monarchy. Those of Notre Dame de Paris (1163–1220) and Chartres (1194–1220) were, in their main structures, completed in the reign of Philip Augustus, and those of Reims and Amiens were begun in 1211 and 1220 respectively. Their stupendous height, so wonderfully combined with lightness and strength, dominated the country for miles around, and constituted a memorial of the fact that the glory had returned to the Kingdom—that there was now a worthy successor to Charlemagne in ' sweet France '.

But even though the Carolingian legend had given glamour and *élan* to his achievements, the kingdom which Philip had constructed was very different from that of his great predecessor. So far from being universal in conception, it was strictly local. Philip Augustus derived his strength from the fact that he was capable of concentrating all his energy on the single task of administering and enlarging his demesne. He did not allow any visions of external glory to distract him from his aim. In contrast to Richard I of England—who was happy to be fighting a crusade in Palestine because he thought that military glory, wherever attained, was an end in itself—Philip had made his stay in the Holy Land as short as possible, since energy spent outside his kingdom was, in his opinion, energy wasted. Similarly, when Baldwin IV, Count of Flanders, had in 1204 joined the Fourth Crusade and thought himself fortunate because he became the Latin Emperor of Constantinople, Philip Augustus stayed at home and marvelled at the luck which had thus removed a potential enemy. Even when Pope Innocent III had begged him to take part in a crusade against the Albigensian heretics, he had refused to be moved from his purpose. ' I have at my side ', he had written, ' two great and terrible lions, the Emperor Otto and King John ; therefore I am unable to leave France [*Francia*].' To him, Toulouse, Narbonne, and Béziers were like foreign territory, because they were not part of his demesne, and no prospect of military glory could turn him aside from his self-appointed task of establishing a feudal monarchy.

In that respect the secret of his success lay in the attention which he paid to detail. For him monarchy was a business. He had no use for the traditional offices of royal administration, which were held by nobles and were used by them in order to magnify their own splendour and power. He left the chancellorship vacant in 1185 and suppressed the stewardship, on the death of Theobald of Blois, in 1191. Instead he governed through comparatively humble men, Bernard the prior of Grandmont, William of Garlande, Peter the Marshal, and Adam the Clerk, who were prepared to devote their time to the supervision of bailiffs, the keeping of accounts, the drawing-up of charters, and all the varied office-work that was inseparable from the efficient administration of either a landed estate or a kingdom. Just as in the time of Louis VI, ceaseless vigilance was necessary if royal rights were not to be lost because they were not exercised. Precise agreements had to be drawn up between the king and his new vassals, in order that the feudal obligations, on both sides, might be explicit and precise. All useful customs had to be committed to writing and preserved. If the king was to administer his greatly-enlarged demesne, it was necessary that he should, metaphorically, be in several places at once. He had to be able to keep his bailiffs informed of all his rights, and he had to keep a check on their activities in order to ensure that they were serving him loyally. There was an immediate need for bureaucratic control and a plethora of documents ; the word which was most in use was the Latin word *subscribite* !—' Write it down ! ' If the king was to make the whole of France his feudal monarchy, the details of land tenure and feudal obligation which had to be remembered were innumerable, and the work of government could only be efficiently performed in a writing office. The earliest registers of the royal chancery come from his reign, and consequently it is to him that can be attributed the creation of an efficient French bureaucracy. That, perhaps, was the most important of all his achievements, for it gave continuity and order to the administration of the French kingdom, and made it not just an honour but an institution.

Gerald of Wales tells the story how Philip Augustus, at the age of seventeen, was asked by one of his barons what he was thinking about, and replied that he was wondering whether God would ever allow him to restore the Kingdom of the Franks to the pristine glory which it had enjoyed in the time of Charlemagne. While the emperors sought to fulfil this ambition by devising grandiose schemes of conquest, Philip Augustus sought it in the strict attention to practical details, and created a feudal monarchy which, in spite of its tedious bureaucracy, or rather because of it, was the New Leviathan and the arbiter of Europe.

APPENDIX

A Charter of Philip Augustus [1]

In the name of the holy and undivided Trinity. Amen. Philip by the grace of God King of the Franks. Be it universally known to all men, present and future, that on account of his faithful service, We are giving and granting in perpetuity to Ralph d'Estrées and his heirs by the wife to whom he is now married, everything that We have at Moreuil, both in the town [*villa*] and its appurtenances, to be held peacefully and quietly from us in liege homage,[2] which he himself has done to Us for it. We are also giving to him at Roye-sur-le-Matz seven measures of oats by the measure of Roye and eleven pounds and sixteen shillings of rent which We have there, to be paid every year to the same Ralph on the day after All Saints in this way, *viz.* :— that if the rent is not paid by the men who owe it at the aforesaid term, Ralph can, without doing any injury, take the balance of the rent from their belongings, as well as ten shillings fine for the several days on which they have detained it. And the said oats shall be rendered to Ralph and shall be transported as far as it used to be transported for Us on the day after All Saints. In order that this grant may remain in perpetuity, We confirm this present charter with the authority of Our seal and of the monogram of the royal name noted below.

Done at Les Andelys in the year 1203 of the Incarnate Word, and in the 24th year of Our reign, there being present in Our palace [*palatio nostro*][3] the people whose names and signa are below.

---

[1] Translated from the text printed by Brunel, Delaborde, and Petit-Dutaillis in *Recueil des Actes de Philippe Auguste Roi de France*, tome ii (1943), p. 335 (no. 762).

[2] Ralph d'Estrées thus accepted the king as his liege lord, which meant that he became his vassal without reserve, so that his duty of serving the king overrode all obligations that he might have to any other feudal lord.

[3] The allusion is not to a building but to the king's court, which was itinerant. Philip was in fact beginning the siege of Château Gaillard (the 'saucy castle' of Richard I).

There being no steward.[1] *Signum* of Guy the butler. *Signum* of
Mathew of the chamber. *Signum* of Drogo the constable.
Given, while the chancellorship was vacant, by the hand of
brother Guérin.[2]

Further Reading

CHARLES PETIT-DUTAILLIS. *Feudal Monarchy in France and England* (tr.
E. D. Hunt). London. 1936.

W. M. NEWMAN. *Le Domaine Royale sous les premiers Capétiens* (987–
1180). Paris. 1937.

ROBERT FAWTIER. *The Capetian Kings of France* (tr. Lionel Butler and
Robin Adam). London. 1960.

F. L. GANSHOF. *Feudalism* (tr. P. Grierson). London. 1952.

HENRI WAQUET (ed.). *Suger : Vie de Louis VI le Gros* (Les Classiques de l'Histoire de France au Moyen Age series). Paris.
1929. Latin text with French translation.

---

[1] The stewardship, being an office previously held by great nobles, was suppressed by Philip Augustus after 1191.

[2] The chancellorship was similarly left permanently vacant after 1185. Brother
Guérin was a Templar and the chief minister of Philip Augustus. He controlled
the palace, ecclesiastical affairs, and the chancery, commanded the royal army at
the battle of Bouvines (1214), and in the same year was made Bishop of Senlis.

VI

THE EMPEROR FREDERICK I BARBAROSSA

(1152–1190)

FREDERICK BARBAROSSA is the last of the medieval emperors to be regarded as a national hero in modern Germany. Since the sixteenth century he has gradually displaced his grandson, Frederick II, as the central figure of the Kyffhäuser legend. It was said that he never died but simply disappeared from the world, to sleep in a cave on the mountain until Germany should once again be united. At intervals of fifty or a hundred years he would awake and look out of the cave to see if the destined time had come—it was to be announced to him by the ravens—but he always looked in vain. That, at least, was the legend as Jakob Grimm heard it, but subsequently the Germans thought that the ravens had come. In the late nineteenth century, the artists of the Prussian court delighted to paint pictures of his last, and joyful, awakening in 1871, when the sky was full of ravens since a second German Empire had been called into existence. Statues of Frederick Barbarossa and Kaiser Wilhelm I were placed side by side to symbolize the 'fact' that where one had left off, the other had begun.[1]

But besides being a central figure of German history, Frederick Barbarossa played an important part in the history of Italy, and it will be most convenient, at any rate for the first part of his reign (1152–76), to discuss these two aspects of his work separately.

1. GERMANY

At Frederick's accession, the power of the crown was very weak indeed. Germany was given over to civil war, for though

[1] The best example of this art is to be seen at the *Kaiserhaus* at Goslar. The legend was originally told of Barbarossa's grandson, Frederick II, but was subsequently (and more suitably) transferred to Barbarossa himself.

the Investitures Struggle had been formally brought to an end
by the Concordat of Worms (1122), the country was still divided
between those who had opposed and those who had supported
the Emperor Henry IV, the most famous conflict being that
between the Guelfs and the Ghibellines. The Guelfs, though
popularly known as papalists, were really the supporters of the
dynasty of Welf, which included in its ramifications most of the
former enemies of Henry IV and continued to oppose his
descendants as if by hereditary instinct. The Ghibellines, though
popularly known as imperialists, were the supporters of the
dynasty of Hohenstaufen which claimed the Empire by hereditary
right.[1] (See the genealogical table.)

It is not necessary to say much about the origins of this dispute.
It had first become acute in 1125, over the election of a successor
to the Emperor Henry V. The German crown, like all those of
Western Europe in the twelfth century, had hitherto been bestowed by a combination of election and hereditary succession.
Though it was the act of election which was essential, it was
normal for every king to have his eldest son elected and crowned
as his successor during his lifetime, even if he was only an infant.
Henry V, however, had died childless and a large party of nobles
and churchmen had seized the opportunity of making the election ' open '. Ignoring the claims of Henry's nephew Frederick
the One-eyed, Duke of Swabia (Ghibelline), who was heir to his
private estates, they deliberately picked a man who not only had
no hereditary claim whatsoever but was also renowned as an
enemy of the Salian dynasty.

This was Lothar of Supplinburg, Duke of Saxony. He was
one of the ' new men ' who had risen to eminence during the
civil wars occasioned by the Investitures Struggle; he had
married the granddaughter of Otto of Nordheim, the inveterate
enemy of Henry IV, and proceeded to secure his position by
marrying his only daughter into the house of Guelf. Her
husband Henry the Proud was Duke of Bavaria, and since she
could expect to inherit Saxony in her own right the power of the
family was overwhelming. Consequently, when Lothar died

---

[1] Guelf and Ghibelline are Italianized forms of Welf and Waiblingen. Waiblingen was one of the chief towns of the Hohenstaufen demesne in Swabia, and
was used by their followers as a war-cry.

GUELFS AND GHIBELLINES

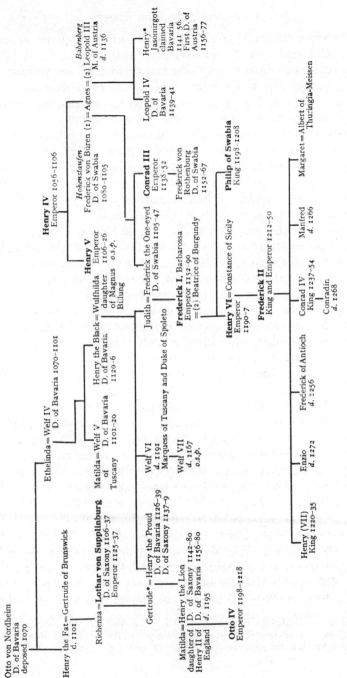

* Gertrude married, secondly, Henry Jasomirgott of Austria.

(1138), the nobles took fright and elected in his place not a Guelf but a Hohenstaufen, Conrad III (1138–52).

Conrad owed his election to the fact that he was comparatively weak, and for that very reason his reign was not successful. He was uncompromising in his hostility to the Guelfs, but lacked the power to crush them. On the ground that no one should hold two duchies at once, he declared Henry the Proud to be deprived of first one and then both of his duchies ; but the declaration merely led to civil war. By 1142 he had been forced to recognize Henry the Proud's son, Henry the Lion, as lawful Duke of Saxony, while in Bavaria, even though he was able to maintain his two step-brothers of the house of Babenberg as successive dukes, the Guelf opposition was not abandoned. When Conrad III died in 1152, Henry the Lion was still demanding his hereditary rights in Bavaria, and civil war was imminent.

It was in these circumstances that Frederick Barbarossa was elected to the throne. He was a Hohenstaufen, being Conrad's nephew, and had been designated by the dying king, but he owed his election, in no small degree, to the additional fact that his mother was a Guelf. It was universally hoped that in his person he would be able to reconcile the two families, put an end to civil war, and re-establish law and order ; and it was in the ardent desire of fulfilling this hope that Frederick inaugurated a policy of collaboration. The Guelf and Hohenstaufen were both to recognize each other's hereditary claims, the one to the monarchy and the other to the duchy of Bavaria.

It was four years, however, before the Bavarian affair was settled, because, anxious though Frederick might be to placate Henry the Lion, he was equally anxious not to betray his old ally of the house of Babenberg, Henry Jasomirgott. If the latter was to be persuaded to surrender the duchy, he had to be re-warded handsomely, and it was long before an acceptable compromise was found. Finally it was arranged that the East Mark, in which the main strength of the Babenbergs lay, should be detached from Bavaria and raised to the dignity of an independent duchy, Austria. As a further inducement, the terms on which it was granted to Henry Jasomirgott were made especially favourable to him. According to the document known as the *Privilegium Minus*, the duchy was to be held in fee by him and his wife jointly. It was to pass to their children whether male or female, and if they should be childless they might bequeath it by will. All justice in the duchy was to be administered by the duke or his agents, and the only services required of him were attendance at imperial diets held in Bavaria and military service in the lands bordering the new duchy. Such terms might be considered excessively generous, since at first sight they seem to constitute an abdication by Frederick of some of the most valuable of his royal rights. But in fact the grant contained nothing that Henry Jasomirgott could not have seized for himself. It secured the surrender of his claim to Bavaria, which he might have attempted to gain by force, and it ensured that he would faithfully defend the south-eastern frontier of Germany against the Hungarians.

That was the secret of Frederick's dealings with the German princes : he came to terms with them on the basis of mutual self-interest. He was a realist, and though he was determined to revive the power of the crown he had the courage to face the facts of the situation. He did not pursue an ' anti-feudal ' policy of the sort which has been attributed to his contemporary Henry II of England and most other medieval kings who restored order after a period of civil war, because such a policy was impossible for him. The Empire had been torn by civil war for the greater part of seventy-five years, and though the main contestants had been Pope and Emperor, Guelfs and Ghibellines, none of them had won. The only victors had been the nobles who, being free to adjust their policy to the varying fortunes of war, had succeeded in transforming the political aspect of Germany by usurping valuable rights from both the ecclesiastical and the secular authorities.

Ever since the ninth century, the simplest way for a noble to advance his fortune had been by becoming the patron or ' advocate ' of a monastery. In theory it was then his duty to defend it and to represent it in secular courts of law, but in practice it became his privilege to despoil it. The monks, being religious, were anxious to shed all secular responsibilities, and had no desire to govern immunities in the Emperor's name. They wanted to be free, and would consequently decide to appoint some local magnate to defend them against oppression and, acting as their servant, to relieve them of all worldly cares.

They called him their ' advocate ' (*advocatus*),[1] and since they did not wish to be responsible for the shedding of blood, which was an essential part of medieval justice, they employed him to exercise their jurisdiction for them, rewarding him with a share (usually one-third) of the profits of justice. They thought that such an ' advocate ' would be harmless, since he owed his appointment to the monastery and was its servant. But they forgot that in putting the defence and jurisdiction of their lands in his hands, they were giving him the powers of a prince. It was not until it was too late that they discovered that the tyranny of an ' advocate ' might be as bad as, or worse than, that of the Emperor. During the seventy-five years of civil war, every ' advocate ' exploited the duty which had been entrusted to him, enlarged its profits, and treated it as a hereditary property. Sometimes he even sold the rights which had been entrusted to him, without consulting the abbot or convent. If he was an able man, he would collect the advowsons of several monasteries and, by means of purchase and exchange with other advocates, consolidate his lands so that they formed a little lordship or territorial principality.

The Emperor had been despoiled by methods which were even more direct. During the civil war it had naturally happened that he had been unable to exercise all his rights. In many places, for example, it would have been impossible for him to exercise the right of receiving hospitality or provisions for his court. What was to happen in such circumstances ? Was the peasantry to be exempted from all the services which this hospitality had entailed ? Or would it not be better for the local magnates to preserve the proprieties of feudal society by seeing that the peasants' services were still rendered, though to themselves rather than to the king or Emperor ? No medieval knight could be expected to stand aside and watch a valuable right disappear for lack of use, and consequently the Emperor's rights, so far from ' vanishing ', were usurped by hundreds of local magnates. They seized crown lands, usurped rights of jurisdiction and taxation, and built castles from which to terrorize the surrounding countryside. They made themselves lords of the land in a truly feudal sense, owning what they governed, and

---

[1] The literal, and most expressive, translation of the word is ' protector ', but historians have come to use the word ' advocate ' as a technical term.

governing what they owned. Thus, though their family origins might be obscure, they cut a figure in the world and rose to positions of great eminence. Even the Hohenstaufen were parvenus before they married into the Salian dynasty; they derived their name from a castle which they had built on the Swabian Alb, and collected lands, advowsons, and regalian rights in the same way as any other families of the new nobility.

It was for this reason, perhaps, that Frederick Barbarossa was so ready to appreciate the fact that during the Investitures Struggle a new nobility had emerged ; he belonged to it himself, and knew that its feudal lordships could not suddenly be destroyed. He realized that any attempt to recover the full rights of the crown as they had existed in Germany a hundred years before, would provoke universal rebellion, and he therefore made a virtue of necessity by making formal grants, on feudal terms, of all the various rights and territories which had already been lost. In 1152 he recognized Berthold of Zähringen as Duke of Burgundy in return for the feudal service of 1,000 knights in Burgundy, or 500 knights and 50 arbalasters in Italy. He bestowed ducal titles and privileges on the Rhine Palatinate (1156), the bishopric of Würzburg (1168), and Styria (1180). The grants he made, however, were always of lands and privileges which he was no longer in a position to control. They cost him nothing, but brought him feudal services. The magnates, on the other hand, were eager to co-operate with him, since the formal grants which they received were the legal recognition of the position which they had won for themselves during the Investitures Struggle, and a guarantee that the Emperor would not attempt to revindicate his rights by force.

The supreme example of this realistic feudal policy was to be found in Frederick's attempt to collaborate with the Guelf. He saw that he could not afford to incur the enmity of Henry the Lion, and that his claim to the two duchies of Saxony and Bavaria was both popular and just ; and he therefore determined to face the fact and rule in partnership with him, since nothing else was possible. Thus, while he devoted himself to the grander designs of empire, he left Henry in virtual control of northern and eastern Germany. While Frederick was busy in Italy, Henry was conquering lands from the Slavs east of the Elbe and colonizing them with German and Flemish settlers. He extended the frontier into East Holstein, Lauenburg and West Mecklenburg and was granted regalian rights in the newly-conquered districts, sometimes enjoying even the investiture of bishops. He encouraged the economic exploitation of the new lands, built cities such as Lübeck and Munich, and (provided that they recognized his lordship) encouraged their commercial development. He cleared the Baltic of Wendish pirates, pursued a vigorous foreign policy towards Denmark, and conducted himself almost as if he were the colleague of the Emperor.

Frederick gave him a completely free hand and encouraged him, because he thought that the simplest way of securing peace in Germany was to keep the Guelf contented. He wanted to re-establish the imperial power in Italy and consequently had to pursue a policy of collaboration in Germany. The question was whether it would work. Could he always rely on the loyalty of the Guelf? Or were the past enmities not easily forgotten?

2. Italy

Although in Germany Frederick Barbarossa was a realist, in Italy he tended, at any rate during the first twenty-four years of his reign, to be a romantic reactionary. He was profoundly influenced by the antiquarian spirit of his age, exemplified by the revival of classical studies and Roman law, and was determined to be a Roman emperor. He delighted in the thought that he was the successor not only of Charlemagne and Otto the Great but also of Constantine, Theodosius, and Justinian. When he issued a constitution in favour of the university of Bologna he ordered it to be inserted in the *Novellae* among the laws of Justinian, and when at the end of his reign he sent a formal challenge to Saladin he identified his empire fearlessly with that of ancient Rome:

Do you pretend not to know [he wrote] that both the Ethiopias, Mauretania, Persia, Syria, Parthia (where the fate of our dictator Crassus was sealed by the Parthians [1]), Judaea, Samaria, Maritima, Arabia, Chaldaea and also Egypt itself (where, alas ! a Roman citizen called Mark Antony, an outstanding man, was robbed of his virtue and transgressed the bonds of temperance . . . by enslaving himself

[1] In 53 B.C.

to the dissolute love of Cleopatra [1])—do you pretend not to know that Armenia itself and numberless other lands are subject to Our sway? [2]

This passage, extraordinary as it is, forms an admirable introduction to the claims which Frederick made in Italy. He demanded all the rights which he thought were due to a real Roman emperor, meaning thereby not just those rights which had been exercised by his predecessors during the previous half-century, but also those which had been exercised in the remote past. He wanted to go back, as it were, not just a century but a great deal farther, in order to revive the glories of an empire that was past; and in so doing he not unnaturally incurred the bitter hostility of the three most important powers in twelfth-century Italy, the Normans, the Papacy, and the Lombard communes.

The power of the Normans had grown enormously since the end of the eleventh century. Whereas Robert Guiscard had simply been Duke of Calabria and Apulia, Roger the Great (1130–54) was King of Sicily and all Italy south of the Garigliano, and was one of the richest and most powerful monarchs in Europe. Since many of his civil servants were Greeks or Arabs, his government was a model of bureaucratic efficiency. His navy controlled the central Mediterranean and threatened the coasts of both North Africa and the Byzantine Empire; and his army dominated central and southern Italy. He was the inveterate enemy of the Empire, but felt sufficiently sure of himself to oppose the Papacy too whenever he felt it necessary. When Pope Innocent II had dared to excommunicate him for supporting an anti-pope, Roger had fought him, defeated him, captured him, and forced him to make an abject peace (1139). In southern Italy he was supreme, and the Papacy, unable to withstand him single-handed, was faced with the choice either of co-operating with him or of seeking help against him from the Empire.

It was in these circumstances that the Papacy inherited its policy of a balance of power in Italy. Its own state, the 'patrimony of St. Peter', was roughly in the middle of Italy, and on either side of it a perfect equilibrium had to be maintained. When the Normans were too powerful it supported the Empire,

[1] 41–31 B.C.
[2] Text from *Itinerarium Regis Ricardi*, ed. W. Stubbs (R.S.), pp. 35–6.

and when the Empire was in the ascendant it reverted to its alliance with the Normans. In order to maintain its own security it was determined to keep Italy divided, and it was therefore a foregone conclusion that it would only support Frederick Barbarossa as long as he was a failure.

There was, however, a second reason for papal hostility to the revived Empire, and this was ideological. For Frederick brought a new *ethos* to the imperial ideal. As a ' Roman ' emperor he discovered Roman Law and found in it an effective philosophical reply to the doctrines of sacerdotal supremacy. The *Digest*, by its careful analysis of the whole range of human activity, provided a counterblast to the accepted ideas of spiritual government and the two swords. It gave supremacy not to the priestly office or the soul, but to law.

> Law is . . . something which all men ought to obey for many reasons, and chiefly because every law is devised and given by God, but resolved on by intelligent men, a means of correcting offences both intentional and unintentional, a general agreement on the part of the community by which all those living therein ought to order their lives. We may add that Chrysippus [said] ' Law is the king of all things, both divine and human ; it ought to be the controller, ruler and commander of both the good and the bad.'

It was an argument that carried conviction not only because of its antiquity but also because of its comprehensiveness and orderliness, which gave men a new view of the world about them.

> All law deals with either persons, or things, or actions. . . . Now the main division of the law of persons is this, that all human beings are either free or slaves. . . . The main division of things ranges them under two heads, some being subjects of divine law, some of human. Subjects of divine law, for instance, are things sacred and religious. . . .

One appreciates why it was that in the twelfth century a doctor of Paris would go to Bologna to unlearn what he had taught, and then return to Paris to teach what he had unlearnt. Roman Law made a new philosophical view of the world possible, laying the emphasis on human observation rather than on divine wisdom.

Frederick Barbarossa was full of admiration. The Archbishop of Milan told him that his will was law, since *Quod principi placuit, legis habet vigorem*, and he himself declared that, following in the footsteps of his predecessors, the ' divine ' (*divi*) Emperors Constantine, Justinian, Valentinian, Charles, and Louis, he venerated the ' sacred laws as if they were divine oracles '. He believed that he derived his Empire from God and consequently called it the ' *Holy* Roman Empire ', and in accordance with this same belief procured (from his anti-pope) the canonization of Charlemagne. He regarded his Empire as the secular equivalent of the Papacy and welcomed the idea that all the kings of Europe were subordinate to him ; even so powerful a king as Henry II of England found it diplomatic to address him in the most obsequious terms, declaring that his kingdom was subject to the Emperor's sway, so that all things might be determined ' at his nod ' (*ad nutum*).

Perhaps the most striking example of Frederick's exalted conception of the imperial authority was when, in 1158, he raised Duke Vladislav II of Bohemia to the rank of king. The novelty lay not in the Emperor's claims over Bohemia, nor in the notion that he could receive the allegiance and fealty of a king (for that was not unusual), but in the idea that he could create a king where previously there had been no kingdom, for kings were normally thought to receive their power from God, through the hands of the clergy. When Pepin the Short had wished to become King of the Franks, he had thought it necessary to secure the collaboration of the Pope (p. 131), but now Frederick Barbarossa acted as if it was sufficient to have the authority of the Emperor alone, since he, in the words of his court historian, was ' the sole ruler of the world '.

Pope Hadrian IV not unnaturally refused to accept such views. He insisted that Frederick held his Empire only by grace of the Papacy. He refused to crown him until he had shown due reverence to his holy office by holding his bridle and stirrup as if he were his vassal (1155), and he altered the order of the coronation service so as to make it clear that the Emperor's position was in no way comparable with that of a bishop, and that his authority was derived not from God direct but from the Pope. He conducted a sort of propaganda-war, in which he displayed a picture of Frederick's predecessor, the Emperor Lothar, as a vassal of Pope Innocent II, and he took every opportunity of minimizing the importance of the imperial office. Finally, at the imperial diet of Besançon (1157), there was a furious scene when Frederick denounced a papal letter in which Hadrian claimed to have ' conferred ' the Empire on him as a *beneficium*, the word usually used to denote a fief. Though Hadrian eventually attempted to explain his words away, by claiming that he had used the word in its non-technical sense of ' benefit ' or ' good deed ', all the old passions of the Investitures Struggle had been revived. Once again there were imperialist and papalist parties among both clergy and laity, and when Hadrian IV died in 1159 the whole issue came to a head in the question of whether his successor was to be an imperialist or a papalist, allied to Frederick Barbarossa or the Normans of Sicily. The two parties were represented by the Cardinals Octavian and Roland, both of whom claimed to have been lawfully elected as Pope, the one as Victor IV (1159–64) who received little support outside the Empire, the other as Alexander III (1159–81).

In fairness to Frederick, it must be admitted that the claims and counter-claims of the two rival popes were genuinely confusing. But none the less he showed singularly little foresight when, relying on the precedents of Constantine, Theodosius, Justinian, and ' more recently ' of Charlemagne and Otto the Great, he used his own authority to summon an ecclesiastical council at Pavia (1160) to decide between the two popes. He should have known that all the precedents of ancient history were as nothing to the events of the previous century, and that since the Hildebrandine reform it was a fundamental tenet of ecclesiastical doctrine that no emperor could sit in judgment on a pope. He was apparently surprised to find that the claimant who refused to submit to imperial judgment, Alexander III, was considered by that very fact to be the rightful Pope ; and that the rest of Europe regarded him (Frederick), like Henry IV, as the mere supporter of an anti-pope.

Judged in purely material terms, the consequence of Frederick's break with the Papacy was that by 1160 he had driven two of the major Italian powers, the Normans of Sicily and the Pope, into an alliance against him. This alliance made his chances of success remote, but he might still conceivably have established his authority if he had not added yet further to his enemies by his failure to understand the new situation which had been created in northern Italy by the rise of the city-states or communes.

This last failure was disastrous, but not in the least surprising, since to anyone who, like Frederick, had been reared in a feudal society, the communes were almost bound to be incomprehensible. They constituted a complete reversal of the normal feudal order, for they were not monarchies but republics, and their wealth was founded not on land but on trade ; and whereas in Germany one would have expected to find that towns belonged to a feudal lord, in Lombardy almost all the feudal lords were subject to the towns. The communes had conquered, not only the fields around their walls, but also whole counties. By far the greater part of Lombardy was subjected to their rule, and this in spite of the fact that many of their most prominent citizens were not nobles but tradesmen and ' workers of the vile mechanical arts '.

How had such a curious state of affairs arisen ? In the cities themselves, men liked to imagine that their republican government was the result of an unbroken tradition from the ancient world, for they lived in an atmosphere of *Romanitas*. Their towns had been amongst the most important of the Roman world—in the fifth century Milan had been the seat of imperial government in the West—and still preserved many tangible remains of their former greatness. Roman fortifications, bridges, temples, and amphitheatres were everywhere to be seen. The language spoken was recognizably like Latin, the law in force was Roman Law, and the magistrates were elected annually and called consuls.

But in spite of all this apparent antiquity, it cannot be denied that the rise of the Lombard communes to political power had been both rapid and recent. The truth of the matter was that they owed their importance not to their antiquity but to their trade. They were the richest cities in Europe and formed the central entrepôt for almost all the trade which passed between the eastern Mediterranean and northern Europe. When the volume of trade had been small, as in the eighth, ninth, and tenth centuries, the cities of Lombardy had been weak and subjected to the power of bishops, counts, and marquises. When the eastern trade revived, as it did in the second half of the eleventh century, the cities began to have political ambitions of their own.

As good fortune would have it, the period of economic expansion had coincided with the period of the Investitures Struggle, and the Italian cities had benefited from it in the same way as the feudal lords of Germany. While Emperor and Pope had disputed the headship of the world, they had cared only for their own independence. If they had embraced the programme of ecclesiastical reform, it had been in order to gain the right of electing their own bishops and to deprive them of their temporal power. If they had supported the imperialist cause, it had been to defeat a papalist bishop who was threatening their liberty. They had played one side against the other and gradually usurped all the governmental rights which had been exercised in the Emperor's name by bishops, counts, or marquises. They had subdued the surrounding countryside, so that every city had its *contado* or dependent county, and they had forced the feudal nobility to recognize their authority. By the middle of the twelfth century the Marqu's of Montferrat was, in the words of a contemporary, ' practically the only one of the barons of Italy who could escape the authority of the cities '.[1]

Frederick Barbarossa, however, was most unwilling to recognize the importance of the revolution which had occurred. Though in Germany he was prepared, as we have already seen, to be a realist and to abandon with a good grace the rights which he had already lost, in Italy his attitude was different. All the prejudices of his feudal upbringing were involved, for the Lombard communes were plebeian, a fact which, in his view, was in itself sufficient to explain the chaos of their political life. Almost every town was at war with its neighbours—Bologna with Modena, Mantua with Verona, Brescia with Cremona, and Milan with all her neighbours—and complaints of corruption amongst the elected magistrates were rife.

Order had to be re-established, and Frederick, who considered the wars of the communes to be but the aftermath of the Investi-

[1] Otto of Freising, ii. xv. (tr. Mierow, p. 129).

tures Struggle, thought that the only remedy was to restore the imperial authority to the position which it had enjoyed before the reign of Henry IV. He put Milan, the most aggressive of the communes, to the ban of Empire and after a month's siege accepted its surrender (1158). Then, having demonstrated the extent of his power, he held an imposing diet at Roncaglia where, with the help of the bishops, he revindicated all the regalian rights which had been lost by neglect or usurpation during the previous century. Representatives of all the cities were present, but they were too frightened to resist his claim and restored the *regalia* into his hand. On being asked what the *regalia* included,

> They assigned to him dukedoms, marches, counties, consulates, mints, market tolls, forage-tax [*fodrum*], wagon-tolls, gate-tolls, transit-tolls, mills, fisheries, bridges, all the use accruing from running water, and the payment of an annual tax, not only on the land but also on their own persons.[1]

The list, which is characteristically medieval, included two main types of regalian rights, governmental and financial. The first consisted in the Emperor's right to appoint, or at any rate to invest in their offices, all dukes, marquises, counts, and consuls. In Germany the right would have been accepted as a matter of course, and in Italy the nobility could be expected to recognize it without demur. But so far as the communes were concerned, admission of the right was disastrous, as it meant the end of their liberty, since Frederick, observing that every city was divided by internal factions, attempted to establish law and order by appointing to every city a chief magistrate or *podestà* who was a foreigner to it, drawn either from the Emperor's entourage or from some other city.

It was in many ways a realistic scheme, but it failed because the communes did not value law and order as highly as their independence. They bitterly resented the loss of the right to elect their own consuls, and they were driven to fury by the financial demands that were made in the Emperor's name. The loss of the various tolls to the Emperor was a serious blow, but even that was not the most serious of their complaints. In

---

[1] Rahewin, Bk. iv. vii (Mierow, p. 238).

Milan the imperial *podestà* demanded one-third of all the produce which was paid to landowners as rent; imposed a tax of 3*s.* a year on all freemen and of 12*d.* on all yokes of oxen and oil-presses; and exacted forced labour for the building of castles ` and palaces. It was hardly surprising that the citizens found Barbarossa's rule an insupportable tyranny and revolted against the Emperor for the second time in 1160–2. But it was all to no avail. As in 1158, Frederick besieged the town and forced it to surrender. But this time, instead of treating it with comparative leniency, he had it razed to the ground, dispersing its inhabitants amongst four open villages, so that the whole of Lombardy might learn to respect the ' Roman ' name.

When, in 1162, he returned to Germany, he probably thought that his Italian policy had been crowned with success. Terror-stricken, the whole of Lombardy had submitted to him. Piacenza and Brescia hastily agreed to dismantle their walls, the Emperor's regalian rights as defined at Roncaglia were universally enforced, and *podestàs* were installed in every city. In the case of the three most loyal cities, Pavia, Lodi, and Cremona, Frederick allowed the citizens to elect their own *podestà*, but elsewhere he made the appointment himself.

Nevertheless, in spite of the apparent submission of Lombardy, the position in which Frederick found himself was really untenable, for he had committed himself to a policy of annihilation. To him it was a matter of little or no importance that Milan had had a continuous history for some fifteen centuries and that it had proved itself to be the natural commercial and strategic centre of the Lombard plain. Now that its continued existence was incompatible with the imperial design, Frederick Barbarossa declared that it should be not simply destroyed, but abolished; in future there was to be no such place. Frederick was so convinced of his destiny as a Roman emperor that he made little or no attempt to make his ambitions conform with the actual facts of Italian politics. He seemed to think that he could re-draw the map of Italy to his own liking, and proceeded to plan further, in 1164, for the abolition of the Norman kingdom of Sicily. In return for naval assistance, he promised Genoa the city of Syracuse, 250 knights' fiefs, and one street with a church, bath, and bakehouse in every town that should be conquered. To

Pisa he promised half of Palermo, Messina, Salerno, and Naples and the whole of Gaeta, Mazara, and Trapani.

With such ambitious schemes it was hardly surprising that he failed. Even though in 1167 he captured Rome, he could not expect the greater part of Europe to accept his anti-pope. His army was decimated by malaria, he was unable even to attempt the conquest of Norman Sicily, and in his rear Pope Alexander III was successfully inciting the Lombard communes to bury their old feuds and unite in the cause of liberty. In face of the common danger, cities which had previously been inveterate enemies agreed to co-operate. Already in 1164, Treviso, Vicenza, Verona, Padua, and Venice had entered into a formal union, and in 1167, after the failure of Frederick's projected Norman campaign, a far larger alliance, of sixteen cities, was formed.

This was the Lombard League (*Societas Lombardie*). Its object was to recover the liberty of the communes, but it did not wish to overthrow the imperial power completely. Its members wanted to restore the *status quo ante*, being prepared to pay the Emperor such services and dues as they had paid him during the previous century, but no more. Their appeal, as was almost invariably the case in a medieval rebellion, was to their ' ancient customs ', but their methods were novel. The consuls of each city took an oath, subsequently repeated by every citizen, to unite for the recovery of the common liberty ; no private war was to be allowed between one city and another ; the common affairs of the League were to be determined by a central body of magistrates elected by the various cities and known as rectors ; and the common army was to be permanently maintained with contingents from the cities in proportion to their resources. Finally, they resolved to assist each other in repairing in common any damage which had been suffered by any of their members in the cause of liberty, and in pursuance of this principle decided to rebuild the city of Milan. On 27 April 1167, contingents from Bergamo, Brescia, Cremona, Mantua, Verona, and Treviso arrived on the site and started the work of reconstruction.

It was an act of open defiance, but Frederick was unable to punish it. He had to return to Germany for reinforcements, and owing to the troubles which he experienced north of the Alps, could not return to Italy (for his fifth expedition) till 1174. In the meantime the Lombard League had won control of all the central and eastern passes of the Alps, and had defended the western approaches of the Lombard League by founding a new city, called Alessandria, in honour of Pope Alexander III, at the junction of the Tanaro and Bormida (1168). Its defences had to be erected in haste, and the imperialists boastfully called it a ' city of straw ', but when Frederick returned to Italy, even though he besieged the city for six months (1174–5), he found himself unable to take it. All Lombardy had been aroused in its defence.

In his previous expeditions, Frederick had been able to make considerable use of Italian troops in his army, for the enmities between the various cities had been so consistent that he had always found allies amongst them. Now, however, his only remaining allies were the Marquis of Montferrat and the city of Pavia, and consequently he found himself in urgent need of reinforcements from Germany. Most of his vassals responded to his appeal, but the one who was most important refused his service. That was his cousin, Henry the Lion, the head of the house of Guelf. Frederick appealed to him personally at an interview at Chiavenna, but without avail. He had to march against the Lombards without his support, and on 29 May 1176 he was decisively defeated at the battle of Legnano.

3. Revenge

The battle of Legnano was the turning-point of Frederick's reign. He acknowledged that he was defeated and hastened to reverse his previous policies. He came to terms with Pope Alexander III, the Normans, and the Lombards, renouncing all the extravagant claims that he had previously made in Italy. To Germany, on the other hand, he took not peace but a sword. Since he attributed his defeat at Legnano to the defection of Henry the Lion, he determined to punish him by destroying the power of the house of Guelf completely.

In Italy Frederick had no option but to make peace, but he had the sense to see that the only chance of securing tolerable terms was to act with speed and divide his enemies. He therefore concentrated on making a separate peace with the Pope, and within five months of his defeat he had succeeded. By the treaty of Anagni (October 1176) he agreed to abandon his antipope, to recognize Alexander III, and to restore any property which he had taken from the Church. Subsequently he concluded truces with the Normans and Lombards, who were offended with the Pope for having made a separate peace, and finally, on 24 July 1177, he submitted to Alexander III in person at Venice. The meeting took place outside St. Mark's church. Frederick approached the Pope, threw off his imperial garment and prostrated himself at his feet. The Pope, with tears in his eyes, raised him, embraced him, and led him into the church, where he gave him his blessing. Afterwards Frederick held the Pope's stirrup as he mounted his palfrey and showed himself willing, if the Pope had not excused him, to lead him to his barge.

On Frederick's part it was a complete submission, and on Alexander's a whole-hearted reconciliation; and though definitive treaties had not yet been made with the Lombards or Normans, the truces which had been arranged proved enduring, since Frederick made it clear that he was at last prepared to accept the facts of the political situation in Italy. He did so, not out of mere defeatism, but because he wanted to have his hands free in Germany, so that he could take his vengeance on Henry the Lion.

Frederick's opportunity for revenge came in 1178–9 over a dispute between Henry and the Bishop of Halberstadt, which threatened to involve the whole of Saxony in civil war. Both parties appealed to the Emperor, and eventually Henry found himself on trial for sorely oppressing the liberty of both the Church and the princes of the Empire ' by seizing their possessions and by threatening their rights '. He was tried first by the Swabian princes according to Swabian law (for the family of Guelf was not of Saxon but of Swabian extraction), and secondly by the princes of the Empire according to feudal law; but as he refused to obey the summons to either court he was found guilty of contumacy and was sentenced to be deprived of all his fiefs.[1] He resisted the sentence with arms, but after two years of civil war (1180–1) was driven into exile.

It might well be asked where Frederick had found the necessary power to enforce so drastic a sentence against his greatest

---

[1] He possessed allods also, but these (since they were not subject to feudal law) could not be confiscated. *Cf.* p. 296.

vassal. It came from two sources. The first was his demesne, to the consolidation and exploitation of which he had devoted increasing attention. Like his Salian predecessors, he realized that land meant power, and had been active in acquiring territorial lordships. By process of purchase and exchange he had done everything possible to round-off his possessions. He had become the ' advocate ' of innumerable monasteries and bishoprics, had taken all the German houses of the Cistercian and Premonstratensian houses under his ' special defence ', and had not hesitated to enfeoff himself with their lands whenever they occupied a strategic position. He had built castles to control the main highways, founded new towns, and taken the main trading-centres under his imperial protection, so that eventually the main trade-route from Italy passed through the imperial towns (*Reichstädte*) of Regensburg, Donauwörth, Dinkelsbühl, Nördlingen, Rothenburg, and Nürnberg. A great deal of research has recently been done in order to show the extent of his demesne-lands. It was mainly in Swabia (which included much of modern Switzerland and Alsace), the Rhine-Palatinate and Franconia, with an important share of the eastern territories, as in Vogtland—so called because it was administered by imperial agents (*Vögte*)—Egerland, and the province of Pleissen, which, being ' new ' lands free of dynastic lords, were capable of intense exploitation under an organized scheme of forest-clearance and internal colonization.

But more important than the geographical distribution of Frederick's demesne-lands was the way in which, following the example of his Salian predecessors, he arranged for their administration by unfree servants known as *ministeriales* or *Dienstmänner*, who formed a class of society with no exact parallel in France or England. Since they were technically unfree they could not properly marry into the nobility, and consequently they had no share in the dynastic factions that beset the kingdom. They had their own laws, their own customs, and their own traditions of loyalty. In many ways they must have resembled the vassals of Carolingian feudalism.[1] They served as knights in the imperial army, and held fiefs which were hereditary but could not be

[1] It should perhaps be stressed that it was not only the king but any great landowner who would have *ministeriales*.

subinfeudated, and their responsibilities varied enormously. Some *ministeriales* would only administer a village, others would command royal castles or govern whole provinces. One *ministerialis*, Markward von Anweiler, rose to such eminence that, on the same day as he was given his liberty, he was created Duke of Ravenna and Marquis of Ancona ; and eventually he became Regent of Sicily. Indeed the prospect of advancement was such that sometimes a freeman would enter servitude in order to accept a *ministerial* fief, for though he would thereby set himself in a class apart he was likely to make his fortune.[1]   The Emperor, for his part, found it worth his while to offer attractive terms to those who would bind themselves absolutely to him as serfs, since in a crisis, such as that of the year 1180, he would then be sure of the nucleus of an army with which to fight his enemy the Guelf.

If the first source of his power arose from his demesne and the *ministeriales* who administered it for him, the second arose from the feudal nobility itself. During the early part of his reign, he had maintained a sort of balance of power within Germany by supporting Henry the Lion (who, it will be recalled, was Duke of both Saxony and Bavaria) against all the other nobles, and now he simply transferred his support from one side to the other. In future he was to rule not in partnership with the over-mighty Guelf but by grace of the ' princes '.

The ' princes ' were not royal officials, but were the greater feudal nobles—usually lords of two or more counties—who had in effect converted their fiefs into territorial states. What they wanted, and got, in return for their support against Henry the Lion, was the right to be the sole representatives of the royal power in their territories. Like the Babenberg dukes of Austria, they wanted sovereignty (*Landeshoheit*) (p. 318). Thus, in contrast to a country like England where the monarchy was strong and the earls had little or no control of their counties, in Germany the princes (whether dukes or margraves) demanded not only that they alone should be entrusted with the exercise of royal

---

[1] In consequence of this development, the dividing line between *ministeriales* and nobles became less rigid towards the end of the century. By the thirteenth century, the wealthier *ministeriales* had been accepted as a ' new nobility ' ; the poorer *ministeriales*, however, remained unfree.

rights, but also that they alone should be tenants-in-chief. They regarded society as a strict hierarchy which, according to the order of the *Heerschild*, could be set out as follows :

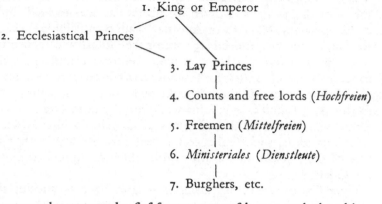

1. King or Emperor
2. Ecclesiastical Princes
3. Lay Princes
4. Counts and free lords (*Hochfreien*)
5. Freemen (*Mittelfreien*)
6. *Ministeriales* (*Dienstleute*)
7. Burghers, etc.

Anyone who accepted a fief from a man of lower rank than himself was considered to be (quite literally) degraded, and no opportunity was given to the king or Emperor to ally himself with the lower classes of society. All authority had to be delegated step by step, so that the king soon found himself unable to enfeoff a count except through the agency of the princes.

This conception of a strictly-graded feudal hierarchy, though peculiar to Germany, was no sudden invention ; it had been developing gradually throughout the twelfth century. But after 1180 Frederick gave it what might be described as his ' official blessing ', since in return for assistance against Henry the Lion he agreed to recognize the princes as a closed corporation, the *Reichsfürstenstand*. Their solidarity as a class was assured by the fact that their number could not be increased except by their own consent ; and their dominance over the land was secured by their recognition as the necessary intermediaries between crown and nobility.

From this time forward, the princes played an ever-increasing part in the politics of medieval Germany, and their power was immediately demonstrated by the fact that they shared the fiefs and honours of Henry the Lion among themselves. It used to be thought that in allowing them to do this Frederick was elaborating a legal principle called *Leihezwang*, whereby the crown was obliged to make grants of all escheated fiefs within a year and a day. In fact no legal principle seems to have been involved. It was simply a question of practical politics. Without the help of the princes Frederick could not possibly defeat the Guelf or deprive him of his lands, and the only way of ensuring their co-operation was to promise them a share of the spoils. As a result the German inheritance of the Guelfs was carved up so as to form five separate duchies. Bavaria, which was conferred on Otto of Wittelsbach, whose dynasty survived till 1918, had already been separated from Austria in 1156 and was now deprived of Styria also. Saxony, conferred on Bernard of Anhalt, was deprived of the districts west of the Weser which were formed into a new duchy of Westphalia for the Archbishop of Cologne.

In this way the ' tribal ' duchies of medieval Germany, so far from being united into a greater whole, were destroyed. Frederick Barbarossa, the mighty Caesar who brandished the club of Hercules, was himself unable to stem the tide of events. In spite of his dreams of glory, he had not only to witness, but also to assist in, the fragmentation of Germany. The dismemberment of the Guelf inheritance was but the first step in the process of division and subdivision, which was to culminate in the seventeenth century with an ' empire ' consisting of more than 300 separate political bodies.

So far as Barbarossa was concerned, the failure of his policy may not have been apparent. He hoped to control the new estate of princes by means of the bond of feudalism. When, in 1184, he held an impressive Diet at Mainz to celebrate the resettlement of Germany, the spectacle was impressive, and it might have seemed that under the new *régime* his power would be restored. But feudal control could only be effective if it was exercised with concentrated attention, since a successful overlord had to insist on all his rights no matter how inconvenient their exercise might be. If continual absences caused him to neglect them, the reality of feudal power would disappear. That was why the decisive factor in the subsequent history of Germany was not the settlement which Frederick made, but the fact that, having made it, he turned his attention away to Italy.

There he showed considerable activity. In 1183 he had concluded the Peace of Constance with the Lombards whereby he definitively renounced his more extravagant claims in the matter of the *regalia*, but received in return an oath of allegiance from all citizens between the age of fifteen and seventy. He made an alliance with Milan for the security of Tuscany and the rest of the Matildine inheritance, and, having thus secured his position in northern Italy, proceeded to create an entirely new situation in the south by entering into an alliance with the Norman kingdom of Sicily. He married his eldest son, Henry, to Constance the heir-presumptive of the Sicilian throne (1186) and thus, whether consciously or unconsciously, prepared an entirely new basis for imperial policy.

Before he could develop this new Italian policy further, he was recalled to yet another aspect of his duty as Emperor. In 1187 Jerusalem fell to the Moslem forces of Saladin, and Frederick, very conscious of his responsibilities as the secular head of Christendom, determined to lead a Crusade for the recovery of the Holy Land. In so doing he demonstrated not only that he had the interests of the Christian Church at heart, but also that he intended to perform all the functions pertaining to his office. Like Charlemagne he was determined ' to defend the holy Church of Christ with arms against the attack of pagans and devastation by infidels from without '. He rallied the Germans to his plan, and on 11 May 1189 set sail down the Danube to join the main body of his army at Vienna and lead it to the Holy Land. The ensuing Crusade was in many ways a miniature of his whole career. Instead of transporting his army by sea, he chose the more difficult overland route which had been followed by the First Crusade. The hardships of the journey were stupendous, and in spite of Frederick's heroic leadership, his army suffered enormous losses. At last, when it had almost fought its way through to Antioch and the greatest difficulties had been surmounted, Frederick was accidentally drowned in the River Saleph (10 June 1190), and his army was so dispirited that it disintegrated.

It was left to Frederick's son, Henry VI (1190–7), to develop the grand Italian design. One year previously he had inherited (in his wife's right) the crown of Norman Sicily. He was opposed by a local candidate, Tancred of Lecce, but by 1194 he had defeated the opposition completely, and had not only Sicily but also the greater part of Italy in his power. He dreamt, like King Roger II before him, of establishing a Mediterranean Empire, married his brother, Philip, to a Byzantine princess in the hope of uniting the eastern and western Empires in their line, and finally gathered an enormous fleet for a crusade which, if it had ever been launched, would probably have been directed against Constantinople rather than the Holy Land.

Like his father before him, he considered himself to be the secular head or overlord of the Christian world, and did not think it at all incongruous that the kings of Cyprus and Armenia should wish to do him homage. He had not the slightest qualm in holding King Richard I of England prisoner on his return from the Third Crusade, until, in addition to the payment of a huge ransom, he surrendered his kingdom and received it back as a fief of the Empire ;[1] and there is good reason for thinking that he had similar ambitions with regard to the French and almost every other European kingdom. As Emperor, he regarded himself as the feudal overlord of the world.

But there was one fatal weakness in his power : the succession was not secure for his line because the imperial crown was still elective. In France and England the hereditary principle had been established and the monarchy was strong, but in Germany the princes were well aware of their power. In 1125, and again in 1138, they had made use of their privilege as electors to see that no one with an overwhelming preponderance of power was elected emperor ; and now that the power of the Hohenstaufen was firmly established they were beginning to regret the enthusiasm with which they had overthrown the Guelf. Consequently they refused to consider Henry's request that they should make the crown hereditary in his line. They wanted to preserve their freedom of action, and did not think that the Emperor's government should be as strong or as centralized as that of the Angevins and the Capetians. If the Emperor was to number kings among his vassals, could it not be argued that his authority

---

[1] The reason why Henry had kept him prisoner was that Richard was the brother-in-law of both Henry the Lion and Tancred of Lecce, and was suspected (with reason) of wanting to form an alliance with them against the Hohenstaufen.

was merely supervisory ? The princes were determined to make themselves sovereigns in their own territorial states. It was therefore a decisive blow against the imperial power when, in 1197, Henry VI died at the early age of thirty-three, leaving only an infant son aged two as his heir. That son, as the Emperor Frederick II, was later to shake the foundations of the Western world, but on his father's death it was a foregone conclusion that the princes would ignore him. They had been waiting for an opportunity for a ' free ' election, and they took it. The majority elected Henry's brother, Philip, as his successor, but a minority, fortified by English gold, elected the second son of Henry the Lion as Otto IV, and thus re-opened the war between the Guelfs and the Ghibellines, so that the Empire once again became a powerless institution.

Further Reading

KARL HAMPE. *Deutsche Kaisergeschichte in der Zeit der Salier und Staufer.* 10th ed. by F. Baethgen. Heidelberg. 1949.

MARCEL PACAUT. *Frédéric Barberousse.* Paris. 1967. Particularly valuable for Frederick's dealings with the papacy.

PETER MUNZ. *Frederick Barbarossa.* London. 1969.

MARC BLOCH. *Land and Work in Mediaeval Europe* (trans. J. E. Anderson). London. 1967. The first and third essays are on Hohenstaufen Empire and the administrative classes in France and Germany.

C. C. MIEROW (tr.). *Otto of Freising : The Deeds of Frederick Barbarossa.* Columbia. 1953. Including Rahewin's continuation.

See also the works by Barraclough, Fisher, and Mitteis listed on p. 231.

VII

THE CRISIS OF THE CHURCH

1. INNOCENT III (1198–1216): ORTHODOX REFORM

INNOCENT III ascended the papal throne in 1198, at a time of general disillusion. The great hopes of the previous century had been disappointed and Christian zeal was almost extinguished. Gregory VII had cried aloud, had spared not, had lifted up his voice like a trumpet, and had declared unto the Lord's people their transgressions. He had thrown the greater part of Latin Christendom into chaos by initiating the fratricidal wars with the Empire, in order that the Kingdom of God might be built upon earth; but one hundred and thirteen years later, though the wars with the Empire still continued, it had to be admitted that the Kingdom of God was more distant than ever. Secular rulers still succeeded by devious means in choosing most of the bishops they wanted, the greater part of the lower clergy still failed to observe the rule of clerical celibacy, and the Emperor's power in relation to the Church had revived. The Crusade had failed; Jerusalem had been won and lost again, largely (it was thought) because of treachery in the Christian ranks (p. 292), and the Emperor Henry VI had not scrupled to hold a returning crusader to ransom. The monastic enthusiasm of the earlier part of the century was exhausted; even the Cistercian monasteries, those former strongholds of asceticism, were already earning themselves a reputation for wealth and miserliness. On all sides laymen were criticizing churchmen for their pride, incompetence, or wealth. Anti-clericalism was common, and in many parts of Europe, more especially in southern France, it developed into anti-sacerdotalism and heresy. The Manichaean doctrines of the Cathari—that God created the spiritual world but the devil the material—were spreading like wild-fire, and it seemed as if the Christian Church, for all its outward splendour, was in danger of losing its spirit.

That was the situation which confronted Lothario de' Conti when, on 8 January 1198, he was elected Pope as Innocent III. He could not ignore the fact that religion was rapidly becoming an ideal of the past, and he could not condone as an ' inevitable development ' the change from an Age of Faith to an Age of Disillusion. As Pope it was his duty to stem the flood of un-belief and heresy and to lead a reaction in favour of Christianity. How was it to be done ?

Innocent III believed that the most effective way was by making a proper and effective use of the authority which his holy office conferred upon him. He was absolutely convinced that, as Pope, he was Christ's Vicar on Earth, charged with the duty of wielding the spiritual sword, so as to uphold religion, justice, and morality everywhere. He claimed the very fullness of power (*plenitudo potestas*) over the whole of Christ's people, and during his pontificate of eighteen years punished seven kings and two rival emperors with excommunication or interdict. Even at the time of his coronation, his views were clear :

> What am I [he said] or what is my father's house, that I should be admitted to rule over kings, to possess the throne of glory ? For it is to me that the words of the prophet apply : ' I have established thee above peoples and kingdoms, that thou mightest uproot and destroy, and also that thou mightest build and plant.' It is to me that it was said : ' I will give thee the keys of the King-dom of Heaven, and whatsoever thou shalt bind on Earth shall be bound in Heaven.' [1]

It should be added, however, that Innocent III was a truly remarkable man. He was elected Pope at the age of thirty-seven —his predecessor having been an octogenarian—and was blessed not only with vigour and determination but also with sanity and commonsense. It may be that he lacked imagination, but he was quite exceptionally clear-sighted. He invented no wonderful new remedy for the sins of the world, and expected no miracles, but simply concentrated on doing what was possible.

---

[1] A. Luchaire, *Innocent III : Rome et l'Italie* (1905), p. 26.

He accepted the institutions of the Church as they were, but determined to make them work efficiently. In this respect his treatment of the problem of anti-clericalism was typical. The main ground for the criticism of the clergy was, as he could not but recognize, that they were too wealthy and conformed more to the appearance of Jewish high priests than to the ideal of the Gospels. Even in the first half of the twelfth century, Arnold of Brescia (*c.* 1100–1155) had found in Italy (and especially in the city of Rome itself) enthusiastic support for the notion that the Church should live ' of its own ', that is to say on the revenues of tithes, surrendering all its temporalities to the laity. Later in the century the Poor Men of Lyons, or *Waldenses*, itinerant preachers who walked the roads of southern and central France barefoot, proclaimed the doctrine of apostolic poverty. What was necessary for the salvation of man, they said, was not a luxurious undergrowth of ecclesiastical institutions but the reading of the Bible—one of the first hints of the new religious thought which was to culminate in the Reformation. But even those of the laity who had no such deeply-rooted convictions joined enthusiastically in the criticism of luxury and in a demand for the redistribution of clerical wealth. Sancho I of Portugal, for example, was said by Innocent III to have suggested that since the clergy ' only simulated religion ', their property should be confiscated and given to the knights who defended the kingdom against the Moslems.

Innocent III was not prepared to tolerate such views, but he was far too great a man to shut his eyes to the fact that there was real ground for discontent. It was true that there were scandals in the Church, and unless they were remedied the critics would continue to be vociferous. There was the question of the circulation of bogus holy relics, for example, which was bringing part of the Church into disrepute. Innocent dealt with this by proclaiming that no new relics were to be venerated unless they had first been approved as genuine by the Papacy itself. Similarly he worked out an elaborate system for the detection of forged papal privileges, the fabrication of which was a favourite hobby in many religious houses. But his main efforts were directed towards the improvement of the most ordinary standards of clerical life. He renewed the edicts against pluralism and, like so many of his predecessors, prohibited the purchase or inheritance of ecclesiastical benefices. He forbade clerics to frequent taverns, take part in warfare, keep company with *jongleurs*, or hunt with the hawk or hounds. He forbade them to wear extravagant clothes, complaining particularly of red and green garments with long sleeves and pointed shoes, and compelled them to wear the tonsure and a standardized clerical dress. A shaven head and black clothes, of the same general type as are still worn by the Roman Catholic clergy, would serve to remind priests of their order, and would help them to realize that their allegiance was not to the world but to the Church.

It was one thing to issue reforming edicts, however, and another to get them obeyed. Previous Popes had proclaimed many similar reforms; where they had failed was simply in getting them carried out. The bishops were the only men who could execute the actual work of reform and they, overwhelmed by the amount required, had grown accustomed to receiving orders which they found it impossible to obey. To them it seemed that the Papacy was always thinking in terms of a divine society, forgetful of the fact that on earth it was composed of mere humans. The stress laid on the rule of clerical celibacy, for example, could only seem artificial in an age when most of the country clergy failed to observe it. The difficulty lay not in depriving the married clergy of their benefices but of finding suitable unmarried men to take their place. There were so many vested interests in every parish, and so much human nature in clerics, that bishops often found it prudent to turn a blind eye to the lesser irregularities and to attempt reform only where it seemed possible.

Such an attitude did not suit Innocent III. He complained that the Church was suffering from inertia, and when bishops or archbishops failed to carry out his orders literally he took prompt disciplinary action against them, no matter who they were. Thus when his old friend and teacher, Pierre de Corbeil, failed to execute a sentence against a relative of the king, Innocent suspended him from his functions ' so as to give the whole episcopate a lesson ' :

When We nominated you bishop [he wrote], We thought that We were doing a service to the church of Sens and the whole of France.

In raising upon a candlestick the light that had been hid beneath a bushel, We thought that We were giving God's flock a shepherd and not a mercenary. But now your light is out ; now it is nothing more than the smoke of a snuffed candle. The moment you see a wolf, you desert your flock and run away ; you are like a dog that is dumb and cannot bark.[1]

The problem of finding loyal lieutenants, however, was one that Innocent never solved to his own satisfaction. For bishops, archbishops, and even papal legates, seemed only too often to be incapable of viewing their difficulties with the calmness and sobriety which were necessary for a man of God. Some were too rigid in their interpretation of the law, others too flexible, judging all things by the criterion of convenience. Consequently Innocent once declared that if the interests of the Church permitted it he would rather do everything himself. He was always ready to review ecclesiastical judgments, and the number of appeals to Rome, already large at the beginning of his pontificate, increased enormously. Abbots who were revindicating their privileges against bishops or archbishops, candidates who considered themselves cheated of a bishopric, and learned clerks who were anxious to display their knowledge of canon law, all flocked to the papal court, together with others whose difficulties were more serious. The Bishop of Tiberias, for instance, had been converting Moslems to Christianity, and wanted to know if their previous marriages were valid, even if polygamous. Innocent, faithful to his axiom that mercy should be exalted on the judgment-seat, quoted the precedents of Abraham and the patriarchs, and permitted the polygamous marriages provided that they had been made before conversion. Similarly, when asked if a husband might divorce his wife if she became a heretic, he replied with an emphatic negative ; in so serious a matter he did not wish to encourage false accusations.

Innocent was untiring in his attention to detail. ' Nothing which happens in the world ', he wrote, ' should escape the notice of the supreme pontiff ' ; and he did his best to see that it didn't. He thought that it was a part of his special duty to watch over the conduct of kings, and to see that they set a good example to their subjects in upholding morality and justice. He

---

[1] A. Luchaire, *Rome et l'Italie*, p. 4.

interested himself particularly in their matrimonial affairs, and punished Alfonso IX of Leon for attempting to marry within the prohibited degrees of affinity, and Philip Augustus of France for attempting to divorce his wife unlawfully (p. 305). In both cases the weapon he used was that of laying an interdict on the whole kingdom, so that all church-services except the baptism of infants and penance for the dying had to be suspended ; and though kings were always able to find royalist bishops who would ignore the sentence, it was usually effective in causing public opinion to force them to return to the paths of righteousness. When more extreme measures were necessary, as in the case of King John of England, whose crime was the refusal to recognize the Archbishop of Canterbury nominated by the Pope, Innocent inflicted the further penalty of excommunication and even threatened physical force, in this case by encouraging the French to invade his kingdom.   John was only able to receive absolution after he had surrendered his kingdom to the Papacy, to be held in future as a fief for the service of 1,000 marks a year.   Other vassal-kingdoms of the Papacy were Hungary, Portugal, and Aragon, and there can be little doubt that to Innocent's mind it was there that the correct relationship between the spiritual and temporal powers was to be found.

This can most easily be seen in his attitude to the Empire, which, it will be recalled, was both the traditional enemy and the necessary associate of the Papacy.   The hostility was due in the first place to the Investitures Struggle, but had been inflamed by the Italian policy and oecumenical claims of the Hohenstaufen. No Pope could remain unmoved when Henry VI's courtiers told him that he, as Emperor, was ' God's vicar ' and ' possessed the earth '.   Association with the Empire, however, was none the less necessary.   For if the Pope was to take upon himself the moral guidance of the world, it stood to reason that he needed a secular arm to execute commands at his nod, lest the sternness of his edicts should become as sounding brass or tinkling cymbals. How could the kings of this world be made to obey the Word of God unless the admonitions of the Pope were supported by the sword of the Emperor ?   Innocent III, being clear-sighted, knew only too well the limitations of ghostly thunderings, and considered it axiomatic that only the most perfect concord between Pope and Emperor could secure ' the tranquillity and glory of the Christian people '. Concord, however, did not necessarily imply equality. On the contrary, Innocent likened the two powers to the sun and the moon :

> Just as the moon receives its light from the sun, which is greater by far, owing to the quantity and quality of its light, so the royal power takes its reputation and prestige from the pontifical power.

The Empire, he claimed, ' belonged ' to the Papacy, both because its origin was in the alleged transfer of imperial power from the Greeks to the Franks, effected by Leo III when he crowned Charlemagne, and because its end was the union of all Christian people in the Church. Reversing the roles played by the Emperor and the Pope at the Synod of Sutri in 1046 (p. 233), he welcomed the opportunity, afforded by the death of Henry VI (1197), of setting himself up as judge over the rival claimants to the Empire.

Unfortunately, however, he misjudged his men. The candidates for the imperial throne were three in number. First there was Frederick II, the infant son of Henry VI, who had already succeeded to the kingdom of Norman Sicily by hereditary right. He was not acceptable as Emperor either to the princes (because he was barely three years old) or to Innocent (who feared the danger that would ensue to the Papacy from the continued union of the Empire with Sicily). Secondly there was Henry's brother, Philip of Swabia, an honourable and clerkly man, who was supported by the great majority of the princes but was mistrusted by Innocent because he was a Ghibelline. And finally there was Otto IV, the son of Henry the Lion, who, though he had won but little support in Germany, was favoured by Innocent because he was a Guelf.

In supporting Otto, however, Innocent made a blunder. For while Philip was alive he had no hope of establishing himself— a fact which Innocent eventually had to recognize (1208)—and after Philip's murder (which Innocent hailed as a ' Judgment of God '), he proved unfaithful to the Papacy, even to the extent of invading Norman Sicily (1210). Innocent, therefore, although he had already changed his front twice, felt compelled to change it a third time and to support the imperial claims of the young Frederick, now almost seventeen years old, even though this greatly increased the danger of a union between the Empire and Norman Sicily. Though he received from Frederick a promise to abdicate the Sicilian throne as soon as he was crowned Emperor, there was little likelihood of the promise being fulfilled. The truth of the matter may have been that Innocent never expected Frederick to succeed in defeating Otto, and that he realized too late the disastrous possibilities of his victory.

Innocent died before the danger of a revived Empire had been fully realized, so that during his lifetime his policy seemed, though versatile, to be successful. But he was well aware that a mere re-organization of Christian government was not enough. Lawyer though he was, he saw that what was needed was not simply revised regulations but a new spirit of Christian enthusiasm. The aspirations of the previous century had to be revived, so that religion might once again become a real force in the lives not only of the clergy but also of the laity. How was it to be done?

The remedy which Innocent proposed was traditional but unimaginative. He decided to preach a Fourth Crusade, thinking that a new Crusade would inevitably revive the old crusading spirit. In fact it did nothing of the sort. An enthusiastic group of French knights started off from Champagne for the Holy Land, but having insufficient money for the journey, which they wisely proposed to make by sea, they sold their services to the Venetians, undertaking—in return for their passage to the East—to capture the Christian town of Zara on the Adriatic coast from the King of Hungary (1202). Innocent III excommunicated them for their pains, but subsequently forgave them, only to find that, lured on by the combination of Alexius Angelus, a Byzantine pretender, Philip of Swabia, Boniface of Montferrat, and Enrico Dandolo, the blind Doge of Venice, the crusaders had determined to make the city of Constantinople their next objective. The greatest Christian city of the East, which for five centuries had borne the full brunt of the Moslem attack, was now to be assaulted by men who claimed to be the soldiers of Christ. When, on 12 April 1204, they finally captured it, they looted wildly for three days. Harlots besported themselves in the sanctuary of Santa Sophia, and the value of the booty officially declared to the commanders was 800,000 silver marks.

When Innocent heard of the outrages that had been committed he was furious :

How is the Church of the Greeks, when afflicted with such trials and persecutions, to be brought back into the unity of the Church and devotion to the Apostolic See? It has seen in the Latins nothing but an example of perdition and the works of darkness, so that it now abhors them as worse than dogs. For they who are supposed to serve Christ rather than their own interests, who should have used their swords only against the pagans, are dripping with the blood of Christians. They have spared neither religion, nor age, nor sex, and have committed adultery and fornication in public, exposing matrons and even nuns to the filthy brutality of their troops. For them it was not enough to exhaust the riches of the Empire and to despoil both great men and small ; they had to lay their hands on the treasures of the Church, and what was worse its possessions, seizing silver retables from the altars, breaking them into pieces to divide amongst themselves, violating the sanctuaries and carrying off crosses and relics.[1]

Innocent did not exaggerate. Amongst the holy booty which was transported to the West were the head of St. Philip, an arm of St. Stephen, some of the flesh of St. Paul, a tooth of St. John the Baptist, and the dish into which Judas dipped his fingers at the Last Supper. The desecration committed by the crusaders was an outrage which reverberated throughout Christendom, and made the schism between the Greek and Roman Churches definitive. Instead of reviving Christian enthusiasm, the conquest of Constantinople demonstrated the cynical lust and depravity which had overcome the Latin West.

What was the cause of this debasement of the ideals of the previous century? To Innocent III it seemed to lie in the fact that the fundamental tenets of Christianity were no longer understood or sincerely believed by a large part of the population. In the great towns of northern Italy and southern France the rapid growth of population had far outstripped the parochial organization, with the result that many people, receiving none of the proper ministrations of the Church, had fallen a prey to false doctrines, and particularly to Manichaeism. This was a heresy of Eastern origin, founded by Mani in the third century, and it

[1] Migne, *P.L.*, ccxv, col. 701 (letter cxxvi).

had spread to the West primarily through the agency of traders. By the end of the eleventh century it had churches in Constantinople, Bosnia, Roumania, Bulgaria, and Dalmatia, and during the twelfth century it was more or less officially tolerated by the municipal authorities in towns such as Milan, Viterbo, Ferrara, Florence, Prato, Vicenza, and Spoleto, while in the south of France, particularly in the region of Albi, its success was even greater, since the Count of Toulouse and the ruling factions in many of the towns were said to be numbered among its converts.

The central belief of these heretics, who were usually called Cathari, or Albigensians, was in the dualism of the Perfect and Imperfect, the Eternal and the Temporal, the Spiritual and the Material, the Good and the Evil. They believed that God, being perfect, had created only the world of the spirit, which was eternal, and that the material world, being corruptible, had been created by an evil God (Satan, Lucifer, or Lucibel) who was to be identified as Jehovah, the God of the Jews. Consequently, they not only rejected the Old Testament, but also denied Christ's Incarnation (for how could God have had a body which was the creation of Satan ?). Having thus rejected the central doctrine of the Christian Church, they proceeded to undermine the fundamental institution of society, which was the family. Carrying their belief in the wickedness of all matter to its logical conclusion, they held that it was a sin to add to the amount of evil in the world by the procreation of babies ; and while they preached chastity for the ' perfect ', they declared that prostitution was normally a lesser evil than motherhood.

It stood to reason that the Church could not allow such doctrines to go unchallenged, and for sixty years, at least, vigorous preaching campaigns had been conducted in the disaffected areas. But even though the preachers had included such men as St. Bernard himself, the results achieved had been negligible. Innocent, therefore, at the beginning of his pontificate, intensified the efforts of the Catholics. He sent papal legates, notably Pierre de Castelnau, to the south of France and enlisted the active support of the Cistercian Order. In 1205 he encouraged two Spaniards, Diego, Bishop of Osma, and his sub-prior St. Dominic, to abandon their original intention of going as missionaries to

East Prussia, and to preach against the Albigensians instead. But even though they travelled the country on foot and were remarkable for their learning, so that they were able to vanquish the leaders of the heretics in public disputations, they were unable to effect large-scale conversions. The heretics remained obstinate because they were encouraged by their temporal rulers.

That was the root of the problem, and it became evident to all when, on 15 January 1208, the papal legate, Pierre de Castelnau, was murdered at a crossing of the Rhone near St. Gilles. Rightly or wrongly, it was universally believed that the murder had been committed at the instigation of Raymond VI, Count of Toulouse. Raymond was a typical product of what all good churchmen considered to be the decadent and immoral civilization of the towns of southern France. He was the idol of the troubadours and the paragon of courtly love. He himself was suspected of heresy, and was said to have received the murderer of the papal legate in public and to have congratulated him on his deed. Though excommunicate, he remained unrepentant.

In these circumstances it seemed to Innocent, and indeed to the vast majority of Christians, imperative that some definite action should be taken. He therefore approached Raymond's feudal overlord, Philip Augustus, King of France, and enjoined him to confiscate his lands as a heretic. From Innocent's point of view, all would have been well if only Philip had agreed to play the part allotted to him. Unfortunately however, he refused, since, being already at war with King John of England and the Emperor Otto IV, he could not afford to dissipate his military strength in the south. Innocent therefore took the matter into his own hands and preached a Crusade against the Albigensians.

The call to arms met with a wide response. The barons of northern France coveted the wealth of Languedoc, and were only too eager for a holy war in which the prizes were both tempting and conveniently near to hand, and on 24 June 1209 a vast army assembled at Lyons. Raymond of Toulouse was in despair. Thinking resistance impossible, he announced his repentance, submitted to the papal legates, and in the hope of being allowed to retain his dominions joined the Crusade against his own people. But unfortunately for him his repentance was too late. Even though Innocent apparently believed in the sincerity of his conversion and tried to save him from ruin, he found that events had passed out of his control. Once the Crusade had been launched, there was a massacre at Béziers and an *auto-da-fé* at Minerva (1210), and nothing could stop the progress of the holy war. Even though many of the greater barons, such as the Duke of Burgundy, eventually returned to their fiefs, the lesser barons, under Simon de Montfort,[1] continued the war of conquest and won a decisive victory at Muret (1213). They were convinced that they were fighting in the cause of righteousness, and enjoyed the full support, if not of the Pope, at least of his legate.

If Innocent was haunted by the fear that the crusaders might have proceeded beyond the bounds of absolute justice, he contrived to conceal his feelings from the world at large. The Crusade was outwardly successful; the heretics were defeated and the Catholic faith vindicated. At the fourth Lateran Council which he summoned in 1215, Innocent was able to give a most impressive demonstration of the unity of the Church and the strength of papal leadership. It was attended by 405 prelates from Italy, Germany, Flanders, France, the kingdoms of the Iberian peninsula, England, Scandinavia, and (thanks to the Latin conquest) Byzantium itself. It was a most impressive assembly, since even the fact of attendance signified obedience to the papal summons. In many ways it could be compared to the ' Marchfield ' of the Merovingians (p. 115) or to the solemn crown-wearing of a king. It was an expression of the Church's innate unity and of its desire to maintain a single discipline by means of papal authority. Detailed plans were made for the reform of both the regular and the secular clergy, and the archbishops were instructed to hold annual synods in their provinces in order to ensure that the reforms were carried out. The manners and customs of bishops, monks, and parochial clergy were reviewed with the calm eye of apostolic authority, and even the laity was brought within the purview of reform. Every Christaiŋ was enjoined to declare any knowledge that he might have of heretics, and all secular rulers were informed that it was their duty to extirpate heresy in their dominions.

---

[1] The father of the Simon de Montfort who played such a large part in the history of England in the reign of Henry III.

More important still was the decree that all adult Christians were, on pain of excommunication, to confess to their own parish priests at least once a year, and to communicate at Easter. By this means, Innocent was able to ensure that in every parish the priest would have firm control of his flock. The maintenance of the true faith, he thought, could not be left to the fortuitous inspiration of the virtuous. It was a matter which required organization and discipline. He, as Christ's Vicar on Earth, would supervise the archbishops ; archbishops would supervise the bishops ; bishops would supervise ordinary priests ; and priests would guide the laity into the paths of righteousness.

That was the real meaning of Innocent's claim to ' possess the throne of glory ', and the reason why he declared that nothing which happened in the world should escape his attention. His was the office on which the whole Church depended, and he thought that he, and he alone, could organize its effective defence. The qualities which he brought to his task were in every way remarkable—clear-sightedness, efficiency, a deep-rooted sense of justice, courage, and faith. He spoke with the tongues of men and of angels, and no one can deny him his greatness. But unfortunately he lacked the spark that might have kindled sympathy and enthusiasm, and all his reforms might have been ineffectual if it had not been for the intervention of St. Francis of Assisi.

2. St. Francis (1182–1226) : Inspiration and Authority

Innocent III had met St. Francis in 1210, had given him his blessing, and after some hesitation had approved his primitive Rule, though only verbally. A less broad-minded or less courageous Pope might easily have refused to do as much, for on the surface St. Francis and his eleven companions were very similar to such heretics as the *Waldenses* or Poor Men of Lyons. They were laymen who had been ' converted to Religion ' [1] but who had refused to enter any of the monastic orders. They lived by a rule of their own, interpreted the doctrine of apostolic poverty so strictly that they refused even to possess houses or books, decried book-learning, and wandered about the countryside

[1] For the significance of this term, see p. 260.

preaching. Innocent saw, however, that in spite of these superficial resemblances to the heretics, St. Francis and his followers
were different. They were not anti-clerical, but showed an
immense reverence for the priesthood in general and the Papacy
in particular. They were prepared to obey the Church, and
therefore, in spite of their wild and unconventional ways, there
was a chance that they might be able to serve it. It was true
that they might eventually develop heretical views, but the risk
was worth taking. Inspiration was what the Church needed,
and, provided he did not break loose, St. Francis was clearly the
man to provide it.

St. Francis (1182–1226) was born at Assisi, a hill-town in the
vale of Spoleto, and he owed his name to the fact that his father,
a merchant of the town, was away in France at the time of his
birth. After a gay youth, in which he served in a war against
Perugia and was on the point of becoming the squire of a local
noble, he underwent one of those sudden conversions to Religion
which were so typical of the Middle Ages. It was said that after
a banquet, at which he was master of the revels, he and his companions went round the town singing. Gradually he dropped
behind them, so that they shouted back to him to ask what he
was thinking of. ' Was he thinking of getting married ? ' they
asked. ' You have spoken the truth,' he replied, ' and you have
never seen a nobler, wealthier or more beautiful bride than I
intend to take.' He was referring to his Lady Poverty.

He did not, however, enter Religion in the conventional way,
for he remained a layman and did not join any Order. The
story, as it was known to his closest companions, was simply
that one day he went into the ruined church of St. Damian, outside the walls of the town, and prayed before the image of Christ
crucified. The image spoke to him and said ' Francis, do you
not see that my house is being destroyed ? Go and repair it for
me.' Francis obeyed. He rode into a neighbouring town, sold
his possessions, and attempted to give the money thus acquired
to the priest. The priest, however, refused to touch the money,
and wisely, for Francis's father brought an action against his
son for absconding with his property. Francis was summoned
to appear before the civil authorities, but refused, claiming, as if
he were a cleric or a monk, that he now owed obedience to

God alone. He was therefore summoned before the bishop. This time he obeyed, and on the bishop's advice, he solemnly renounced his patrimony.

> Going into the bishop's chamber, he cast off all his garments, and laying the money on the clothes before the eyes of the bishop, his father and all who were present, he stepped naked before the door and said : ' Listen all of you, and understand. Up to now I have called Pietro Bernardone my father, but as I am now resolved to serve God, I give him back the money about which he was so perturbed, as well as the clothes I wore which belong to him, and from now on I will say " Our Father which art in Heaven " instead of " my father Pietro Bernardone ".' [1]

From that time forward St. Francis owned no property. He had been converted to Religion and had renounced the world. But he was in an agony of doubt whether to be a hermit or a preacher. He tended lepers, retreated to the seclusion of *Rivo Torto* and *Carceri*, and eventually sought to end his dilemma by an appeal to authority. But the authority he sought was not that of the Church. As ever an individualist, he was insistent on seeking the authority of God in his own way. He asked two friends, Brother Silvester and St. Clare, to pray to God for a sign, and it was the revelation which they received from God which determined him to live a religious life not only on his own account but also for the purpose of winning souls for God.

Thenceforward he determined to preach as well as to pray, and from Portiuncula he travelled round the countryside, preaching repentance. He always went barefoot, and in the early days he took a broom with him so that he could sweep any of the churches that he found dirty. In the intervals between his journeys he would live the life of a hermit. After two years, that is to say in 1209, he was joined by his first two companions, Bernard of Quintavalle, formerly one of the richer men of Assisi, and Peter Cathanii, and together they determined to live according to the rule which Christ had given to the apostles, obeying his instructions literally, particularly in regard to the following three texts :

[1] ' The Legend of the Three Companions ' : O. Karrer, *St. Francis of Assisi* (Sheed & Ward, 1947), p. 12. The conversational quotations on the previous page are from the same, pp. 6 and 8.

If thou wilt be perfect, go and sell that thou hast and give to the poor. (Matthew xix. 21.)

Take nothing for your journey, neither staves, nor scrip, neither bread, neither money ; neither have two coats apiece. (Luke ix. 3.)

If any man will come after me, let him deny himself, and take up his cross, and follow me. (Matthew xvi. 24.)

They renounced property in the most absolute fashion possible. They had no fixed habitation, and begged for food from door to door, finding the very act of begging an exercise in humility.

In some ways this renunciation of property must have tempted people to doubt whether St. Francis was a Catholic or a heretic, for the ' perfect ' of the Cathari adopted a similar position. But while these latter rejected property because they thought that all things material were the work of the devil, St. Francis made his renunciation simply as a step towards humility. He wanted to be not a person in authority but a ' brother underling ' (*frater minor*), and when the Bishop of Assisi told him that the life he was proposing would be difficult, he replied as follows :

My Lord, if we possessed property, we should have need of arms for its defence, for it is the source of quarrels and lawsuits, and the love of God and of one's neighbour usually finds many obstacles therein ; that is why we do not desire temporal goods.

It was this ardent interpretation of apostolic poverty that caused St. Francis to break with the established tradition of Benedictine monasticism. For though St. Benedict had laid great stress on the principle of ' stability ', thinking that every monk should enter one particular monastery and vow never to leave it till he died, St. Francis thought that he and his brethren should spend their lives travelling. This was partly because he wanted them to preach, but it was also because the notion of ' stability ' did not accord with his view of apostolic poverty. He was insistent that he and his brethren should own no money, that they should beg for food from door to door, and that they should own no houses. He would not allow himself or his companions to live in any dwelling which they could call their own, and the idea of a monastery built of stone struck him as a contradiction in terms. When the citizens of Assisi built a house for him and his friars, he climbed on to the roof and tore down the tiles with his own hands.

Poverty, humility, and simplicity were his guiding ideals, and he aimed to win souls not so much through the force of argument as by the power of love. Unlike St. Dominic, he did not lay any great stress on learning, preferring that he and his friars should be ' accomplished in charity rather than smatterers in research '.. It was not by scholarship that he tamed the wolf of Gubbio ; and it was only the ardour of his love for the ' lower and irrational creatures ' that prompted him to preach to the birds. Similarly when, in 1219, he went to Egypt and passed from the camp of the crusaders to that of the Moslems, he was not relying simply on his natural eloquence ; the power on which he relied was the boundless love of God. That was why, for all his emphasis on good works, he kept the sacraments as the central point of his religion.

> If I chanced to meet at the same time [he said] any saint coming from heaven and any poor priest, I would honour the priest first, and would sooner go to kiss his hands ; and I would say to the other : ' Oh, wait, St. Laurence, for this man's hands handle the Word of Life and possess something that is more than human.' [1]

The appeal that St. Francis made was such that men flocked to sell their goods and became his brethren or friars (*fratres*). By 1220 his followers were to be numbered in thousands, and no one could mistake the fact that here at last the Church had found its inspiration. It was also clear, however, that the Church would have to regularize and organize the new movement. The licence which could be given to one man who was a saint, or even to his more intimate associates, could not be given so freely to the commonalty of men. For St. Francis acted as the spirit moved him. We read how he said his prayers in the rain, discovered that there were devils in his pillow, took off his clothes before the brothers, cursed a cruel pig, cured the cattle at Fonte Colombo, and made Peter of Cathanii drag him through the streets ; and in his case we are still left in no doubt of his sanctity—indeed, our certainty of it is increased. But however

---

[1] II. Celano, § 201 as quoted by Moorman, *Sources for the Life of St. Francis*, Manchester (1940), p. 124.

great might be the respect in which he himself was held, it was only natural to wonder whether it was right for his conduct to be copied by all and sundry. His followers were beginning to cover the earth, and the thought of them all acting as the spirit moved them must, to ordinary people, have been a little alarming. Was not some form of control desirable, or even imperative?

The difficulty was that St. Francis disliked the thought of any elaborate organization. In the early days he had watched over his converts himself, and had quite rightly insisted that the best way to train them was not to issue them with a set of rules and regulations but to inspire them with the love of God. But with the rapid expansion of the Order he could no longer supervise his friars individually, and some delegation of authority became imperative. In 1217, the year in which missions were first organized to countries outside Italy, he went so far as to designate territorial provinces and appoint 'ministers' to supervise them in his name; but he was still unwilling to frame any definite regulations for their guidance. He valued spontaneity for its own sake, and trusted that the inspiration of his own example would remain with the brethren even in his absence.

The authorities of the Church, however, were understandably perturbed at the lack of consistent discipline. As one observer wrote in 1220:

> To us this religious order [*religio*] seems exposed to a great danger, for it accepts not only the perfect, but also the young and imperfect who ought to be trained and tested by a period of conventual discipline, and it sends them out, two by two, to all quarters of the globe.

It was true that in the early days St. Francis had never sent out any of his friars until they were fully prepared. But now the very success of the Order had increased its danger. Were all the thousands of converts convinced of their vocation? Had all the ministers of the Order caught the inspiration of their founder? And might not the friars, if inadequately trained, fall victim to the very heresies which they were supposed to counteract? Pope Honorius III decided that the danger was indeed great, and in 1220 he issued the bill *Cum Secundum* which imposed a novitiate of one year on all who wished to enter the Order.

This was the first direct intervention which the Papacy had made in the internal affairs of the Order. Its indirect influence, however, had been considerable for some time past, at least since 1216, when Pope Honorius III had appointed Cardinal Ugolino (subsequently famous as Pope Gregory IX) to be ' the father of the saint's family '. Ugolino was a remarkable man. He had a deep and intuitive sympathy for St. Francis and his ideals, and yet thought instinctively in terms of ecclesiastical organization. He had vision, and saw not only what St. Francis and his companions were, but also what they might become. He realized that their ideals were complementary to those of St. Dominic, and that, if combined, the followers of the two saints would form a spiritual army against the heretics of the time. But though St. Dominic was deeply affected by the Franciscan ideal, St. Francis himself would not unite with him, since he was not anxious to accept the Dominican emphasis on learning, and hated any suggestion that he or his brethren should be given positions of authority.

My lord [he said to the cardinal], my brethren have been styled Lesser [*minores*] that they may not presume to become Greater [*majores*].[1] Their calling teaches them to be in lowliness, and to follow the footsteps of Christ's humility, that thereby at last they may be exalted above the rest of the Saints. If you would have them bear fruit in the Church of God, hold and keep them in the state to which they have been called, and bring them back to lowliness even against their will. Therefore, father, I pray you by no means to let them rise to high office, lest their pride should be proportionate to their poverty and they should wax arrogant against the rest.[2]

None the less, the movement towards authority was irresistible. After the creation of provinces and the appointment of provincial ministers, the need for a definitive Rule was all the more pressing. There was, it is true, the primitive Rule (*Regula primitiva*) which St. Francis had written in 1210, and to which Innocent III had given his oral approval; but this Rule, designed only for the first eleven companions, consisted to a large extent of precepts

[1] People in authority were often called *majores*, whence the English word *mayor*.
[2] II. Celano, § 148 (tr. A. G. Ferrers Howell, Methuen, 1908).

from the Holy Gospel and lacked the precision and definition needed for the organization of a great religious Order. Cardinal Ugolino therefore persuaded St. Francis to write a new and fuller Rule, the *Regula Prima* of 1221, and then, when that proved unacceptable, to start again and write the *Regula Secunda* of 1223. Rules which did not meet with the approval of the ecclesiastical authorities were, like the *Regula Primitiva* and first draft of the *Regula Secunda*, conveniently lost or destroyed.

It was not surprising therefore that St. Francis withdrew to an increasing extent from the activities of the Order which he had founded. In 1220 he resigned the position of Minister General, being succeeded first by Peter Cathanii, who died within six months, and then by Elias of Cortona, whose views were more or less in accord with those of Cardinal Ugolino. St. Francis withdrew to live a semi-eremitical life at such places as Portiuncula, La Verna, or Fonte Colombo, wooing his Lady Poverty, devoting himself to prayer, and defending by the example of his life the ideals for which he had originally stood and still did stand.

The development of the Order began to pass out of his control. Changes were made which could not have met with his approval, and the rule of poverty was gradually modified. In spite of his insistence that anyone who became his friar should first sell all that he had and give it to the poor, the *Regula Prima* added that this was ' if he wishes and can do so in a spiritual way and without impediment '. The brethren were allowed to possess service-books, and for clothing they were allowed not one tunic but two. Most important of all, however, was the weakening of the provision that the friars should have no papal privileges and no churches of their own. As early as 1222 Pope Honorius III gave them the privilege of saying Mass in times of interdict. ' We accord to you,' he wrote, ' permission to celebrate the Sacrament in time of interdict in your churches, *if you come to have any* '; [1] and this, be it noted, was during St. Francis's lifetime.

That was the tragedy of the situation, and it was hardly surprising that during his last years St. Francis showed a very deep anxiety to prevent his Order from being corrupted by its own

---

[1] Quoted from Moorman, *Sources for the Life of St. Francis* (Manchester, 1940), p. 32.

ministers. Most particularly was he determined to see that no Rule should be allowed to force the brethren out of the primitive way of life. Consequently, in spite of the extreme importance which he laid on obedience, he was always endeavouring to secure the right of the individual friar to disobey his superiors on a matter of conscience :

> If any of our ministers should give to any brother an order that is contrary to our life or his conscience [*animam suam*], that brother is not bound to obey him. For that in which a fault or sin is committed is not obedience. (*Regula Prima*, Chapter 5.)

Such a declaration was contrary to every previous religious Rule and to the whole spirit of the medieval Church. St. Benedict, for example, had firmly declared that a monk was to obey his superior, even when ordered to do an impossibility, and from the eleventh century onwards the Papacy had insisted, with ever-increasing force, that disobedience was as the sin of witchcraft. But St. Francis, foreshadowing in this respect one of the central features of Protestantism, was convinced that, important though obedience was, the conscience of the individual was more important still. In the *Regula Secunda*, Ugolino and Elias were able to modify many of the more uncompromising features which they had not been able to keep out of the former Rule ; but in the matter of obedience St. Francis stood firm and had his way. Though the phrasing was altered in order to shift the emphasis, the essential provision remained :

> The brothers, who are subjects, must remember that on account of God they have renounced their wills. Whence I firmly order them to obey their ministers in all things which they promised God to observe *and which are not contrary to their conscience or our Rule.* (*Regula Secunda*, Chapter 10.)

More direct was the appeal which St. Francis made in his Testament, the document which he dictated on his deathbed (1226). In it he stated quite simply how his conversion had been marked by the change in his attitude to lepers, whom he had previously shunned but subsequently tended. He declared his faith in the priests of the Roman Church—'even if they should persecute me '—and his belief in and devotion to the sacraments.

He related how, having no one to show him how to govern the brethren, God had shown him what to do, revealing to him that they should live according to the rule of the Gospels, dividing their possessions among the poor, and being content with a single tunic, patched inside and out. He told how he and his companions had worked with their hands and begged for bread from door to door. He forbade his brethren to have any church or habitation built for them, and he forbade them to ask for letters of privilege from the Papal Curia. He declared his obedience to the Minister General and exhorted his brethren to obey their ' guardians ' (*guardiani*).[1] Finally, he explained that this was not ' another rule ', but a ' reminder, admonition, and exhortation —[his] testament '. He commanded that it should be read alongside the Rule, with nothing added, nothing deleted, and nothing explained away :

> But as the Lord has given me [grace] to say and write the Rule and these words purely and simply, you are to understand them simply and purely, without glosses, and you are to observe them in blessed charity to the end.

On 3 October 1226 St. Francis died in a little hut at his beloved Portiuncula. On the following day the Minister General, Brother Elias, announced to the world the miracle of the stigmata which had taken place some two years before. Barely two years later, on 16 July 1228, St. Francis was canonized by his old friend Ugolino, now Pope Gregory IX ; and on the following day the foundation-stone was laid of the great basilica which was to be built in his honour at Assisi, as the *caput et mater* of the whole Order. In 1230 St. Francis's body was translated to the new basilica, so that the faithful might honour him more devoutly ; and in the same year Pope Gregory IX declared authoritatively that the friars were not bound to observe the injunctions of the Testament, since St. Francis had had no right to lay commands on them without the consent of the Chapter General, and no power to commit his successors in any way. Now that he was officially raised to the company of the saints, it seemed as if the

---

[1] A *guardianus* or *custos* was the word used to describe the head of a Franciscan convent. It would seem, therefore, that convents were already in existence, though in such cases the property would be *owned* by the donor or town-authorities.

wishes of the *poverello* could at last be ignored. The final blow came in 1245, when Pope Innocent IV declared that the followers of St. Francis might enjoy the *use* of any property, such as houses, land, furniture, or books, so long as the legal ownership was vested in the Papacy.

Although the Order had thus been transformed, many of the more intimate friends of St. Francis—brothers Giles, Leo, Angelo, and Rufino for example—refused to be divorced from their Lady Poverty. They were known as ' observants ' or ' spirituals ' and fought a long, though losing, battle against the ' relaxing ' or ' conventual ' party. The ministers were normally against them, and so sometimes was the Rule (the *Regula Secunda*), but they appealed boldly to the authority of St. Francis's own life. They told and re-told the stories of his strict poverty—how he would not have more than one tunic, how he would not let a novice have a psalter, and how he insisted on abandoning a hut because, rough shelter though it was, it had been described as ' his '. The officials of the Order therefore realized that the only way of restoring unity was to have but a single authorized Life of the saint, which, while being truthful, would not insist too much on the points that were controversial. The early ' legends ' (*i.e.* readings), such as those of the ' three companions ', the writings of Brother Leo, and the two official Lives written in 1228 and 1244 by Thomas of Celano, were all, for one reason or another, considered unsuitable, and in 1260 St. Bonaventura, the Minister General, was commissioned to write a new one. It was a masterpiece of saintliness and tact, and in many ways it drew a picture of St. Francis which was accurate and true. But though it quoted some of St. Francis's own sayings about learning, it modified their force ; though it recounted St. Francis's views on poverty, it somewhat softened the hardship of his early life ; and it never mentioned the Testament at all. It was a Life written not so much for St. Francis as for the Franciscan Order, and in 1266 the Chapter General not only approved it, but decreed, though fortunately without success, that all previous ' legends ' should be destroyed. Unity was to be purchased at the expense of a little tactful silence.

That is not to say, however, that the Order was not a wonderful achievement. Ugolino had diverted the Franciscan ideal into the main channels of ecclesiastical organization and had created a veritable army of missionaries where St. Francis had envisaged only a small band of ardent souls, loosely-knit in a form of personal union. He had seen that St. Francis could save the Church and he had thought it important to see that no modesty or idiosyncrasy prevented him from doing so. He revered his sanctity and sympathized with him as a man ; but he was determined that he should fulfil what he considered to be the Lord's purpose.

The crying need of the time was for priests who would be brothers to the poor and help them, who would be at home in the squalor of the new industrial towns, and who would be accepted by the unprivileged classes as equals and friends ; who would preach as St. Francis had preached, tend the sick as he had tended the lepers, and revive the Christian faith and Christian charity. Ugolino saw that the friars could supply the need. He recognized the genius of St. Francis and saw at once its full potentialities. But he realized also that what St. Francis could do spontaneously and by divine inspiration, could only be attempted by others after much training. He tried, as it were, to bring the saint to earth, and to show him what a wonderful contribution his followers could make to the life of the Church, if only he would let them be organized on a grand scale. He understood the necessity for rules and regulations, discipline and learning, and saw that, to be effective as missionaries, the friars would need not only to visit the poorer quarters of the towns but also to live in them, even at the cost of having houses. Given the means, he saw that they could reconvert the lost portions of Christendom.

And he was not mistaken. The expansion of the Order was remarkable. In England, for example, the first Franciscans (four clerks and five laymen) arrived in 1224, two years and twenty-three days before the death of St. Francis. By 1230, when Ugolino, as Pope Gregory IX, declared the Testament not to be binding on them, they had founded houses in sixteen of the most important towns of the kingdom—Canterbury, London, Oxford, Northampton, Norwich, Worcester, Hereford, Salisbury, Nottingham, Leicester, Lincoln, Cambridge, Stamford, King's Lynn, Bristol, and Gloucester. Their success was astounding :

They illuminate our whole country [wrote the Bishop of Lincoln in 1239] with the bright light of their preaching and teaching. . . . If your Holiness could see with what devotion and humility the people run to hear from them the Word of Life, to confess their sins, to be instructed in the rules of living, and what improvement the clergy and regulars have gained by imitating them, you would indeed say that ' upon them that dwell in the valley of the shadow of death hath the light shined '.[1]

The Church apparently had been saved, and Christendom was secure. But in order to effect this it had been necessary to damp the ardour of a saint, to regularize his sanctity, and almost (one suspects) to break his heart. Yet who can say that Ugolino was wrong ? Had he not served his Master well in finding the souls that were lost, and in making possible so wonderful a Christian revival ?

APPENDIX

I

The Novice who wanted a Psalter [2]

It happened that the blessed Francis came to the hermitage where a certain novice . . . was staying, and one day the novice said to him : ' Father ! It would be a great consolation to me to have a psalter, but though the General is willing to give me permission, I would not have it without your knowledge.' The blessed Francis answered him saying : ' The Emperor Charles, Roland and Oliver and all the paladins, robust men who were strong in battle, pursuing the heathen with much sweat and labour even unto death, had a glorious and memorable victory for their pains, and in the end were martyred, dying in battle for Christ's sake. And [now] there are many who want to receive honour and human praise simply by telling the story of the things which they did.'

Another time, when the blessed Francis was sitting by the fire, warming himself, this [brother] spoke to him again about the psalter. And the blessed Francis said to him : ' When you have a psalter you will begin to long for a breviary ; and when you have

---

[1] Robert Grosseteste : quoted from A. G. Little, *Studies in English Franciscan History* (Manchester, 1917), p. 134.
[2] From the ' Intentio Regulae ', printed in L. Lemmens, *Documenta Antiqua Franciscana, Pars i, Scripta Fratris Leonis* (Quaracchi, 1901), pp. 92 ff.

a breviary, you will sit on a throne like a great prelate and say to your brother : " Fetch me my breviary." ' And speaking thus with great fervour of the spirit, he took some ash with his hand and put it on his head, rubbing his hand around his head as if he was washing it, and saying to himself : ' I a breviary ! I a breviary ! ' repeating the words over and over again, ' I a breviary ! ' as he rubbed his hand on his head. And the brother was astounded and afraid. Afterwards the blessed Francis said to him : ' I also was tempted to have books, but so that I should know the will of God on this matter, I took a Gospel Book and prayed to God that in the opening of the book He should deign to show me His will on this matter. And when I had finished my prayers, at the first opening of the book I came across these words of the holy gospel : " Unto you it is given to know the mystery of the Kingdom of God, but unto them that are without, all these things are done in parables." ' And he said ' There are many who would eagerly ascend to the knowledge that the man who is blessed is he who makes himself sterile with the love of God.'

II

Conversion without Tears [1]

[The following story shows how quickly the Franciscan ideals could be debased. The writer, Salimbene, was himself a Franciscan Friar and knew Gerard well. Gerard was a leading member of the Order and had once been one of St. Francis's companions.]

One thing I must not omit, namely that, at the time of the aforesaid devotion [the Alleluia of 1233], these solemn preachers were sometimes gathered together in one place, where they would order the matter of their preachings : that is, the place, the day, the hour, and the theme thereof. And one would say to the other, ' Hold fast to that which we have ordered ' ; and this they did without fail, as they had agreed among themselves. Brother Gerard therefore would stand, as I have seen with my own eyes, in the Piazza Comunale of Parma, or wheresoever else it pleased him, on a wooden stage which he had made for his preaching ; and while the people waited he would cease from his preaching, and draw his hood over his face, as though he were meditating some matter of God. Then, after a long delay, as the people marvelled, he would draw back his

---

[1] Translation from the Chronicle of Fr. Salimbene by G. G. Coulton, *From St. Francis to Dante* (London, David Nutt), 2nd ed., 1907, p. 25.

hood and open his mouth in such words as these : ' I was in the spirit on the Lord's day, and I heard our beloved brother, John of Vicenza, who was preaching at Bologna on the shingles of the river Reno, and he had before him a great concourse of people ; and this was the beginning of his sermon : Blessed are the people whose God is the Lord Jehovah, and blessed are the folk that he has chosen to be his inheritance.' So also would he speak of Brother Giacomino ; so spake they also of him. The bystanders marvelled, and, moved with curiosity, some sent messengers to learn the truth of these things that were reported. And having found that they were true, they marvelled above measure, and many, leaving their worldly business, entered the Orders of St. Francis or St. Dominic. And much good was done in divers ways and divers places at the time of that devotion, as I have seen with my own eyes.

Further Reading

A. LUCHAIRE. *Innocent III.* 6 vols. Paris. 1905-8.

M-H. VICAIRE. *St. Dominic and his Times* (tr. Kathleen Pond). London. 1964.

L. E. BINNS. *Innocent III* (Great Medieval Churchmen series). 1931. A brief but useful introduction.

S. RUNCIMAN. *The Eastern Schism.* Oxford. 1955.

P. SABATIER. *Vie de Saint François d'Assise.* Final edition. Paris. 1931. A nineteenth-century classic, first published in 1894.

J. R. H. MOORMAN. *The Sources for the Life of St. Francis.* Manchester. 1940. See also the critical review by M. Bihl in *Archivum Franciscanum Historicum*, xxxix. 1 37.

S. RUNCIMAN. *The Mediaeval Manichee.* Cambridge. 1947.

C. R. CHENEY and W. H. SEMPLE. *Selected Letters of Pope Innocent III* (Nelson's Medieval Texts). London. 1953. Latin text with English translation of letters referring in the main to English affairs.

A. G. FERRERS HOWELL (tr.). *The Lives of St. Francis of Assisi by Brother Thomas of Celano.* London. 1908.

O. KARRER. *St. Francis of Assisi ; the Legends and Lauds,* translated by N. Wydenbruck. London. 1947. Includes translations from most of the main sources other than Celano, but unfortunately refers to several by different titles from those used by Moorman.

M. R. B. SHAW. *Joinville and Villehardouin : Chronicles of the Crusades.* London. 1963.

VIII

THE NEW ERA IN MONARCHY

IN the Middle Ages the people of Western Europe regarded themselves as a single society, which they often likened to the seamless robe of Christ. They considered themselves to be 'the Christian people' or the Church, and professed obedience to the government of Christ as it was exercised through the agency of two powers, the Empire and the Papacy. The one was supposed to exercise all temporal, and the other all spiritual power; and though there might in fact be several independent kingdoms and a schism between Orthodox and Catholic Christianity, these latter were not regarded as essential features of the order of creation, but simply as accidents or the consequence of sin.

Eventually, however, this hierarchical view was abandoned. It was replaced by the conception that kingdoms or nation-states were natural units in themselves and, in some respects at least, superior to the law. It was a change which has always been taken to mark one of the clearest divisions between medieval and modern history, and it is usually said to have occurred as a result of the Renaissance, and in the fifteenth century. In fact, however, it is clearly visible as early as the thirteenth century, in the history of the Emperor Frederick II (1197–1250) and King Louis IX of France (1226–70). The reigns of these two monarchs seem to mark the end of one era and the beginning of a new one.

1. FREDERICK II (1197–1250)

The Emperor Frederick II was born on 26 December 1194 at Jesi near Ancona. Through his father, the Emperor Henry VI, he was the heir of Frederick Barbarossa; through his mother, Constance, he was the heir of King Roger II of Norman Sicily; and he spent his life attempting to fulfil the ambitions of both, in spite of the overwhelming odds against him. Since he was scarcely three years old when his father died, the German princes did not elect him as successor. His mother died a year later, and though he then succeeded to the crown of Norman Sicily by hereditary right, he was a minor in the wardship of his feudal overlord, Pope Innocent III. Innocent preserved him his kingdom, which was gravely distraught by rival factions of Germans and Normans, but did surprisingly little for his education. He made no attempt to introduce him to his own entourage—in fact he never even saw him till he was seventeen—but allowed his education to look after itself in the *Regno* of Norman Sicily.

The *Regno* was a kingdom of unrivalled wealth and splendour, the meeting-place of all the cultures of medieval Europe, and it afforded an intellectual atmosphere where none of the simpler traditions of the Latin West could long remain unchanged. How could one fail to modify one's view of the universality of the Roman Church in a kingdom which contained significant survivals of the Greek Church and a large number of Moslems? Or how could one fail to be excited by the cosmopolitan and scientific learning that flourished at Salerno, the oldest medical school of Western Europe? Even the royal court had a tradition of intellectual brilliance. King Roger II (1130–54) had been the patron of al-Idrisi, the Moslem geographer, and the chancellor of King William I (1154–66) had translated Plato's *Phaedo* and' *Meno* into Latin from the Greek. Most spectacular of all, however, were the art and architecture of the kingdom. The Palatine Chapel at Palermo was one of the most gorgeous buildings in Christendom, designed and decorated in an eclectic style which was partly Norman, partly Byzantine, and partly Islamic. Like the civilization of the *Regno* as a whole, it did not fit into any of the accepted conventions of the medieval world, but stood out as something splendidly unique.

It was in such surroundings that the young Frederick was educated. He imbibed learning rapidly, and soon made a reputation for himself as both a sceptic and the ' wonder of the world '. But so far as the rest of Europe was concerned he was for a long time forgotten, while attention was concentrated on the wars of Innocent III with Philip of Swabia and Otto IV (p. 347). It was not till 1211, when Philip was dead and Otto had fallen foul of the Papacy, that the Ghibelline princes in Germany recalled the existence of this young scion of the Hohenstaufen and elected him to the Empire.

It was a sudden change of fortune, and seemed complete. For even though it had previously been one of the prime aims of papal policy to ensure that the Empire and *Regno* were never united in the same hands, Innocent III gave Frederick's election his approval. He demanded certain safeguards in respect of his position of feudal overlord of the *Regno*, but otherwise seems to have acted on the assumption that the civil war between Otto and Frederick would be both lengthy and inconclusive. If this was so, it was a disastrous mistake. Frederick crossed the Alps with only sixty knights, entered the town of Constance three hours before it was due to be occupied by Otto IV, and won the most amazing successes. The decisive victory was won for Frederick by his ally, Philip Augustus of France, when in 1214 he defeated Otto at the battle of Bouvines (p. 310). In 1215 Frederick was crowned at Aachen, sitting in the marble throne of Charlemagne. In 1218 Otto IV died. And in 1220 the aged Pope Honorius III crowned Frederick as Emperor in St. Peter's basilica at Rome.

But no matter how often, or how solemnly, the young Frederick might be crowned, the question remained whether the Empire could be revived. The German and Italian dominions of the Empire had been in a state of spasmodic civil war since the death of Henry VI in 1197, with the inevitable result that, as in the Investitures Struggle, the royal or imperial administration had broken down almost completely. In Germany the ecclesiastical and lay princes had consolidated their position, and Frederick, following in the footsteps of his grandfather Barbarossa, legalized the usurpations which he was no longer able to challenge. In 1216 he renounced the *jus spolii* whereby the Emperor had previously enjoyed for a year and a day the revenues of all vacant bishoprics and abbeys, and in 1220 he issued a constitution in favour of the ecclesiastical princes which secured them in their temporal dominions. In Italy he was less accommodating, but even there he was careful to learn from the experience of his grandfather and did not insist on any rights which were lost beyond recall. He realized that if his Empire was ever to be a reality, he needed first to concentrate his resources and establish a new basis of power.

He therefore turned his attention to the *Regno* or Norman kingdom of Sicily, where the foundations of an absolute monarchy and bureaucratic government had already been laid. It was the only kingdom of Western Europe in which the links between the central and local government had been so firmly forged that there was no need for the court to be ambulatory. The king had a capital city, Palermo, and there in the splendours of an oriental palace he lived with his *harem* and his eunuchs. The court etiquette was derived from that of the Byzantine Empire, and the king was rarely seen by his subjects except on ceremonial occasions. Those who were so fortunate as to be honoured with an audience had to prostrate themselves before him and to treat him with the reverence due to a power which was almost divine. It was considered sacrilege to dispute his judgments or decisions, since that which pleased the ruler had the force of law. At a time when legislation was but rarely practised by the kings of Western Europe, King Roger the Great had established a tradition of legislating on the grand scale: his ' assizes ' of 1140 constituted a code of law which, in spite of certain elements derived from feudal practice, canon law, or local custom, was unmistakably based upon the Roman law of Justinian and his successors.

The *Regno* had an established civil service. Though there were also feudal lordships, feudal liberties, and feudal justice, there was a solid core of professional judges (κριται), in cities, provinces, and the royal court itself. They were rewarded not with the grant of fiefs but with salaries paid by the king's financial office (σεκρετὸν or *diwan*) which was largely staffed by Moslems. The revenues were derived only in part from the normal feudal sources. Export duties were levied on corn (which was sent in large quantities to the coastal towns of Moslem Tunisia), woollen and linen goods, steel, timber, butter, cheese, and fruits. Tolls were paid at the entrance of all towns, and foreign ships which put into port on their way through the Straits of Messina (the direct route from Pisa or Genoa to the Orient) had to pay harbour dues. More important still were the state-monopolies, a device which had been borrowed from Byzantium. They included the forests, the manufacture of pitch (which was important for the fleet), fisheries (especially of the tunny-fish), salt, iron-mining, stone-quarrying, dye-works, and the manufacture of silk ; the royal silk factories stood cheek by jowl with the royal palace in Palermo.

The *Regno* was the wealthiest kingdom of Western Europe, and one of the most powerful. It could even control its trading cities, those of Gaëta, Naples, Salerno, and Bari being reduced to a state of subjection which none of the communes of northern Italy would have tolerated for a moment. The Norman kings of the *Regno* had been able to support their authoritarian claims with overwhelming force. They had a navy which was second only to that of Byzantium and was able to exercise an almost complete control over the central Mediterranean. They had an army which was composed, not only of Norman knights, but also of Moslem mercenaries. These latter had been used on the mainland as early as 1098 ; Roger the Great and his successors found them invaluable, especially as they were immune to the effects of papal excommunication.

It was to the *Regno*, therefore, that Frederick turned in his search for a new basis of power. The Norman inheritance was, in his opinion, more important than the German ; it was to be not just an appendage of the Empire but its very core. First, however, it had to be put in order. It had suffered from the troubles of the previous thirty years like every other part of his dominions, the towns and nobles having been rewarded with grants of royal rights and privileges whenever their loyalty had seemed in doubt. But whereas in Germany Frederick was prepared to confirm and even enlarge the grants which had been made, in the *Regno* he attacked them boldly. In the assize *de privilegiis resignandis* (1220) he revoked all privileges granted since the death of King William the Good (1189). On the island of Sicily itself he waged war against the Moslem communities, which were in open revolt (1221–3) ; and when at last he had defeated them, he deported them *en masse* to the mainland, where they were settled in specially selected garrison-towns as his mercenaries—at Lucera the city was emptied of its previous inhabitants and the cathedral converted into a mosque. This bold policy was really no novelty, since in the Balkans it was one of the traditional Byzantine remedies for troublesome barbarians. But in the West it made a very deep impression, especially as it was reported that any attempt to convert these mercenaries to Christianity was forbidden. Frederick knew that the religious protection which he gave them was the surest hold on their loyalty, and, when the Pope protested, he excused himself by saying that he was driven to wage many wars and, since blood had to be shed, the souls of Moslems were surely of less consequence than those of Christians.

Having thus pacified the *Regno* and established an army, Frederick proceeded to make provision for the civil service. He needed an almost unlimited number of clerks, lawyers, and financial officials, and realized that he would have to train them himself. Accordingly, in 1224 he founded the University of Naples. This, so far as the Latin West was concerned, was a startling innovation, since learning lay within the province of the Church, and the existing universities, such as Paris and Bologna, were ecclesiastical institutions for the training of churchmen. Frederick's university was the first state university in Europe. In the charter of foundation he stated explicitly that it was his aim to train shrewd and intelligent men for the imperial service, and he proceeded to set out, in the manner of a prospectus, the advantages of the place. Naples, he said, was a wealthy town, easily approached by sea and well furnished with provisions and halls of residence.

> We keep the students within view of their parents ; we save them many lengthy and toilsome journeys ; we protect them from robbers. They used to be pillaged while travelling abroad, but now, thanks to Our liberality, they may study at small cost and a little distance from home.

Apparently, however, he thought the arts of persuasion would prove insufficient to establish the popularity of the new university. He therefore gave it a monopoly of learning within the kingdom. No natives of the *Regno* were allowed to study elsewhere, and those who had already entered foreign universities were ordered to return by Michaelmas. Frederick did not want his ablest subjects to be drawn away to Paris ; nor did he want them to become churchmen, theologians, or papalists. In the manner of a Byzantine emperor or Islamic caliph, he regarded learning as an essential function of the State and one of the attributes of his majesty.

All this was very modern, and it might well be asked what was the attitude of the Papacy towards it. It might have been thought that the Pope's hostility would have been immediate and uncompromising, but in fact Pope Honorius III (1216–27) made a serious attempt to collaborate. The reason for this was not that he approved of Frederick's Sicilian policy, but that he could not conceive of the Papacy without the Empire. In this respect Honorius was a traditionalist. He considered that the two powers, the spiritual and secular arms of the Church, were complementary to each other, and that nothing but harm could be caused by a conflict between them. He had before his eyes the results of the Investitures Struggle—the failure of political authority and the appalling growth of heresy—and he considered that the first essential for the reform of the Church was the restoration of harmony between the two heads of the Christian world. Returning to the ideal of Peter Damian, he thought that they should live ' in the union of perfect charity ' and ' prevent all discord among their lower members '.

In terms of practical politics, this meant that Pope Honorius III was prepared to help Frederick restore the imperial power, if he in return would assist the ecclesiastical authorities in the extirpation of heresy, and unite the laity of Christendom in a crusade to recover Jerusalem. In the first respect, Frederick was not unhelpful. At the time of his coronation at Rome, he issued a constitution of ten articles which, in addition to the usual provisions for the freedom of the Church (exemption from taxation and lay jurisdiction, etc.), inaugurated strong measures against heretics. He put to the ban of Empire all those who remained excommunicate for more than a year and a day, and similarly condemned ' all Cathari, Paterines, Leonists, Speronists, Arnaldists, Circumcisi, and heretics of either sex ', ordering their property to be confiscated and their sons to be disinherited, since it was ' more serious to offend against the eternal than the temporal majesty '. Most important of all, however, was the order that all civil magistrates (*potestates vel consules vel rectores*) were to take an oath to purge their territories of heretics on pain of expulsion, for Frederick thus provided the ecclesiastical authorities with the basic collaboration which was to make the Inquisition an effective weapon for the defence of Catholic Christianity.

But if Frederick's measures against heresy proved satisfactory, his attitude towards the proposed crusade was not. He took the cross for the first time, at his coronation at Aachen in 1215. He took it again at his imperial coronation in 1220, and after that made a habit of proposing dates and delays *ad nauseam*. Eventually, when even Honorius III was beginning to show signs of impatience, he made a formal promise, under pain of excommunication, to set sail for the Holy Land in August 1227 and to maintain a thousand knights there for two years.[1]

But still there were many who, having observed the endless excuses and delays, thought that Frederick would never redeem his vow. When Honorius III died (18 March 1227), it was not surprising that the cardinals elected a less compliant man to succeed him. Their choice fell upon Cardinal Ugolino, who adopted the ominous name of Pope Gregory IX (1227–41).

Gregory was eighty-six years old at his accession—and he lived to be a hundred—but he had still the same religious insight and ruthless determination which he had shown in his dealings with St. Francis. He had lost none of his vigour, and his pontificate was memorable for his many-sided activity. He founded a new university at Toulouse and was almost a second founder to that of Paris ; he regularized the Inquisition and brought it under papal control ; he issued the *Decretals*, a codification of the new material added to canon law during the previous two centuries ; he presided over the expansion of the Franciscan and Dominican orders, and canonized St. Francis. Surveying the state of Christendom with the cold eye of a man of affairs, he decided that the alliance between Empire and Papacy must be destroyed.

There were two main considerations which led him to this

---

[1] An interesting detail which emerges from the terms was that every knight was expected to have three horses.

decision. First was the belief that in all his dealings with the Papacy, Frederick, having frequently proved himself faithless, was only pretending to have the interests of Christendom at heart. Gregory was not prepared to trust him in anything. He was convinced that he would never set out on crusade unless threatened with firm measures, and when in 1227 Frederick did set sail, only to return within two days because an epidemic had broken out on board, Gregory jumped to the conclusion that it was all a pretence, and excommunicated him. When in the following year Frederick set out again, though still unabsolved, Gregory renewed the excommunication. To him it made no difference even that the crusade was successful. Frederick, by skilful diplomacy, persuaded the Sultan of Egypt to surrender Jerusalem, Bethlehem, and Nazareth, and placed the crown of Jerusalem on his own head in the Church of the Holy Sepulchre. But Gregory, having committed himself to disapproval, was ruthless. He released Frederick's Sicilian subjects from their oath of allegiance and invaded the _Regno_.

It was not an edifying sight to see the Pope invading the lands of a successful but excommunicate crusader. But part at least of Gregory's anger may be understood when it is recalled that a crusade should have been a religious exercise. Before the Second Crusade, St. Bernard had described the taking of the cross as a means of salvation :

> Have confidence, O sinners ! God is good. If God wanted to punish you, He would not ask for your service ;—even if you had offered your service, He would not have accepted it. If then, He has need, or pretends to have need of you, it is because He desires in return to help you in your need.

Frederick Barbarossa, Richard Cœur de Lion, and Philip Augustus had all, whatever else might be said of them, made sacrifices to go on crusade. But Frederick II had gone only when it suited him, and for his own purposes. He had visited Cyprus in order to remind its ruler that it was an imperial fief ; he had married the heiress of the Kingdom of Jerusalem and received its crown ; and he had behaved as though the object of the crusade had been not to revive the zeal of Christendom but simply to acquire a certain strip of territory. In Gregory's view he had failed to understand what the crusade was about because he was fundamentally out of sympathy with the thought and ideals of the Church. Consequently, even though Frederick might be all-powerful on his return from Palestine, and might force the Papacy to come to terms for the time being (1230), Gregory was clear that he constituted a force which had to be destroyed.

The second consideration which determined Gregory in his opposition was even more potent than the first. Since Frederick, in his dual capacity as King of the *Regno* and Emperor, was in a position to unite the whole of Italy under his rule, the freedom of the Church was imperilled. In the narrowest and most immediate sense, this meant that the security of the Papal States was threatened, but in a wider sense it meant that the whole structure of the Church was in danger. For the medieval Church was conceived not as a voluntary society but as a divine institution, the City of God upon earth. The Papacy had been entrusted with the government of its spiritual life, and had been established over peoples and kingdoms, to uproot and destroy, to build and plant; it had been given the keys of the Kingdom of Heaven, so that whatsoever it bound on earth would be bound in Heaven; and it had to protect these mystical powers, since God had entrusted them to its keeping. It could not allow them to be subjected to the threat of force, or to fall into the hands of a secular ruler. The Pope had to be secure in his own city. The temporal security of the Papal States was but the necessary condition of the spiritual freedom of the Church. Consequently, when the patrimony of St. Peter was surrounded, both on land and sea, by the power of an Emperor who had already demonstrated his lack of sympathy with the ideals of the Holy See, it could legitimately be said that the Church itself was in danger.

Gregory IX found it his duty, not only as an Italian potentate, but also as the Vicar of Christ on earth, to raise up enemies against Frederick wherever he could. Not surprisingly, he met with the greatest success among the city-states of northern Italy, where Frederick was doing his best to restore some form of imperial control, largely through the agency of imperial *podestàs* or supreme magistrates. Gregory incited the communes to resistance, revived memories of the Lombard League which had been formed against Barbarossa, and assisted the formation of a new one. Open war broke out in 1237.

By the very nature of the Italian political scene, however, it was impossible for either Pope or Emperor to win a speedy and decisive victory, for the communes of Lombardy and Tuscany were divided against each other by the same feuds which had divided them in the twelfth century. Territorial disputes, commercial rivalry, and the opportunity of restricting a rival's trade, were sufficient to ensure that Milan would almost always be opposed by Cremona, Pavia, and Parma ; and if the one declared for the Pope, the others would have no hesitation in being imperialist. At the foot of the Brenner Pass, there was a similar rivalry between Verona and Padua. On the main trade route through Tuscany, Florence and Lucca (which were usually papalist or 'Guelf') were opposed by Siena and Pisa which were Ghibelline ; while Pisa, which was a considerable naval and mercantile power, had also to contend with the rivalry of Genoa. It was the same all over central and northern Italy ; every town was normally in a state of war with its neighbours.

Every city was also a house divided against itself, being rent by feuds between the various noble families, who fortified their residences with towers and thought little of fighting pitched battles in the streets. In Florence, for example, the Buondelmonti were opposed to the Ubertini, and since the one family was Guelf, the other was naturally Ghibelline ; they fought on every possible occasion, and when the Ubertini staged a successful rebellion (1249) the city was unexpectedly imperialist for a period of eighteen months. To complicate matters still further, there were in every town additional feuds between the nobles and the non-nobles, and between the commercial magnates (*popolo grasso*) and retail traders (*popolo minuto*). Every trade was organized into guilds and was concentrated in a separate street or quarter of the city, with gates which could be shut as a defence in times of internal warfare.[1] All was confusion, and no government or alliance could be stable.

Yet Frederick tried to build an empire out of this mass of

---

[1] Thus, in Florence the guild of silk merchants was known, from the place of their residence, as the Guild of *Porta Santa Maria*. For a similar reason, the dressers of foreign cloth were known as the *Calimala* (*Calis mala* = street of ill repute).

warring cities. He claimed that he was ' overfilled with justice ', and organized the government of Italy under captains-general, such as his illegitimate sons Enzio, Frederick of Antioch, and Richard of Theate. But though they were splendid and attractive warriors, they could not control the situation with which they were confronted. Even the unspeakable Eccelino da Romano, the tyrant of Verona and Friuli—who was said to have condemned as many as 50,000 men to death—was unable to protect himself from the shifting plots and intrigues of Italian politics. Loyalty to the Empire was a quality which did not exist ; the only realities were the city and family. Though there were personal loyalties in the inner circle of Frederick's court, they rarely proved permanent. ' The Emperor could keep no man's friendship ', wrote Salimbene ; ' nay he boasted that he never nourished a pig but that he had its fat.' [1] At the end of his reign he relied almost entirely on the fear inspired by his informers and his Saracen hangmen.

Wherever he travelled he was accompanied by his chief officials, his judges, his jesters, his executioners, and his Moslem bodyguard ; and the procession was completed by his treasure and his menagerie. This latter included leopards, lions, panthers, bears, ostriches, and even an elephant and a giraffe, a fantastic sight which lent colour to the belief that Frederick was the Antichrist, or Beast of the Book of Revelation. He was the emperor who wrote poetry, who kept a *harem*, who composed an expert treatise on falconry, who wanted to revive the art of ancient Rome, who was full of scientific curiosity, and who was absolutely lacking in human feeling. According to Salimbene

> He fed two men most excellently at dinner, one of whom he sent forthwith to sleep, and the other to hunt ; and that same evening he caused them to be disembowelled in his presence, wishing to know which had digested the better.[2]

His religious scepticism was notorious, and shocked Moslems as well as Christians. He joked at the ' ignorance ' of God in commending a land so infertile as Palestine to the Jews, he

[1] Quoted by G. G. Coulton, *From St. Francis to Dante* (Nutt), 2nd ed., 1907, p. 121.
[2] Coulton, *op. cit.*, p. 243. The physicians pronounced in favour of the sleeper.

mocked at the sacraments, and took a pleasure in uttering blasphemies. According to Pope Gregory IX, he openly asserted that ' the world had been deceived by three men, Jesus, Moses, and Mohammed '.

In consequence the war between him and the Pope was fought against a background of religious excitement. The friars were already sending out their best preachers to conduct religious revivals in the towns, and in 1233, the year of the great *Allelulia*, many cities had entrusted their government to popular preachers, with dictatorial powers to remodel the laws as they pleased. Huge crowds would assemble to hear their message, and wonders and miracles were expected, and provided, with astonishing simplicity. One Franciscan who preached from a portable wooden belfry was reputed to have been heard, and understood, at a distance of thirty miles. He was so eloquent on the subject of the Last Judgment that his audience trembled like a rush and begged him ' for God's sake to speak no more of the matter '.[1]

Apocalyptic speculation had a fatal fascination for both populace and preachers, especially when taken in conjunction with the doctrines and prophecies of Joachim of Flora (*d.* 1202). Joachim had taught that the history of mankind fell into three ages or dispensations : the reign of the Father when men lived under the Law ; the reign of the Son in which they lived under the rule of Grace ; and the reign of the Holy Ghost (expected by some for the year 1260) in which they would live in a plenitude of love, untrammelled by partial laws and revelations. But before this stage could be reached there would be the coming of Antichrist, who would be to the Church like a flail. Was he not already amongst them, the unbelieving and excommunicate Emperor ?

> There has arisen out of the sea a Beast, wrote Gregory IX, full of words of blasphemy ; which, formed with the feet of a bear, the mouth of a raging lion, and in its other limbs a leopard, is opening its mouth in blasphemies against God's name, and is attacking His saints.[2]

The struggle that ensued was of titanic proportions. Frederick began the subjection of Lombardy in 1237 with a victory over

---

[1] Compare ' Conversion without Tears ', *supra*, p. 366.
[2] T. L. Kington, *Frederick II* (1862), ii. 117. Cf. *Revelation*, xiii. 1–7.

the Milanese at Cortenuova, but Gregory IX immediately began to inspire a spirit of resistance. He used the friars as his secret agents—the Franciscan Salimbene carried messages in cypher— and sent them out to preach not only repentance from sin but also rebellion against the Emperor. He excommunicated him in 1239, and faced his fury undismayed. When Frederick marched on Rome and the citizens were inclined to support him, Gregory rallied them with a solemn procession of the relics of St. Peter and St. Paul (1240). When Frederick appealed to the cardinals, Gregory summoned a General Council of the Church to Rome. It was his intention there to depose the Emperor, but Frederick prevented the Council from meeting by sending his navy to capture the Genoese convoy which was transporting thither one hundred prelates and two cardinals. Flushed with success, he marched on Rome to overthrow his enemy; but before he could force a decision, Gregory, now past his hundredth year, died—resisting him still (1241).

Frederick was still excommunicate, and could not be absolved except by a new Pope. He therefore strained every nerve to secure a favourable papal election. He threatened and cajoled the College of Cardinals, as also did the Romans in their own interest, and the See of St. Peter was vacant for the greater part of two years. At last Frederick was successful, and a Ghibelline, Sinibaldo Fieschi, was elected Pope as Innocent IV (1243-54). But once enthroned, Innocent, realizing that no Pope could remain a Ghibelline, proved himself an antagonist even more formidable than Gregory IX. For though he lacked the religious insight and heroic qualities of his predecessor, he had more diplomatic skill and sense of strategy. He fled from Rome to take refuge in Lyons—at that time not in the Kingdom of France but within the Empire—and summoned a General Council of the Church. Though attended by no more than 150 prelates, and those mainly from England, France, and Spain, it proceeded, on 17 July 1245, to the solemn deposition of the Emperor.

Frederick accepted the challenge and prepared to march on Lyons as previously he had marched on Rome, but an unexpected delay was caused by the defection of the city of Parma, control of which was essential for his communications. A group of seventy exiled nobles had ridden into the city and captured it while all the Ghibellines were at a marriage-feast—the history of the period is full of such curious chances—and Frederick had no option but to besiege it. He thought that its capture would be a comparatively simple affair, and encamped his army at a place which he prematurely named Vittoria. It was there that the papalist cities united their forces, defeated Frederick's army decisively (1248), and broke his power. Two years later he died, at Castel Fiorentino, not far from the camp of his Saracens at Lucera (13 December 1250). His body was taken to Palermo and buried in the cathedral beside that of his father and grandfather, in an urn of red porphyry, supported by four lions. On it was placed the following inscription :

> Si probitas, sensus, virtutum gratia, census,
> Nobilitas orti possent resistere morti,
> Non foret extinctus Fridericus qui jacet intus

(If it were possible for honesty, understanding, excellence, wealth, and nobility of birth to resist death, then Frederick, who lies within, would not have died.)

It is an epitaph which might equally well be applied to the medieval Empire itself. With Frederick's death it virtually came to an end. His son Conrad IV survived him for four years, and after that an illegitimate son, Manfred, set himself up in the *Regno*. But the Pope invited a French prince, Charles of Anjou, to evict him, and his ' crusade ' (for such it was called) was crowned with success in 1266. Two years later, the final challenge came from Frederick's grandson, Conradin, who, though only fifteen years of age, crossed the Alps to reclaim his patrimony. He was defeated at Tagliacozzo, captured, tried, and beheaded in the market-place at Naples (1268). Thus perished the last of the ' brood of vipers '. The Papacy had won its battle against the Empire, and had exposed itself to the peoples of Europe as relentless in the pursuit of vengeance. It had uprooted and destroyed the Empire. Time would show if it could do without it.

2. Louis IX (1226–1270)

Louis IX of France, St. Louis, contrasts strangely with Frederick II, the ' Antichrist '. Frederick, so modern in his manners, with the scepticism and cruelty of a Renaissance prince, was the last medieval Emperor. Louis, so medieval in appearance, realized a new pattern of monarchy by divine right. He was, at first glance, the sort of king who might have stepped out of a stained-glass window. He yearned for the life of a monk, and was prevented from abdicating his crown only by a strong sense of duty. He was a crusader not once but twice, and died on crusade. He was the builder of *La Sainte Chapelle*. He has been immortalized by his friend and steward, the Sire de Joinville, who wrote the history of his life, and described his saintly simplicity with the most delightful naïvety. The picture that springs immediately to mind is that of St. Louis doing justice beneath an oak-tree in the forest of Vincennes.

> Maintes foiz avint que en estei il se alloit seoir ou bois de Vinciennes après sa messe, et se acostoioit à un chesne, et nous fesoit seoir entour li. Et tuit cil qui avoient afaire venoient parler à li sanz destourbier de huissier ne d'autre. Et lors il lour demandoit de sa bouche : ' A-il ci nullui qui ait partie ? ' Et cil se levoient qui partie avoient. Et lors il disoit : ' Taisiés-vous tuit, et on vous deliverra l'un après l'autre '.[1]

His honesty was a by-word ; he would not even deceive the Saracens. On his first Crusade he was captured by the Egyptians and had to pay a heavy ransom for his release (1250). But when Philip of Nemours told him that he had cheated the Saracens of a total of ten thousand pounds,

> the king was very angry and said that he desired them to render the ten thousand pounds before they left the river [Nile]. Then I [Joinville] trod on the toe of my lord Philip, and told the king not to believe it, because what he was saying was not true, since the Saracens were the greatest calculators on earth. And my lord Philip said that I was speaking the truth, because he had only been speaking in jest. And the king said that such a jest was out of season : ' And I order you ', he said to my lord Philip, ' on the faith which you owe me as my vassal, that if the ten thousand pounds have not been paid, you are to pay them '.[2]

The incident was typical. Louis IX was scrupulous not only in regard to his own rights but also in regard to those of others.

[1] Joinville, *Vie de St. Louis*, ch. xii (ed. de Wailly, 1867), p. 34.
[2] Joinville, ch. lxxvi.

He governed ' according to God and the Church and for the profit of his kingdom ', embarking on no new conquests, but rather consolidating his kingdom by making it willingly loyal. Under Philip Augustus and Louis VIII, the greater feudatories had supported the crown, but with circumspection, fearing that one day their own rights might be imperilled by the growth of royal power. Under Louis IX they supported it without reserve, for he won their trust by interpreting the mutual obligations of lord and vassal fairly. He insisted on his own rights but kept within them. When a disturbance broke out in a house where he was staying, he would punish no one until he had first established that the place was one where he had jurisdiction. Before he set out on his first Crusade (1247) he was alarmed at the thought of leaving his subjects to the mercy of his bailiffs who, trained in the harder school of Philip Augustus, were often merciless in their demands. He therefore sent out a commission to enquire, not which royal rights had been lost but which had been abused. The commissioners were to

> receive in writing and examine all the complaints which can justifiably be brought against us or our ancestors, as well as statements concerning the injustice and exactions of which our bailiffs, provosts, foresters, sergeants and their subordinates have been guilty.[1]

It was the sort of reform for which the barons of England were perpetually asking King Henry III in vain. Louis granted it of his own initiative, and did not weaken his throne thereby.

It would be a mistake, however, to imagine Louis IX as the inaugurator of liberal monarchy. His government was absolute, and on some matters he could be exceptionally severe. This was particularly the case in matters of religion. He punished blasphemers mercilessly—once burning the lip and nose of a burgher of Paris for this offence—and he was himself largely responsible for the organization of the Inquisition in France (1233). Previously religious persecution had been the prerogative of the secular clergy, but now it was handed over to the expert talents of Dominican friars who, protected by the mandate of the Pope and the presence of royal sergeants, burnt heretics by the score in Burgundy, Champagne, and Flanders.

[1] Quoted from Ch. Petit Dutaillis, *Feudal Monarchy in France and England* (Kegan Paul, 1936), p. 298.

The ruling passion of Louis' later years was the desire to recapture the Holy Land, and consequently he led two Crusades. The first (1249–54) captured Damietta, but subsequently ended in disaster, since, through the folly of Robert of Artois, the army moved against Cairo and, like a previous crusading force, allowed itself to be surrounded in the maze of streams that constitutes the Nile Delta. Louis was captured and had, as we have already seen, to pay an enormous ransom for his release, after which, though he remained four years in Palestine, he merely occupied himself with the fortification of the great seaports and achieved nothing of note. His second Crusade (1270) achieved even less, being diverted against Tunis because of the fantastic report that its Moslem ruler was prepared to be converted to Christianity.[1] Louis himself died of fever on the site of ancient Carthage, and his army returned home demoralized.

In matters which affected his conscience, Louis could be obstinate. He acted as though under divine inspiration, and was prepared to flout the advice of his whole council. The most famous case concerned the negotiations for the Treaty of Paris (1259), by which he allowed King Henry III of England to retain Périgord and the Limousin as fiefs, although he could have expelled him from France entirely. The council opposed the treaty unanimously, on the grounds that Henry's father, King John, had been deprived of those lands by judgment of the court of France. But according to Joinville,

> The king replied that he well knew that the King of England had no right to it but there was a reason for which he really ought to give it him. 'For our wives are sisters and our children are cousins-german, and for that reason it is important that there should be peace between us. There is very great honour for me in the peace which I am making with the King of England, since he is now my vassal, which before he was not.'[2]

The majority of historians have taken the same view of the matter as the council, and have claimed that a firmer and more ruthless policy would have put an end to English domination in

---

[1] It is uncertain whether Sultan Beibars of Egypt or Charles of Anjou was the more responsible for the circulation of this report. Charles, being King of Naples, was probably anxious to revive the exploits of Roger the Great in North Africa.

[2] Joinville, ch. xiv.

France, and so have prevented the outbreak of the Hundred Years War. But the incident should not be treated in isolation. Louis made his family relationships a major instrument of policy, and normally found them more profitable than not.

His father, Louis VIII, had by the terms of his will made provision for all his sons. Only the eldest could inherit the kingdom, but the others were to receive, as a sort of consolation prize, important fiefs known as ' appanages '; Robert was made Count of Artois, Alphonse, Count of Poitou and Auvergne, and Charles, Count of Anjou. The situation thus created had its dangers, which were to become apparent in subsequent centuries, but at the time it offered great administrative advantages. For Philip Augustus and Louis VIII had, by the defeat of the Angevins and the Albigensian heretics, enlarged the royal demesne by about five times ; and it was only to be expected that the administration of the new territories might be difficult. Great attention had to be paid to local custom, lest grievances should arise which would encourage a revolt in favour of the Angevins. In the case of Normandy, both Philip Augustus and Louis IX made frequent progresses through the duchy so as to keep its administration under their own personal view, but all the newly-conquered territories could not possibly be visited with the same personal interest. In most of them it was therefore essential for the king to delegate his authority to men on whom he could rely implicitly, and he consequently found the appanage system useful. So long as the king could keep the peace in his own family the kingdom would be secure.

The family relationships, however, could have still further uses if the brothers married suitable heiresses. Alphonse of Poitiers married Jeanne, the daughter and heiress of Raymond VII, Count of Toulouse, and on the death of his father-in-law (1249) succeeded to his county, which comprised the western part of the Languedoc. Charles of Anjou married the youngest daughter of the Count of Provence, and by good fortune and good management inherited the whole of his territory. He governed it so firmly that the Pope invited him to lead the proposed ' crusade ' against the Hohenstaufen in Sicily, with the result that by 1266 Charles, in addition to all his other honours, was King of Naples. It could almost be said that the reason why it paid Louis IX to keep the peace within his own family, was that he was related to most of the crowned heads of Europe. By the following century, wise marriage alliances had given the French royal family an extraordinary predominance, with close links in England, Aragon, Castile, Navarre, Provence, Sicily, Bohemia, Hungary, and Poland. The popes were generally French and resided at Avignon which, though technically in imperial territory, was within the French sphere of influence, and at one time even the titular emperors were Frenchmen from the house of Luxemburg.

The age of Louis IX marked the beginning of a period of French predominance in Europe which was to last for five centuries and more, and Louis himself played a considerable part in establishing it. He was the very pattern of a Christian king, a realization of the ideal for which churchmen had been praying for centuries. He was held up to the admiration of Europe, and earned for himself a reputation for fairmindedness and justice which was superior to that of the Pope, with the result that he was often asked to act as arbitrator in disputes between men who were neither his subjects nor vassals. The most famous case was his arbitration between King Henry III and the barons of England, but there were a number of others which involved the territory of the kingdom of Arles and Vienne, the King of Navarre, and imperial fiefs in the Low Countries and Lorraine. His judgments were not always wise, but his impartiality was universally respected.

We must not allow his personal sanctity, however, to blind ourselves to the peculiar ascendancy that he had thus gained for the kingdom of France. In the previous century, no one outside the kingdom would have dreamt of approaching the French king as a supreme arbiter. Recourse would rather have been had to the Pope, or just conceivably to the Emperor. Now the situations were reversed. It was Louis IX to whom the powers of Latin Christendom appealed; Louis IX who was continually urging moderation on Pope Innocent IV; and Louis IX who promised him protection if Frederick II were to march against him at Lyons (1247).

The truth of the matter was that the King of France was acquiring an independent standing as the moral arbiter of Europe.

He did not assume that ecclesiastics were always right or that their justice was necessarily better than his. On the contrary, when the bishops asked him to distrain the goods of those who remained excommunicate for a year and a day, Louis replied that he would do so only if the bishops could prove the justice of the sentence in each individual case, ' For it would be against God and against reason to force people to receive absolution when the clerics were doing them wrong.' In justification of his stand, he cited the case of the Count of Brittany who had been unjustly excommunicated for seven years before establishing his innocence in the papal court. But if the King of France was to maintain an oversight of excommunications, where was the line between the secular and spiritual jurisdictions to be drawn ?

St. Louis was not content with criticizing the conduct of his own bishops. When the occasion demanded, he criticized the Pope himself. Thus in 1247 he presented a whole series of complaints to Pope Innocent IV, remarking that, as the most Christian and devout son of the Church, he would have remained silent, pretending all was well, if it had not been for the fact that the abuses were getting worse every day. He complained of the papal taxation of the 'Gallican' Church and of the use made of excommunication to enforce it ; of the unprecedented extent of the papal collation to benefices ; of the fact that the collations were often made before the benefices were vacant, ' so that every day the live canons see those who are waiting for them to die, like crows waiting for corpses ' ; and also of the fact that many of the papal nominees were non-resident. If Innocent's successor exceeded Innocent in his exactions by the same extent that Innocent had exceeded his predecessors, the native clerics would have no option but to clear out of the kingdom themselves, or clear the foreigners out. He admitted that Innocent was in difficulties because of his ' persecution ' by Frederick II, but he could not see why he wanted so much more money than his predecessors who had been ' persecuted ' by other emperors. He admitted that the Pope had the right to do what he wanted, but thought that even though he did possess the ' fullness of power ' (*plenitudo potestatis*) he should restrain himself in the use of it. Previous popes had done so, and Innocent would do well to follow their example.

Innocent might well have replied that though some of his collations had been made in favour of friends and relatives, the greater number had been due to his desire to put the ' civil servants ' of the papal curia on a professional basis, with salaries and pensions provided by all the churches of Europe. But in our present context what is important is not the justification or condemnation of the Pope, but the fact that the King of France, saint though he was, had risen in defence of the ' Gallican ' Church against the Pope. He did not dispute the Pope's spiritual authority, but simply insisted on his own prerogative.

> The lord King, he said, whose predecessors founded the churches of the kingdom and endowed them with their goods for the maintenance of the worship of God, . . . has the right to take all the treasures of the churches and all their temporal goods as if they were his own, in order to meet the necessities of himself and his kingdom.[1]

That was a statement which in the previous century and a half would have been disputed fiercely by the Papacy ; indeed one would have expected it to be made only by the unholiest of kings, such as Henry II of England or the Emperor Frederick II himself. The fact that in the thirteenth century it was made by a king who was subsequently canonized is the best illustration possible of the breakdown of what had previously been the traditional conception of the Church. From St. Louis, the universal arbitrator who reproved the Pope but is depicted in sculpture or glass on so many of the cathedrals of France, it is but a little distance to his grandson, Philip IV, who did not scruple to lay hands on Pope Boniface VIII, and to declare that before there were clergymen, the King of France had the custody of his kingdom. *Antequam essent clerici, rex Franciae habebat custodiam regni sui.*

Few things can be more certain than that Louis IX had not intended to damage the Papacy or to lay the foundations of a national Church. He would have wept most bitterly if he could have seen whither his policy was leading. But owing to the special grace which God had given to kings, he thought he had

[1] Matthew Paris, *Chronica Majora* (ed. Luard, 1882), vol. vi (Additamenta), p. 110.

seen the right quite clearly and openly, and consequently he had spoken his mind. He viewed himself, as old-fashioned church-men had always wanted to view the king, as ' the minister of God '; but unlike his predecessors he had the personal sanctity which could bring the ideal to life. ' Divine right ', which had previously been little more than a scholastic theory, appealed to the popular imagination, and was understood when St. Louis did justice under the oak-tree at Vincennes. Henceforward the King of France was regarded as the incarnation of religion and justice. He was the Lord's Anointed, and his ascendancy over the Church was complete.

After nine-and-a-half centuries, the problem posed by Con-stantine's conversion was still unsolved. The Empire had fallen and the Papacy had overstepped the pinnacle of its power, but the words of Hosius of Cordova had lost nothing of their urgency :

> Into your hands God has put the kingdom ; the affairs of the Church He has committed to us. . . . We are not permitted to exercise an earthly rule ; and you, Sire, are not authorized to burn incense.

Further Reading

T. L. KINGTON. *History of Frederick the Second, Emperor of the Romans.* 2 vols. London. 1862. Still useful.

G. BLONDEL. *Étude sur la politique de Frederic II en Allemagne et sur la transformation de la constitution allemande.* Paris. 1892.

P. CHALANDON. *Histoire de la Domination Normande en Italie et en Sicile.* 2 vols. Paris. 1907.

ERNST KANTOROWITZ. *Frederick II* (tr. E. O. Lorimer). London. 1931. Both learned and readable in spite of its extremist viewpoint.

MARGARET WADE LABARGE. *Saint Louis.* London. 1968.). 231

CH. PETIT-DUTAILLIS. *Feudal Monarchy in France and England from the tenth to the thirteenth century* (tr. E. D. Hunt). London. 1936.

JOINVILLE. *Histoire de St. Louis*, ed. N. de Wailly. Paris. 1874. Old French text with modern French translation, and excellent notes and appendices. There are several English translations, of which the most recent is by M. R. B. Shaw (see p. 367).

IX

EUROPE IN THE MIDDLE OF THE THIRTEENTH CENTURY: AN ECONOMIC SURVEY

BETWEEN the tenth and thirteenth centuries the economy of Western Europe expanded rapidly, but that of Byzantium and Islam began very gradually to contract. In the middle of the thirteenth century Constantinople was still a very wealthy city, but the days of its Mediterranean supremacy were past, and it was losing trade steadily to the merchants of the Italian city-states. Indeed it would be hardly too great an exaggeration to say that while Western Europe was laying the foundations of a capitalist society, the countries of the eastern Mediterranean were becoming more feudal. In the Byzantine empire, economic power had passed from the State into the hands of the ἄρχοντες, 'feudal' lords who had benefices (πρόνοιαι) and vassals (καβαλλάριοι = chevaliers). In Egypt, though there were flourishing merchant communities at Cairo, Alexandria, and Damietta, the government belonged to the Mamlukes who, in return for grants of land, maintained bands of soldiers at their own charge.

The main cause of this retrogression in the East was probably the lack of external security. In the case of Islam the disruptive force was that of the Mongols who, though they opened up a new overland route from the Black Sea to Cathay, dislocated the traditional channels of trade and put the whole Near East into a state of perpetual alarm; Baghdad, captured in 1258, never recovered its former prosperity, and the great towns of Syria found themselves exposed to sudden raids, Aleppo being sacked in 1260 and 1280, and Damascus in 1260 and 1300. In Byzantium, however, the insecurity dated from an earlier period. The rich provinces of Asia Minor had been lost to the Seljūk Turks in 1071, and those of the Danube to the Bulgars in 1186; while the crusaders, having first established trading-posts from which they could deal with the East direct, had subsequently turned against Constantinople itself and captured it (1204). (See p. 348.) Though that city was to be recovered by a Greek dynasty in 1261, it could no longer pretend to be the mistress of the Mediterranean. It was but a shadow of its former self, a fortress beleaguered in turn by Asiatics, Slavs, and westerners of every kind.

When we turn to the West, however, the situation is very different. There, in spite of the fears of a Mongol attack, the frontiers were steadily expanding. The Germans were advancing eastwards against the Slavs, with such effect that by 1252 the Teutonic knights had founded Memel ; the Christian kingdoms of Spain, having received the surrender of Cordova (1236) and Seville (1248), were left with only Granada to subdue ; and the mainland and islands of Greece had been divided between Venice, Genoa, and the French participants in the Fourth Crusade. It was evident that Western Europe was increasing rapidly in territory, population, and wealth.

One of the outward signs of the new prosperity was the growth of towns, which were no longer sheltered fortresses as they had been in the tenth century, but flourishing industrial and commercial communities. Most of them were self-governing communes and seemed extraordinary phenomena in a feudal world. Surrounded by walls, they formed little islands of liberty. The traveller who entered their gates passed from the ordinary jurisdiction of the land into that of the commune, in the same way as if he had entered the ' immunity ' of a bishop or baron. But when he reached the market square he would find himself confronted not with the palace or castle of a lord but with the *Palazzo Comunale, Hôtel de Ville, Stadthaus*, or Town Hall, for the extraordinary thing about a medieval town was that it had the privileges of a feudal lord. The commune, or community of citizens who had sworn to unite in a single corporation, had, by a legal fiction, taken on the attributes of a baron, so that it controlled its own territory, held its own courts, and had its own palace or hall. This latter was important ; it was built with the utmost magnificence, was adorned with statues, and was crowned by an imposing belfry from which the whole body

of citizens could be summoned to deliberation or war. It was
a symbol of the commune's status and lordship. So much so,
that when Frederick Barbarossa wanted to crush the spirit of
the Milanese he forced the citizens to build *him* a palace in the
middle of the city, as a public declaration of the fact that they
had renounced their own lordship in favour of his own.

Stadtluft macht frei ; town-air made a man free. A villein or
serf who entered a free town and resided in it for a year-and-a-
day, was automatically regarded as free, since he had acquired
a share in his own lordship. But that did not mean that he was
free to work, or buy and sell, as he liked. On the contrary,
every commune regulated its own industries and trades with the
most scrupulous care, organizing them into guilds which controlled prices, standards, and working-hours. The interests of
both consumer and producer were protected, the former by
controlling the quality of the materials and craftsmanship employed, and the latter by the elimination of competitive trading.
No manufactured goods might be imported from other towns
except at fair-time, and within each town prices were rigidly
controlled. Inspectors were employed to see that no craftsman
undercut his fellows or advertised his own wares as against theirs,
and there were usually regulations prohibiting him from inventing new tools, from using the unpaid labour of his wife and
children, or from working before the town bell had rung in the
morning or after it had rung at night.

For food, every town was dependent on the produce which
was brought to its market from the countryside, and the authorities soon recognized that if the townsmen were not to be exploited mercilessly, the organization of the weekly market would
have to be supervised with care. The great danger was that
enterprising merchants might attempt to ' corner ' the entire
supply of some essential foodstuff with a view to selling it at
famine prices, and the policy of every town, therefore, was to
prevent the rise of ' middle-men ' by making the peasants sell
direct to the individual townsmen. With this end in view, it
was decreed that all buying and selling of foodstuffs had to be
done in public and within the walls. The peasants had to take
their produce straight to the market-place and expose them to
the public view. Until a stated hour they might not make any

sale except to burghers, and there were inspectors present to see that no one bought beyond the needs of himself and his family. No butcher was allowed to keep a stock of meat in his cellar, no baker to build up reserves of flour. All the food that was sold had to be consumed promptly.

The two most important economic centres of the thirteenth century, and those where the greatest towns were to be found, were the coasts of the North Sea and Baltic on the one hand, and of the Mediterranean on the other. The one might be described in general terms as a centre of primary products and basic manufacture, while the other was the centre of high-class luxury-goods. Economically they were complementary to each other, and therefore they were united by several overland trade-routes and had what might be described as a central clearing-house in the Fairs of Champagne.

The most important factor in the economy of the northern region was the cloth industry. It was controlled by the great merchants, who purchased raw wool in bulk from England, shipped it across the channel to Bruges, had it dyed and woven in the cities of Flanders and Picardy, and finally sold it for export as finished cloth. It was an operation which required not only considerable capital but also a well-organized industry, and between the Scheldt and the Somme there were a large number of cloth-towns, which formed a sort of medieval 'black country'. Ghent and Ypres were the giants of the group, but St. Omer, Lille, Tournai, Arras, Cambrai, Douai, and Amiens were also of importance. It is probable that rather more than half their population were employed in the cloth trade. In Ghent, for example, where the total population can hardly have exceeded 30,000, it is known that there were 4,000 weavers, each employing one or two men and an apprentice. But it must not be imagined that they worked in factories. Every merchant would distribute his wool to individual weavers, who would have one or two looms in their shops. He would pay a stipulated rate, and perhaps provide the weavers with tools on hire. The weavers in their turn would employ casual labour from the floating-population of 'blue-nails' (so called from the dye on their fingers), who would wander from town to town in search of work, and who formed an impoverished proletariat, excluded both from the guilds and from the rights of citizenship. Flanders cloth was the manufacture *par excellence* of Western Europe. It clothed Germans, Swedes, Norwegians, Danes, Englishmen, Frenchmen, Portuguese, Castilians, Catalans, Italians, Slavs, and sometimes even Greeks and Moslems. The merchants from the south would travel overland to buy it at the Fairs of Champagne ; those from the north would go by sea to buy it at the great mart of Bruges. There, the trade was dominated by the Hansa merchants or ' Easterlings ', who were by far the most active seamen in northern waters. From Lübeck, Hamburg, Visby, Rostock, Stralsund, and Danzig they would transport corn from the new colonial lands of eastern Germany, herrings from Scania, salt and wine from La Rochelle and Oléron, and wool from London, Yarmouth, Lynn, and Kingston-upon-Hull.

But even the Hanseatic merchants were not nearly as rich as the merchants of Venice, Genoa, Pisa, Milan, Florence, and Siena, who had fallen heirs to the wealth of Byzantium. The basis of their wealth was the trade in ' spices ' which were bought in the ports of the eastern Mediterranean and exported over the Alps to France, Germany, England, and Flanders. ' Spices ' (*species*), however, is a somewhat misleading term, since in the Middle Ages it was used to denote a large number of different products. One early fourteenth-century treatise listed 288 different sorts of spices, including almonds, alum, borax, cinnamon, cloves, coconuts, copper, cotton, cummin, dates, elephant-tusks, frankincense, gall-nuts, ginger, ginger-bread, glue, gum-arabic, indigo, linseed-oil, liquorice, mandrake, musk, mustard, myrrh, nitre-salt, nutmeg, olive-oil, pearls, pepper, pine-resin, pitch, quicksilver, raisins, sandalwood, silkworms' eggs, sugar, tin, turpentine, and wax. Nearly all these products came from the southern or eastern shores of the Mediterranean, and commanded great prices in the north. The first necessity for a successful career in trade was therefore a ship.

The Italian ships of the thirteenth century had remarkably short lives. They were incapable of withstanding the Atlantic seas, and even in the Mediterranean fell out of commission in five or six years. Consequently the demand for new ships was incessant, and ship-building was a major industry in its own right.

The two biggest shipyards were those of Venice and Genoa. The former was known as the Arsenal (from the Arabic *Dar Sana* or 'house of work') and was, along with banking and the salt-trade, one of the state-owned industries of the Republic. Genoa, on the other hand, favoured private enterprise, and built (and navigated) ships for the benefit of Tuscans, Lombards, Frenchmen, or anyone else. An average-sized ship cost about £2,000 to build, the most costly single item being the mast (a fir about 65 ft. tall) which might cost anything from £200 to £300. A large ship could carry 600 tons dead cargo weight from Tunis to Genoa, and we know of one ship, the *Oliva*, which in 1248 carried 11,000 pilgrims to the Holy Land and charged them £2,887½ for the single journey.

The major Italian cities, such as Venice, Pisa, and Genoa, had trading-stations or *fondachi* at Constantinople, in the towns of the Holy Land, and at Alexandria. They gave material assistance to the crusaders, jockeyed each other for power in the Byzantine Empire, and sold ships' timbers, pitch, and tar to the Sultan of Egypt for his navy. They coasted between Morocco and Asia Minor, carried cargoes from port to port as the occasion offered, and served Christians and Moslems indiscriminately. It was a lucrative business. A voyage to Acre and back, lasting from spring to autumn or autumn to spring, might easily realize a profit of 150 per cent. net.

If the profits were great, so also were the risks. For quite apart from the danger of shipwreck from natural causes which, since the mariners hugged the coasts, was a comparatively common event, there were the added dangers of piracy and war, which were even more immediate. The Italian cities were, as we have already seen (p. 378), permanently divided against each other, and did not hesitate to plunder their rivals' commerce as well as their territory. When Genoa was at war with Pisa (as it usually was) Genoese merchants would invest in privateers 'to win profit from the enemies of Holy Church' (for Pisa was Ghibelline), and hoped to see a return of £3,000–£5,000 on an outlay of £250. Venice, acting as usual as a corporate state, found it necessary to organize her merchantmen in convoys for the East, and even the inland cities suffered losses from Guelf and Ghibelline marauders.

In these circumstances it was not surprising that the merchants of the Italian cities quickly developed a business technique for spreading their risks. Rather than lock up their capital in one particular voyage or one particular ship, they would form companies and buy shares (*loca*) in several ships. At first the most common way of doing this (and it is found as early as 1072) was for two or three merchant-capitalists to ' commend ' money to an active partner with a ship. While the ship was trading, the *commendatores* stayed at home and awaited results : if the ship was lost, so also was their money ; but if it returned they regained their capital together with a half or three-quarters share of the total profit. By the thirteenth century, however, a more elaborate form of enterprise had come into vogue—the company proper (*compagnia*) in which all full members, whether active or not, bore a joint and unlimited liability for the conduct of their affairs. By this time it was also possible to insure a cargo, the form of words employed being like that of a contract for sale, except for a final clause which stated that the contract would be cancelled if the specified goods were to arrive safely at their destination.

The most important people in the world of Italian commerce were the money-changers or bankers (so-called because they kept their piles of money on a bench). By the middle of the thirteenth century they could, at any rate in Florence and Genoa, keep their accounts in double-entry, and they not only exchanged money of different currencies, but also traded bills of exchange, so that a French merchant might obtain Genoese money at Genoa for subsequent repayment in the currency of Provins at (say) the fair of Lagny. Exchange-rates fluctuated, and the bankers were not above speculating in them. But, as is always the case, their most important business was money-lending. They were aware that the Church prohibited usury, but that did not prevent them from charging interest at rates varying from 8 to 20 per cent., though they sometimes had the grace to conceal the fact by making out their bonds for a larger sum than had originally been lent. They knew that the Church would not penalize them, because the Papacy itself was amongst their clients. Pope Innocent IV, for example, had required money for his wars against the Hohenstaufen and had borrowed it from the bankers of Tuscany, some of it on the security of a tax to be levied on the English Church ; and it was with Florentine gold that Charles of Anjou raised the ' crusading ' forces that won him the crown of Sicily (1265-6).

Until the end of the thirteenth century, the central clearing-house of European trade and finance was to be found in the Fairs of Champagne. Of these there were six, which followed each other in succession throughout the year, and which lasted six weeks each. One was at Lagny, one at Bar-sur-Aube, two at Provins (in May and September), and two at Troyes (in June and October). They owed their importance, at a time when direct navigation from the North Sea to the Mediterranean was impracticable,[1] to the fact that they were on the direct land route from Italy to Flanders, at a point which was equally accessible from the Hanseatic towns of North Germany, the Rhineland, Provence, and Catalonia. They were international gatherings, in which the local population played but a minor part. Each fair was controlled by its own police (*custodes nundinarum*) and was divided into two distinct periods, the first for commerce and the second for the settlement of accounts. The merchants sent wares to their agents—we have a contract of 1248 for the transport of two loads (*caricae*) of pepper from Marseilles to Troyes for seven pounds of Vienne—and the Italian bankers sent agents who issued letters of credit which could be cashed in almost any stated currency and in any part of Europe.

Finally, one industry which was very much in evidence in Champagne should perhaps be mentioned here, though it does not fall into any of the normal categories of trade—building. It represented an enormous capital investment in the thirteenth century, as the surviving monuments testify. It is hardly necessary to recite the famous names—Reims, Amiens, Beauvais, Paris, Chartres, Bourges, Burgos, Toledo, Assisi, Siena, Cologne, Magdeburg, and Ypres—for monuments of the first part of the thirteenth century are to be found everywhere, and it requires little effort of the imagination to appreciate the extent of economic organization which their construction involved. After the site

---

[1] It was not till the very end of the thirteenth century that Italian merchantmen began to make regular sea-voyages to England and Flanders. Before then their ships had not been strong enough to make Atlantic voyages.

had been cleared, it was necessary to procure a plentiful supply of timber and building-stone. If the quarries were at a distance, arrangements had to be made for the transport of the stone, preferably by water since the cost of cartage overland might double the cost in twenty-five miles. Tessellated tiles were needed for flooring, lead for covering the roofs, sheets of stained-glass ('pot-metal') from Lorraine as material for the glaziers, and bells which might come from the foundries of Dinant on the Meuse.

The greatest problem of all, however, was probably that of labour, since vast numbers of workmen were required in different places and at different times. In England 435 men, including 130 masons, were employed on the building of Westminster Abbey at midsummer of 1253, and at the end of the century King Edward I kept a labour force of about 3,000 men building his new castles in Wales. Richard I admittedly built his Château Gaillard in a hurry, but the partial accounts that survive for the year 1198 (when wages varied, according to skill, between 2*d.* and 4*d.* a day) are none the less astonishing. They include the following items : Woodcutters £2,320, Carpenters £3,350, Minor tradesmen £9,730, Miners for cutting the fosse and cellars out of solid rock £1,780 19*s.*, Quarrymen £2,600 5*s.*, Freemasons £2,600, Ships and barges for the carriage of timber and stone £1,700 5*s.*

The workmen employed on such undertakings necessarily lived a migratory life, moving from place to place as cathedrals, castles, abbeys, parish-churches, or town-halls were begun and finished. But, even so, employers often found difficulty in getting sufficient labour for their larger enterprises. Kings were able to exercise the right of 'impressing' labour, and could order their sheriffs, bailiffs, or provosts to round up masons and carpenters from every corner of their kingdom. Others, such as mere bishops, dukes, and counts, had to send agents round the countryside, advertising for labour wherever they could find it. Consequently masons were much-travelled men. One French master-mason, Villard de Honnecourt, kept a sketch book on his travels, which still survives and shows how he visited, or worked at, Cambrai, Vaucelles, Laon, Reims, Meaux, Chartres, and Lausanne. His greatest journey, however, was to Hungary, most probably undertaken in 1244–7 in order to rebuild churches which had been destroyed by the Mongols.

His career furnishes an admirable example of the economic unity of Western Europe in the thirteenth century. Before 1250 there were no national customs-systems, no ' tariff walls ', and no restriction on the movement of merchants, ecclesiastics, scholars, or labourers from one country to another. The Pope ' presented ' Italians to English benefices ; English scholars studied in Paris where the great master was Thomas Aquinas, the son of a German baron from the *Regno* of Naples and Sicily ; Catalan mercenaries were employed in the Byzantine Empire ; and Italian merchants resided at Lübeck and Bruges. Even though a feeling of hostility towards foreigners was beginning to grow in some countries, especially England, during the first half of the thirteenth century, it was not yet strong enough to threaten the essential unity of the European economy.

The most striking example of the mobility of population is to be observed in the eastward expansion of Germany and the colonization of the ' new ' lands east of the Elbe, which had (except for a brief period under Otto I) constituted the boundary between Germans and Slavs from the age of Charlemagne to the twelfth century. (Berlin, Schwerin, Leipzig, and Dresden are Slavonic place-names which bear witness to their medieval origins.) The movement first became important during the reign of Lothar III (1125–37). In 1150 Albert the Bear acquired Brandenburg, and by *c.* 1250 his successors had advanced to the Neumark east of the Oder. Farther to the north and east, the Teutonic knights had by 1241 conquered East Prussia between the Vistula and the Pregel. But conquest was one thing, colonization another. The pressing need was to cultivate the ' new ' lands.

The Slavonic population was unequal to the task, both in numbers and technique ; they did not have the heavy plough, did not know the use of ' three-course ' farming, and eked out a miserable existence. What was needed to make the country prosperous was an agricultural revolution. Some princes therefore made large grants of land to Cistercian monks, who were renowned for their agricultural technique ; it is recorded that the abbey of Leubus in Silesia, which was founded in 1175, had by 1233 been endowed with 5,900 *Hufe*, which probably represented about 177,000 acres of land. But even monks could not cultivate these vast areas of land unaided, and found, like every other landlord on the eastern frontier, that it was absolutely imperative to recruit a new peasant population from the West.

They therefore built attractive villages, usually with the houses arranged symmetrically along a straight road and with the fields divided into rectangular blocks, and made arrangements with a ' middle-man ' or *locator* to find peasant colonists who would inhabit them. The *locator* ' advertised ' for colonists in all the over-populated areas of Europe, especially Westphalia, Flanders, and the Netherlands, and offered attractive terms to the adventurous. The colonists could expect to receive about forty acres of land and a house, and they were promised a considerable amount of freedom. Labour services were either non-existent or negligible, for the lord's demesne (if any) would be very small in size. Rents were reasonable, and the initial purchase-price (which could be paid on mortgage) low ; it was even permissible for a colonist to sell his holding, if he so desired, and return to his home-country. The *locator* was rewarded for his pains with a holding about six times the size of that of the peasants, and became the *Bauermeister* or *Schultheiss* of the village.

Colonists came in multitudes, for there were always many younger sons of villeins who, unable to inherit their father's land, had to set out on their own to make a fortune. By their skill and industry they effected an agricultural revolution. By introducing the heavy plough with wheels, mould-board, and iron plough-share (which had been known for centuries in the West) they were able to till the heavy soils which had previously lain waste. They introduced three-course farming and the cultivation of wheat (the Slavs had grown millet), and exported vast quantities of grain to Flanders and even England. They introduced water-mills, mined precious metals in the Erzgebirge, established vineyards, and in general converted what had previously been one of the poorest lands of Europe into one of the richest. The effects were such that even the neighbouring Slavonic princes were anxious to secure German colonists in order to improve their lands ; a bishop of Gnesen is said to have built colonial villages to such good effect that in one district he increased his revenue from 1 mark to 800.

The colonial movement was on such a vast scale that it was not long before its effects were to be felt in the West. Some of these were commercial and have already been noticed—the importance of the Baltic trade and the emergence of the Hansa— but others were of more direct consequence for agriculture. The constant drain of peasants away from the West to the East, for example, made it impolitic for lords to treat their villeins too harshly. If they wished to keep sufficient labour to maintain their lands in prosperity, they had to treat their tenants with consideration. Labour-services were often commuted for money-rents, and once fixed remained immutable. They were not raised even to compensate the steady rise in wages and prices, for the lords were afraid of driving their peasants to run away and make their fortunes in the East. The peasants therefore grew richer, while the lords, having fixed incomes in an age of inflation, grew poorer.

The new conditions also made it possible to grow specialized crops, since with a money-economy and plenty of surplus grain in the East, it was no longer necessary for every village to grow its own food. In Champagne and along the Atlantic sea-board of France, whole territories could specialize in the cultivation of the vine, the Gascon wine-trade being particularly profitable because of the easy communication with England and Flanders by sea. In northern France, the Toulousain, and the Po valley, there was concentration on the plants necessary for the dyeing industry, and in England the general tendency was to specialize in sheep-farming.

The economy of Europe had developed fast since the time of the *Polyptych* of Abbot Irmino. Feudalism had grown to its full development, and by the thirteenth century was already in decay. The wealth of every kingdom was no longer in its land but in its trade, the English king being rich because he could tax the export of wool, and the French king because of the revenues received from Flanders and Champagne. Even barons and knights were prepared to admit the importance of money. They knew from bitter experience the ever-growing cost of clothes, armour, buildings and all the luxuries of life, and often found it expedient to perform additional knight-service in return for pay. Commercial activity increased and new denominations of money had to be struck. Frederick II and Louis IX both struck gold coins, as also did Henry III of England, and in 1252 the Florentines struck the first examples of a coin that was to have a long history, the *florin*. Most of the modern forms of currency and exchange were coming into vogue, and the age of capitalism had been born. Prosperity was great, and the disasters that were to befall the European economy in the fourteenth century were as yet unsuspected.

Further Reading

Cambridge Economic History of Europe, vol. i (2nd ed., 1966) and ii (1952). The first volume concerns agriculture, the second trade and commerce.

W. HEYD. *Histoire du Commerce du Levant au Moyen Age.* French edition by Furcy Raynaud. 2 vols. Paris. 1885–6.

H. PIRENNE. *Mediaeval Cities* (tr. F. D. Halsey). Princeton. 1925.

FRITZ RÖRIG. *The Medieval Town* (tr. Don Bryant). London, 1967. Mainly concerned with Germany.

EUGENE H. BYRNE. *Genoese Shipping in the twelfth and thirteenth centuries.* Cambridge, Mass. 1930.

R. S. LOPEZ and I. W. RAYMOND. *Medieval Trade in the Mediterranean World.* Columbia and London. 1955. Select documents in translation, with bibliography.

R. D. FACE. 'Techniques of Business in the trade between the Fairs of Champagne and the South of Europe in the twelfth and thirteenth centuries.' *Econ. Hist. Rev.* 2nd series, X (1958), 427–38.

EPILOGUE : THE MONGOLS

IN the middle of the thirteenth century, Europe was menaced by a new and unexpected danger, the Mongols. Under their 'universal emperor', Jenghiz Khan (1162–1227), they had conquered the whole of central Asia, from Peking to Lake Balkash, and in 1222 they broke through the Caucasus and invaded southern Russia, overwhelming the Cuman Turks who lived in the region of the Crimea. In 1238–40 they overran Muscovy and destroyed Kiev, and in 1241 they launched an offensive against Western Europe.

> They are inhuman and beastly [wrote an English monk], rather monsters than men, thirsting for and drinking blood, tearing and devouring the flesh of dogs and men, dressed in ox-hides, armed with plates of iron, short and stout, thickset, strong, invincible, indefatigable, their backs unprotected, their breasts covered with armour.... They have one-edged swords and daggers, are wonderful archers, spare neither age, nor sex, nor condition. They know no other language than their own, and no one else knows theirs ; for until now there has been no access to them, nor did they go forth [from their own country].[1]

They were a nomadic people, grazed enormous herds on the steppes of central Asia, and travelled with their huts on carts, which gave the appearance of a whole city on the move. Their empire was vast ; an idea of it can be gained from the fact that from the Crimea it required a journey of about three-and-a-half months to reach its centre, near Caracorum in Mongolia. There, the Great Khan or emperor had his golden tent (*ordu*), from which he sent his generals forth to conquer the world.

The offensive against Europe in 1241 was boldly planned as a converging movement by two separate forces. One passed

---

[1] Matthew Paris, *Chron. Maj.*, iv. 76 ff. Trans. from W. W. Rockhill, *The Journey of William Rubruck* (Hakluyt Soc., 2nd series, no. 4 ; 1900), pp. xv–xvi.

through Poland, destroying Cracow on its way, invaded Silesia, defeated its duke at the battle of Liegnitz (9 April), and moved on to Moravia. The other, led by the great Batu, invaded Hungary and annihilated the forces of King Bela IV at Mohi (11 April). It seemed as if the Mongols would have the whole of Europe in their grasp, especially as the struggle between the Emperor Frederick II and Pope Gregory IX was absorbing most of the military effort of Germany and Italy. But in the hour of victory the Mongol generals received the news of the death of the Emperor Ogodai, and returned to Mongolia to assist in the election of his successor. In fact they were never to return to Europe again, since Batu eventually settled down as Khan of the Golden Horde, with his capital at Serai on the Volga. But this was an eventuality which, in 1242, no one could have foreseen. To most people it seemed more likely that the Mongols would return.

It is easy to understand the horror which they inspired, for they were a threat not only to the frontier districts but to the whole Christian world, to Byzantium as well as Rome. The only encouragement to be gleaned was the fact that they were equally a threat to the existence of Islam. In 1231–3 the Mongols had conquered Persia, and it was possible that they would advance still farther to Baghdad and destroy the caliphate. Consequently, some of the more optimistic Christians came to the conclusion that the Mongols could be used for God's work. If only they could be converted to Christianity they might join in a combined onslaught to destroy Islam and liberate the Holy Places for the Christian Church!

Accordingly, in 1245, at the Council of Lyons, Pope Innocent IV decided to send two missions to the Mongols, and entrusted them to Franciscan friars. One of them, consisting of Friar John del Pian di Carpina and Friar Benedict the Pole, was successful in making the journey to the Great Khan and back, though the double journey took just over two years (1245–7). They travelled by way of Kiev and the Dnieper, and, passing north of the Caspian, eventually arrived in Mongolia in time to witness the election of Guyuk as Great Khan (1246). They were not successful in converting Guyuk to Christianity, however, and obviously did not favour the thought of him as an ally; Friar

John records that he did not invite Mongol ambassadors to accompany him back to Europe since ' if they saw the dissensions and wars among us, . . . it would encourage them to march against us '. Nevertheless, his report that there were Nestorian Christians at the Great Khan's court, and that they were employed as his clerks, was sufficient to keep the hopes of the optimists alive. Soon it was reported from various unreliable sources that the Great Khan was actually on the point of becoming a Christian.

Louis IX heard these reports in 1248, when he was in Cyprus at the beginning of his first crusade, and he seized upon them with joy. He dispatched a Dominican friar, Andrew of Longjumeau, to the Great Khan, and he, like Friar John before him, made the double journey with success. He arrived just after Guyuk Khan had died (1248), but received letters from the regent, which informed Louis bluntly that if he wanted peace he would have to pay tribute. According to Joinville, Louis then repented of ever having sent the embassy. But four years later we find him hopeful again, sending a Franciscan, William of Rubruck, not as an ' ambassador ' it is true, but on some form of ' unofficial mission ' to the Mongols (1253–5) which had no more success than its predecessors.

It must be admitted, however, that the friars who undertook the missions showed less disappointment at their failure to convert the Mongols, than enthusiasm for exploration. The accounts which they wrote of their journeys deserve to be ranked among the great travel-books of the world. The *History of the Mongols* by John del Piano di Carpina and the *Itinerary* of William of Rubruck show that these two friars were born explorers, cheerfully braving the desert in both the heat of summer and the snow of winter, and observing the country and its inhabitants with an accuracy and detachment that did credit to their intellectual training.[1] They abandoned any false preconceptions which they might previously have entertained, and recorded what they saw and heard in language which is both sober and exact. William of Rubruck remarked that the Mongols seemed like people out of another world (*seculum*), but none the less made a determined (and successful) effort to understand them. His

---

[1] Both works are printed in translation by Rockhill, *op. cit.*

account of their manners and customs is fascinating. He described how in Russia the Mongols moved in winter to the south, and in summer to the north, in search of grazing for their flocks ; how their dwellings were built, and how they were transported on carts, even though they might be 30 ft. across—he said he had seen one cart drawn by twenty-two oxen, ' eleven abreast across the width of the cart and the other eleven before them '. He recounted how it was the women's duty ' to drive the carts, get the dwellings on and off them, milk the cows, make butter and *gruit*, and to dress and tend skins which they do with a thread made of tendons ' ; how the men cut their hair, and how they dressed ; how their favourite food was *cosmos* or mare's milk, and how they also ate meat that had been dried in the sun, and sausages made with the intestines of horses ; how the great lords had villages in the south from which millet and flour were brought for the winter ; how they derived great revenues from the salt-lakes of Perekop, since ' from all Russia they come thither for salt, and for each cartload they give two pieces of cotton worth half an yperpera ' ; what offences were punished with death—and in this respect William did not think the Mongols harsh—and so on. It is no mere ' traveller's tale ', but the result of patient and accurate observation.

One passage may be quoted in full to show the practical spirit which dominates the whole work. It relates to Friar William's journey home. When he was passing through the Caucasus the Mongols had to provide him with an escort of twenty men against the Alans and Lesgi who were still unsubdued.

And this pleased me much, for I hoped to see them [the Mongols] under arms ; for I had never been able to see their arms, though most anxious to. When we came to a dangerous passage, out of 20 only 2 had haubergeons. I asked them how they came by them, and they said they had got them from the Alans, who are good makers of such things, and excellent artisans. So it seems to me they have few arms except arrows and bows and fur gowns. I saw given to them iron plates and iron caps from Persia, and I also saw two who had come to present themselves before Mangu, armed with jackets of convex pieces of hard leather, which were most unfit and unwieldy.[1]

[1] William of Rubruck (tr. Rockhill, *op. cit.*, p. 261).

From a geographical point of view it may also be remarked that Friar William was the first westerner to indicate the true sources and course of the Don and the Volga, to appreciate that (in spite of the teaching of Ptolemy) the Caspian was an inland sea, and to mention the wild ass or *kulan*. For historians, an important point is that both he and Friar John noticed the settlements of Goths in the Crimea (relics of the fifth-century migration), remarking that they were Christians and still spoke a Teutonic language.

To contemporaries, however, the most fascinating parts of the friars' descriptions were those which bore on the possibility, or otherwise, of a Mongol alliance. On this matter, both friars were quite firm. There was no chance of the Mongol rulers becoming Christian. There were Nestorian Christians at the Mongol court, who were always circulating rumours of impending conversions, but the Nestorians made a habit of saying things ' ten times greater than the truth '. Indeed, the friars did not like the Nestorians, and though they managed to keep on terms of outward friendliness with them they never forgot that they were heretics. The people they did find helpful were the Europeans whom they found most unexpectedly at the court of the Great Khan. There were several Hungarians, presumably captives from the offensive of 1241 ; an Englishman born in Hungary ; a French goldsmith (who sent ' endless salutations ' to Louis IX) ; and, finally, a monk called Sergius who had come from Jerusalem in obedience to a divine revelation, to tell the Great Khan that ' if he became a Christian, all the world would come under his rule, and that the Franks and the great Pope would obey him '.

This last caused Friar William great indignation, and not a little alarm. For, to him, the prospect of a Mongol invasion of Europe was still a real terror, as witness the care which he took to describe the armament of the Mongols and the attempts which they made to hide it from him. He did not dismiss the Mongols as an absurdity. He knew them for the danger that they were. Their advance seemed irresistible. In 1258 Hūlagū, the brother of Kubla Khan, took Baghdad, sacked it, and brought the Abbāsid caliphate to an end, sewing up its last representative in a sack and trampling him to death with horses. Refugees streamed westward to Cairo (with important consequences for the culture of Moslem Egypt), and told terrible tales of the destruction wrought. In 1260 Damascus and Aleppo fell, and it looked as if the Mongol Empire would soon reach to the shores of the Mediterranean. But once again Europe was saved, this time by the Egyptian Mamlukes, who won a decisive victory at Goliath's Well, near Gaza (1260). Christendom had been spared the Mongols by the valour of the Moslems, but as yet it did not know that it was secure, and it awaited the coming of the Antichrist with a mixture of expectation and fear.

The Mongols symbolized all the mysterious forces which were threatening the established order of medieval Europe. The impact which they made on the imagination was as great as that of the apocalyptic utterances of Joachim of Flora. Like the Emperor Frederick II they were held to be the flail of God and the precursors of a new era, for in every sphere of life it was evident that the foundations of the old order were dissolving. The Augustinian philosophy, which had held the field for close on eight centuries, was in full retreat before the new Aristotelianism. The stability of monks was giving place to the vagrancy of friars, the rule of psalmody to the allure of popular sermons, and the learning of the cloister to the disputations of the university. Latin literature was being replaced by the vernacular, and Romanesque art by Gothic even in Germany and Italy. Manor and castle, though still in evidence, were overshadowed by the wealth of towns. But most important of all was the fact that the Christian Empire had been destroyed. The spiritual and secular arms of the Church had failed to live in the union of perfect charity, had engaged in deadly conflict, and had shattered the unity of the Christian people. The ideals of Constantine the Great and Charlemagne, alike with those of Gregory VII and Innocent III, could no longer be realized. And it seemed like a judgment of God that the Mongols were now at the gates.

That is why the middle of the thirteenth century makes a natural ending to the history of medieval Europe. The conservative might lament the passing of the old order and try to reconstruct it, but the task was beyond them. The significant figures were the friars who set out to find the Mongols and explore the unknown however fearsome it might be.

Appendix I

GREGORY AND BENEDICT

THE extent to which the monasticism of Pope Gregory the Great was truly Benedictine has been called in question by K. Hallinger ('Papst Gregor der grosse und der hl. Benedikt' in *Studia Anselmiana* xlii (1957), 231–317), who goes so far as to suggest that the pope can never have examined Benedict's *Rule* closely. He reaches this conclusion from a detailed study of Gregory's writings, being particularly impressed by the way in which Gregory uses some of the key-words of the *Rule* in a sense different from that of St. Benedict. He uses *Opus Dei*, for example, to denote the work of God generally (as in the case of missionary work), although in the *Rule* it is a technical term for church services; and the term *praepositus* for almost anyone in authority—pope, king, bishop or abbot—though in the *Rule* it invariably refers to the prior or second-in-command of the monastery. It is true that a man who had been schooled in the Benedictine *Rule* from infancy, or even from the age of 19 or 20, would probably have become so used to these words as technical terms that they would have become part of his language, but for a man who became a monk at the age of 34 the case might well have been different. By then his language would have become 'set', and it would surely have been natural for him to continue using words in the old sense outside the monastery, even if he knew that inside the monastery they had a specialized meaning. What matters is not whether Gregory adopted Benedict's language, but whether he was sufficiently inspired by the *Rule* to become Benedictine in outlook.

Hallinger has shown that on various points of detail Gregory's views were not identical with those of St. Benedict—he thought that the novitiate should be longer and harder, and that greater

411

stress should be laid on seniority in the election of abbots—but these differences are neither fundamental nor surprising. Recent research has emphasized that in the sixth century several monastic Rules were in circulation in the West—one of them, the so-called *Regula Magistri*, has been the centre of much controversy and is now thought to have been one of the main sources of the *Rule* [1]— and it looks as if the eventual pre-emine   of the Benedictine *Rule* was due to the fact that it embraced the best points of most of them. It would not be in the least surprising if Gregory considered St. Benedict's *Rule* to be, not the only Rule for monks, but the best. One can study many Rules, and yet be inspired by only one of them.

The reason for thinking that this was the case with Gregory the Great is that he wrote the earliest Life of St. Benedict in the second book of his *Dialogues*. In the prologue he stated that he drew his information from four of St. Benedict's disciples, one of whom (Valentinian) ' for many years ruled the Lateran monastery in Rome '. He praised the *Rule* for its discretion and lucidity, and referred his readers to it for further information about St. Benedict's life. Though the biography is primarily a collection of miracles, several of them illustrate the main themes of the *Rule*, e.g. Humility (ch. 20), Stability (chs. 24–5), Obedience (ch. 28 and Bk. III, ch. 16), the wickedness of keeping (and concealing) personal gifts (ch. 19), and manual work in the fields (ch. 32). It is self-evident that Gregory the Great had the utmost admiration and reverence for St. Benedict, and in the second book of the *Dialogues* (which had an enormous circulation) he undoubtedly publicized the virtues of both the man and his *Rule*.

[1] See ' The *Regula Magistri* and the *Rule* of St. Benedict ' in David Knowles, *Great Historical Enterprises* (London, 1962), 139–95.

Appendix II

THE VIKINGS

SINCE this book was published a great deal has been written about the Vikings. Among the problems which have been most fiercely debated, the following may be singled out for brief comment :

(1) *The causes of the Viking irruption.* In spite of the work of modern scholars, it is still widely believed that because the Vikings were polygamous Scandinavia had an exceptionally high birth-rate, that the rapid increase of population led to a shortage of food, and that the shortage of food caused the Vikings to set out in search of new lands. In fact polygamy does not necessarily lead to an increased birth-rate, because it does not increase the number of potential mothers but merely allocates them to fewer men. Prior to the invention of contraceptives the so-called ' birth-rate ' was really an inverse reflection of the rate of infant mortality. The real question was not how many children were born but how many survived, and this depended on the amount of food available. It seems, therefore, that the increase in food supplies would have had to come before the raids, not after them.

It is important to see the problem in perspective. There is no direct evidence to suggest that the increase in population was sudden. On the contrary, there is a great deal of evidence to show that Scandinavia had been overpopulated for centuries, and that its natives had a tradition of emigration on a scale similar to that of modern Ireland. Between the fifth century B.C. and the fifth century A.D. the emigrants from Scandinavia included the Goths, Vandals, Burgundians, *Cimbri*, and Anglo-Saxons. The Vikings were merely the last of a long succession

413

of emigrants, and it may well be that they were also encouraged by the economic conditions of the time. See Appendix III.

(2) *The numbers of the Vikings.* As in the case of the Germanic invaders of the Roman Empire, it is impossible to give an accurate estimate of numbers. The only source which seems reliable is the Alfredian section of the *Anglo-Saxon Chronicle* in which the movements of the Vikings are traced, as if for military intelligence, on the Continent as well as in England. It suggests that during the course of the ninth century the size of the Viking forces increased considerably. In the first half of the century the largest fleets recorded were 35 ships (or about 1,000 men), but in 892 we are told of one which (according to various versions of the *Chronicle*) had 200, 250 or 350 ships (6,000–10,000 men). Part of the increase seems to have been due to the fact that the smaller Viking forces tended to coalesce as the opposition grew stronger, so that the army of 892 would have consisted of a considerable part of the total number of Vikings in the West—but this, of course, would have been in addition to the Varangians in the East.

Armies of 1,000 or 6,000 men may not seem very large today, but in relation to the population of medieval Europe they were far from negligible, and once one begins to make sober calculations it is difficult to see how so many men could have been produced by Scandinavia alone. It seems that insufficient emphasis has been placed on the fact that, in the course of their raids, the Vikings not only made many captives whom they took home to Scandinavia (as shown, for example, in Rimbert's Life of St. Anskar), but also gained recruits, as in the case of King Alfred's nephew Æthelwold who in 899 went over to the Danish army in Northumbria and was accepted by them as king. The *Jomsvikingsaga* assumes that those who 'joined the fellowship' of that mysterious band would not necessarily be Scandinavian, and early in the eleventh century Wulfstan Archbishop of York took it as a matter of course that an English thrall 'might run away from his lord, leave Christendom, and become a Viking'. Such recruitment would explain not only why it was that the armies tended to get larger and larger, but also how it was that the Vikings took so easily to the language and customs of the countries which they conquered.

(3) *The extent of destruction.* Recent historians, notably P. H. Sawyer (*The Age of the Vikings* (London, 1962)) and Albert d'Haenens (*Les Invasions normandes en Belgique au IXe siècle* (Louvain, 1967)) have belittled the amount of destruction caused by the raids. Of course it is true that all life did not come to an end with the raids, and that the fields did not cease to be cultivated. But the sort of argument used by d'Haenens could be used equally well to minimize the destruction caused by aerial bombardment in the Second World War. In both cases one can point to towns and villages which escaped unscathed, but that does not alter the fact that the total amount of destruction was immense. Sawyer lays great stress on the *Anglo-Saxon Chronicle's* statement (*s.a.* 897) that ' by the grace of God the [Danish] army had not on the whole afflicted the English people very greatly ', but the context suggests that the chronicler was making a triumphant claim, pointing out at the end of a heroic defensive campaign that the efforts of the English army had indeed been worthwhile, since otherwise there would have been as much destruction as before.

(4) *The settlements.* It follows from what has been said about the numbers of the Vikings that the settlements which they made in Britain and Europe can hardly have been settlements *en masse* with every village populated by Scandinavian peasants. I have argued the case in detail in the case of East Anglia (*Trans. Royal Hist. Soc.*, 5th series, V (1955), 23–39), but in general the evidence suggests that the Vikings ruled the territories they conquered from fortified towns such as the ' five boroughs ' in England, their settlement of the country being more a matter of lordship than of manual labour. Sawyer (pp. 98–9) thinks that they used the money which they got as loot or danegeld in order to purchase land in the conquered territories, but no such transaction is known—indeed the whole notion of colonization by legal conveyance seems somewhat ridiculous at this period. The large number of Scandinavian place-names in England is often taken as evidence of a settlement *en masse* in the ninth century, but it could be explained equally well as the result of a very long and gradual immigration from Scandinavia, continuing into the tenth and eleventh centuries.

Appendix III

NUMISMATICS AND THE PIRENNE THESIS

THE advance of numismatic studies has led to a further criticism of Pirenne's thesis. Pirenne seems to have assumed that the change-over from gold to silver coins implied some form of economic disaster, but it now seems more likely that the reverse was true. The old coins may have been satisfactory for hoarding, but their small size and high value must have made them very inconvenient for traders. The new coins were larger and stronger—easier to handle and less easy to lose—and their value was about right for purchasing the more ordinary commodities of life. We know that Pepin III and Charlemagne both made great efforts to provide a standardized coinage, and that Charlemagne more or less succeeded in doing so ; it was he who decreed (in 780) that the pound (*libra*) should consist of 20 shillings (*solidi*) and the shilling of 12 pence (*denarii*) —thus providing the £ s. d. equation which has been preserved in England until 1970. All this surely suggests trade, as also does Charlemagne's attempt (in the *Admonitio Generalis* of 789) to standardize weights and measures.

It may be suggested that where Pirenne went wrong was in his assumption that the Mediterranean was the only sea which lent itself to navigation and trade. The Baltic surely had many of the same advantages. Like the Mediterranean, it was small enough for the fearful mariner never to be far from land, yet large enough to open the most exciting possibilities. By exploring the rivers which flowed into it from central Europe, a route could be found to Constantinople, while the mariner who emerged into the North Sea could follow the coast of the Low Countries down to the English Channel. That these routes were actually used is proved by a large amount of archaeological evidence ; the grave goods of the seventh-century king buried in his ship at Sutton Hoo in Essex, for example, include a helmet and shield from Sweden and a large silver dish from Constantinople. From the eighth century onwards, imported pottery was common in southern and eastern England, the bulk of it coming, we are told, 'from factories in the middle Rhineland between Bonn and Cologne ' (G. C. Dunning in *Medieval Archaeology*, iii (1959), 50). We may recall that when Pirenne assumed that the Moslems of Tunisia took to piracy, he assumed also that there was a Mediterranean trade for them to practise piracy on. We know that the Vikings took to piracy at the end of the ninth century. Would they have done so if there had been no traders to attack ?

INDEX

(Persons are indexed under their first name)